CL16

Gloucestershire
COUNTY COUNCIL

Items should be returned to any Gloucestershire County Library
on or before the date stamped. Books which are not in demand may
be renewed in person, by letter or telephone.
0845 230 5420

HC

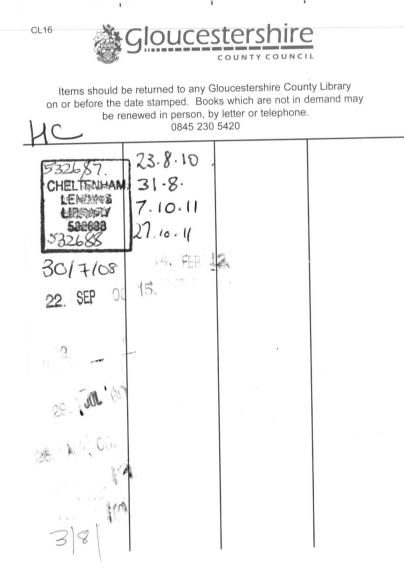

532687.	23.8.10		
CHELTENHAM LENDING LIBRARY 532688	31.8.		
532688	7.10.11		
	27.10.11		
30/7/08	14. FEB 12		
22. SEP 08	15.		

3/8/

Also by James Naughtie

The Rivals: The Intimate Portrait of a Political Marriage
The Accidental American: Tony Blair and the Presidency

The Making of Music

A Journey with Notes

JAMES NAUGHTIE

JOHN MURRAY

First published in Great Britain in 2007 by John Murray (Publishers)
An Hachette Livre UK company

1

A CIP catalogue record for this title is available from the British Library

ISBN 978-0-7195-6254-9

Typeset in Bembo by Hewer Text UK Ltd, Edinburgh
Printed and bound by Clays Ltd, St Ives plc

John Murray policy is to use papers that are natural, renewable
and recyclable products and made from wood grown in sustainable
forests. The logging and manufacturing processes are expected to
conform to the environmental regulations of the country of origin.

John Murray (Publishers)
338 Euston Road
London NW1 3BH

www.johnmurray.co.uk

In Memory of Ronald Center, 1913–73

Contents

Preface

MUSIC IS A personal affair. Although we enjoy it collectively, and mass music-making is exhilarating, the reason why it inspires a passion in so many people is that it strengthens our individuality, lifting us up or helping us through, often making us think and, at its best, speaking in a language that can't be imitated and has irresistible power. This book is written in that spirit, an account of a journey through time that is also a personal voyage. It follows that I am not attempting a conventional history – neither pretending to offer a comprehensive account of how music has changed over the centuries, nor giving all the great composers the attention and space they deserve – but trying to paint with brushstrokes an alluring picture that captures something of the richness of the tradition we've inherited. Above all, I hope the story explains how that stream carries with it more than the precious originality or even the genius of particular musicians, and speaks to us of our past.

I hope the result will be enjoyed by those who spend a good deal of time listening to classical music, by casual listeners with diverse tastes (like my own) and, above all, by those who sometimes find it scary or strange. If I can persuade them that there is nothing to fear, and that an adventure is about to begin, I'll be content.

The origin of this book is a phone call I received one day from the controller of BBC Radio 4, Mark Damazer, while I was descending into the depths of the Underground on an escalator at Waterloo station. We had a quick conversation. By the time I had reached the bottom I had agreed to write some kind of music series – probably sixty episodes, he said alarmingly – and I got on the train wondering what I had done. But I have no regrets. We had to decide how wide to cast our net – this would be the story of what we tend to call classical music, set in a European context, and it would explore the connections between that tradition and our broader history. I am no musicologist, and wanted to make clear that I would not (*could* not) venture into spheres which were the territory of others. For detailed explanations of thematic development in the score of the Ring cycle, or of the tell-tale signs in Prokofiev's First Symphony that tie it to the neo-Classical movement, or of the guiding principles used by Pierre Boulez in his radical 'Structures Book 1' in 1952, people would have to turn to the admirable voices of BBC Radio 3. This would be different.

In this book, I have tried to preserve the spirit of the series that emerged from those conversations, *The Making of Music*. Though I love a great deal of music that doesn't sit in the classical mainstream – rock, some jazz, traditional folk and the songs of the great American writers for the musical stage and the piano bar – that story will have to wait for another day. This is a journey that begins in the churches of the Dark Ages and then winds its way across Europe, picking up the sounds of the Renaissance composers, the Baroque, the Classical age of Haydn and Mozart and the Romantics, before we reach the twentieth century and the music that we still call modern, even if it was written just after the First World War.

In writing the radio series, I was fortunate to work with an outstanding production team. Rosie Boulton, Sara Conkey and Lucy Lunt were wonderful colleagues, bringing energy and sparkle to my sometimes chaotic efforts. Philip Sellars oversaw the series, and Tony Sellors at Radio 3 brought his characteristic enthusiasm to bear on a project that was designed in part to break down the artificial barriers that sometimes exist between BBC networks, allowing Radio 3 to play the music that was being talked about on Radio 4, an innovation about which Roger Wright, Radio 3 controller and director of the BBC Proms, was enthusiastic from the start. Ivan Hewett and David Huckvale did sterling research for the series, Stephen Johnson lent some of his formidable expertise, and above all I want to thank Roderick Swanston, distinguished academic and proselytiser for music, who had the difficult role of steering me back when I had wandered off course and whose care and commitment I treasured, even if some of my scripts were returned marked as if they were rather inferior

GCSE exam answers. I tried to produce a series that did what radio does best, combining a narrative thrust with the informality of the spoken word and, for once, infused with music. I think we all enjoyed it.

Writing for radio and the ear and writing for the page are quite different tasks. This book has been my effort alone, and I must emphasise that no one else has any responsibility for the judgements made here, nor for interpretations with which some readers may disagree. I know how seriously people take their music. Any mistakes are mine alone. Roland Philipps has been a wonderful publisher, Peter James a meticulous copyeditor, and my agent Felicity Bryan her usual inspirational self.

As always, my colleagues on *Today* have been supportive. They are a great gang. And, of course, I have been sustained by Ellie, Andrew, Catherine and Flora who all have my love and who know that, although books are fun to write, they exact a price. I hope that they will find the effort worth while.

I

Thursday Nights

~

THE OLD MANSE is still a rather handsome building, sheltered by trees along the curving path that leads to the house from inside the high gates. Each Thursday night I would push them open and set off for the front door with its crescent of light above. I would climb the stairs and seat myself on a rather uncomfortable straight-backed chair for a few minutes to wait my turn. Behind the door beside me I would hear someone playing the piano.

These nights are sharp in my memory, though they began when I was only five years old. I was never a dedicated pianist – I share the blushes of the many who wish that they'd understood then what they know now – but even in those years, which began in the 1950s and lasted until the late 1960s, I was conscious of a certain quality in those hours. Occasionally I would dodge a lesson for a football match, and sometimes turn up with the exercise book obviously unopened from last time (which would earn a gentle whack on the knuckles with a carved ruler), but mostly I would enjoy myself. Most of all, I enjoyed the teacher.

He was called Ronald Center, and he loved music. When I was a teenager we would often talk instead of listening to my playing of another Chopin nocturne that was ill prepared or a bit of Bach that I simply couldn't handle with my feebly exercised fingers. I can understand his choice. He would talk about why he had studied organ and piano, and sometimes he would play Debussy or Skryabin or Bach (his first love) to give me a glimpse into his world.

'Mr' Center – it would never have occurred to me to address him less formally – was a magician. He could cast music's spell, and explain how it worked. He was formidably talented on the keyboard but had given up school-teaching in middle age because, frankly, he couldn't stand it. As time went on, I discovered why. Late in the evenings, and in the mornings before the pupils started to come in, he was what he wanted to be: a composer.

Years later, long after he died at the age of sixty in 1973, I opened a cardboard box in the National Library of Scotland and looked at some of his manuscripts. His output was modest – though there were many songs set for his wife Evelyn, a soprano who sang professionally – but it included a stunning piano sonata, three string quartets, a divertimento for strings and elements of a symphony, 'The Coming of Cuchulain'. It was an experience that moved me, not least when I found a scrap of paper that I recognised. It was the crudely cyclostyled programme for the annual concert in which his pupils would play (and his wife's pupils would sing) at one of the local church halls in the town, Huntly, Aberdeenshire. On one side were a scribbled stave and the fragments of a song setting, probably jotted down in an odd moment late at night. I turned it over, and saw the list of the performers in that year's parents' concert in which I appeared as a six- or seven-year-old, playing, as I recall, some cowboy tune.

They were events that we all dreaded as we sat waiting in line in the room off the hall where the ladies made the tea, in which there always seemed to linger the smell of newly laundered socks. But the pro-gramme swung me back in an instant to those Thursday nights, and the conversations we had had. Though I didn't understand it fully as a schoolboy, and though there were many times afterwards when my engagement with music was casual – even at times quite distant – they leaped into my mind again as if they'd happened last year. Why do you think Bach *works*? Just listen to how Mozart does this; imagine the mind that can construct a chord sequence like that. He explained to me why I might like opera, why a string quartet was a thing of wonder and how the accompaniment to a song was as important as the words. Above all, I remembered the sheer commitment to the piano and what it could do and the insistence that music would always repay what you gave to it.

Leaving aside those who have the talent and concentration to have studied music or make it a career, everyone who plays an instrument and many who can't will understand those feelings. They bubble up, they are insistent, and they are important. My luck was to encounter an original, slightly eccentric man whose gentleness and considerateness formed the outer skin of a passionate personality. His sonata, written just after the war, burns with a near-pacifist passion, and his song cycle *Dona nobis pacem* has a moving, plangent simplicity. Having an idealist as a teacher was a better deal for me than the attentions of someone concerned above all to put me through the hoops (Mr Center – I treasure the memory – didn't believe in exams) and I was fortunate to get suggestions for unheard-of novels to read, as well as quite natural instruction in how to imagine the life of a composer and to understand the techniques that lay behind the notes on the page.

My Thursday nights were the beginning of a journey. It seems to me a more and more important one as the years go by. In the grip of a celebrity culture, where worth is so often measured simply at the supermarket till or in the size of the tabloid spread, we all need to remind ourselves of where worth lies – in conviction and persistence. Above all, in talent. I think of my teacher with his manuscript paper – he seldom spoke directly about it – labouring over his suite for cello, and wondering if it might be played on the Third Programme (which became BBC Radio 3 in 1967), as some of his music was, from Glasgow in the late 1950s and early 1960s. More than the nostalgia, I enjoy the reminder of how rewarding music can be and how much it mattered that the barriers to that realisation were removed.

How wearisome it is to hear, again and again, the argument about access and 'elitism' posed as if the broadening of the audience and the pursuit of excellence were opposites, or should be. It is the most destructive of arguments, setting those who care about quality against those who care about artistic freedom and a certain kind of democracy, as if they were enemies, when they are usually the same people.

It remains something of a mystery why a football fan is not considered elitist in asserting that, in general, Arsenal play better football than Accrington Stanley. It is possible to compare them, and come to a conclusion. Excellence is what matters, and nothing else, and the reason why doors to concert halls and opera houses should be opened wider is so that the message can be shouted more loudly. More people should be encouraged to make their minds up. Music isn't there to be lapped up by some supine audience like a doctor's potion; it is there to be tasted and assessed, and no one who cares about it should avoid the responsibility of making a judgement.

There are social barriers that have been erected over the years which discourage many people from making that leap – more's the pity. Without constant reassessment and comparison, the effort to distinguish music of quality from the mediocre, the landscape loses its contours and is flattened. I cherish the description of a precocious (and overrated) pianist by Sir John Drummond, a great figure in his day at the Edinburgh Festival, the Proms and BBC Radio 3, who listened and said: 'He looked like a hairdresser and played like a blacksmith.' That might seem to have an air of lofty arrogance about it – with the authentic Drummondesque ring – but you would be wrong to think it an exercise in bitchiness, or worse, snobbery. It's an honest judgement: rough, but genuine. If the emperor has no clothes, say so. As our journey through its history will show, music depends on criticism and argument. It must never be allowed to atrophy, because then it loses its meaning and its purpose.

The visceral thrill of live music comes in part from the relish of a player or a singer or an orchestra for performance, and also from the challenge to an audience to consider what it has heard. Did they pull it off? If there is a threat to the place of serious music in the future it comes not from the possibility of composers ceasing to compose – they won't, for better or worse – but from a dilution of that excitement. If orchestras don't adapt, if concert halls and opera houses don't find ever more ingenious ways of competing against other attractions, they will wither on the vine. A tradition can't be taken for granted.

Sometimes the weather turns nasty. Think, for example, of the recording industry, which can bolster the health of classical music, or drain it. Dark days come, like the one that saw the end of EMI in May 2007, a titan of the recording industry, which began at the end of the nineteenth century as the Gramophone and Typewriter Company and is now in the hands of an equity firm and probably on its way to Hollywood, there to end up as a piece of a bigger corporate jigsaw where it will take its chance with a studio, a TV company or a sprawling media empire. The smaller recording companies are doing a magnificent job in bearing the responsibility that's been thrust on them, but when a great tree falls, the ground shakes.

This was the company that in the 1950s, with Decca, preserved on disc the performances of a generation for an audience that will stretch far into the future. When Walter Legge recorded Maria Callas in *Norma*, or Wilhelm Furtwängler conducting Beethoven's Choral Symphony at Bayreuth, or Elisabeth Schwarzkopf singing Richard Strauss's *Four Last Songs*, he was bequeathing a legacy that will not fade. Like John Culshaw's first studio recording of Wagner's Ring cycle, for Decca, from 1958 these discs are the precious reminders of performances that should be allowed to shimmer in the mind for years. They catch for ever a moment of poignant grief, or laughter, or an orchestral pause of trembling excitement. The early 1960s set of Herbert von Karajan's Beethoven symphonies boom down the years with a power that doesn't fade; a Pierre Monteux conducting Stravinsky or a Gunther Wand conducting Bruckner is an experience on disc that reminds us what it is like to be in a concert hall when the tuning stops and the music is about to start.

We all remember the moments. I sat once in the early 1980s in the very back row of the amphitheatre – the gods – at Covent Garden, with my back against the wall, to watch a production of Verdi's *Otello*, with Plácido Domingo in the title role and Margaret Price as Desdemona. The conductor was Carlos Kleiber, who would only come down from his mountain-top a few times a year, for a performance to which he felt committed. He came into the pit, gave a curt bow, raised his arms and we were off: the opening storm and Otello's first cry of 'Esultate!' carrying us away. At the end, more than three hours later, I remember sitting still against the wall in a state that was something like a trance. What was it that had caused that particular conductor, on that particular night, to forge that golden pact with the orchestra? They'd played it often before; everyone knew the score. What had happened? None of us can know the answer, which is how it should be.

Music involves mystery. The here-and-now should fade away when you hear the start of Schubert's String Quintet in C major or a Chopin étude or a simple-sounding song by Ivor Gurney. These are moments of transformation.

Yet the mystery is not mystical. Composers are real people. They work, they struggle and fiddle about; they're sometimes cantankerous and jealous and they aren't always nice to their friends. I dare say some of them only bathe once every three or four days. Let's not imagine for a moment that music emerges in some holy stream from a sacred mountain, flowing towards a temple where devotees can drink and be cleansed. It is real, sometimes a balm and sometimes an irritant, a cause of solace but something that can also rouse you to anger or despair. Above all, music is the product of human inspiration, a force that's engaged with the world around us.

Romantic music wouldn't have taken its course without the chance upheavals of politics that changed the lives of those who succumbed to its spell. Opera might not have produced Verdi or Puccini if the Italians hadn't found that its temperament and style provided a happy sounding board for their politics as well as their lifestyle, because it might have drifted out of fashion. Who can explain the achievement of Janáček or Bartók without understanding their nationalism, or Debussy without understanding how he wanted to find an expressiveness that would match what the painters in Paris were beginning to produce?

The thread that leads you through the story is the commitment they showed to their music. Sometimes composers had to produce to order – even Bach would write cantatas for the coffee house as required, and marches for the funerals of the Leipzig great and good as they came along – and their practical skills weren't honed by accident. Yet underneath there's conviction and steadfastness. When Bartók longed for Hungary in America he *had* to write about home; when Hector Berlioz heard Beethoven's Third Symphony, the 'Eroica', he felt 'an antique sadness' that wouldn't leave him. The business of making music is a fusion of feeling and brilliant craftsmanship. One without the other produces nothing much.

Sometimes musical people are tempted to cut themselves off. They're irritated by a culture that seems to devalue the original and the new, or they feel easier in the company of those who share their insights and tastes. Just like those who refuse to open their ears to music they don't know, or denigrate the classical tradition because of some imagined 'snobbery', they're undermining the spirit that needs to be preserved. A symphony or a string quartet or a song is a leveller. We're all in the same state when the prelude of *Das Rheingold* draws us into the waters of the Rhine and the sinuous maidens begin to lose their grip on the magic gold. A surrender to the feeling is no less than the music deserves, and requires. The answer to the strange social divisions that have sprung up in the arts – everywhere, not only in Britain – lies in the music itself. Prejudice and pig-headedness have to be abandoned. Religions preach humility (though some don't practise it), and music does the same.

I was struck once when talking to the pianist András Schiff about a cycle of Beethoven sonatas on which he was just launched. He had waited until the age of fifty before taking it on, because he said he felt that he had needed to be ready. Approaching Beethoven was approaching the summit. We talked for an hour or two about his feelings and about his approach to the music. He spoke of how important the audience was to him, how he would sit in the hall the night before a concert to take the measure of it and how, at the start of a recital, he would regard the playing of the first note as the moment when the crucial engagement was made with the listeners. Without that connection, and the knowledge that a current was passing between them, all was lost.

He also spoke about his beliefs. As a Hungarian Jew, he left Austria in the 1990s in protest against a particular right-wing lurch and eventually became a British citizen. He talked with feeling about the importance of his politics. As he showed me out of his house he gestured towards two grand pianos side by side in the room where he worked. He put his hand on one of them – an elegant old instrument – and seemed to offer it a gesture of love. 'That', he said, 'was Furtwängler's piano.' There was a moment's silence: Wilhelm Furtwängler, the stern denizen of Bayreuth and Berlin, who had stayed (controversially) in Germany through the Hitler years, never giving the Nazi salute but shaking hands with the Führer, was remembered here, with awe and humility.

That shared feeling is the gift of music. It is powerful precisely because it is not abstract, living in a distant sphere, but speaks of people and their sensibilities. The European tradition is only part of the history of music-making, which took different paths elsewhere, but it is one of the great stories, springing from our history and bearing its mark. Without it we would live more impoverished lives, and it isn't fanciful to say that we need it. That is why composers and listeners are participants in music. Each needs the other.

My teacher may often have disappeared upstairs to worry about a chord or the resolution of a song, but his activity was not a solitary indulgence. It was humane and generous. That generosity is revealed in the story of our music, which reminds us how important it is that it should be preserved and refreshed.

2

Beginnings

Monks, Troubadours and Burgundians

~

SEARCHING FOR THE source of a European musical tradition is like trying to find the beginning of a great river, following little springs and streams up a valley and wondering where the flow begins. The place to start is where the river first gathers pace and runs strong.

There are monasteries across Europe where you can imagine echoes of the plainchant that marked the holy hours – and many where you can still hear it – and you can still pick up traces of the rhythms and sounds that came from the east or from North Africa, sounds from ancient instruments that became absorbed into the notes of a scale that was the template for western music, the notes that are imprinted on the minds of even those who think of themselves as having no well-developed musical sense, let alone a musical education.

Many places bear witness to those beginnings, eked out over many centuries. But if you want to mark a moment and a place where the evolution took a leap forward, go to Notre Dame in Paris. It was there, more than anywhere else, that music grew up and here that some of the founding figures of European music gathered in the twelfth and thirteenth centuries. This church, too, saw a movement that it is not too fanciful to describe as the birth of the composer.

Even on the skyline of modern Paris, and from the cacophony of its streets, the Cathedral rises with a physical presence that still asks for attention, and a moment's silence. The stones embrace a story that's nearly 900 years old – since the first drawings for the building were scratched in the dust by the Bishop of Paris on the Île de la Cité in the Seine – and ever since the city began to grow around them, the walls and twin towers have been more than an adornment; they've been a living part of the city's history. France has worshipped here, celebrated victory and mourned defeat; Napoleon had himself crowned emperor here, insisting that the Pope attend as an observer but not as a participant in the ceremony. This great church has encouraged, allowed, even demanded one of the great movements in music.

We have some evidence of what was going on there from an English monk known as Anonymous IV, who was studying at the Sorbonne. He is still a shadowy figure, but is thought to have been in Paris around 1280. His notes on musical form, and his account of the rules that governed composition at that time, were found in two later copies which turned up in the fourteenth and fifteenth centuries, giving an insight into the techniques the composers were using when he was in Paris. The city was the intellectual heart of Europe and musicians were drawn there for an accompanying reason: as well as an atmosphere of innovation and discovery, the building of Notre Dame meant that there was a huge church that had to be filled with music. It was an invitation for plainchant to be stretched and adorned. According to Anonymous IV − the witness whose name gives him an appropriate air of mystery − the master composer was Léonin (we know him only by that name) whose *Magnus liber* was the great book of organum, the form that was turning plainchant into something new.

Organum was simply the form that used a chant and placed another melody above or below it, a simple two-part composition. It had been developing for several centuries, first in a form that placed one musical line a set distance apart from another − usually a perfect fourth or fifth, the intervals between notes that are the foundation of the simplest harmonies − and then in a more flexible way, which began to let them move independently. It was in Paris in the thirteenth century that it flowered, and polyphony − multiple voices singing in harmony − began to flourish. Anonymous IV wrote of Léonin:

> He wrote the Great Book of Organa, for the Mass and Office, to enlarge the divine office. The book was used until the time of the great Pérotin, who shortened it and rewrote many sections in a better way. Pérotin was the best composer of descant − he was even better than Léonin − and he

wrote the best four-part organa, such as Viderunt and Sederunt, with the most ample embellishments of harmonic art.

In these words, written by someone about whom we know almost nothing, you sense the excitement that was hatched in Notre Dame. It came about in part because of the sheer scale of the place. The roof is a hundred feet above the floor, the vastness of the nave is intimidating, the rose window at the west lights up with fire when the evening sun strikes it. Paris was going through its own renaissance in the twelfth century when the Cathedral was being built (it took more than 200 years to complete) and Notre Dame was a soaring monument to God, one of the greatest of the church buildings that were meant to make a statement of power and devotion.

Composers began to work there. Léonin and Pérotin produced organa that were heard alongside the familiar plainchant, now turned into polyphonic music, with different lines mingling together, that carried music forward with a spring in its step. Several voices sang simultaneously, sometimes one or more simply as a drone on one note, but gradually they began to sing lines that depended on each other, and seemed to have a relationship. This had certainly been going on for centuries, quite crudely, but by the time that Notre Dame was rising over Paris – the first great European city of the medieval world, growing fast at a time when the early universities were being founded in Europe – this music took on a new quality of simple beauty.

Most of the singing was unaccompanied. In the course of the fourteenth century the organ began to appear in church but it would only begin to develop into the pipe organ we know today in the following century, becoming established in more or less modern form by about 1500.

Though they are spare, the melodies of Léonin and Pérotin are recognisable to us today. They seem part of a culture that we know, connected through the centuries to the kinds of tunes, arrangements, that we hear every day, filtered through a classical tradition in western Europe and also drawn by a folk strain that is a familiar undercurrent to it.

Notre Dame represented at that time the magnetism of Paris. People attracted from the countryside could live without being subjected to the rules of rural feudalism, and the city was an intellectual crossroads where theologians, philosophers and the curious would meet to exchange ideas from all of Europe and from Byzantium to the east. At the centre of it was the Church, the conduit for all learning and education, and the Church was the home of music.

The expansion of the musical language, after centuries in which it had developed slowly, was dramatic. The sounds were alive with new possibilities – new sounds, new voices, a new vocabulary. It wasn't an accident, a chance discovery by some genius in a musical laboratory, but a product of places like Notre Dame, which were dramatic evidence of human progress in an age when ideas too were reaching for the heavens. In Paris at that time, Peter Abelard was arguing that religion should be a matter of reason rather than mysticism, and engaged in philosophical debates with Islam about the nature of the Christian texts. There was vision – the Bishop of the city himself, Maurice de Sully, had arrived here penniless and on foot, but had enough oratory and charisma to acquire power in the Church (and therefore great temporal power), and the imagination in the middle of the twelfth century to plan Notre Dame.

We shouldn't get carried away. The intellectual muscularity of people like Abelard didn't stop him being put on trial for heresy. His books were burned. Yet the spirit that was loose here couldn't be snuffed out. In particular, the musicians who clustered round this church – and who had the thrilling task of trying to fill it with sound – were able to become themselves, to write as composers. It was the first time it had happened on this scale.

Anonymous monks were turned into clerks or canons of the Cathedral who were, in practice, full-time church musicians. How could you have a building like this and not have sounds that were appropriate to its size, its magnificence? It became a practical matter for the church: the bigger the cathedral the greater the demands on the musicians. Notre Dame, after all, is a building which would eventually have an organ with nearly 8,000 pipes. It's a space that demanded glorious sounds.

You can understand how it happened. Looking at the elaborate stonework high above, at the delicacy of the tracery in the window set in that grand façade, you seem to hear music starting to weave sounds together in ways that hadn't been heard before. The first dance-like rhythms heard in church, basic harmonies that sounded very bold in their day, the simple melodies of the past wrapped up in something that was meant to echo the ambitions of the builders and masons and carpenters who were working here for two centuries to produce the building we know today.

You hear two impulses at work. One is the sheer excitement of the musical landscape that was opening up. The stage on which they could perform was bigger, the ideas that were flowing around these embryonic cities were bringing new inspiration with them, and the instruments were starting to get better. And, secondly, there was still the desire and the obligation to praise God. The Church that wielded power and was the repository of learning – just as it was the only source of literacy itself – ensured that for its own purposes, the noblest purposes, music was to be written.

So, within these walls, great sounds were created. They were meant to uplift the soul, but there was a practical objective too. The Church was interested in power: the universal gospel had to be an influence that would reach everywhere, shape everything. Its buildings would be huge towering things; its music would be beautiful. The liturgy would be burnished by these sounds, though the notion of glamour was one that would have been quite foreign to the clergy and musicians of the time. As a sermon or homily might strengthen devotion, so might a magical union of voices. It was also a way of separating the world outside from the world inside a Gothic church, where the worshipper was led typically from the darkness inside the west door, with only a few fragments of light stealing through the stained glass, to a high altar where the windows were designed to illuminate the focal point of the Cathedral and to keep the rest of the interior in reverential dimness. The elaborate music was part of the same message, and part of the same journey.

The history of music for hundreds of years afterwards was entwined with that of the Church, sometimes in harmony and sometimes in conflict, and this is where its modern story began.

Paris was already a glittering destination: in the course of the thirteenth century it would become the biggest city in the world known to Europeans, with probably a quarter of a million inhabitants.

Learned men trekked here from far across Europe and beyond, bringing their ideas with them. They were tiny in number, of course, and their learning was something that wouldn't be available to most of their countrymen and women for centuries. But the city was throbbing, and even without the ability to read, people could gather in Notre Dame and places like it and hear things which might lift them out of the here and now, satisfying their devotional obligations, but hearing too sounds which they might begin to savour and which could make them marvel. A Pérotin mass contains sounds which are surprisingly modern to our ears – dissonance that feels daring still, across the centuries.

In those harmonies, that arrangement of sound, you can hear so much that rolls down the years. It's striking that the composer Steve Reich (born in 1936), a scion of the school of late-twentieth-century minimalist composers, has drawn on Pérotin in particular in his work, because he says he can hear in him the kinds of sounds that he's searching for in his effort to simplify music and find something new. Pérotin was elaborating; Reich simplifies from the elements in that early polyphony, drawing them back to their roots. So we have these two periods of change nearly a millennium apart and striving in different directions: one back to the foundations of western music to search for its essence, the other turning a corner into the future, almost by instinct and without a plan.

Sometimes, music does stand still for a while. A style is established – conformity sets in – composers and performers enjoy their moment and make the most of it. But it never lasts for long. Styles change, innovators arrive and a new horizon appears. When a genius emerges who startles the world, or a new form excites a generation of composers, people hear a different sound and respond – just as the composers who worked and worshipped in Notre Dame heard in their heads a new melody that could run above one they already knew, and started to put them together. The history of such places – and their very shape and size – is bound up in the story of music itself.

Stand on the Île de la Cité with the Seine running alongside you and Notre Dame in front. Listen to the sounds of Paris – the traffic, the horns, the chatter, the rattle of a bike on the cobbles, sense those smells carried on the evening breeze that tell you exactly where you are, watch the dusk creeping over the city, little spirals of mist on the river. You will know – because this is how we react to buildings and places like this – that there is something profound at work: sometimes we respond to it and sometimes we don't. But it's there for us if we want it.

To visit that Cathedral is to remember for how long that impulse has been part of our history. Music flows from us, but it's also a product of time and place. There, among these great stones, are some of the foundations of our music: it was there that it took on a new complexity and a new beauty. It was here that the anonymous monks slipped into the dark, and men of music began to work, to display their skills with relish, to be revered, and to enjoy the adulation. It only takes a modest flight of fancy to think of Notre Dame as the birthplace of the composer.

The church was the cradle but it would be a mistake to think of religious devotion or practice as the only source of early European music. There were the troubadours. These men have remained fabled figures in our culture, pale-faced and lovelorn serenaders singing to the maiden in a tower at nightfall. Romantic twaddle, of course, but the tradition of the travelling musician who became an adornment at court and a conduit for the expression of love was important in carrying music across Europe and in establishing it as a means, outside church, of capturing the emotions of everyday life.

What was it was like to be serenaded if you were a fine lady in the middle ages? There are about 1,700 tunes surviving and we have the poetry used by forty or so troubadours – a fragment of the picture but enough to get an idea of the style, which was one of the musical adventures of the age. For example, we can listen to music written by Bernart de Ventadorn for the woman who was successively queen consort of England and France, the embodiment of power and attractiveness in her time, Eleanor of Aquitaine. He wrote for her about the time that she crossed the English Channel in 1152 with her husband Henry II, and the music is a badge of its era – echoing from the strange formalities of courtly love, which was the way of life in Aquitaine for those who exercised power and those who clustered around them. Running alongside the music of the church there was a rich stream of secular music.

Music in church was simply a mechanism of devotion. Inspiration came from God; and he had to be praised. Now, across Europe, in courts and great houses, poetry and music were beginning to celebrate the human as well as the divine. And the result was a kind of social commentary that sometimes celebrated the rigid conventions of what we've come to know as courtly love – but pricked them too, with irony and sometimes savage satire. Here are the words that Bernart de Ventadorn used to describe Eleanor. At the beginning she seems to be the object of all his desire:

> When I see the lark beating
> Its wings in joy against the rays of the sun
> That it forgets itself and lets itself fall
> Because of the sweetness that comes to its heart
> Alas! Such great envy then overwhelms me.

He describes in that verse a scene he witnessed when Eleanor was still married to Louis VII of France. Bernart was the court poet, and he had arranged to hide himself in Eleanor's bedchamber to watch the woman he adored. Unfortunately, what he saw was her ravishing at the hands of a knight, rather than of her husband the King, and her apparent enjoyment of every moment of it. His song uses code – she is the lark, the knight is the sun – but soon his rage and disillusion bursts out: 'I despair of ladies . . . I will never trust them again . . . because I know very well that they are all alike.'

It is, of course, a love song. In those words you can hear the stirring of centuries of musical inspiration. For the first time, notes – tunes that we might recognise today – were being used to picture the vagaries of human nature, to express sadness and ecstasy, anger and hurt. Music was the mirror in which Eleanor's infidelity, Bernart's anger and a scandalous tale could be captured.

Leaving aside her adventures in the bedroom with the knight of the song, she's a figure who reveals so much about this change, because it was in the court of Aquitaine in which she grew up that the conventions of courtly love became a famous way of life. Eight or nine centuries later it's quite difficult to grasp how those conventions worked, because they were much more than a charter of good manners, a pattern of behaviour that might be expected between men and women of some social status. There were rules, elaborate codes – a knight wearing green would be sending a signal of fidelity – and a form of courtship that came something near to worship of the woman concerned. She was usually married to someone else, and would be further up the social scale than the knight who had decided to give her his devotion. He was almost like a servant to a feudal lord. They were partners in a dance that had complicated and precise steps. Naturally, it was often an illusion. On the surface the rules were obeyed, but they were a mechanism for deception and betrayal too. How could it be otherwise?

In the troubadour songs that survive you can hear the distant stirring of a musical form – a kind of singing – that survived for centuries, because the picture of the lovesick knight, the disappointed suitor, the lover trying to express the inexpressible in music, is one of the most powerful impulses in our tradition. Think how Richard Wagner used the song contest in his opera *Tannhäuser* to explore the difference between divine love and something lustier and perhaps less admirable. The myth that Wagner used in his story is Germanic (of course) but it has its roots back in those years when the love song was beginning to be heard in France, in England, anywhere in Europe where courts were at play. The character at the heart of it was the troubadour.

What a picture that word conjures up – the moonlit windows, the bandy-legged youths warbling below, dusty figures on the road with a song for every occasion and almost certainly an anachronistic guitar, though there were none. Indeed there were almost no instruments, only voices. But the troubadours did travel to the great houses and they were a special breed.

They were most numerous in the Languedoc in south-west France, the territory associated with a religious movement particularly bound up with the culture of the travelling poets – the Cathars. They saw themselves as primitive Christians, pure and undefiled – unlike the Catholic Church, which they thought greedy, corrupt, almost Satanic in its ambitions for power. Their belief in sexual abstinence and their admiration for suicide as an escape from a corrupted world hardly offered a recipe for procreation and survival, but their influence was enough to scare the Church. By the end of the twelfth century they were being persecuted, because they were becoming dangerously popular. The Pope organised a crusade against them in 1181, and for a generation afterwards they were hunted down and driven from their lairs. They've passed into legend as guardians of religious secrets – most famously or notoriously the Holy Grail itself – but one of their legacies was in the poetry and music of the troubadours.

One of the most famous was called Chrétien de Troyes, who sang about King Arthur and the Holy Grail and spread the stories that would ooze down the centuries, picking up new characters and legends as they went. Singers and poets like him were men of high birth, well known at court, and they began to embroider their performances with music and with clowns and jesters who started to be figures on the scene from about the end of the twelfth century. Some virtuosity was beginning to creep in. Formal though the manners were that they had to adopt in the company of the rich and great, melody lines that echoed through the cloisters of the monasteries were being transformed into something different – something secular, calculated to appeal to the senses.

A song like Bernart de Ventadorn's 'Quan vei l'aloete' was familiar enough to be used as a tune for different sets of words, and the troubadours themselves became celebrities in the grand circles in which they moved. This was quite new, and a contrast to what was happening inside the churches. Bernart wrote in Provençal, not in Latin, and eventually the troubadours would all use the languages of the people. Recognisably English songs were developing – Eleanor's court had brought the tradition with it – and could there be a more memorable symbol of the minstrel age than her son, Richard the Lionheart himself, whose fate it was to never be pictured in a school textbook without lute or guitar in his hand? He certainly sang, and represented that part of the troubadour way of life that had found its way to England.

In church there was a gushing of polyphonic music as composers began to revel in the patronage – and frankly the fame – that they could find at the altar. The vaulted roofs rang to music which seemed enticing and daring, though to us it seems calm, controlled, even bare, springing from an age of refreshing simplicity. At a time of mass illiteracy, with printing still a couple of centuries away, and the Church the rigorous guardian of all learning, the idea of the divine was being given a new voice.

Outside, however, there was another voice. It spoke of human things, both lovely and loathsome. The troubadours had a travelling storehouse of tales of love and betrayal, and in the places where the rich and powerful gathered round their tables and their fires they were the entertainers of their time.

The songs were a contrast to the music of religion, though they drew on the same wellsprings, and they represented something that owed part of its attraction to the fact that it was dangerous. Though they spoke of love as a reflection of the love due to God, theirs was an art that was essentially secular – they sang of warriors and spies, lust and betrayal, as well as the ideal of courtly love. So they flirted with ideas that found no place behind the church doors – especially, perhaps, in the treatment of women, who in the surviving poetry of the time begin to appear less as idealised objects of adoration and more as flesh and blood.

The music was personal, human. New ideas were also travelling faster than before, the pace of learning was quickening, and in music new possibilities were starting to gleam in the minds of those who heard the troubadours and listened to what the church musicians were now creating.

Imaginations were at work, and an age of discovery lay ahead, all over Europe. There had been music in England that travelled across the Channel in earlier times, but by the middle of the fourteenth century there was a composer in London who may have been the best known in the world. More than 600 years later, only scholars and enthusiasts for the period know his name, but John Dunstable was a star.

You would have heard talk of him if you had visited the King's court at Sheen Palace by the Thames to the west of London, established by Richard II in 1383 (and eventually turned into Richmond Palace by Henry VII in the late fifteenth century). The tapestries on the walls would have come from Bruges or Ghent, the stained glass would have been from the continent too, the fashions imported – but the music would probably have been English. And in France the composers of the day were full of him: he was the most admired of composers and when he died, on Christmas Eve 1453, they wrote on his tomb that he had 'secret knowledge of the stars'. This shadowy figure is important. He and those who followed him, copying and refining his techniques, brought music to a new pitch: they were the bridge between the medieval and the Renaissance, the precursors of a golden age.

Dunstable was probably born in the town that bears his name in Bedfordshire; we don't know precisely in which year. He is thought to have travelled to France in the service of the Duke of Bedford; his biography is only a sketch. We do know that his music travelled far and that it was admired throughout Europe, in all the places where rich men were reaching for music as an accoutrement of power, a badge of culture and wealth. He was especially revered in the medieval court that was the most powerful and ambitious of them all – Burgundy.

You can hear his influence in the music of Guillaume Dufay (?1400–74), a composer who was said by one French poet to have given music 'an English countenance'. Dufay wrote for the Duke of Burgundy, who presided over a court that was much more than a rich household with thousands of hangers-on of the sort that you would find all over Europe. Burgundy wasn't exactly a nation but it behaved like a state. It was not merely the territory we think of now as the land of vineyards and canals south-east of Paris, but reached north into Flanders and Brabant – the Low Countries – and east away beyond Alsace and Lorraine with Dijon as its capital. It had riches and political power, but it was also the summation of medieval culture – fashionable, learned, stylish, often extravagant, and musical. There was singing at court, which rang to the sound of bagpipes and early recorders, drums and harps and, after about 1450, the dulcimer.

The Burgundy of Duke Philip the Good in the mid-fifteenth century that nurtured composers like Dufay and Dunstable was an example of a phenomenon that comes along from time to time in the story of music – the chance collision of power and enlightenment, a flash of genius that makes a country, or a city, for a short while the centre of the world: Vienna in the 1820s, Paris in the 1840s, New York in the 1920s. In Burgundy the music of Europe was distilled.

Nothing on this scale had been seen in Europe since the ancient world had passed away. Burgundians dressed in their own style – cone-shaped hats, butterfly veils, distinctive fur-trimmed robes – they ate and drank with gusto, had the biggest chapel in the world, and fought with France itself for pre-eminence. In their swagger could be found an echo of the stories that traders brought back to Venice from the east, where they'd seen the most exotic sights; yet this was Europe. And the court of Burgundy was never observed in a more spectacular or perhaps more arrogant guise than at the moment when Christendom suffered its greatest defeat.

In 1453 Constantinople fell to the Turks, and the Byzantium which had stretched eastwards for more than a thousand years was no more. The eastern Roman Empire had dissolved; the Catholic Church was shaken; Europe saw the enemy at the gate. So, of course, there had to be a crusade to fight the infidel. And in February 1454 the Duke of Burgundy and his Order of the Fleece – a kind of Arthurian order of knights – held a feast that was meant to be the prelude to that expedition. In the event the crusade never set sail, but the banquet on the Feast of the Pheasant would be remembered for a long time. To the music of Dufay, the Burgundians indulged in a bacchanalian entertainment that was extraordinary, even by their standards.

As they ate, they watched a tiger fighting a serpent and falcons being set on a heron, and camels, bears and even an elephant appeared, accompanied by a giant figure dressed as a Saracen, the enemy. On the elephant's back a nun popped out of a model castle and introduced herself as 'the Holy Church' pleading for a crusade. And on a table in the middle of the banquet was a vast pie, holding twenty-eight musicians who played for the guests from its depths, blowing their horns, banging the drums and working the Burgundian bagpipes. It was bizarre and extravagant, evidence of something remarkable behind the frolics – the idea of music as something worth paying for. The patron had arrived.

Philip the Good was less interested in political power and influence than in his antecedents and was more engrossed in the culture of his duchy. He wasn't literally the first patron of music – the troubadours did quite well in their wanderings – but in the whirlpool of his court you can feel the change. The composers writing for him were celebrities, and musical invention was valued. Never before had this happened on such a scale. The monasteries had been the repositories of the musical tradition for centuries, absorbing sounds that had come from beyond Europe as well as from earlier generations and turning them into something of their own. There was a tradition of secular song already, carried round the courts of Europe. In the scale and ambition of Burgundy at this time a new chapter opened in the story of music. If you listen to Dunstable's songs for a number of voices, there is confidence in the blending of those different voices in counterpoint, producing something quite different from the simpler lines that he himself had heard as a young man. He was revealing music's next phase.

That was the attraction to the French composers, in particular Dufay and Gilles de Bins Binchois (1400–60). Binchois was at the centre of the Burgundian court for thirty years and had heard English music. There had, after all, been an occupying English army in France. The Hundred Years War was going on its weary way. Binchois, Dufay and Dunstable were the most famous exponents of the Burgundian style. It was admired everywhere. A Flemish composer, Joannes Tinctoris, wrote this rather florid account of how lesser beings were in thrall to these stars:

> At the present time, there flourish whether by the force of some celestial influence or by the force of assiduous practice, countless composers . . . who glory in having studied this divine art under John Dunstable, Gilles Binchois and Guillaume Dufay. As Virgil took Homer for his model in that divine work the *Aeneid* so I, by Hercules, have used these composers as models for my modest works.

Throughout Europe, musicians realised that there was fertile new ground for them. The sounds of a Dunstable or Dufay were enticing in their possibilities: you could hear in them a different kind of music, more satisfying in its complexity, maybe more fluid, certainly suggesting that a melody – a tune with an appealing line – could be embroidered, shaped and turned, in ways that hadn't been done before. That was their achievement and their promise.

You can hear it in Dunstable's music for church (which is mostly what he wrote), where he was able to use the *cantus firmus* – the fixed song, the basic line – to build up a choral sound. He wrote what became known as cyclic masses, because they had a structure from the same tune, which linked the movements of the mass together, but which displayed an invention and even daring that was new.

His is confident music. The devotion of the monastic tradition had something else now: a feeling of power, of potential. Patrons, like the dukes of Burgundy, were going to pay for it, to encourage composers and to search for talented performers. They would boast of their culture and celebrate the new. The consequence was that musicians stepped out of the cloisters into the world. Though many of them would still write most of their music for church, and religion would remain the highest inspiration for generations to come, in the glamour of Burgundy and the atmosphere of excitement around its composers, you can hear a fuller sound than anyone had known before.

In learning, in art and architecture the Renaissance thinkers were now establishing the foundations of the European culture that has shaped our own world. Music was now part of it. There's no building that embodies the spirit of that time better than the Cathedral, the Duomo, in Florence. Filippo Brunelleschi won the competition to design it, and his dome, with its two shells one inside the other, became one of the wonders of the world. The Cathedral was dedicated on 25 March 1436 and Guillaume Dufay wrote the music for the occasion.

He'd done something extraordinary, writing a song in which he worked out the proportions of the Cathedral in minute detail and embodied them in his time signatures for the music, so that, like the dimensions of the Great Pyramid at Giza, they seemed to have some inner secret balance and power. He offered a homage to Brunelleschi and a private display of the musician's own craft, matching the architect's meticulous planning and his ability, in this Cathedral, to build a colossal dome that was supported by means that had once been thought impossible. Brunelleschi had shown that there was some mystery in the skill. Dufay wanted to show that, in music, you could do the same.

On that day in Florence, under Brunelleschi's dome, they played Dufay's 'Nuper rosarum flores' during the service of dedication. The Renaissance involved a rediscovery of ancient arts and learning that built up, layer upon layer. The dedication of the Duomo in Florence is an occasion on which you can see, and hear, the beginning of its culmination. After three centuries of invention and experiment, in which musical ideas and forms started to travel more quickly across Europe than ever before, a moment of maturity had been reached. In the century that followed music would flower more quickly and more spectacularly than it had ever done before.

3

The Renaissance

Florence, Trent and the First Opera

~

WE CAN LOOK back at the time when Brunelleschi's dome rose above Florence and enjoy the fantasy of imagining that this was the moment when the High Renaissance was born. Nonsense, of course. Who knows how to put a date to the beginning of an age of change? Sometimes there is a treaty or a coronation, a significant discovery or a death that becomes a marker. More often, the tide creeps up slowly until – suddenly it seems – everything is at the flood. The Renaissance was a patchwork of ideas, inspiration and expressions of genius that came together gradually over centuries. Although it is true that a painting by Giotto or later a drawing or sculpture by Michelangelo captures the brilliance of an era, and that there is music that still speaks of the power that artists began to feel they had rediscovered, there is no simple way of catching the moment.

For musicians it was less of a recreation of classical civilisation than a harnessing of the power of the idea. Such pieces of music as there were from early times, assumed to have been passed down over many centuries, were hardly an inspiration in themselves because they were mere fragments, no more than a suggestion of what might have been played or how it sounded. Poets, however, had spoken of the power of these sweet sounds. The music of the Renaissance came from a belief in that power.

Think of what it must have been like to be in Ferrara, about eighty miles south-west of Venice, at the beginning of the sixteenth century. At the Duke's court, one of the grandest and most ambitious in Italy, you would have heard the music of Josquin Desprez, the greatest composer of his time.

Josquin (as he is usually now known) was born in the middle of the fifteenth century, probably in 1460, and he was a pupil of Johannes Ockeghem, who may have been taught by Binchois and who led a Flemish school of composition that became influential over the next generation. The fact that no one can be quite sure of the Binchois connection at one remove is a useful reminder that the effort to pluck out the streams of thought and musical technique from the middle ages is fraught with danger. We are dealing with uncertainties. Whatever preceded the relationship with Ockeghem, it is known that Josquin was, with Dufay, one of the great stars in the Burgundian firmament, that his teacher Ockeghem was Flemish, and that he passed on to Josquin a subtle style of polyphony which was carried on from Burgundy to Italy, where it became part of musical life.

Ferrara was an encapsulation of the boldness and excitement of Italy at that time. It wasn't Venice or Rome or Paris, but here at the court of one ambitious duke they came to hear music that was avant-garde (a concept that would have seemed something from outer space at the time, if such a realm had existed), catching the spirit of their time. Duke Ercole d'Este I had ambitions. In a Europe of cities that sprawled and festered along their rivers and at their trading ports, he decided to lay out a network of streets and squares, with a citadel in a perfect pentagram at the centre, so that Ferrara would become a standing boast, and evidence of the rediscovery of classical line and form and a physical homage to Greece and Rome, which was the new intellectual obsession.

He wanted more than physical beauty, and the satisfaction of reviving the classical dramas that he staged in his theatre. He needed music, and by now there was competition for the greatest talent, which was being traded as a precious commodity. For a couple of hundred years the Church had been patron to the composers who discovered that it was – perhaps surprisingly – the vehicle for experiments in music as well as a career. Now along came Josquin, born in northern France, who had been a student in Flanders, and then a singer and composer in Milan, where his talent made him one of the best-paid musicians in the civilised world, at that time assumed to be synonymous with a fairly restricted western Europe. The Duke of Ferrara's secretary advised his master to employ Heinrich Isaac, because he was cheaper than Josquin and would compose to order when required. Josquin would be more wilful, but he was better. The Duke decided he would have him. Martin Luther, who admired Josquin's music, said of him: 'He is master of the notes; others are mastered by them.'

At the outset of the sixteenth century, Josquin was snapped up by the court in Ferrara – the Duke wanted composers who would be talked about – and what is perhaps the most important piece he wrote there, the 'Missa Hercules Dux Ferrariae', is a musical landmark. It was born of a way of thinking that had been developing gradually for centuries, but now took a leap forward – the idea that the scholars of the day called *umanismo*. It became known to us as humanism, a word attached to it in the nineteenth century. There was, emphatically, no break with the Christian tradition that was part of the Renaissance, but there was a new interest taken by the artist – whether a painter, a sculptor, a musician – in man, not just in God. In music it had a practical consequence that would change the way composers worked.

Humanism sought clarity of exposition. The meaning of words had to be obvious, so musical rhythms and textures became more subtle, more expressive, trying to tease out the text, which was more important than before. In the 'Hercules Mass', the structural basis of the composition wasn't traditional plainsong – always the foundation of church music, the stream from everything else had flowed – but the very syllables of the Duke's own name. Here in the mass, sung in church, the celebrants and the congregation heard the glorification not of God but of a man – a patron, a duke, a landlord. Josquin was not trying to turn his employer into a deity, but merely paying the kind of compliment which hired musicians at court were required to pay. Nonetheless, he was confronting the assumption that such music was inappropriate for a setting in which no figure should challenge the omnipotence of God.

The secular and the sacred had flowed together for centuries. The idea prevalent in medieval times that everything had the potential to be divine meant that there need not be a 'sacred' source for music used in church. Anything could be crafted to a divine purpose. Josquin was writing for the Duke of Ferrara with an absolute belief in the capacity of music to serve simultaneously its purpose in church and the glorification of the man who had paid for it.

By this time, with the fifteenth century just gone, the music at court was almost unrecognisable compared to the sounds that had been heard generations before. This is a description by a pupil of Desprez called Coclico of how the master worked:

> My teacher Josquin . . . never gave a lecture on music or wrote a theoretical work, and yet he was able in a short time to form complete musicians, because he did not keep back his pupils with long and useless instructions – but taught them the rules in a few words, through practical application in the course of singing. And as soon as he saw that his pupils were well grounded in singing, had a good enunciation and knew how to embellish melodies and fit the text to the music, then he taught them the perfect and imperfect intervals and the different methods of inventing counterpoints against plainsong. If he discovered, however, pupils with an ingenious mind and promising disposition, then he would teach these in a few words the rules of three-part and later four-, five-, six-part, etc., writing, always providing them with examples to imitate. Josquin did not, however, consider all suited to learn composition; he judged that only those should be taught who were drawn to this delightful art by a special natural impulse.

That account reveals the leap that Josquin made. Having absorbed the techniques of his teachers from Flanders, he twisted the straightforward lines of plainsong into a new form. New rhythms were added, with new harmonic patterns, new textures with voices beginning to overlap and carry the melody forward.

This was innovation. Around Josquin, the world was looking at itself in a new way. He was a contemporary in Milan of Leonardo da Vinci, engineer and scientist as well as painter and sculptor, who painted the *Mona Lisa* around that time. In that first decade of the sixteenth century Raphael was at his peak, working on frescoes in the Vatican, and Michelangelo was revealing his genius – he completed the statue of David in 1504. In Florence, in the shadow of Brunelleschi's cupola – the greatest in the world – painters, under the patronage of the Medici, were luxuriating in the inspirations of a golden age. Music was rather different. There was no clear classical model to which to turn. No one really knew what Greek or Roman music had sounded like.

Palladio could look to the ancients for architectural inspiration – he knew how Rome had been built – and artists could find classical perfection in statuary. Musicians instead wondered how the profound impact of music that the ancient poets had described could be replicated. The idea of *feeling* in music would arrive later, but the beginnings of that revolutionary change were rumbling beneath the surface. Rather than remaining almost a branch of mathematics, as it had seemed to be in the previous century, composition had adopted a subtlety and complexity.

Most sacred music at this time was heard in the private chapels of the princes. A greater array of instruments was appearing: alongside the recorder and the dulcimer would be a range of viols, the bass viol de gamba being the deepest and most powerful, giving guts to the sound, though much sacred music was still unaccompanied. In the course of the sixteenth century the harpsichord would become as familiar as the sackbut (the primitive Renaissance trombone) or the lute. You could hear the first faint whisper of what would become an orchestral sound.

The technical business of music-making was advancing fast, and the idea of music's purpose had changed too. Church music was still a shining centrepiece, and the inevitable stream from which most else flowed. Rome, with the first stirrings of the Protestant Reformation reaching its anxious ears, was an ever more diligent patron of the finest sounds, the grandest compositions. But the humanism of the Renaissance gave man a new status alongside God – in painting, in sculpture and in music. Artists looked at the classical world and compared it with their own: they were learning not only about the glories of the past but about how different their own society was. Historical inquiry was the intellectual fashion. They might still look to the stars and the heavenly places, and try to represent the divine, but now they were also interested in humankind. And that intellectual change was irreversible, though sacred music was still written for the purpose that the Church demanded, one that seemed perpetual and inviolable.

An age remembered for artistic genius in its canvases and statues, when western art glowed with certainty and boldness, was also an age of upheaval. The ideas sweeping through the universities that were springing up and establishing links between themselves across borders were even suggesting that some day they might challenge the power of the Church itself. While in Italy, in the first decades of the sixteenth century, the achievements of painters and musicians alike spoke of confidence and stability, in Germany Martin Luther (1486–1546) was challenging the very foundations of the religious teaching that had nurtured them. He was fomenting a revolution of his own; and it would have its own music.

The sound of the Protestant Reformation that was shaking Europe in the middle of the sixteenth century was a break with the tradition of the Church. The theology of Luther constituted the principal offence in Rome's eyes, but his music presented a challenge of its own. Not only were worshippers joining in the singing in church – itself something of a heresy – and singing in German instead of Latin, but the words were clear and understood. Luther himself produced a German translation of the Bible. Instead of soaring away above the congregation, in an almost mystical way, church music had come down to earth. Something had to be done. The Church had already grasped that the power of secular music needed to be understood, and was already making an effort to ensure that the words of sacred music were clearer. But the pressure was becoming much stronger.

That argument was part of the extraordinary conference convened in northern Italy in 1545, at Trento in the foothills of the Dolomites, to decide what to do about Luther and the other heretics who were causing such consternation. This was no panicky summit: it lasted for eighteen years, a diplomatic and theological circus of the sort that has never been seen since. As well as worrying about doctrine and discipline, the delegates who came and went at the Council of Trent during those long years eventually turned their minds to music. They did so under the sombre and miserable heading 'Abuses in the Sacrifice of the Mass'. This is what the Council said: 'All things should indeed be so ordered that the masses, whether they be celebrated with or without singing, may reach tranquilly into the ears and hearts of those who hear them, when everything is executed clearly and at the correct speed.'

It was a necessary compromise, an admission that although nothing was to be allowed to interfere with the glorious sound – the richness of praise – the Church now accepted that what was being sung should be clear and comprehensible. 'In the case of those masses which are celebrated with singing and with organ, let nothing profane be intermingled, but only hymns and divine praises. The whole plan of singing should be constituted not to give empty pleasure to the ear, but in such a way that the words be clearly understood by all.'

Where did this leave composers who'd been revelling in the Renaissance style, playing with more complicated harmonies in the many-layered vocal lines of polyphony and with new instruments? Churches were ordered to allow only 'heavenly harmonies', whatever they might be, and all instruments other than the organ were banned. 'They shall also banish from church all music that contains whether in the singing or in the organ-playing things that are lascivious or impure.'

That injunction, issued in 1562 when the Council of Trent was limping towards its end, might have been a disaster for music. It was not. Perhaps this was because the Church had already absorbed some of the creativity that was developing in secular music, and because the Council spoke in generalities. A good illustration of how the secular tradition of composition was absorbed with ease into church music, whatever the nervousness in Rome, comes in the 'Missa Papae Marcelli' by a musician called Giovanni Pierluigi but always known by the name of the town near Rome where he was born in the 1520s – Palestrina.

He wrote more than a hundred masses and became one of the most famous church composers of his day. His clarity and flowing style, and his ear for gorgeous melody, happened to be exactly what the Church needed, though there is no evidence that he was influenced by what was happening far to the north of him in the Alpine foothills. We need to remember the panic that was now flowing through the Vatican in the early 1540s. When it looked northwards to the rest of Europe, there seemed to be trouble everywhere, fomented by Luther in Germany and John Calvin in Switzerland. Beyond continental Europe, in England Henry VIII (by now on wife number six, Catherine Parr) had dissolved the monasteries in a violent campaign and was at war with the Church. In Scotland, reformers and priests were murdering each other, and John Knox, Calvin's disciple, was starting to preach.

How would composers manage to reveal their texts more plainly – so that 'the words [would] be clearly understood by all' – without abandoning the intricate forms that they were now using, and which were promising so much? Palestrina, perhaps by chance, appeared to be providing part of the answer. He said he 'blushed and grieved' to think that he had once been one of those depraved men who used the love songs of poets to make music – though he had resorted to a secular melody as the mainstream, the *cantus firmus*, of his mass 'L'Homme armé'. You can hear in his music not just the impulse of someone wanting to fill a church with beautiful sound, and to glorify the mass, but a composer who got his inspiration everywhere.

He had a smoothness of line, and a delicacy in handling harmony, distinguished by balance and simplicity. He's an extraordinary example of how musicians can rise above the narrow rules forced on them, responding to them with an easy arrogance. The pattern has been repeated again and again since those distant days in Italy when the Church was engaged in a struggle which for musicians (quite apart from ordinary Christians) in later centuries seems almost bizarre in its intensity. The Council of Trent was engaged in a kind of censorship. It's a familiar story: panic, followed by the cry 'Something must be done,' then a little bit of compromise with the enemy, and finally a decree couched in absolutist language. In painting, artists like Titian (1485–1576) and El Greco (1541–1614) had the genius to react to the demand for unsullied religious images by producing something even greater than the Church had expected; Palestrina turned what might have been a restrictive and regressive regime in church music into something new, perhaps without realising what he was doing. The negative became positive.

The truth is that music was going its own way, and it was impossible to stop the passing on of ideas from one composer to another, just as it was impossible to stifle the ability of an original musician to learn from what he'd heard. Decrees from the princes of the Church might govern the liturgy, or the behaviour of priests and bishops, but they could not stop the musical explosions that were being heard everywhere. A ban might work for a short time, but there appears to have been an understanding that imagination was having its way and couldn't be eliminated. Expecting a composer to ignore the 'depraved taste' of secular songs in writing for the Church was to expect him to go against nature, as was obvious from the number of masses that took secular inspiration for their *cantus firmus*. In Palestrina you hear all the strands intertwined. He'd studied the French and Flemish composers, grown up with the sounds of the Renaissance music that was flooding Italy in the early sixteenth century, and heard the new instruments that were changing the accompaniment to the voice.

The result was that although this was the age of the Inquisition, the banning of books, the zealotry of the Jesuits, music wasn't confined at all. Indeed in the second half of the sixteenth century it bounded forward. What you would hear in Italy, especially in Venice, was music that had the complexity of an age still to come. It didn't look back at all, and though the Church may appear to have wanted in theory to be restrictive in its proclamations, in practice for most composers' church music it was business as usual. The innovation that was exciting composers throughout the late Renaissance couldn't be stifled.

In any case, the Council of Trent wasn't as clear in its thinking as it wanted everyone to think. Titian painted a session in 1555 (after it had been sitting for ten years) in which all was order: the delegates seated in neat rows, gazing towards the altar, and the leaders of the Church sitting in front of it. But, for all its prescriptive language, the declaration on music was confused. They wanted clarity, but also a kind of sensuous opulence that would inspire awe. To a composer with the talent, that was a marvellous ambiguity.

Musicians were being encouraged to be sensual, and that was to be part of the experience that would cement the faith. Let the Protestants sing their hymns and listen to their preachers in black in their bleak German churches; Catholics would hear the finest music and emotional oratory, enjoy the spectacle of churches filled with colour and light, and experience the 'ecstasy' – a favourite word at the time – of the divine presence.

Imagine how Palestrina's music sounded when he was working for the Pope in the Capella Giulia, which become the Sistine Chapel. The music of the Counter-Reformation had power: that was the point. And it was one of the successes of the fightback by Rome against Protestantism. But it failed to sap the strength of the Lutheran movement that was its target. Indeed Lutheranism was prospering too, and just as Palestrina's heirs would benefit from his ability to exploit the desires of his Church, so Bach and others in the seventeenth and eighteenth centuries would draw inspiration from the other side.

Music had now become important as a voice of the institutions and states that were competing for power. The popes wanted it to conjure up ecstasy, to show that music was a representation of their power, which was probably as important to them as any aesthetic aspect. To Luther it was the voice of the people; in Philip II's Spain and Elizabeth's England composers were establishing parallel traditions of their own with a similar intent. Europe was sunk in religious conflict and war, but its music was alive.

The Catholic Church, from the middle ages and throughout the Renaissance, was a patron of music, and an inspiration for it, the conduit for musical ideas. Composers clustered round the huge churches and cathedrals that had to be filled with sound; and just as the architects tried to send their spires higher and higher, the musicians produced more glorious music, richer and fuller. There was no greater purpose for the artist than the praise of God. Meanwhile, beyond the church doors, the powerful men of the age encouraged court music that was not designed for religious purposes, and there was an oral culture in the streets that kept tunes alive across the generations. The sacred and the secular lived side by side, and had to be harnessed for the proper purpose.

Luther, of course, believed precisely the same thing. In his rebellion against the Church, in which he began as a reformer and became almost a revolutionary figure, he believed that sound was important. The voices of the people – the faithful – were the evidence of the changes in worship and church practice that he wanted to bring about, thereby shaking Rome. When, in protest, he nailed his ninety-five theses to the door of the church in Wittenberg in Germany in 1517 he was challenging the Church's system of allowing papal 'indulgences' to be sold – these effectively promised an easier entry into heaven for those who could afford to pay the clergy at the going rate. Luther thought it was corruption that had to be exterminated, and he is remembered above all for that act of defiance, which became the symbol of the reforming Christian tradition in Europe.

Yet there was much more to it than an argument about money and the question of whether God's grace could be bought. Luther, who'd been ordained a priest in 1507, wanted to reform the mass to bring it closer to the laity as part of his belief in a relationship between the worshipper and God that didn't need the intervention of a priest. His central belief was in 'justification by faith alone', the belief that sinners were redeemed by the exercise of devotion and the strength of their faith. Part of that reform would be in the way congregations spoke to God, in their own language. He didn't want to dispense with Latin, which was still the language of learning and praise for God, but he did want to introduce German into the liturgy. The natural way to do it was with music.

He'd been trained to sing as a boy; in the quadrivium, the course taught to students of the arts at medieval universities, you studied music (the science of the 'music of the spheres') alongside arithmetic, geometry and astronomy. He learned about intervals between notes, about harmony and polyphony, and found himself able to write tunes, which doesn't always follow. Contemporary accounts say that he had a soft tenor voice in later life, perhaps not the one we would first associate with the black-clad figure, always pictured looking grim, nailing his pieces of paper to the church door. Anyway, he sang, and music was important to him.

He knew the work of the Renaissance composer Josquin, the greatest of those working in Luther's era at the beginning of the sixteenth century. This familiarity was made possible by the fact that music was beginning to travel more easily, not only because musicians were on the move all the time between the European centres of learning, but because musical scores could now be printed, initially on wood blocks and then with movable type, first used in Venice at the very opening of the sixteenth century. It was primitive, and only towards the end of the century would printed music begin to circulate widely, but for the first time a beautifully illuminated manuscript was not needed to show what a composer had written.

As usual, there was a patron in the background. He was Duke Frederick of Saxony (known as 'the Wise'), who encouraged Luther to replicate some of Josquin's skill with polyphony, which he wanted to do because he thought it was like 'the song of the finch' – so natural. He had a profound interest in music. This is an extract from a letter he wrote to the composer Ludwig Senfl in 1530, revealing how his idea of the 'truth', which he thought the Church had abandoned, could be revealed in the way music was used in church: 'The prophets did not make use of any art except music. It was not as geometry, or arithmetic, or astronomy, but as music that they delivered their theology. For them theology and music were closely bound together and they proclaimed the truth through psalms and songs.'

You could put one of Luther's most important ideas in those terms – turning the mass from a sacrifice to God by a priest on behalf of the people into an offer of forgiveness and grace to them from God. And the response from the people would come in music. So he started to circulate broadsheets in Wittenberg which helped people to learn the tunes, and the words, and this is how he described them:

> These songs were arranged in four parts to give the young – who should at any rate be trained in music and other fine arts – something to wean them away from love ballads and carnal songs and to teach them something of value in their place, thus combining the good with the pleasing, as is proper for youth . . . I would like to see all the arts, especially music, used in the service of him who has given and created them.

It is almost as if he is saying what General Booth, founder of the Salvation Army, said when he entered a theatre in Worcester more than three centuries later and was introduced to the crowd with a music-hall song. 'Why should the devil have all the best tunes?' Booth asked. The carnal songs would pass away, Luther hoped, but the truth is that their influence would remain – because, whether he liked it or not, Luther was one of the causes of that mingling of the secular and the sacred which was one of the strongest currents flowing through our story at this stage. Congregational singing of the sort we know today was a radical thing – a new sound in church – and we get from Luther those building blocks that would be taken by so many composers, including those of genius like Bach, and turned into some of the greatest musical constructions we know.

The Reformation, despite the religious wars it spawned across Europe for much of the next two centuries, was a cultural reawakening. It broke the rules; new ideas were on the loose; so were new sounds. Behind the power struggles within the Church and among the monarchies across the continent, and regardless of the ebb and flow of the reformers' influence, that fact was inescapable. Just as word had travelled from Italy to Germany to France and to England of the achievements of Josquin and his like, the songbooks that Luther was now able to print in Germany began to circulate. He said of Josquin that he 'made the word stand before our eyes' and continued to insist that the key to reformed religion was understanding on the part of the faithful: there must be no force-feeding. It was an important influence in the campaign in church music to clarify the text, just as madrigals were beginning to celebrate the sensitivity of the word revealed by music.

Perhaps it is not surprising that the dynamism of this new kind of worship was popular – with congregations singing in their own languages as well as hearing the Latin they expected in musical settings of the creed. There were powerful patrons who rather liked the radicalism for other reasons – anything that loosened the grip of Rome on land and money was useful to them, after all – and they could therefore celebrate the Lutheran movement, having saved its founder from the heretic's fire into which he had nearly been thrown. In the chorales sung in these churches you can feel some of that sense of release.

Luther played the lute and the flute and it would have been natural for him to pick up the tunes – folk melodies we would call them now – that were common currency in Germany (unless of course they seemed too carnal) and adapt them to higher purposes. In doing that he was an exemplar of the mobility of music, which is one of its most formidable secrets. It flows, from one sphere to another, from street to church and back out again, across borders, through languages and cultures, carrying ideas and inspiration as it goes. And, in an era like Luther's, it is part of the political and religious discourse. You can hear the Reformation in these chorales, in the German words finding their way into church, in the bravado with which these tunes and arrangements were used to challenge the way things had been. For the learned Protestant leaders, and the people who decided to follow them in northern Europe, these were sounds that described the tumult.

These are confident melodies and harmonies, with simple lines and clear rhythms – familiar to us still, perhaps even cosy. In their day they were subversive and dangerous, and the established Church had to respond to the challenge they represented – hence the Counter-Reformation. And almost as if music was a weapon as powerful as the most charismatic preacher, or even the most radical theological idea, that response would be heard in the instruments and the voices that accompanied the Church's answer to Luther. As well as much religious strife, and many bloody acts in the name of God, out of this tormented argument would come music that aspired to the sublime.

Although Rome was aware that church music should acknowledge the need for understanding – and musicians like Josquin had written for voices in ways that would allow the notes to interact carefully with the words, setting up a pulse that would put the emphasis in the right place – one of the paradoxical developments in the second half of the sixteenth century was an urge to greater splendour in such music. Simplicity, but glory too. The wealth and excitement of Renaissance Italy meant that, while comprehensibility in words might be deemed admirable by the authorities in Rome, religious devotion was bound to be expressed in polyphony that would become richer and grander.

The rebirth of the Renaissance also led to discovery. In trying to replicate what was imagined to have been classical perfection in music, as painters, sculptors and architects were doing, composers were keen to experiment. Perhaps the most significant innovation took place in Florence. It would be good to put a precise date to the moment opera was born. That can't be done, though we can pinpoint the day when the earliest extant opera was first performed. It was 6 October 1600. The occasion was appropriately auspicious, the wedding of one of the Medicis to Henry IV, King of France, in Florence's Pitti Palace.

There were three operas heard on each night of the wedding celebrations, one by Jacopo Peri (1561–1633), the others by Giulio Caccini (?1550–1610) and Emilio de' Cavalieri (1550–1602). They are names we hardly hear now; but in the Florence of that time these men were innovators and stars. They called themselves the Camerata, and though none of them was a composer who would survive in the regular repertoire – someone else was going to be the first operatic genius in this world, and quite soon – collectively they were the founders of opera.

They had got the idea from the distant past. The Florentine Republic was trying to strengthen itself against rival city states by looking back to the ancient models of Greece and Rome, and one of the by-products was the discovery by the Camerata that drama and music could be brought together, as they imagined the Greeks had shown. They wanted a change from the madrigals – sophisticated part-songs for several voices – to exploit the solo voice. They believed that only a solo singer could express emotion. In a polyphonic piece one voice might be going up when another was going down (indeed, that was almost bound to happen). How could that express a moment of ecstasy or sadness? They wanted to tell a story in music.

Everything that lay ahead – from Handel to Verdi to Wagner to modern opera – can be traced back to these early performances. This was because, like scientists watching a spectacular chemical reaction, the Camerata stumbled across something extraordinary: music drama gave audiences something that they loved, an experience like no other. Florence wanted more. The dukes of Mantua and Ferrara, whose courts were about showing off as well as about power, wanted similar music and spectacle. Soon dozens of theatres would rise up, forty of them in Venice alone.

Among the aristocrats of Florence music drama became a craze. Italy had always loved spectacle, and here was a chance to indulge. All sorts of performances adopted music: parades, mock naval battles, cere-monial jousting contests, crude equestrian ballets, and even a ball game called the *calico* which had players dressed in costume who sang – it was primitive football to a soundtrack. The most popular was the *mascherata*, in which the masked dancers stopped from time to time to sing, with mechanical sets behind them. Although there had always been music of the streets, passed on down the years, this was different from the church music that had dominated everything in an earlier age. Now there was a stage on which anything could happen.

Performers responded. They started to compete with each other in their histrionics. Effects were everything. A contemporary diarist, Vincenzo Giustiniani, said of the ladies of Ferrara and Florence that they manipulated their voices to change the mood:

> breaking off sometimes with a gentle sigh, now singing long passages legato or detached [from each other], now groups, now leaps with long trills, now with short, or again with sweet running passages sung

39

softly . . . to which one sometimes heard an echo answer unexpectedly. They accompanied the music and the sentiment with appropriate facial expressions, glances and gestures, with no awkward movements of the mouth or hands or body, which might . . . express the feeling of the song.

He was probably describing the kinds of madrigals that were the forerunner of early opera and that incorporated various pieces that collectively told a story. They turned into a form that spread like wildfire throughout Italy, harnessing the genius of Claudio Monteverdi and then advancing a few decades later into France.

From these hesitant beginnings, the music of the Renaissance was able to encompass a new way of expressing feeling. The arguments between the established Church and the Reformers were about the proper way for the faithful to relate to God. Echoes of that debate were heard in music, in the way Luther saw directness as the key to his truth and the Catholic Church tried to encourage clarity in its religious music. There was a political and theological conflict here. But music is not a cipher for these collisions. It comes from the inspiration of composers who absorb what is around but also delve into themselves. The Renaissance was a time of athletic exploration in music, both in church and outside.

As the century of the High Renaissance ended, the stirrings in Florence were proving to be as momentous as anything the Council of Trent had to say about 'proper' music in church. The Camerata were the trailblazers of a musical invention that would, in the next century, conquer new territories in the imaginations of composers, musicians and those who were able to hear their work.

4

A Seventeenth-Century Journey

Venice to Paris to Cremona

∿

IT IS NATURAL to think of the story of music as a journey because so often it is impossible to separate a sound, or the personality of a work, from its physical surroundings. Sometimes, the notes seem to spring from the ground or from the particular byways of a city. A landscape, a bleak stretch of seashore, the feel of a city square or a church can be caught and held for a moment: a phrase, a simple arrangement of notes, an atmosphere, seems to speak of the place, and take you there.

Listeners often arouse such feelings within themselves almost as an act of will, making music say something that the composer never intended, but it is obvious that much music bears the stamp of time and place. Whether it is the raucous street politics of Italy in Verdi, the melancholy reed-beds of the Suffolk coast in Benjamin Britten or the grand swagger of Paris in Berlioz, the sound can't be ripped from its setting, even when a composer is not conscious of writing music which is meant to tell a contemporary story or paint a picture of something familiar. Sometimes that is not the point – would you know, or should you worry, that Mozart wrote his First Symphony not in Salzburg but in London? But from time to time, in a particular place, that influence – the sheer insistence of the place that it should shape the music – becomes overwhelming.

At the end of the period we think of as the Renaissance, when Italy regarded itself as the world's teacher and guide, you can begin a sensuous journey into the seventeenth century in a city that was in love with itself. If you visited Venice on Ascension Day in 1600 you would have heard trumpet fanfares announcing the *sposalizio*, the wedding of the city to the sea. Where else would they have dared?

Each year on the same day, the Doge who ruled the city state would renew the pledge of his ancestors that Venice would always reign supreme over all the oceans, leading a procession in which the precise hierarchy of the city was replicated: by your place in his train your position in society, and your power, was revealed. He would then take to his ceremonial ship – *il bucintoro* – with 168 oarsman and 40 sailors on board, a magnificent craft with a figure of justice at the prow and a throne for the Doge in the stern. Canaletto's several paintings of the scene in the 1730s show a mustering of gondolas on the Grand Canal evoking both contentment and settled glory, a festival of colour and style.

The Doge would seek his blessing for the ceremony in the basilica of St Mark's, which was his private chapel, in the square that Napoleon later called the finest drawing room in Europe, and once again Venice would have its place confirmed as the most civilised city in the world. By the beginning of the seventeenth century, of course, this was already becoming a hollow boast. Power was ebbing away; in trade, Venice was no longer the envy of Europe. The city state that had once ruled all the passages to the east and dressed itself in silk and ivory was in decline, though it hardly knew it yet.

Its music, however, was in its prime. To imagine how the city sounded, think of St Mark's itself. It is enormous, overpowering and strange, because the basilica seems to owe debts that are far greater than loyalty to the orthodoxies of Renaissance Christianity. As Jan Morris wrote, at the height of her love affair with the city in 1960, 'there is a tremendous sense of an eastern past – marbled, hazed and silken'. The church had a 'rich barbarism . . . like a great Mongolian pleasure pavilion or a fortress in Turkestan'.

That commitment to pleasure was reflected in the music of the church. Some of the most famous musicians in Venice at the start of the seventeenth century were from the Gabrieli family, providing the kind of glorious sound that would fill St Mark's and do justice to its finery and its mystery. Because of its position as the Doge's chapel, where the important ceremonies of state often took place, St Mark's had the luxury of being outside the day-to-day control of Rome, and to some extent able to strike out on its own. The surge of the Renaissance, and the religious collisions of the sixteenth century, had already moulded music, encouraging it to become richer, more subtle in construction, and now many composers were striving for more sensual power, even in church. It was in Venice that everything came together.

Here in this basilica, had you come in through one of the five great doors opening on to the square, under the four bronze horses on the façade, into the swirl of incense and the flash of gold in the dark from priestly vestments and hangings, you might have heard one of the madrigals by Giovanni Gabrieli (1557–1612) or his organ music, which was exceptionally rich. He was the director of music at the Scuola Grande di San Rocco, where many of the musicians from St Mark's also sang and played, and it was there that he developed a polychoral style – for multiple choirs and orchestras – that became one of the glories of the city. They would be played in a sumptuously decorated hall, graced with paintings by Tintoretto, including his *Crucifixion*, executed in 1565, which the novelist Henry James said contained more of human life than any other painting. In that setting Gabrieli directed music that reflected the spirit of a city, unrestrained in its appeal to the senses.

The sound of Venice was confident and rich when it was able to look out contentedly across its protective lagoon to the world. Its traders were bringing treasure back from the east; the oligarchy that controlled it was secure; it hadn't yet acknowledged that its power was on the wane. And from all over Europe artists and musicians were drawn to La Serenissima, the most serene Republic. They heard some of the best organ music in Italy and choral singing that had a special new fullness. Gabrieli, whose uncle Andrea (1510–86) was principal composer at St Mark's before him, used the church for musical invention. The idea of a dialogue between two choirs or groups of musicians found a natural home here. The basilica became a magnet for visitors. They would marvel at the Byzantine architecture, the mosaics on the walls laid on a gold background, the dusky light filtering through narrow windows, and they would listen.

They heard groups of brass and string instruments which weren't yet common elsewhere, the musicians following written instructions that told them when to play loudly and when softly, which was also uncommon. Everything seemed to point forwards, to new sounds and new styles. We think of Venice now as a grand old lady – slightly bent but dignified, faded and crumbling a little. When Gabrieli was writing for St Mark's it was the most modern place in Europe.

The city was flamboyant and throbbing with commerce. Its seventy or so churches were set in a city that was cosmopolitan and that was proud to think of music as an important part of its civic as well as its religious life. When the Doge was carried through Venice, the show was accompanied by music designed to capture the sheer confidence and even the arrogance of power. Contemporary accounts speak of an overwhelming experience. Thomas Coryat, a slightly eccentric English writer and traveller who came to Venice in 1608 having travelled much of the way on foot, left a vivid account of his time in the city in his travelogue *Crudities*. He enjoyed eating fried frogs, excoriated the whores whom he had encountered around the Rialto, noted approvingly that women were allowed to play parts in the theatre (in Shakespeare's England, boys were still playing female roles) and for the first time heard the singing of a castrato (who, he was surprised but apparently relieved to find, was not a eunuch at all but was simply blessed with a voice that could explore areas that most men found beyond them). He wrote that one concert he went to:

> consisted principally of musicke, which was both vocall and instrumental, so good, so delectable, so rare, so admirable, so super excellent, that it did even ravish and stupefie all those strangers that never heard the like . . . For mine own part I can say this, that I was for the time even rapt up with St Paul into the third heaven.

Having visited the Scuolo San Rocco, where he gazed at Tintoretto's ceiling while listening to Gabrieli's music, performed by a choir of twenty, two dozen instrumentalists and seven organs, he heard one singer who impressed him to the point of ecstasy: 'I thinke the country where he was borne may be as proude for breeding so singular a person as Smyrna was of her Homer, Verona of her Catullus, or Mantua her Virgil. But exceeding happy may that Citie, or towne, or person bee that possesseth this miracle of nature.'

Travellers discovered that music was part of the city. The Venetian historian Francesco Sansovino wrote that at Christmas services in St Mark's about this time he saw a congregation 'stupefied' by the eight-,

ten-, twelve-, sixteen-part settings and added that those from outside
the city 'confessed to having heard no finer music in many parts of the
world'. He was describing a church service, but one which had the
same theatricality as the Doge's procession down the Grand Canal. St
Mark's had a special dispensation from the Pope to have the first mass of
Christmas before midnight, which would begin in darkness before, one
by one, more than a thousand candles would be lit during the office of
Matins. Sansovino described the effect: 'an illumination brighter than
one might see at midday, which astonishes everyone standing to admire
the number and density of the candles . . . one could not see grander,
richer, more splendid, more noble or more illustrious illuminations
anywhere in Italy or indeed in Christendom'.

That nobility was important. The city evinced a limitless confidence.
Coryat described the loggetta, the meeting place for the powerful men
of Venice at the foot of the campanile next to St Mark's (which
collapsed without warning in the summer of 1902 and was patiently
rebuilt over ten years). This was where disputes were settled and deals
arranged. Here stood a statue of Apollo, one of four bronzes in the
loggetta, of which Sansovino wrote:

> Apollo is the sun, which is singular and unique, just as this Republic, for
> its constituted laws, its unity, and uncorrupted liberty, is a sun in the
> world, regulated with justice and wisdom; furthermore it is known how
> this nation takes a more than ordinary delight in music, and Apollo
> signifies music. Moreover, from the union of magistracies, combined
> with the equable temperament, there arises an unusual harmony, which
> perpetuates this admirable government: for these reasons was Apollo
> represented.

The sounds that filled St Mark's were intended, like the candles, to
startle and to leave the listeners slightly dazed with grandeur. They
would think on higher things. With patrons willing to pay for new
music, travellers flocking to Venice to experience its excitement,
musicians vying with each other to have their music played, there
was a thriving culture of discovery. By the time Gabrieli died in
1612, Venice was a celebrated centre of music; and Gabrieli's
successor Claudio Monteverdi (1567–1643) was ready to conquer

new territory in music, like an ambitious Venetian merchant setting off for the east.

The fame of this music spread. The influence of Venice abroad was beginning to shrink, but at the start of the seventeenth century there was still nowhere else quite like it. In Germany they copied Gabrieli's style; there were composers in Slovenia and Poland who wrote polychoral works as if they had their own St Mark's. Gabrieli's students carried the message everywhere.

Although there was a celebrated Venetian school at work, complete with its conservative and liberal factions, few of the composers' names are widely known today – Adrian Willaert (c.1490–1562) is remembered as a master of the Venetian style – but Baldissore Donato, Giovanni Croce and Claudio Merulo are among those whose reputations nowadays are familiar only to enthusiasts for the period. This is an example of a musical movement that had much greater significance in its time than is sometimes recognised today. Subsidiary composers whose work would have been as celebrated as that of Gabrieli lose their place in the pantheon as the years pass, though the creativity of the city was partly theirs.

This was happening at a time of expansionism in Europe when minds were turning outwards. The Spanish Empire extended across the Atlantic, English adventurers were laying the first tracks of their own empire, and the world that had been known a century earlier (before Magellan sailed round it in 1519–20) seemed tiny. Though Venice was no more than a city squeezed on to the islands of a lagoon in a tiny corner of the Adriatic, and its political power was past its apogee, it expressed that excitement in music. A happy conjunction of talent or genius, money and confidence can turn a particular place at a particular time into a furnace of creativity.

The Italian experience throughout the sixteenth century – the triumphs of Renaissance art and the travails of the Church – meant that the musicians who lived into the seventeenth century in its cities carried with them a cultural legacy that was rich and complicated. Their techniques were subtle now, their instruments capable of a wider range of sounds, their boldness in harmony and vocal line greater than before. Theirs was the music the rest of Europe wanted to hear; and it contained the first hints of the Baroque style that would dominate music-making for a century and more.

There was something else in Venice that made it extraordinary: the theatricality of its music. Whether we think of it as a place of masked balls and self-indulgent entertainment, or of processions of gondolas, or of Byzantine churches, it has drama embedded in it. Everything was a show, and the music in the late Renaissance thrived on that boastful vigour. This was new. Whether or not there were two or three choirs performing together in St Mark's, as they did on special occasions, Venice seemed to have a penchant for the spectacular. As well as the sensuality of the music, the love of melody and line and the mingling of voices, these were sounds that told a story. It is not at all surprising that it was here that there would be the first genuine flowering of one of the most exciting, most tantalising and maybe most peculiar art forms of all, the opera that the Camerata of Florence had started to develop, almost as if it was an experiment – edging forward to see what might come of it.

The spark of genius came from Monteverdi. He invented a style and touched it with brilliance. The first operatic performances in Florence were awkward, more like simple street theatre. The music was ordinary and quite dry. In Monteverdi's first opera, *L'Orfeo*, first heard in 1607 and performed in Venice two years later, it is immediately obvious that a change has taken place. The score is heavy with his own sadness; his wife was dying in Cremona, his home town, and the opera is invested with an unmistakable humanity. Even in its infancy, the form was already expressing the personal and the unspeakable, using the direct-ness of the dramatic moment to transfix an audience with emotion coming from within a character.

Monteverdi used a bigger group of musicians than the Camerata. There were trombones, recorders, a variety of strings for a richer sound, and the story is told with an attempt at psychological realism. The characters try to draw the audience into their predicament, almost appealing for sympathy. The writing is sensuous and delicate. The madrigals in the opera (that is really what they still were at this stage) add up to something much more than a score with musical numbers for the singers scattered through it. For the first time an audience was getting the idea of opera as a flowing composition, in which words and music helped and illuminated each other. Monteverdi's librettist Ottavio Rinuccini was able to devise words which inspired the composer to respond, in that instinctive way that marks the greatest opera scores in which the sympathies of dramatist and musician seem fused.

It was the start of an operatic career for a composer who was already famous across Italy for his madrigals. He'd been born just across the street from the Cathedral in Cremona, where his family had a pharmacy, and he was given a good musical education, drawing on the Church tradition. He was writing in his early teens, and he followed a well-worn path to the court of the Duke of Mantua, who was always on the look-out for young talent. There he plied the composer's trade, and in *L'Orfeo* all his originality poured out.

Monteverdi's achievement was to turn a fashion into a tradition. By the time he died, in Venice in 1643, opera was an established form with rules and conventions, and singers were casting an eye on the stage as a place where they could create magic, as they've been doing ever since. Monteverdi was once asked to write an opera that gave personalities to different winds (composers are asked to do some odd things). He wrote back to the librettist, who'd already produced the words, saying that since winds didn't speak he couldn't imitate their speech in music; moreover, audiences were moved by the heroine of his opera *Ariadne* because she was a woman and by Orpheus because he was a man. Neither, he pointed out, was a mere wind.

There you have it. He wanted to use music, and the drama, to move an audience by involvement. He understood that the difference between the performance of a familiar song and the opera was that new dimensions opened up on stage for the composer and the audience: the monochrome could blaze with colour.

For *L'Orfeo* he assembled a band that consisted of two harpsichords, two organs, two viols and two bass viols, three six-stringed viols, a chiterone (a form of lute), four violins, a harp, four trombones, recorders, two cornets and a trumpet. Later operas had smaller ensembles, but Monteverdi was an original, breaking new ground. One of his dramas is remarkable for an effect that no one else had ever used before. *Il combattimento di Tancredi e Clorinda* was written, probably for a coronation, in 1636. At one point in the story Tancredi, the knight, charges on his horse towards another armed figure whom he thinks is his rival in love: it's actually his lover in disguise. And Monteverdi produces an accompanying sound that could almost be from a film score. He said he tried repeated crotchets, then semi-quavers, and 'matched them one-to-one with a speech connoting anger and disdain' to get the effect he wanted. He was one of the most masterful orchestrators of his time.

It was in Venice, where he spent most of his life, that Monteverdi became a prolific composer. After his wife had died, in the year *L'Orfeo* was first performed, he wanted nothing more to do with the court at Mantua. He wasn't being paid on time, so he went off to Venice, from where he later told the Mantuan court that the difference there was that his music was well performed and he was paid regularly. He eventually took charge of music at St Mark's, where one of his sons sang in the choir. Much of this sacred music has survived, and of course it's sung today – his Vespers, written before he got to Venice, is one of the greatest devotional pieces of music we know. And those of his operas that have survived (most have been lost) are triumphs of originality.

Where there had sometimes been apparently random songs that hardly seemed to be connected, there was now a sensuous mixture of emotion and musical drama. The characters and the music began to speak to each other; for the first time the possibilities of opera were revealed. You could see the point of people singing on stage, because the music was becoming less of a backdrop and more part of the story. Monteverdi probably wrote nearly twenty operas, though only three survive complete, and one in part. They present modern conductors with problems because the musical instructions are limited, so there's an element of invention in every performance. What should never fail, though, is the power of the musical voice that Monteverdi found.

He wrote his last opera in 1642, the year before he died. It's *L'incoronazione di Poppea*, the story of Nero and his mistress, at once erotic and dripping with gore. Although he'd been ordained into Catholic orders ten years earlier, Monteverdi wasn't interested in conventional or safe opera by this stage. *Poppea* is passionate, human, dramatic and touching – it does the things that opera does best, and perhaps alone can do. Listening to Monteverdi, it's tempting to think of the last duet from *Poppea* as the summation of his style, uplifting and impassioned as it is. Nero and Poppea sing a duet to celebrate the power they've achieved, bloodstained but touched by love. Unfortunately, he didn't write it. It was added later. As in the studio of a leading portrait painter where a student or a junior associate might finish the routine parts of a picture – adding the feet or a piece of jewellery – the opera has some work by other hands. In a way, it is evidence of what had occurred in the circle in which he moved. Venice – confident, colourful and energetic – produced the first great composer of opera, and he left his mark on those around him.

Venice, fabled destination of those who took the Grand Tour of Europe, is a natural starting point for a journey into the seventeenth century. Nowhere was finer, and music rose to its challenge. But within a few decades Paris would be making similar claims. No one had ever used music quite like Louis XIV of France. An absolute monarch needed to be surrounded with glory – how else could it be? – and it was not enough that the court should look splendid. It had to sound magnificent too.

The Sun King came into being in 1653, ten years after the boy Louis became king. In one of the great halls of the Petit Bourbon Palace in that year the fourteen-year-old King took part in a pageant called Ballet de la Nuit in the course of which he was drawn on to the stage in a chariot pulled by a figure representing Dawn. The king was dressed as the Sun. One of the most important artists at court – we don't know definitively who he was – left this account:

> Dawn pulls a superb chariot bringing the most beautiful Sun that one had ever seen, which at first dissipated the clouds and then promised the most beautiful and the greatest Day of the World; the Spirits came to render him hommage, and they formed the grand ballet. The sujet is vast and in all its extensiveness completely worthy to exercise the steps of our Young Monarch, without detracting from the scene.

It is possible that these were the words – and the spectacular sycophancy – of Jean-Baptiste Lully, an Italian musician who'd arrived at court as a dancer. Indeed, that night, he even danced with Louis at the party. The music was part of the idea of monarchy that was later embodied in the wild extravagance and beauty of the Palace of Versailles where the King spent the last three decades of his seventy-two-year reign, the longest in the whole history of the kings and queens of Europe.

Lully (1632–87) demonstrated how music could become part of worldly power. He had to work at it. He was a Florentine who had somehow found his way to France as a young man and got a reputation as a fine dancer. He changed his name from Lulli to Lully, and Giovanni Battista became Jean-Baptiste. That was a start. Eventually he came to the attention of the Paris court of the King's cousin, helping her with her Italian, dancing, and playing the guitar and the violin (one of the most distinctive instruments of the time, whose strings were giving music across Europe a different quality).

After the ballet at which he'd danced with the King he was given the post of Compositor de la Musique Instrumentale de la Chambre, which established him at court and recognised what must already have been known to be a creative talent. Louis XIV's father had set up a famous band of strings, the Vingt-quatre Violons du Roi, and Lully became a member. Before long, he controlled the whole group. He was a character. One historian of the Sun King's court describes him as a 'virtuoso and dancer . . . a wit, a born entertainer, a mimic, a pederast and a libertine'. He had ten children by his wife, Madeleine, but that did not cramp his style.

He directed the music in what was Europe's greatest court, gathered round a king who was appropriating ever more power, presenting himself as an incarnation of France, and who was determined that monarchy should display its power and resilience. When he moved to Versailles in 1682, having already spent forty years on the throne, he was at the centre of the world – the geometry of the gardens was even conceived so that the axis passed through the King's bedchamber. The power that was ruthlessly concentrated there had its sounding board in the musical entertainments that Lully arranged for him.

The *grands ballets* that Lully arranged became famous. The style and formality of dance became a reflection of the perfection of monarchy; the stories, though they might seem to be mythological, were about the grandeur of the King; the spectacle and the scale were evidence of power. We have the words of the King himself to make the point:

The art of dance has always been recognised as one of the most respectable and necessary to train the body and to give it the first and most natural dispositions to every kind of exercise, to that of the arms among others. Consequently, it is one of the most advantageous and useful to our nobility, and to others who have the honour of approaching us, not just in wartime in our armies, but even in times of peace in the *divertissement* of our ballets.

Music was 'advantageous and useful': not a decoration but one of the sinews of power. The cultural ferment around the King was remarkable. You only need to think what French schoolchildren are given to read to this day: the plays of Molière and Racine, the fables of Jean de la Fontaine drawn from Aesop and others. The artists encouraged by the King were making the French style the envy of the world. In the paintings of Poussin (looking back at his native country from Rome in the 1640s) you see an idealised world of beauty and elegance, a classical perfection that was meant also to speak of France.

So Lully – a schemer, a sycophant, a notorious loose-liver, philandering quite happily with both sexes – was an important part of an artistic explosion. Thanks to the King, he controlled stage music in the whole of France. As a result he was bound up in the development of opera in France, which arrived in the 1660s. Cardinal Mazarin, a fellow Italian, imported some opera from Italy, but it was said to have been sabotaged by a jealous Lully. In the 1670s the first French *tragédie-lyrique* was written and Lully himself wrote more than a dozen, as well as many ballet scores, comic and serious. With Molière he famously collaborated on *Le Bourgeois Gentilhomme* of 1670.

Creativity was harnessed to power. Lully, who became a very rich man and owned property throughout France, was a kind of cultural dictator. He didn't like the old instruments such as the shawm (the precursor of the oboe) or the recorder. So the musicians who mastered the oboe and the flute vied for prominence and popularity. Music that spoke of the countryside wasn't suitable for court, so the style that Lully encouraged was one that sounded grand. That was its point.

You can't separate the way music was written and performed from the struggle for influence and power that was going on. It sprang from the desire of Lully and those around him to protect their own position, which meant pleasing the King. One of the habits Louis developed was to listen to Lully's band during dinner and before he retired for the night. This was a *petite bande* that Lully had developed as an offshoot of the old Vingt-quatre Violons du Roi which had provided him with his musical entrée to court circles, and with it he introduced his own style. It was known as the French Overture. The jagged rhythms that Lully used became a craze. Everyone used them. And, as so often happens with a musical style, it was picked up by great composers many years later, who absorbed Lully's innovation. They turn up at the very beginning of Handel's *Messiah*, written in the 1740s, long after Lully (and Louis XIV) were dead.

That goes back to Lully and his little band. It was a time of change, despite the obsession with the centralisation of power, which was turning the King into an absolute ruler surrounded by the apparatus of omnipotence – rather like the sun itself which, in the new science, was acknowledged as the centre of the universe, replacing our small earth. The musical atmosphere produced originality. Distinctiveness was prized. When François Couperin (1668–1733) arrived as an organist at court in the last decade of the seventeenth century, still in his twenties, he became a phenomenon, probably the most famous keyboard player in Europe. His achievement was to take the emerging French style – which would come to be known as its Classical tradition – and bring it together with the story of Italian music. The result was spectacular.

Couperin epitomised the refinement that the France of Louis XIV had developed. Even when the regime came to be dismantled, and the cult of absolutism was excoriated across Europe, there remained the truth that in art and music and literature much had changed for good. Though Jean-Baptiste Lully was almost a caricature of the devious courtier – part Machiavelli, part Rasputin – hated by his rivals, one of whom tried to poison him with arsenic, he was also the agent of change, ensuring the growth of opera in France, the championing of a style that remained defiantly French even when it was exported, and a reverence for the violin – an instrument that was entering its golden era.

You don't have to be a paragon of refinement to make music. Lully was a rogue as well as a brilliant musician, an operator in the undergrowth of royal politics and, of course, a seducer of anyone he could find. A life of drama came to an appropriately macabre and sticky end. It was 1687, and Lully had composed a 'Te Deum' – at a time when he was writing more religious music, perhaps because he thought that the powerful clergy were beginning to turn against him. The piece had a predictable genesis. The King had recovered from an operation, and this was to celebrate his return to health. Lully was conducting the musicians, beating time on the floor with a cane as usual. His stick had a very sharp point, and at a moment of excitement in the performance he stabbed himself in the toe. Gangrene set in; he wouldn't allow the doctors to amputate and a few weeks later he was dead.

Lully's period at court in Paris and Versailles coincided with the transition from the achievements of Italy, inherited from the Renaissance and epitomised in Monteverdi's Venice in the generation before Louis XIV, to the start of the age of Enlightenment. The Enlightenment would revolutionise European society and thought and would see music move from the Baroque age, usually described in loose terms as ending around the middle of the seventeenth century, into the Classical – a misleadingly general term but a useful enough piece of shorthand to describe the era of Haydn and Mozart. It was an era that established the symphony and the chamber music that would give the Romantic age its inheritance, and stretch far beyond it.

From a distance, looking back, the beginning of the Classical age may seem like a metamorphosis. At the time, it was more like practical progress, a natural maturing. Instruments were more varied, more secure in their tuning and resilience in performance, and more subtle in the sounds that could be produced from them. Making music is not simply a matter for composers and the performers who try to do justice to them, but one for technical craftsmen too. The seventeenth-century journey that goes from Venice to another centre of brilliance and invention, Paris, now turns back to Italy, to Monteverdi's birthplace, the city where he wrote *L'Orfeo*. Cremona was to give the world a beautiful sound.

The city became synonymous with one instrument, and a byword for perfection in its manufacture. In the course of a generation it produced many of the finest violins ever made: nowhere has anyone been able to reproduce what happened there. It was extraordinary, and it had consequences: an opportunity and a challenge for composers.

Cremona had a long history. It was a musical centre from the middle ages onwards, enjoying the spread of music-making through Italy in the Renaissance. And in the sixteenth century the city's Amati family started to make violins. At first the instruments had three strings instead of four, but in the course of that century they came to look like the ones we know today. They began to take their place in the ensembles and bands, joining the various viols (which were held upright like a modern cello) and giving them string sections with greater range than before. Monteverdi knew these instruments, whose secrets were being passed on. It was an Amati who taught two of the men who were going to became the most famous instrument-makers of them all, Antonio Stradivari (1644–1737) and Andrea Guarneri (1626–98).

The violin had been around since the early sixteenth century, when Andrea Amati first became famous as a maker, and musicians naturally began to write music for the instrument. His was a celebrated work-shop, even before the most famous period in Cremona, from which a particular Stradivarius instrument sold today can command a huge sum. One of his instruments known as the Hammer was sold at auction in 2006 for $3.5 million. Something about the balance in its design, the size and the finish gives one of his violins (there are probably between 700 and 800 in existence) a perfect tone still. Guarneri violins from the same period are noted for their power. When they were made, the violin was becoming the most popular stringed instrument. Louis XIV's band of fiddlers was a typical adornment of the court – the violin spoke to style; so by the time Cremona's greatest instruments were produced, there was a vast body of work written for it. And the craft handed down through the generations, the subject of experiment and refinement, was now reaching its peak.

The violin was thus the object of every composer's gleaming eye. Among them was the man who was creating a sound world that influenced generations of composers after him and helped to give the early eighteenth century its musical character, Antonio Vivaldi (1678–1741). Vivaldi was a priest who found another vocation in music. At an orphanage in Venice he was master of music to girls who were often the illegitimate children of daughters of noble families in a convent round the corner, and he was known as the Red Priest because of the colour of his hair. It was here that Vivaldi taught the violin, buying the new hand-crafted instruments when he could, and began to compose. He was prolific. By the time he was finished he'd written more than 500 concertos for soloists and orchestra, many of them for the violin, as well as forty-six operas and much chamber and church music. He'd established the three-movement form that would become the standard concerto structure, and he'd demonstrated what a modern violin could do. Indeed, in his lifetime he may have been known as much for being a player as for being a composer.

The violin-makers of Cremona were doing for the instruments what Vivaldi had been doing for the music. The way they adapted the design of the old Amati violins – giving the arch of the back a new shape, altering the two f-shaped sound-holes, experimenting with different woods and varnishes – allowed composers to do things differently. The favourite solo instruments until then had been the trumpet, the lute and the harpsichord. You used them to deliver a great tune. Now there was a chance to do something new.

Composers like Arcangelo Corelli (1653–1713) had written exciting music for the instruments in the 1660s and 1670s, the generation before Vivaldi, but it was Vivaldi's sonatas, because they allowed for delicacy, ornamentation and a display of virtuosity, that became perfect vehicles for the modern instruments. More than that they seemed to echo the subtlety of the human voice better than any trumpet could. Alongside brilliance and drama, you could produce great tenderness and lyricism. Musicians had more power at their fingertips: here was a richer range of colours for their palette. The fingerwork that became possible, the potency of the instrument, the way a broken chord or an arpeggio could be played across the strings – all suggested opportunities for invention.

Vivaldi could use this instrument to formidable effect. He was an attraction and a curiosity in Venice. One visiting German music-lover wrote in his diary that he'd heard a fantasy being improvised by Vivaldi in a way that he said 'really terrified' him – his fingers came 'within a mere grass stalk's breadth of the bridge so that the bow had no room . . . and this on all four strings . . . at an incredible speed'.

It was Igor Stravinsky who said in the twentieth century that Vivaldi hadn't composed a hundred concertos but one concerto hundreds of times – a remark that probably demonstrated how much of his music had disappeared from view. Vivaldi suffered the posthumous fate of so many composers in having immense quantities of his work vanish, condemned as unfashionable and simplistic, only to have it rediscovered by a later age and gazed upon with fresh eyes and open ears. It happened in their turn to Bach, Handel, even Mozart to a lesser extent, and famously, closer to our own time, to Gustav Mahler.

Vivaldi's breakthrough was in showing how the violin could produce a solo concerto that built on the lyricism already achieved with other instruments and with the voice. Without this change, carried to its peak by the patient craftsmen of Cremona, the sound of the early symphony orchestra that was just round the corner in the eighteenth century might never have come our way, and the very character of what we call classical music would have been different. There are few better examples in the history of music of the catalytic effect of an instrument on the imagination. Just as the piano would change social habits, as well as musicians' minds, in the nineteenth century, the arrival of the modern violin was nothing less than the invention of a sound. Composers were fascinated by it, and impelled to write for it.

Tunes had always travelled, first in musicians' heads, next in handwritten notation, and at last in crude and then rather better printed versions. By now, at the start of the eighteenth century, printing had reached a stage where compositions could circulate quite quickly, as they never had before. *L'estro armonico* (The Harmonic Whim) was printed in 1711 by Etienne Roger in Amsterdam (where they used the most advanced engraving and printing techniques) and it was one of the most influential music publications of the first part of the eighteenth century, helping to make Vivaldi especially popular in Germany and the object of jealousy in France. The Italian had become an international star.

Despite his operas, his sacred music, his concertos for trumpet and the rest, you can't separate Vivaldi from the violin. He seems to us now to have been a kind of conduit for its sound – that brightness, the ease of moving from one sound register to another, the delicacy at the top of the range – which contributed a change in the formal structure of music. Vivaldi was not the formulaic and rather staid figure that some successor composers used as a caricature; in his lifetime he sounded a note of freedom. He explored harmonic novelties as well as new formal structures in his concertos just as much as he exploited the violin's potential, both as a lyrical and as an exciting virtuoso instrument.

The viols of an earlier age now seemed antique. The violin had taken centre stage – sounding better, the wood shining through with new varnishes, the leader of the band. It seemed that you could do and say anything with it. The English poet John Dryden put it this way in his 'Song for St Cecilia's Day':

> Sharp violins proclaim
> Their jealous pangs and desperation,
> Fury, frantic indignation,
> Depth of pains, and height of passion,
> For the fair, disdainful dame.

In Vivaldi – the red-haired priest who became a musical phenomenon – you can hear the development of virtuosity on the violin, the tradition that flowed back and forth from the orchestra to the concert platform so that Nicolò Paganini in the nineteenth century or Jascha Heifitz or Yehudi Menuhin in the twentieth might make the instrument sing with a seemingly human capacity for tenderness. Without Vivaldi, and without the torrent of music written for the instrument at this time – some of it brilliant, some of it dull, much of it lost for a couple of centuries – the story of eighteenth-century music, when the Classical period took shape and imprinted itself on Europe, would have followed another route. The orchestra that Haydn took in his hands; Handel's opera scores; the chamber music that would grow in complexity and power in the next century – everything would have taken a different turn without the excitement of that modern violin, and its sounds.

When a young violinist in our time begins to sense a promising career, and the patrons cluster round, they often start to look for an instrument that will match the talent. There have been great violin-makers all over the world, whose instruments are cherished, but the chances are that the search will switch back to northern Italy, to Cremona, and the first thirty years or so of the eighteenth century. They'll look for a violin made by Stradivari or Guarneri or one of their pupils. These men were craftsmen who were more important than many composers, now long forgotten: they made music with their hands.

Cremona takes its place in the story of music, the chance location of one of its most important scenes. Like Venice at the end of the Renaissance, with its incorrigible confidence, or the Sun King's Versailles, it was a place that seems still to shine, and to tremble with music. Cremona, Venice and Versailles can't be separated from the sounds they bequeathed. Their story flows into the eighteenth century when the Baroque period reached its peak and the symphony and chamber music for strings and the opera entered a golden age. Many streams come together. One, with a distinct personality, was English music.

5

England

Elizabethans, Puritans and Purcell

~

ENGLISH MUSIC BECAME one of the glories of the Elizabethan age, matching and sometimes surpassing what was being written elsewhere in Europe. But it was a struggle. The two composers who more than any others turned the end of the sixteenth century into a shining era were on the wrong side of the religious divide. Their lives as composers are, in part, a story of survival.

If you listen to William Byrd's consort song 'Look and Bow Down' you hear a celebration of the defeat of the Spanish Armada in 1588, with words by Elizabeth I herself. Byrd was glorifying a national triumph. Yet he and his teacher, Thomas Tallis, the two men who did for English music what Marlowe and Shakespeare were doing for English literature, were not natural adherents to the Protestant Queen. They were members of a Catholic community which was being persecuted, and which suffered particularly badly after the Armada was sent by Philip II to avenge the execution of Mary, Queen of Scots in 1587. Its proud ships might have been sunk and remnants sent in flight to the northern isles, but a residue of fear was left behind.

Rich Catholic families who had refused to accept Elizabeth's state-decreed Protestantism were celebrating secret masses, and carving out hiding places in the walls of their great houses to conceal priests from the authorities. Byrd and Tallis not only survived, their talent (and their popularity) was such that they held positions at court – musicians whose brilliance encapsulated the ambiguity of a time when politics was fractured and bloody, but artistic creativity was confident and apparently unstoppable.

Thomas Tallis was born near the beginning of the sixteenth century – probably in 1505 – and lived through the reigns of four monarchs. He was playing the organ at priories and monasteries when Henry VIII dissolved them and went to war with the Church, and Tallis had to stay ahead of a tide of destruction that lapped at his heels. After the brief and insipid interlude of Edward VI, Mary Tudor restored Catholicism and for a short time it became a little easier for composers. With the accession of Elizabeth in 1558, the bespoke Protestantism of Henry VIII was restored and life became difficult for Tallis once more.

These changes involved ingenuity on the part of composers. When Henry decreed that Catholic music was too grand and too ornate, church music – in English instead of Latin – took on a simpler form. But the lack of ornamentation seemed dull, and in Mary Tudor's brief reign church music was allowed to recover some of its elegance and by the time Elizabeth came to the throne there was an English style for the liturgy that, despite the monarchical upheavals of thirty years or so, had emerged intact. It was this that Tallis and Byrd were able to exploit and dignify. Byrd, who was probably born in the 1540s and died in 1623, produced free-flowing melodies, and the delicacy with which he could bring voices together and send them apart again gave his music a character that was unmistakable. He was not writing to any formula; he was creating an original sound of his own.

Composers had to be pragmatic. You would write a madrigal to gratify the Queen – such as Byrd's 'This Sweet and Merry Month of May' – because loyalty of that sort, beamed towards the person of the monarch, was necessary. But you might also get away with some church music – all of which was written for the Anglican liturgy – that spoke quietly of a lost religion, much as it has sometimes been argued that Shakespeare's persistent return to the themes of broken realms and poisoned inheritances was in part a reflection of his own lingering commitment to Catholicism and his feeling of loss and betrayal (though these are deep waters best left to literary critics for their sport).

An underground community was in place. Father William Weston was thought to be the only Jesuit in England when he arrived back home from Rome to lead the Society's mission in the 1580s. Thereafter he moved in the shadows. In his autobiography he recounted one visit to a recusant:

we left the city and went out nearly thirty miles to the home of a Catholic gentleman, a close friend of mine . . . In the house was a chapel, set aside for the celebration of the church's offices. The gentleman was a skilled musician, and there were an organ, other musical instruments and choristers both male and female. During those eight days it was just as if we were celebrating the octave of some great feast . . . Mr Byrd the very famous musician and organist was among the company.

These were double lives, but it seems that neither Byrd nor Tallis was ever in danger of his life. They had the brilliance to pull it off, Byrd managing to write memorable church music despite being investigated on at least one occasion and having his house searched after his name had appeared on a list of secret papists, a crime for which others were being imprisoned or strung up. His work *The Great Service* was as fine as anything being produced anywhere else in Europe, a peak of invention (the 'great' is a reference to the service for which the music was written). Its six sections, from the 'Venite' to the 'Nunc dimittis', show Byrd at his majestic best.

The music which Elizabeth herself could hear, and which was used for Anglican services across the country, was now full of energy and confidence. Just as in the theatre, and in poetry, its power transcended the religious politics of the composers. They could sidestep the regular Catholic purges, which were fuelled by fears of Spanish conquest and by the near-obsession with the Jesuits intent on reconverting the English throne, whose imagined footprints were seen everywhere. The truth was that Elizabeth understood that Tallis and Byrd were artists who were adornments of her age. Not only were they tolerated, they were celebrated. In 1575 she granted them the exclusive right to print and publish music. They controlled its production and therefore its style, though they in no way resembled the cultural commissars of a later age. When they published their collection of Latin motets *Cantiones sacrea* in the same year as their appointment by the Queen they were hoping that the thirty-four choral compositions would be more popular than proved to be the case.

Within a couple of years they submitted a petition to the Queen complaining that they needed more money. Compared with some of their counterparts on the continent – those from the Low Countries who were being collected like treasure trove by Italian dukes, for example – their incomes were modest. But they had positions in society. Despite their complaints, they were serving a Queen who valued them. In the preface to *Cantiones sacrae* the composers praise her in terms that she would have expected from all her obsequious courtiers.

By successfully combining devotion to the Queen with their own religious impulses, these two composers were able to use their positions to bring English music to a new height. Tallis's 'Spem in alium' written for five eight-part choirs – and, it's thought, to celebrate the Queen's fortieth birthday in 1573 – was spectacular. No English composer had written like this before. It is harmonically detailed and rich, confidently scored for many voices, utterly assured in the way it brings all the melodic lines together.

Tallis's pupil Byrd was an even mightier figure. Elizabeth's enlightened decision to give these men their position and their power represented a landmark in British cultural history. Until his death in 1585, Tallis was an organist and composer in the service of the Queen; and Byrd, though he had many friends among the recusant families, was a pillar of the Chapel Royal, where he had no choice but to follow its firmly Anglican practice. He was a beneficiary of Elizabeth's private tolerance, a tolerance which acknowledged that vast numbers of her subjects were still in thrall to traditional ways of worship, and that loyalty to the Crown in times of trouble was probably more important to her than loyalty to the early Book of Common Prayer which was now the state-sanctioned foundation of worship (predating the 1662 version still treasured by so many today).

Byrd and Tallis were remarkable examples of artists who were able to surmount the political squabbles and dangers that seethed around them. Byrd's output, in particular, was prodigious. He wrote for solo voice, choir and more or less every instrument available to him – madrigals, motets and dance and song variations to be played on the virginals. The virginals (or virginal – the singular form is maybe less peculiar), the most popular instrument in England at the time, was a kind of oblong harpsichord with horizontal strings parallel to the keyboard. Each note had one string, plucked when a key was pressed, as with a harpsichord.

The best record of what was happening in keyboard music in the second half of the sixteenth century is embodied in a volume called *The Fitzwilliam Virginal Book* which contains more than 300 works and reveals how Byrd and others developed techniques that would influence composers who flourished long after them.

Byrd, whose music is still heard in Anglican churches every Sunday, more than four and a half centuries after his death, was probably the greatest keyboard composer of his time, anywhere in Europe. His music bridged the religious distance he maintained from his Queen. Elizabeth had a lingering affection for the Latin liturgy, which had been suppressed after the reign of Mary Tudor, except at Oxford and Cambridge and at three schools (Winchester, Eton and Westminster), where Latin remained the language of scholarship. Byrd could exploit that contradiction for his own purposes. He wrote more than 200 Latin motets, a number of which were effectively laments for the plight of his fellow Catholics and were performed privately. In public, the Queen and her court would hear his works in English rather than Latin. They were able to satisfy her wish for an English Protestant liturgy and her affection for the past, quite happily.

By the last decade of the century, he was bold enough to write three Latin masses which seem likely to have been used at the home of his Catholic patron, Lord Petre. They were not sung publicly, though they were printed and would be available for those who knew of their existence. They are beautiful, with a certain melancholy which may well reflect Byrd's feeling that his public work in the service of the Queen could not be complete since his faith had to be formally disguised, even concealed. There was much official hypocrisy involved – the Queen had close courtiers who were resolute Catholics to the end – but form had to be observed.

There's not much point in the argument about who was the greatest composer in any tradition – was Henry Purcell in the next century a bigger figure in English music or not? It's more sensible to say simply that William Byrd was a giant. With Tallis, and surrounded by a host of lesser figures, he towered over his age, though it was populated by many musicians of stature – Orlando Gibbons (1583–1625), Thomas Weelkes (?1575–1623) and John Wilbye (1574–1638) among them. At a time when dramatists and poets were gilding Elizabeth's reign with words, these composers were giving it a musical character. In church, among the singers of madrigals, among the talented players of the primitive keyboards of the day, they were bringing English music to a new pitch.

By the end of the sixteenth century, a new cultural epoch was flowering across Europe, the legacy of the Renaissance. The religious turmoil on the continent – with Rome and Luther engaged in a struggle for supremacy, and in an argument about truth – was reflected in the music that was sung in church and that composers were being asked (and paid) to write. The Church wanted music that was clear as well as uplifting – it had to make its point – but in Italy, especially, there was a simultaneous movement towards the glorious and the grand in the courts of those, like a doge or a duke of Ferrara, who considered themselves to be no less powerful and better arbiters of taste than the Pope and the bishops, clerks and draughtsmen of the Council of Trent.

In England, a glittering path had opened up. Literacy was increasing fast – maybe a third of the male population was now able to read. In London, a city of less than a quarter of a million souls, it's thought that 15,000 people were going to the theatre each week. While Byrd was writing his three masses in the mid-1590s, Edmund Spenser was publishing the ninety sonnets in *Amoretti* and Shakespeare was writing *Romeo and Juliet, Richard II, The Merchant of Venice* and the sonnets. Out of the turmoil of an age of religious discontent and violence sprang originality in music. Sometimes what Byrd wrote was a gently ironic commentary on his own awkward position, and on the misery which some of his faith were suffering. His music was also a solid part of the achievement that the Queen wanted to call her own: the country of Shakespeare had its musicians too.

When Tallis wrote 'O nata lux de lumine', or Byrd the instrumental music in *My Ladye Nevells Booke*, they demonstrated how mature English music had now become. With the first printed music for keyboard in 1591, the pace quickened, and these composers, who were at least the equals of their continental cousins, revealed how music had somehow transcended the fractured politics around them, music that had been written for the Queen and her court but spoke across the divides in the realm to those who were on the opposite side. It was bold and it was popular. Keyboard works began to circulate, just as songs had been available for some time, and in years to come these sounds would be associated as closely with the achievements of the age as Shakespeare's words or Spenser's verse. Their names became known across Europe, and Byrd was one of the fathers of the keyboard style that lasted until the time of Johann Sebastian Bach in Germany more than a century later.

This was a time of endless invention with new harmonies, and in music from the sixteenth century – so *English*, so familiar in its resilience down the centuries – you hear a tradition more confident and more adventurous than it had ever been before. When the early-music movement took hold in the 1960s, in London more vigorously than anywhere else in the world, the rediscovery of medieval and Renaissance music was a revelation to many musicians, let alone the public. Part of its energy came from an impatience with the established taste and style of the 1960s, especially in orchestral performance, but it became much more than a revolt against a suffocating Romantic richness in playing.

In the quest for more authentic performance, ensembles like the Early Music Consort and the Academy of Ancient Music were also revealing the depth of a repertoire that had been allowed to become dusty and stale. A new generation of listeners was introduced to the music of a period which they barely knew, and though in those early days of the 1960s there was a brown-rice-and-sandals earnestness about some of the enthusiasts accompanied by a true fundamentalist's gleam in the eye, they rediscovered the simplicity that Elizabethan composers had been able to turn to such purpose.

By the time Byrd died in 1623, English music had a confidence and style that was its own. It came of mixed parentage, since much was written by Catholics who had to pursue lives of careful ambiguity in their public duties, and it sprang from a loyalty to a Queen who embodied contradictions. At war with Catholic Europe, she rewarded and promoted some around her who shared the sympathies of those who were her enemies. The music of the time is therefore a product of tension as much as a celebration of the Queen in the way that Spenser's epic poem, *The Faerie Queene*, depicts an all-powerful and even magical monarch.

The force and sometimes the poignancy of Byrd's masses, the delicacy of his writing for three or four voices, the rise and fall of a Tallis line, or the firm confidence of an Orlando Gibbons melody, all reveal how music seemed able to store and treasure its own energy. These writers were not commenting directly on their time – there was only a cautious echo of events around them, except when they were commissioned to honour a public event or a military victory – but were feeding on a vigorous intellectual atmosphere which drew some inspiration from the rest of Europe and became the fuel for their originality.

At the beginning of the seventeenth century – while Monteverdi was writing for St Mark's in Venice, the first true opera was being heard in Florence, and in France the Parisians were developing a style that would grace the court of the Sun King – English music had developed sturdy sinews of its own that would prove indestructible. In particular, they would survive the period that would often be thought – wrongly – to be a fundamental assault on the purpose and practice of music, Oliver Cromwell's Commonwealth.

Overseen by a pragmatic Queen, the Elizabethan age had ambiguity built into the court and the Chapel Royal, and Cromwell's time was also a study in contradictions. He smashed the organs in churches and closed the theatres, but never had private music-making in England been so widespread. Black drapes were drawn across the public stages, but music flourished. It is an astonishing story.

When he became lord protector after the civil war, with Charles I executed in 1649, the royal family in exile and the monarchy dissolved, part of the culture that Cromwell confronted was the music that had celebrated the King. William Lawes (1602–45), whom Charles I had called the Father of Music, wrote compositions that represented the old order. He died for his King at the Siege of Chester in 1645, the year in which the Royalists effectively lost the war in the rout at the Battle of Naseby in Northamptonshire. In the setting of a pastoral elegy written by his brother Henry, 'Cease you jolly shepherds . . .', you hear his pain expressed in a traditional Arcadian form – all nymphs and shepherds – that had been a feature of the Jacobean court and was now to be expunged. It is a beautiful lament for what had been lost along with the Stuart kings and with Henry's own brother.

Yet victory for the Parliamentarians and the arrival of Cromwell didn't mean the descent of darkness. Cromwell liked music. He had a good voice himself, and enjoyed singing. The rich musical culture that had developed alongside the poetry and drama of the Elizabethan era, and had flourished under James I and then Charles I, was too muscular now to wither away.

Take John Milton, who published his first collection of poems in the year of the Royalist defeat in battle. He was a Puritan, but was steeped in the culture that had flowed from the Renaissance. His father had written madrigals in Elizabeth's time, and Milton himself was imbued with the humanism of the Renaissance. Henry Lawes wrote the music for his masque *Comus*, first performed in 1634, and throughout his life the poet treasured it. Milton, a civil servant in Cromwell's service after the Commonwealth was established, was no caricature Puritan of the sort that would be lampooned for a grim lack of grace and style.

Cromwell's difficulty with music was that, outside church, composers had written largely in celebration of the monarch. So just as music was being silenced in church by the Puritans, banished along with incense and the hated statues and graven images, the court music associated with the King was publicly unacceptable. Privately, it was a different matter. A composer like Henry Lawes found it relatively easy to survive if he made the necessary compromises. He'd been a court musician but after the King's execution in 1649 and the flight of the royal family, Lawes made his peace with the new regime.

Nor was it an establishment with no place for music. The Lord Protector himself was sympathetic. He might have sent his dreaded 'Parliamentary Visitor' William Dowsing to supervise the 'cleansing' of churches – smashing up organs, and shooting bullets into any roof that sported an angel or grinning cherubim – and he might have been rigorous in enforcing the ban on music in theatres, but when he moved into Whitehall Palace in the 1650s, Cromwell wanted music and a surprising degree of elegance.

They weren't allowed to sing in the old way in churches, and the royal court was gone, but Cromwell wanted his own pleasure. Towards the end of his rule, for example, he saw to it that the organ of Magdalen College, Oxford, was spared the axe and carried bit by bit to Hampton

Court by the Thames where he could enjoy it for himself. He had heard that it made a fine noise.

In the England of Cromwell's Commonwealth you find a story that recurs again and again in the history of music – a desire by the state to turn it to its own purposes, and a familiar playing-out of politics in the struggle to control it. That authoritarian effort always fails in the end, though it visits destruction on people caught in its path. In the twentieth century, not too long ago, music was used in the Soviet Union both by the state and by those who were crushed by it and wanted to rebel as best they could. Some artists fled, a few succumbed and played their miserable parts as satraps of the Great Idea, and some survived by subtlety.

Cromwell was caught in a dilemma, determined to purge music from religious and public places but personally moved by songs, by the organ and by the new violins which were beginning to be heard in England. His Protectorate reveals how the inspiration in music, and its hold, is impossible to suppress successfully.

That happens because music cannot easily be appropriated as an instrument of policy, though many have tried and will try again. It has its own life, which touches the world then often draws back again. Music can mirror the world, and always says something about its time, but it is also an abstraction, complete in itself. That, after all, is what saved Shostakovich and others in the Soviet Union when they were able to argue (at least on some occasions) that even under a regime of Socialist Realism music retained an element of the abstract. Even in brutal times a composer can remain an artist, and his music can build and inhabit its own world from which invaders can be repelled. And from the safety of their art they can make forays. It's an old story.

In Cromwell's time, Thomas Tomkins (1572–1656) is an example of this. He was a Royalist and his well-known piece 'O Sing Unto the Lord a New Song' had a title heavy with political irony. Tomkins was organist at Worcester Cathedral, where he saw choral services banned and the Cathedral organ pulled apart. He wrote about the loss of a king – in his 'Sad Pavane for These Distracted Times' – and also about the loss of music, responding to what he thought was a crude and brutal assault on everything he held dear.

But the age of Cromwell was much more ambiguous than that. Outside churches and theatres, private music-making flourished. Cromwell wanted the best music at his daughter's wedding, which was a lavish affair. There was even dancing in the big houses, so long as it avoided anything too lascivious. Settled in power, he wanted the ambassadors to England to be entertained as they might expect. Music was played for them, masques performed. The first full-length English opera, *The Siege of Rhodes*, was staged. In houses around London there was gambling, which was accepted with the same lazy wink of the eye that might be cast towards a speakeasy in Prohibition America.

It was a time of intense intellectual and artistic activity, and in 1657 – five years after Cromwell become lord protector – musicians felt confident enough to petition for official recognition. The Council of State set up a Committee for the Advancement of Music. The truth was that Cromwell was just as interested in building up an image of authority as Charles I had been in presenting a picture of splendour, and music played a part. Though the music he associated with Catholic practice was purged, as viciously as his enforcers stripped the churches of popish embellishments, domestic rather than court music advanced in these years.

It's important to remember in this story of the making of music that there is no straight line marked 'progress' with one composer's innovations inspiring the next to greater efforts in the same direction, each building on the achievement of what had gone before. To think of the story as linear is misleading. Sometimes there are interruptions, reversals, unexpected turns – and the pattern is complicated. The Puritan era, for example, might seem to have threatened the progress that had been made since the golden days of Elizabeth, with Tallis and Byrd in the first rank of European musicians. The Cromwell years weren't as destructive as that. Music just took another path. Songs were published, circulated and sung at home. People learned to play the violin. The skills of the madrigal singers of an earlier time were nurtured.

That first English opera *The Siege of Rhodes* was staged privately (at the home of the Duke of Northumberland), but that was nonetheless remarkable at a time when Cromwell had banned spoken drama, to say nothing of new opera, and the theatres that had presented Shakespeare and Ben Jonson were – as we would now say – dark. The opera was the idea of an interesting character called Sir William Davenant, a poet and impresario who put it about (with no real evidence) that he was Shakespeare's natural son. The music was by Henry Lawes, Matthew Locke (1621–77) and others, and though it doesn't survive we know that it was in Italian-style recitative – words in spoken form over music. And it had a successor, called *The Cruelty of the Spaniards in Peru* (what we might now call a politically correct title).

Drama set to music was deemed less dangerous than straight theatre – perhaps because the public gatherings for popular plays were regarded by the Puritans as lewd and unruly, whereas the masque, performed in a more domestic setting, was refined. Milton and John Bunyan both loved music, Milton writing a sonnet for Henry Lawes in which he said the composer 'First taught our English music how to span / Words with just note and accent'.

Though church music had been stripped down, the English tradition was thriving. Lawes was a master of counterpoint and would work later with Henry Purcell. Locke, who was a Catholic and sympathetic to the monarchy, nonetheless survived to write and publish instrumental music throughout the Cromwell years. Their music was as innovative as ever. Locke's later introduction to his *Consorts of Three Parts* of 1656 is defiant:

> when most other good arts languished Musick held up her head . . . for many chose to fidle at home, than goe out, and be knockt on the head abroad; and the entertainement was very much courted and made use of, not onely in country but city familys, in which many of the Ladys were good consortiers; and in this state was Musicke dayly improving more or less till the time of (in all other respects but Musicke) the happy Restoration.
>
> But for such as either fear or scorn to see or hear with content any but their own thick-skull'd or fantastikall conceits, they are desired to forbear censuring, or dar'd (observing the designe) to mend them. And for those Mountebanks of Wit, who think it necessary to disparage all they meet with of their owne Country-mens, because there have been and are some excellent things done by Strangers, I shall make bold to tell them (and I hope my known experience in this science will

inforce them to confess me a competent judge) that I never yet saw any Forain instrumental composition (a few French corantos excepted) worthy an English man's transcribing.

They were ready, of course, when the King returned. At the moment of restoration in 1660 – after the death of Cromwell and the failure of his son Richard to hold on to power – Lawes wrote an anthem for Charles II's coronation. The King had been in exile in France where he'd been influenced by the brilliant explosion of music at the court of Louis XIV in Lully's time. When he came back he wanted more public encouragement for music. Locke, despite having co-operated sufficiently with Cromwell to prosper, was now writing once more for a king, and with gusto.

The years of the Commonwealth put another layer on the English tradition. The composers who'd worked in that time – like the poets – left their own traces which became part of the music after the Restoration, the era of Purcell. The King who wanted music restored had French sounds ringing in his years, but – partly thanks to Cromwell – it would be a thoroughly English Restoration. It was certainly the occasion for a great noise. The diarist John Evelyn described the King's arrival in London in 1660 as if it were the opening of the epoch for which the whole world had been waiting.

There was a triumph of above 20,000 horse and foot, brandishing their swords and shouting with inexpressible joy; the ways strewed with flowers, the bells ringing, the streets hung with tapestry, fountains running with wine, the Mayor, Aldermen and all companies in their liveries, chains of gold and banners: lords and nobles clad in cloth of silver, gold and velvet: the windows and balconies well set with ladies: trumpets, music and myriads of people flocking even so far as from Rochester, so as they were seven hours in passing the city even from two in the afternoon till nine at night . . . It was the Lord's doing, for such a restoration was never mentioned in any history, ancient or modern, since the return of the Jews from the Babylonian captivity.

The easygoing, even libertine King – now we would call him liberal in habit and sentiment – wanted to be surrounded by fun, music, *activity*. But there were worries. When Matthew Locke wrote 'Be Thou Exalted, Lord' in 1667 he was celebrating a famous victory in the King's first war against the Dutch, though it wasn't the end of the struggle as Charles wanted to believe. And there was trouble elsewhere: the King of England and Scotland wasn't presiding over a settled realm. London had had the plague and the Great Fire; there was war and sharp religious tension, especially north of the border. The King knew that his father, Charles I, had died on the scaffold in Whitehall as a result of his inflexibility. His famous serenity as he walked out of the Banqueting Hall in Whitehall to his death was a reflection of his belief that, if given another opportunity, he would do the same all over again. That mistake couldn't be made this time.

One of the ways in which the King tried to lift the national spirit was through music. And from a bubbling pool of talent, the composer who would eventually rise above them all – coming to maturity after the King was dead – was Henry Purcell. If you listen to Purcell's song for the King, written when he was still in his twenties – 'Welcome, Viceregent' – you hear the sound that would come to define that period in English music and would echo into our own time. It has clean lines, a pure straightforwardness, solid foundations.

Purcell was born only the year before the Restoration, in 1659, and became a choirboy at the Chapel Royal, starting to compose when he was only nine. By the time he was twenty-one he'd become organist of Westminster Abbey and was therefore established as one of the most important musicians in the capital. His first songs suggest a startling confidence in composition: from the first there was a Purcell 'sound' or 'style'. His position meant that his work was heard by the highest in the land; and there was an appetite for it. He rose to the challenge.

The King's enthusiasm for music, and the return of cathedral church music – after the Puritans had expunged it during the Commonwealth years – ensured a congenial atmosphere for someone like Purcell, who was able to write quickly and to order. As composer-in-ordinary to the King from 1677 he would produce short cantatas for state occasions which were known as Welcome Odes and which turned the formal and usually second-rate poetry used for these purposes into serious choral pieces. He had started early, writing a song for the King's fortieth birthday when he was only eleven.

As a result of his brilliance, in songs, masques and short music dramas that were really the beginnings of English opera, in church music and on the keyboard, Purcell was a leader of a revived tradition in England. Because the King's tastes had been formed in France, he was interested in importing the sounds he'd heard from the likes of Lully at Versailles. He seems to have wanted him to come to London. He couldn't get him but employed another Frenchman, Louis Grabu, instead. The power, however, was with the Englishmen, led at first by Locke.

As we have noted, Locke was sceptical about tastes and musical habits brought across the Channel. But despite his irritation, even contempt, the work of Byrd and Tallis in the Elizabethan era a couple of generations before had now absorbed some continental forms. The dancing at court was in the French style and many of the anthems in church were different from those that had been heard in the reign of the King's father. Charles sent one of the most inventive composers of the time, Pelham Humfrey, to France and then to Italy to expand his range. Humfrey's church works, however, do not sound like copies: they bear the stamp of other traditions, but they are his own.

The arts were flourishing. Restoration drama supplied a determined splash of colour and wit to celebrate the reopening of the theatres – and Shakespeare and Ben Jonson were revived – while Purcell was the crest of a mighty wave of musical talent, with composers like John Blow and Humfrey in his wake. They were writing choral music for the church, songs for domestic music-making, and incidental music for the theatres that were soon booming once more. There were also the first – few – public concerts. A coal merchant called Thomas Britton provided a room in his house in Clerkenwell in east London where the public could go. The first gardens were starting to put on concerts in London, the best known at Vauxhall, across the river from Westminster.

In France, fine music was still mainly confined to the great houses or the royal court and the churches and the opera house in Paris. In London you could pay to hear it, and though those who went were still the moneyed classes, music was beginning to become public entertainment. Away from church, away from the Chapel Royal or an earl's drawing room, you could listen to the latest work by the composers of the day. These popular concerts were first organised in the 1670s and they had the interesting innovation that the public could choose the music. If you paid, you had the choice. There was no programme planning by the conductor. He would play what the audience wanted.

Samuel Pepys started his diary in 1660. His account of life in London is a window on the early Restoration years – his women, his food, his diseases, the streets, the weather, the theatres, and his day-to-day life as an Admiralty civil servant. And Pepys was a music-lover. He played several wind and stringed instruments, mixed with musical friends and, from his days as a student in Cambridge, regarded music as one of the most important strands in his life. He even made a music room upstairs in his house. In John Evelyn's diary in November 1679 you get a sense of how much music was flowing into London.

> I dined at the Master of the Mints with my wife, invited to hear Musique which was most excellently performed by four of the most renowned Masters, Du Pré, a Frenchman on the Lute; Signor Bartholomeo, an Italian, on the Harpsichord; and Nicolao on the violin; but above all for its sweetness and novelty the Viol d'Amore of five wyre-strings plaid on with a bow, being but an ordinary violin, played on Lyra way [like a lyre] by a German, than which I never heard a sweeter instrument or more surprising . . .

A different kind of musical life was beginning. Within a few decades, public performances would become an important part of London's entertainment. By Handel's time – a generation ahead – opera audiences would be growing fast; there would be musical spectacles in the public gardens of London; you no longer had to be very rich and well connected to listen to an orchestra or a visiting musician from France or Italy. As the intellectual ferment of the late seventeenth century produced an outpouring of knowledge – this was the time of Christopher Wren, Isaac Newton, Robert Hooke and the powerhouse of the Royal Society – music, like science, was seen as part of the personal equipment of any enlightened, rounded man of stature. Those who travelled to London to hear the scientists of the day speak of their new discoveries, and the excitements that lay ahead, were also patrons of music. They wanted to hear players and composers, to learn what was new.

The New Spring Garden at Vauxhall was one of the earliest public venues. Pepys and Evelyn recorded visits in their diaries. It could be a fairly wild place at that time, full of ruffians and ladies of the night, but in the 1670s musical performances began to be held there, though not after dark. It was at Vauxhall eighty years later that 12,000 people paid to watch Handel conducting a rehearsal of his 'Music for the Royal Fireworks', and the streets along the Thames had to be closed because the carriages of the rich and famous had come in such numbers that there was a huge traffic jam.

Restoration London was a city in transition. Though the King's French taste may have influenced the English style – at least in popularising the continental sound – music was spreading. It was as if the repressive years had allowed pressure to build up, and it was now released. Pepys describes a city that was throbbing with energy in the theatres, the gardens, the streets and the drawing rooms he visited.

In this atmosphere, Purcell, particularly, sought to refine taste and to raise the sights of the people. In the preface to his *Sonatas of Three Parts*, published in 1683, he wrote:

Ingenuous Reader:

Instead of an elaborate harangue on the beauty and the charms of musick (which after all the learned Encomiums that words can contrive commends itself best by the performance of a skilful hand, and an angelic voice) I shall say but a very few things . . . Its author . . . has faithfully endeavoured a just imitation of the most fam'd Italian masters; principally to bring the seriousness and gravity of that sort of musicke into vogue, and reputation among our countrymen, whose humour, 'tis time now, should begin to loathe the levity and balladry of our neighbour.

Purcell is the composer who has come to define the period, not because he exudes any of the rougher charms of the churning city, but because he produced a special kind of refinement. Much of his work is familiar still to those who would barely know the names of Matthew Locke or Pelham Humfrey, and he left one gem that glitters as a perfect remnant of the Restoration period. With *Venus and Adonis*, written by John Blow (1649–1708) – who preceded and then succeeded him at the organ in Westminster Abbey – Purcell's *Dido and Aeneas* is one of the glories of English music.

It is short. A performance takes less than an hour, and it is simple compared with the three-act *opera seria*, on serious or tragic themes, that was already established in Italy, or the five-act *tragédie-lyrique* in France. Taking his story from Virgil's *Aeneid*, Purcell conjures up great emotion in the six short scenes, leading to Dido's death, using minor keys at the beginning and the end to reveal foreboding and anguish. It's also a score – for strings and harpsichord – that has in it a certain melancholy that would always be associated with English music and that seems to us still to run through its history.

This wasn't a time when music in these islands leaped forward – the achievements of a century before were surely greater – but in Purcell the sound of a very English dissonance can be heard: that state of music where the notes seem to be held in suspense, waiting for a harmonic resolution that is held back. Purcell's command of that style, that feeling, is one of his great gifts. At the end of *Dido and Aeneas* he manages to create a sublime moment, of the sort that later operas would take much longer to produce on stage. Aeneas has left for Rome, reminded that he has been born to found the Roman Empire. And Dido, left alone in Carthage in despair, kills herself.

In the strings, you can hear that anguish. A bass line is repeated; above it the other instruments are plaintive, even angry. And Purcell writes for Nahum Tate's words with an assurance that turns a perfectly constructed aria, balanced and measured, into a profound expression of grief. When Dido sings the words 'Remember' and 'Forget', on which hang the weight of her tragedy, Purcell moves the vocal and musical accents to give them the emphasis they need. He is subtle in the pursuit of simplicity.

Henry Purcell died in 1695. His century produced a glorious tide of English music that carried through the tradition established by the Elizabethans in an earlier age. The Puritan years changed the course of that development, but not its power. Drawing on influences from France and Italy, music still had – in that phrase from the middle ages – an English countenance.

It was shaped by religion and monarchy and also by the patronage they provided. Men of brilliance, and sometimes of genius, produced in a century and a half a tradition that matched anything across the Channel. There would never be an era in England quite so fertile again.

6

A Tale of Three Cities

London, Paris and Bath

~

THE POPULARITY OF music in England in the early eighteenth century was hugely influenced by an embarrassing and dangerous problem that beset the royal family. They were having difficulty in finding a Protestant in the line of succession. When Queen Anne died in 1714 the first fifty or so potential successors were all Catholics, and as such had all been excluded from the throne by the Act of Settlement of 1701. The search had already identified Sophie of Hanover as the chosen one, a distant but suitable heir. Inconveniently but hardly surprisingly (she was eighty-four), she died before Queen Anne. So her son George, Elector of Hanover, found himself king. One of the consequences was that George Frederick Handel decided not to return home to Germany and settled in London, where he became music's great populariser.

That chance spin of the wheel gave London audiences the first composer to produce opera that dealt with the feelings of people who seemed real. He transformed a crude form – rickety plots with much formulaic writing – into operas of grace and power that surpassed many of the Italian works which had influenced him in his time in Italy as a young composer. The glories of Monteverdi had not produced the number of successors that might have been expected in the seventeenth century, and when Handel got to London he shone immediately. He seemed to sparkle with the best of the continental style.

The early years turned him into a star, in which his own Italian opera company (which he called the Royal Academy of Music) was the talk of London, filling the King's Theatre in the Haymarket night after night. He was also the toast of the royal court. The first performance of his 'Water Music' in the summer of 1717 was played by a floating orchestra on the Thames, accompanying the royal barge, with the King demanding three repeats – two before supper and one after – and crowds watching from the banks as darkness fell. It's said that harpsichords were left onshore lest the musicians' boat sank, but there were trumpets, bassoons, horns, French and German flutes, violins and basses. It was all extravagant, rather frivolous and popular.

The 'Water Music' was a piece of politics too, in celebration of a king who needed his subjects to feel good, or at least a little better. There was every reason for George I to value his fellow German, apart from the fact that he could talk to him in his own language without embarrassment. His awkward accession had angered many of his subjects. He was mocked in the streets, not least for his preference for German conversation at court, and in Scotland he had to confront a Jacobite rising in his first year on the throne in support of the restoration of the Catholic Stuarts.

Handel (1685–1759) was First Composer to the King, and in that role he was the champion of an international style. Unlike his contemporary Bach back in Germany, he was a traveller. When George was still Elector of Hanover, he wrote for his court, having started at the opera house in Hamburg before going to Italy for four years. There he worked with Arcangelo Corelli, and with Alessandro and Domenico Scarlatti, and had a triumph in Venice with *Agrippina*, first heard on Boxing Day 1709. No sooner had he got back home to the job he'd been given by George as *Kapellmeister* (director of music) in Hanover than he was off to London, where he achieved his first triumph outside Italy – the opera *Rinaldo*.

The Handelian trademark was speed. He wrote *Rinaldo* in two weeks (*Messiah* thirty years later took him not much longer). By this time publishing was big business and arias from the opera were circulating in the streets, along with the political pamphlets that were energising politics (and causing considerable trouble for the King). The number of people who could see complete performances was quite small – about 400 in the theatre in the Haymarket – and the tickets were fairly expensive. So his popular fame came about in large part because of the distribution of his melodies and arias.

Rinaldo was a natural operatic story, an exotic tale with sorcerers, flying dragons, magic gardens. The cast included castrati – male altos, counter-tenors as we would now call them – who were something of a dramatic import, and who took three of the six main parts. Handel was using a form familiar to the well-heeled Whigs who built the theatre and wanted to experience in London the Italian *opera seria* that they'd seen in the course of the Grand Tour.

Handel's gift for a memorable tune was immediately appreciated. 'Cara Sposa' from *Rinaldo* was described at the time as 'Mr Handel's most celebrated air'. He was feeding a hungry public whose imagination had been caught by the Italian style, and he quickly became a famous figure, a musician spoken of in the same breath as Henry Purcell, who had died in the last decade of the seventeenth century and whose place had not been filled.

When George arrived as king, Handel had spent most of the previous three years in London and became a natural ally at court – a German whose English was good enough for him to make friends with the High Tories who had surrounded Queen Anne, as well as with the Whigs who were on the rise, and whose boast was that they had money and an interest in social style. Indeed, the Queen had asked him to compose a 'Te Deum' and 'Jubilate' to be performed in St Paul's to celebrate the Treaty of Utrecht in 1713, which put an end to the War of the Spanish Succession and placed a large British footprint on North America. Technically, the musical commission was illegal, because only Englishmen were permitted to write for such occasions. It demonstrated that even before George I ascended the throne, Handel was a trusted (and successful) figure.

When he set up his opera company in 1719 he began to work at a startling rate. In the course of three years, for example, he produced *Ottone*, *Julius Caesar* and *Rodelinda*, three of his finest operas. London was the place to be. The German composer Johann Mattheson said in 1713 that everyone was heading there. 'In Italy and France there is something to be heard and learned; in England there is something to be earned.' That may be a double-edged remark – many continentals still saw London, culturally, as being in the wings – but there were opportunities.

The merchant class was expanding fast and England as a trading nation was booming. Travel across Europe was becoming easier. London was a centre for printing and publishing, the idea of 'fashion' was taking a hold outside the closed world of the royal court, and despite the early unpopularity of the Hanoverian succession it was a time of optimism.

Handel's music was a natural expression of that opening out: a sound that seemed to suggest something new. And this wasn't opera for a tiny elite, clustered round the throne or gathered in a great man's drawing room. The theatres in London were full, and Handel's arias were the popular songs of their day. You might say that he invented a middle-class audience for music, though in the theatres themselves the aristocracy still made up the bulk of the audience. Outside, in the pleasure gardens that were becoming ever more popular, his music was greatly in demand.

But popularity and fashion are fickle. Handel had become well off and famous, the talk of the town. Yet his very success in feeding a popular taste helped to bring him trouble. He'd produced fine Italianate operas, dealing with classical stories and depending on his mastery of melody to bring his characters to life. But when audiences began to want more, they also wanted something new. John Gay's *The Beggar's Opera*, which came along in 1728, was, in part, an assault on Handel's style, a home-grown story.

The opera was produced in the same year that Alexander Pope published his satirical poem *The Dunciad*, which sprayed venom at the 'hacks and scribblers' who were now such a part of life in London, a city where a Whig political class was establishing itself, a vigorous and often scandalous press was digging itself in, and Jonathan Swift and Alexander Pope were demonstrating what satire could do. In Book 4 of *The Dunciad*, a riotous but sometimes dense commentary on London life that Swift told Pope would be unlikely to be understood by anyone living more than twenty miles from the capital, Pope pokes fun at the decorative Italian style that Handel perfected (and at the audiences that lapped it up) and pricks him for his acceptance of commissions from Ireland, a natural instrument of insult at the time.

'O *Cara! Cara!* silence all that train:
Joy to great Chaos! let Division reign:
Chromatic tortures soon shall drive them hence,
Break all their nerves, and fritter all their sense:

One Trill shall harmonize joy, grief, and rage,
Wake the dull Church, and lull the ranting Stage;
To the same notes thy sons shall hum, or snore,
And all thy yawning daughters cry, *encore*.
Another Phœbus, thy own Phœbus, reigns,
Joys in my jiggs, and dances in my chains.
But soon, ah soon Rebellion will commence,
If Music meanly borrows aid from Sense:
Strong in new Arms, lo! Giant Handel stands,
Like bold Briareus, with a hundred hands;
To stir, to rouze, to shake the Soul he comes,
And Jove's own Thunders follow Mars's Drums.
Arrest him, Empress; or you sleep no more—'
She heard, and drove him to th'Hibernian shore.

Gay's opera used the feel of the street ballad and added the spirit of the pamphleteers who were the public commentators of their day. To its audience it represented the life they saw around them. It was sung in English and dealt with the mysterious symmetries of the moneyed classes and the ruffians of the street, satirising the powerful by putting their values and ideas into the mouths of common criminals. The end, however, was a happy-ever-after affair, which is precisely what audiences wanted and expected.

The doings of Mr Peachum, his daughter Polly and the Macheath gang rapidly became more popular than Handel's stylised tales from ancient Rome. The very liveliness of the theatres, the appetite of the audiences, meant that there had to be something new, and the rival company to Handel's Royal Academy of Music was the winner. In its first London season there were sixty-three performances of *The Beggar's Opera*. Handel's disgruntlement is easily imagined. The eighteenth-century music historian Charles Burney said of him that he was 'impetuous, rough and peremptory in his manners and conversation', but that although his general appearance was heavy and sour, when he did decide to smile the beam emerged like 'the sun bursting out of a black cloud'. The sunburst in Handel's music was a consequence of his operatic difficulties. He continued to write operas, but never again had the success that he'd known at the beginning of his British career.

Instead, he turned to the form for which many still know him best –
writing for choir and soloists in the oratorio. Who has sung in a choir
and doesn't know the greatest choruses from *Messiah*? It is a measure of
Handel's brilliance, and of his adaptability as a musician, that he was
able to turn his skills as an operatic composer to the service of a different
form, and become the inventor of the English oratorio.

Messiah, written at the beginning of the 1740s, has Italianate melodies
of the sort that he'd used on the opera stage, gives the soloists an
opportunity for virtuosity, and produces a rich choral sound. Most of his
audience would have heard that fullness only in Handel's own earlier
work – the 'Te Deum' written at Queen Anne's command and the first
oratorios like *Saul* and *Israel in Egypt*. Curiously for us, *Messiah* wasn't
the most popular of his oratorios at first, though it was eventually so
successful that Thomas Coram's Foundling Hospital was able to benefit
greatly from Handel's gift of the rights to the 'Hallelujah' chorus. Of the
two dozen and more that he wrote, *Samson* and *Judas Maccabeus* were
more often sung, but *Messiah* became one of the foundation stones of the
English choral tradition, a work loved by generations of singers for its
breadth, its glorious moments of surprise, and perhaps also its sheer
singability. Advertise a scratch *Messiah* – where amateur singers just turn
up ready to join in – and you can still fill the Royal Albert Hall.

The reason for that popularity is the combination of high seriousness
and exuberance which makes *Messiah* so remarkable. The Christian
story of redemption is embedded in western culture, the subject of so
much art and music, and Handel took that familiar theme and
transformed it. A performance of *Messiah* should be touching and
shattering all at once. He wrote it in only twenty-three days, so the
story goes, before travelling for the first performance in Dublin,
whence the commission had come. It's a work that catches the essence
of Handel – his endless capacity for melody, his understanding of what
human voices can do together, and perhaps above all his sense of drama.

The *Gentleman's Magazine* reported in 1749 that 12,000 people had
paid 2s 6d (a fairly hefty ticket price) to watch him in the New Spring
Garden at Vauxhall rehearsing the orchestra for a performance of his
'Music for the Royal Fireworks'. So many carriages had come to
deposit the fashionable at the rehearsal that the streets were blocked
for hours.

Big audiences would listen to him in gardens, smaller ones in theatres; people would gather along the river to see him and listen to his music in the elegant drawing rooms of the capital. Handel, the cosmopolitan musician who decided to become a British citizen (and dropped the 'k' from the end of his middle name Frederick as a patriotic gesture), turned the music of his age into a popular pursuit. He helped to create a taste, and satisfied it. Fashions would change and much of Handel's work would be put aside (the operas, for example, would be rediscovered and revered in our own time after long neglect), but his ability to create drama in music wouldn't be forgotten. Mozart, who arranged *Messiah* for a performance in Vienna in 1780s, said of him: 'When he strikes, he strikes with thunder.' That was how the majestic opening of his anthem 'Zadok the Priest' must have seemed to the congregation in Westminster Abbey when George II was crowned in 1727, music heard at every coronation since.

Handel, granted a state funeral in his adopted country, was buried in Westminster Abbey with full honours. There are many pictures of him in commanding postures, exuding what is assumed to be wisdom, but perhaps the best vision of him is the statue commissioned for Vauxhall gardens by Louis-François Roubiliac, which is now in the collection of the Victoria and Albert Museum. It shows him with unbuttoned shirt, a slipper dangling from one foot, a soft cap pulled roughly over his head. He is playing a lyre, with a cherub nestling happily at his feet, but he seems caught in a domestic moment, not in formal communion with the gods. The formal portraits – like Thomas Hudson's in 1756 – show a composer in court finery, his wig freshly powdered against a painted sylvan scene in the background. He is remote and austere. By contrast, the Vauxhall statue avoids idealising the musician, or placing him somewhere else, but presents him in a more affecting and human guise. It was produced in the year he had a stroke, 1737, and captures something of the frailty of this genius (though he hadn't yet gone blind when the statue was executed) who lit up London with his invention and his ability to transform musical ideas, ideas that he picked up like a restless and sharp-eyed magpie. His contemporary, the organist and composer Dr William Boyce, said of him that he 'took other men's pebbles and polished them into diamonds'.

Handel's craftsmanship produced memorable melodies and passages of great drama. The elegance of an opera like *Rodelinda* or *Xerxes* has little to do with briskness in the movement of plot or the kind of dramatic subtlety that would be required for audiences in the future. Handel was popular because of his ability to catch deep emotion in music, which is why the best productions of his operas have a pace that suits the elegance of the structure, everything in its place in a well-ordered world. Balance and rhythm are everything. He wrote fifty operas, and though he was praised by his contemporary Bach and later by Mozart and Beethoven, his operatic output slipped from fashion, into a strange and inappropriate darkness. When the early-music movement took hold in the 1960s it was natural that Handel would be one of the composers who would be rescued as a by-product, because his reputation had rested rather lopsidedly on the oratorios and his instrumental work (particularly the organ concertos) rather than on the operas – although it was on that territory that he displayed a luminous brilliance in understanding the Italian tradition and transforming it for a new age and a different country.

Handel was the principal figure in a time of great musical excitement in London. It seems, in retrospect, a matter of inexorable progress – the understanding of different traditions, principally from Italy, and the moulding of what seems to be a quite distinct national tradition of music-making. However, such developments are not inevitable. The English experience is an individual one, contrasting spectacularly with what happened in the same period in France. Though Handel's Italian style caused his operas to decline in popularity – and, indeed, to be treasured as representatives of an 'older' tradition even in his own lifetime – he was never involved in the kind of extraordinary artistic dispute that convulsed Paris at this time. Sometimes you hear philosophical disputes in unusual places, and in a surprising style. The unlikely *casus belli* among the French was an opera little known today, *La serva padrona* by the Italian composer Giovanni Pergolesi, who was long dead when it caused an intellectual riot in Paris in the 1750s. It is worth a trip across the Channel to recall how music could become a code for deeper arguments.

For a couple of years after that opera was first heard in Paris it was at the centre of a high-minded row that became known as the War of the

Buffoons – a reference to the comedians who were the staple characters of the Italian comic *opera buffa*. Every member of the intelligentsia had to be on one side or the other. The King, Louis XV, and his Queen even took opposing views. It had come about for a familiar and weary practical reason. Audiences were dropping away and the management of the opera house was worried. The diet of French opera, overwhelmingly tragic in its themes, was proving indigestible. So they decided to bring on the Italians.

Not only was the style different; the stories were less often tragic, and the change in the programme at the opera house became a metaphor for something else – the national argument about political reform. It mirrored the philosophical debates led by Jean-Jacques Rousseau, who praised the Italian opera just as he argued the case for a more enlightened monarchy and an end to absolutism. The loyal French musicians at the opera, probably more worried about their jobs than about Rousseau's philosophy, burned him in effigy.

The most important musical figure in France at this time had begun writing in the tradition of the court composer – drawing on the example of Louis XIV's limpet-like courtier Jean-Baptiste Lully – but he was also shaped by the age of reason which would produce the Enlightenment. He was Jean-Philippe Rameau, and he began to talk about music as a science. Rameau's story reveals the profound change in music that was going on in France. Handel was popular in London, riding with the social changes that were producing a bigger audience for music (and patrons from the merchant class as well as the aristocracy). In France there was a similar opening up, but it was embedded in an intellectual debate about monarchy, individual liberty and reason that was being pursued by Rousseau, Voltaire and others.

Rameau (1683–1764) was a prolific composer of harpsichord music, cantatas and motets for the voice, before turning to opera. And he found himself in the middle of the War of the Buffoons. He'd begun as the natural heir to Lully, whom Rameau admired but who saw his purpose as glorifying the King. That duty – obsession even – was now becoming a thing of the past. Rameau was more interested in praising the world around him than in kingship.

He was a composer who was interested in the theory of music, its science. By the 1720s he was starting to write about music in a way that the likes of Lully would have found not only unnecessary but rather heretical. He wanted to know how music was constructed. Bach was already demonstrating this approach. The preludes and fugues of *The Well-Tempered Clavier* are an intoxicating guide to the major and minor keys, one by one. Rameau wanted to explain why.

Take the simple perfect chord – the triad of the first, third and fifth notes of the scale. Rameau saw such chords as the natural component parts of every piece of music and argued that there were philosophical as well as practical reasons for this. In his *Treatise on Harmony* he attempted to prove that every set of sounds could be traced back to those 'natural' musical intervals which reflected a deeper order of things. And he described at great length how a theory of music could emerge from that understanding.

His ideas became important in music-teaching, but at the time they represented a sharp break with the past. Though composers had understood how harmony worked for centuries, and Bach was getting to the essence of music in his work for keyboard and choir, Rameau was trying to show that it had natural origins: that the perfect piece of music was a mirror that faithfully reflected nature. He began to write opera only when he was fifty, and approached it with high intellectual seriousness.

In that respect he was no longer the descendant of Lully but the product of a novel way of thinking about music. Voices in a Rameau opera were woven into the score in a remarkable fashion. It was why Richard Wagner and Claude Debussy, for example, would admire him in years to come. Listening to the voice of Pluto in his first and most popular opera, *Hippolyte et Aricie* (the first version was written in 1733), with the rivers thundering away in the violins, the chorus of demons adding their anger and anxiety to the scene, you hear music and drama fused together. The voice part isn't sung separately, but threaded into the pattern of sound from orchestra and chorus. It's extraordinarily far-sighted.

The problem for Rameau was that his philosophy tended to overwhelm his operas. They were criticised for being too 'learned', over-orchestrated and even unintelligible. He suffered the fate of many opera composers since, in being accused of writing about ideas instead of about people – which is what drama on the stage is supposed to be about. Though there are more than two dozen of his operas, and future composers would study them with admiration, Rameau's experience is a vivid example of how periods of experiment are dangerous and unpredictable for music and musicians.

He was the victim of a terrible irony. Though he was devoted to the pursuit of reason, the watchword of the thinkers of the time, his operas came to be lumped together with the old French tradition. The managers of the Paris opera house concluded that that tradition was running out of steam with the audience, so turned to the Italians. And, much worse for Rameau, he fell out with Rousseau, whose natural intellectual companion he was. He saw music as a science and looked forward, but he was on the wrong side of the War of the Buffoons, with the traditionalists. Rousseau said that Rameau had tried to substitute 'harmonic speculations for the delight of the ear'. In a way, of course, he was right. But how terrible it was for Rameau to find the articles he wrote for the *Encyclopédie* in Paris attacked by Rousseau for worrying more about 'equal temperament' in music than about beauty, which he said turned his work into 'a mathematician's delight but a musician's nightmare'.

The truth is that the pursuit of reason, and respect for nature, meant different things to different followers of the cause. In the waspish exchanges between Rameau and Rousseau you hear a collision, and feel an awkward pause. Enlightenment ideas were rampant and it was a world in which everything seemed possible. In Paris the King's government was starting to tremble – there were military disasters abroad, debt and dissent at home. And that spirit of disagreement had a bizarre outlet in that struggle in the opera house, which spilled into the streets and continued for two years.

Pergolesi the Italian was brought in to cheer up a public apparently beaten down by the gloom and intellectualism of French opera, and poor Rameau, who thought of himself as a progressive thinker, was caught up in a battle in which music (not for the first or the last time) was a cipher for deeper disputes, and an instrument of politics.

The audience in the opera house was a worrying one for the King, because outside the boxes owned by the aristocracy and the richest merchants it consisted of parliamentarians, lawyers, clerks – the very elements active in the movement for reform. As in Handel's London, the audience for opera was broadening. The subscribers who wanted more Italian opera ended up occupying the opera pit, and the King sent soldiers to flush them out; reports of the climactic battle of the opera house were sent to Versailles, it's said, every quarter of an hour. Louis XV won the day. And how did he celebrate? With a French opera by Jean-Joseph Cassandéa de Mondonville, *Titon et l'Aurore*. So the War of the Buffoons was settled, after a fashion.

The character of that time in London was rather different. Though the Enlightenment was throwing up the same questions that were obsessing thinkers in France, the British King and Queen could not be said to be taking opposing sides in a philosophical dispute. George III's favourite piece of music was the 'Hallelujah' chorus; London was not riven by a high-minded argument about what might best represent the state of the nation. Indeed the contrast with Paris was highlighted by the fact that one of the most striking features of British musical life was the extent to which it was spreading in lively fashion away from the metropolis. The Enlightenment was hastening a process that had been obvious half a century before, revealed for example in the spectacular proceedings of the Royal Society: the speed with which ideas and innovations were carried around Britain by informed and original people.

By the time Handel died in 1759, in the last year of George II's reign, Edinburgh was already shaping up as a crucible of the European Enlightenment, its links with the continent happily bypassing London and involving vigorous exchanges of ideas as well as heavily laden ships that carried claret from Bordeaux to the wine merchants of Leith. Elsewhere, the flow of money from the colonies, and through the slave trade, was producing a moneyed class that wanted education and, probably more keenly, style. Travelling musicians from the rest of Europe were prized and celebrated, and the notion of 'society' took hold. By the middle of the century, the Georgian elegance that is still familiar to us was in full flower. Nowhere was it more obvious than in the old Roman spa of Bath.

Nowadays, if you leave the traffic of that city behind you and go into the Assembly Rooms you find a peaceful retreat from the world. Among their pillars and galleries, chandeliers and Georgian windows nestle memories of the eighteenth-century beau monde, when these rooms were a stage for popular music-making. But the decorum that they seem to embody today may be a little misleading. In the 1770s they weren't always quiet and calm. There might be 800 people milling about, the card rooms would be full, the place would be a cacophony of talk and gossip and flirtation. An 'assembly' was a particular kind of entertainment, and music was only part of it. On Sundays there were public teas for sixpence a head; in the evenings there might be a candlelit ball with the musicians playing from the gallery above. It was a place where you wanted to see and be seen.

Music was part of the social fabric in a new way, one of the influences that helped to create the atmosphere in the Pump Room above the Roman springs. If you had a crinoline dress or a fine suit and cravat, and the manners and training needed to navigate the dance floor in the Assembly Rooms, this was your territory for the social game.

Music in Britain in this period has sometimes been portrayed as inferior to the state of affairs on the continent, where in Paris they were rioting at the opera house and in Vienna the Habsburg Emperor was presiding over an arrogant but brilliant cultural realm. But in fact for the British it was a time of invention, originality and popularity. There was trade, wealth and freshly launched newspapers, and Defoe and Fielding were announcing the arrival of the novel. Young ladies would read, and they would learn to play on the keyboard. In the course of George III's sixty-year reign, which began in 1760, the early 'square' pianos would begin to supplant the harpsichord. Things were on the move.

As we've seen, Handel's success in London had made opera a sought-after form of entertainment: and apart from the audiences in the theatres, popular arias were printed and circulated to a wider public. Thomas Arne's imitation of an Italian *opera seria* in English, *Artaxerxes* (1762), for example, was an indication of some of the cross-currents flowing so strongly across Europe. One family illustrates that clearly – the Storaces. Its members had contacts with Mozart in Vienna, where the soprano Nancy Storace was the first Susanna in *The Marriage of Figaro* in 1786, and her brother Stephen was a composer who laboured under the burden of the label attached to quite a few composers of the time, 'the English Mozart'. They were of Italian origin but their father had moved to London and the family had become naturalised Britons. Though Nancy found it difficult at first to get as much work as she deserved, before long they were very well known. Among Stephen's songs was a setting of Gray's *Elegy Written in a Country Churchyard*. That song, 'O Tuneful Voice', was one for the concert hall.

Before Bath became the social centre of Georgian England outside London, the first purpose-built public hall for music in Europe was constructed in Oxford. The Holywell Music Room, whose doors opened in 1748, is still used for chamber concerts and recitals today – an intimate, high-ceilinged, rather bare oval room, with beautiful acoustics and, as one visitor said in the early days, 'not one pillar to deaden the sound'. It was built by public subscription and was soon a magnet for 400 or so of the well-heeled. There was already a flourishing music society in Oxford and it had organised fund-raising concerts in order to provide a room for its activities, though as with Bath it is important to remember that the atmosphere wouldn't necessarily be reverential at a concert. Nearly thirty years after it opened, the Musical Society had to send out a note to its subscribers with a request that dogs should no longer be allowed to come to concerts. They were too annoying, and barked in the wrong places.

Animal noises apart, the concerts there began to attract singers and musicians from continental Europe. In the early days Handel, George III's favourite composer, was still one of the biggest draws, and there were Handel festivals all over the country. There were also madrigal societies and 'glee clubs' which met to indulge in what was a cross between art and community singing. If you had wandered into the Crown and Anchor in the Strand in London on an evening when the Anacreontic Society was having one of its meetings ('for supper and the singing of catches, glees and songs') you would have heard proceedings begin with a song that was the invariable opener, a piece by John Stafford Smith which went on to have another life in the New World: it became the tune for 'The Star-Spangled Banner'.

There was an enthusiastic audience for the concerts at the Holywell Music Room, and a resident orchestra was established. Similar public halls were erected elsewhere. In Edinburgh in the early 1760s, a city buzzing with ideas, argument and bold architecture, St Cecilia's Hall opened to the public. A visiting English scientist said around that time that if you stood on the High Street, on the Royal Mile running down from the Castle, you would before long be able to shake fifty men of genius by the hand. Edinburgh was the city of, among many other distinguished figures, the philosopher David Hume and the first economist Adam Smith, the poet Robert Fergusson, the portrait painter Allan Ramsay, the father of geology John Hutton and Robert Ferguson, who is often described as the first social scientist. The Adam brothers were building a stunning Georgian city, and Voltaire thought it the most interesting place in Europe.

Later generations in Britain sometimes looked towards Vienna where Haydn and Mozart were ablaze, and underrated the cultural excitement at home. Literature was spreading, and music was coming out of the churches and great houses into public places: the audience was still moneyed (and therefore limited) but it was enthusiastic. The music-publishing business was booming, and in an age when adopting new ideas was smart and indeed important, there was an appetite for fresh entertainment.

In Bath, it was managed in part by the extraordinary character of Richard 'Beau' Nash, who became the city's Master of Ceremonies and set about giving it a social reputation. He was a gambler and a rough-cut diamond, despite his dandy's clothes, and was more interested in the glamour of a society ball than in musical refinement. But one thrived on the other. You could gamble, show off, play social games and concentrate on marrying your daughters off to the richest young men; you could also feed on a lively musical culture. At the centre of it was a remarkable family, whose achievements have often been underestimated. They were the Linleys.

Thomas Linley senior organised the subscription concerts in Bath. When the New Assembly Rooms opened up in 1771 as rivals to the old ones – there was a big enough public for that kind of competition – it was Linley who became director of music. A harpsichordist, he was the city's best-known performer, at the Pump Room (where the spa water bubbled up) and at the various assemblies, and he was a singing teacher and a composer too. His son, Thomas, followed him and turned out to be a remarkable musician.

Young Linley is a fascinating product of his time. He was exactly the same age as Mozart (born in 1756), whom he met while he was studying the violin in Italy. He was fifteen when his father became music director of the New Assembly Rooms, and by the time he was twenty he'd written twenty violin concertos. When his father became director of music at the Drury Lane Theatre, in London, Thomas's fame spread and his *Shakespeare Ode* of 1776 was hailed as a work of real brilliance. The *Morning Chronicle* described the piece as 'an extraordinary effort of genius in so young a man . . . the fugue of the overture is masterly'.

That public comment is important. Linley was writing and performing in an age when news was beginning to travel fast. The London press was expanding, and there were nearly three dozen provincial papers. So word of a performer, or of a new work, was passed on quickly. The public appetite for performance, whether at a theatre like Drury Lane or a subscription hall like Holywell, was encouraged by the reviews and recommendations that were starting to reach a wider public.

It was an appreciative one. In March 1778, the *Morning Post* reviewed a performance by Linley in which it was said that the 'warm applause he received last night proves that an English audience will give proper encouragement to true merit and genius'. The paper then added tartly: 'even though it is the production of their own country'. There's an acknowledgement there that Linley was part of a movement, a broadening of musical taste that didn't depend on imported ideas or styles from abroad for its energy. He wouldn't live to enjoy that success for long. In that same year he drowned in the lake in the grounds of Grimsthorpe Castle, Lincolnshire, while boating with friends. He was only twenty-two. With his father, the Linleys' spirit and skill had helped the opening up of music in their time. They were a well-connected family, prospering at a time when money from the East and West Indies (and from the slave trade) was flowing in – that's why the tea houses and coffee houses proliferated. Elizabeth Linley – young Thomas's sister – married the playwright Richard Brinsley Sheridan when he was managing the Drury Lane Theatre, and Thomas wrote the music for his production of *The Tempest* and the score for his opera *The Duenna* in 1775.

By the 1780s more than a hundred musical societies had been set up around the country. Visiting soloists and conductors travelled outside London. Musical entrepreneurs were selling concert tickets, music lessons, even some early pianos for those who could afford them – though that instrument's heyday was still some way off. Printed music wasn't yet cheap but by 1800 a number of music magazines were circulating, and the most successful and longest-lasting ones were those with a musical supplement (as with the cigarette cards of the future, you had to buy them to get the new piece and they became part of your collection). Though in the eighteenth century we are still talking about a segment of society, the days of music as the preserve of the very rich or the royal court and the Church were over.

You could go to subscription concerts in Salisbury or Newcastle or Leeds as well as in Oxford and Edinburgh. When the travelling assizes with their judges and lawyers visited Nottingham or Leicester there were concerts. In Doncaster or York there were special concerts to coincide with the big race meetings. These were run not by rich patrons, but by enthusiasts who wanted to spread the word, if they could raise enough money to keep the concerts going.

Musicians would trundle round the country on a happy progress from hall to hall. They might play in the orchestra in Bath from autumn to Easter then go to country houses and to other towns, playing, conducting, satisfying a public taste. Bath was proud of its reputation. When Joseph Haydn was in London in the early 1790s he travelled down to stay with the celebrated singer and harpsichordist Venanzio Rauzzini, the castrato for whom Mozart wrote the motet 'Exultate, jubilate' (K 165) first performed in 1773. Haydn's visit is remembered in the Canon in B Flat, a round, written to remind Rauzzini of his recently deceased dog, whom he was missing.

You sense the liveliness of the musical scene. It was drawing in sounds from everywhere. The Oxford Musical Society was led by John Baptist Malchair, a German who had settled there in the 1750s, and he became one of the first collectors of folk tunes, rushing home to write down a melody he had heard whistled in the street or the snatch of a song picked up in a tavern.

Public concerts, folk tunes, sheet music, visiting virtuosi – a kind of liberation was afoot and in one respect a particularly important one. Women were becoming prominent in musical life. In the drawing rooms of Bath they were playing the harpsichord or the piano, and listening to music in the Assembly Rooms. By the time Jane Austen arrived in the city in the first decade of the nineteenth century – she was a music-lover herself – she was able to observe a society in which music had become part of everyday life. Isabella in *Northanger Abbey* goes to a ball in Bath; and Mary Bennett, we know, played the piano. Here she is in Chapter 6 of *Pride and Prejudice*:

> Mary had neither genius nor taste; and though vanity had given her application, it had given her likewise a pedantic air and conceited manner, which would have injured a higher degree of excellence than she had reached . . . Mary, at the end of a long concerto, was glad to purchase praise and gratitude by Scotch and Irish airs, at the request of her younger sisters, who with some of the Lucases and two or three of the officers joined eagerly in dancing at one end of the room.

We are not told what she played. A John Field sonata, perhaps? Her character and aptitude suggests not. More probably it was one of Mrs Bolton's tunes, the best known of which is 'The Bluebells of Scotland'. It isn't suggested that Mary was working her way through Book II of *The Well-Tempered Clavier* or a Haydn sonata. You do catch there, however, the way that music had come into the home. There was vanity and lack of talent as well as brilliance and insight, social posturing as well as fun. These drawing rooms were the playgrounds of the upwardly mobile. And they had their own music, written for them. Society was changing, expanding, and absorbing music into its bloodstream.

The musical life of late-eighteenth-century England has tended to be undervalued, despite literary London's flourishing life. But it may be true that even more important musical achievements of the age took place elsewhere. Whatever the delights of Sheridan's theatre and the Linleys' music, it would be the work of Joseph Haydn and Wolfgang Amadeus Mozart (whose father took him to London as a boy in 1764) that would dominate the last part of the century. Mozart would be a beneficiary of Haydn's symphonies and string quartets – more than 180 of them altogether – which were the works that crowned the age of the Baroque. Mozart later said of him: 'There is no one who can do it all – to joke and to terrify, to evoke laughter and profound sentiment – and all equally well, except Joseph Haydn.'

Between them they provided the majestic transition from the sounds and style of the mid-eighteenth century to the Classical form that

Beethoven would inherit and infuse with his own genius. Their music, however, has an antecedent of its own. While Handel was writing in London, and Rameau was writing for the keyboard in Paris and turning his mind to opera, the composer was working in Germany who, more than any other, was building foundations in keyboard music, in writing for voices and for the small orchestras of his time, that would prove some of the deepest and most durable of all.

About a month after Handel was born in Halle in Saxony in February 1685, a couple of hundred miles away in Eisenach, Thuringia, Johann Ambrosius Bach and his wife Maria Elisabeth gave birth to their last child, Johann Sebastian.

7

J. S. Bach

'The Immortal God of Harmony'

~

JOHANN SEBASTIAN BACH was little travelled, a journeyman musician, organist and composer whose religion was probably as important to him as his music. He did a job, and of all the great composers he is probably the one who had least idea of the scale of his achievement and the effect it might have. Three and a half centuries after his death he still inspires awe and a kind of mystical admiration, and remains a source of inspiration, though his life seems remote and strange.

It is strange only because, from the vantage point of our brittle contemporary age of celebrity, Bach breaks the rules that have come to be attached to fame and brilliance in our own time. The notions that accompany success in our day were unknown to him; the way that he worked, and the impulses that drove him, came from a society that many people born in the twentieth century find so distant and different that it is easy to misunderstand. The church where he worked for the last twenty-seven years of his life, which still stands in Leipzig, is an outpost from another world.

When he arrived there to be cantor at St Thomas's School and civic director of music in 1723 he was the most important musician in the city, responsible for the music in its four biggest Lutheran churches. Leipzig was the centre of German Protestantism, not far from Wittenberg, where Luther had nailed his theses to the church door in 1517. It was a commercial powerhouse and a renowned seat of learning with a fifteenth-century university and thought enough of itself to adopt the self-satisfied nickname of Little Paris. Bach was a civic employee, supplementing his income by writing to order for weddings and funerals, and his commitments were those of a musical workman.

His productivity was extraordinary. Of his musical output, more than a thousand works, most were written in Leipzig. Within three years of his arrival there he produced two complete cantata cycles for the church year – a total of 120 pieces for the choir – and three more were written later. Nothing of its quality and depth had been heard in the city before, though Leipzig had a high musical reputation. St Thomas's church looks much as it did in those days, having survived the bombing raids of the last days of the Second World War, a high narrow building painted white with a tall thin tower, steeply sloping roof and an interior that Bach would still be able to recognise. As cantor, he conducted week after week, sometimes starting at 7 a.m. on a Sunday morning with a three-hour service. It was gruelling, serious work and it required an intensity of religious commitment that marks him out. Devotion was an important part of musical life before his time; afterwards it gradually became much more a matter of individual choice. For Bach, reared in the glow of Luther's and Calvin's revolution, it was his life.

Though he wrote a great deal of secular music, for keyboard and choir, his work grew out of his beliefs. He had been an organist at the ducal court in Weimar in his early twenties but it was as a church composer and conductor that he would spend most of his life. Luther's central preoccupation was the idea that the grace of God was granted in return for devotion and faith (and not on the say-so of an intervening priest), and the life to which Bach was attracted was one which demanded a high degree of discipline and commitment. He had been famous as a young organist, his ability on the keyboard (and the organ pedals) being a wonder, and had imbibed the spirit of the great players whom he had heard as a youth when he sang in a choir at Lüneberg and used to walk thirty miles to Hamburg to hear Johann Adam Reincken, the master organist of his time. His life as a composer, however, was increasingly focused on the need to produce music that was worthy of the Church.

In doing so, he became a craftsman who showed how complete mastery of the techniques of composition could produce the sublime – like a mathematician whose understanding of how numbers work is so profound, and so instinctive, that it takes him on to some ethereal plane where the rest of us cannot go. This was music that was perfectly constructed, whether in the patterns of a complicated fugue in which interconnected melodic lines are allowed to go their own way and are then brought together again, or in a cantata for choir. He had an utterly secure understanding of counterpoint, the handling of different melodic lines simultaneously to produce more than the sum of their parts. The craftsman image is not unfair, even for someone who can safely be labelled a genius. To his natural talent he added hard work. He studied composers from the past like the German organist and composer Johann Pachelbel (1653–1706) and contemporaries like the French keyboard master François Couperin.

Bach's achievement was worked at, sometimes wearily. He was a journeyman musician for most of his life, moving to and fro across north Germany, Thuringia and Saxony (and almost nowhere else), and often writing to order. Another mass, another prelude for a wedding, a cantata for the choir, another string concerto for the Duke of Saxe-Weimar – that was his lot. Yet he composed a body of music that, after a century or so of being undervalued, came to represent one of the most precious achievements of western art.

That music was the product of a particular culture: much of it Protestant, devoted to learning, conscious of being different from the traditions of France and Italy, and above all taking music very seriously. The principalities that would gradually come together to form a united Germany in the nineteenth century were a loose collection of mini-states, competing with each other for influence, and driven by the ambitions of princes for whom music was a reflection of their power, and an adornment to it. With that patronage, and the urgings of a Church that wanted more and more music, Bach's brilliance was allowed to shine.

He was a composer who wrote because people wanted his music. If they were rich they wished to boast of having had the cantor of the city's most important church writing for their weddings (and funerals). Bach's achievement lay in demonstrating that productivity and brilliance were not incompatible. He had no need to secrete himself away, to be sheltered from the world, in order to write. When a piece was required, he could provide it.

As a boy in Eisenach (the town where Martin Luther had been born) he developed a voracious musical appetite, secretly copying manuscripts composed or previously copied by his elder brother, Johann Christophe – working at his technique on the keyboard, studying intensely, learning complicated fugues in which the lines of notes are tied together like some perfectly formed knot, then untied and tied again. This came naturally to him, as soon as his hands were big enough to cope. The family was musical, and he would have joined in at the keyboard or on the violin, learning the first principles. Then he had his encounter with the organ, and began to listen to Reincken and others.

Soon he was writing for the instrument. Some of his best-known preludes and fugues for the organ were written when he was in his early twenties, already in command. Nowhere else in Europe was the organ as central to music-making as it was in the German principalities. It filled the churches; dukes and princes were eager to have one built for their great houses and castles; it was a vehicle for invention. The instruments were getting bigger, the complicated mechanisms more secure and more subtle, the pipes producing a greater range of sounds. Their only rivals were in France.

Bach was in demand. He would travel to hear new instruments, to play them, and you get a picture of a culture which was alive to new ideas. The young Bach was writing for ducal courts in which the assumption was that the settled order wouldn't change, but was open to musical invention – though the churches were more conservative institutions. He was stretching the boundaries, and in his hands the keyboard took on a formidable power. He was doing all this at the same time as Domenico Scarlatti, born in that same Bach–Handel year of 1685, who was conquering the sonata form a long distance away in Italy, quite unknown to Bach. They were the keyboard innovators of their age.

But, for Bach, life in Leipzig was often complicated by frustration with his municipal employers:

It pleased God that I should be called here as musical director and cantor of St Thomas's School, even though at first it seemed to me intolerable to descend to the rank of cantor after having been director of music [at Köthen]. That is why for three months I held back my decision. But the post was so favourably recommended to me that finally, and chiefly because my sons appear to be inclined toward study, I dared, in the name of the Almighty, to go to Leipzig. I passed an audition and then moved to the new place where, by the grace of God, I am still.

But I find (1) that the duties are by far not so agreeable as they were described to me originally; and (2) that quite a few of the bonuses attached to the post have been withdrawn; (3) that the cost of living is very high here; and (4) that the authorities are rather strangely hostile to music; that I have to live in a state of almost constant struggle; that envy prevails and vexations are numerous; I find myself, so help me God, compelled to seek my fortune elsewhere.

My salary here is seven hundred thalers, and when there are more burials than usual, the added fees raise this proportionately higher. But whenever the air is a little more healthful, the loss is great. Last year the fees for common burials showed a deficit of a hundred thalers. With four hundred thalers I could support myself in Thuringia more comfortably than here with twice that amount, for the cost of living in Leipzig is exorbitant.

A composer who has to worry about a drop in the number of burials among well-to-do families is far from the picture often assembled of a frenzied genius in the grip of a restless and insistent muse. By the time he arrived in Leipzig and unloaded all his worldly goods from the four wagons that carried them from Köthen, where he had been director of music for Prince Leopold of Anhalt-Köthen since 1717, he was thirty-eight and into the second of the five marriages that would produce twenty children. Work had to be done.

In Leipzig, Bach – organist, violinist, harpsichordist, choirmaster, composer – was now immersed in all the jealousies and bureaucracy of the city council and its hangers-on. It was a hard business – constantly frustrating, and nurturing in Bach the feeling that he had always harboured, that he wasn't being properly appreciated. Somehow, since his early days, he had always seemed to be scrabbling around for money. It never changed.

But the point about Leipzig was that music was taken seriously. It was expected that different settings for services would be heard regularly and that the choir would sing the new as well as the familiar. The city worked him hard; and as he sped from church to church he had to turn out a constant supply of music. It was said of him that he could write a cantata a day. The cantata had developed into a short choral work, with passages for soloists. Bach's were glorious, and they gave him an opportunity to find some extra work outside church.

He found a new challenge in taking over the direction of the Collegium Musicum (Music Society), an orchestra of students and some professional musicians founded by Georg Philipp Telemann in 1702. With one a short interruption, Bach led the society till the early 1740s. The concerts were held once a week, on Friday evenings (and more often during the Easter and St Michael's fairs), in Zimmermann's Coffee House in Katharinenstrasse. When the weather was fine they took place in Zimmermann's gardens, and Bach was grateful. His so-called 'Coffee' Cantata (1734–5) comes close to being an elegant advertisement for the establishment.

In the next seven years or so he produced some of the greatest pieces of sacred music we know, in which all the precision of his organ and keyboard composition is fused with a passion for the poetry of the text. At the same time he was turning out his secular cantatas and keyboard works. For nearly 300 years, choirs have counted on him for a supply of music that manages simultaneously to satisfy singers who want the experience of mass music-making and to rise far above the here-and-now.

In the 1720s in Leipzig, he wrote most of his greatest sacred works – the first version of the *St Matthew* and the *St John* passions (and a lost version of *St Mark*), settings of the 'Magnificat' for Christmas, more than a hundred chorales – hymns – and music for funerals and weddings. You sense in them the seriousness about music that char-acterised the milieu around him, and in the range of his writing for organ, strings, keyboard, choir and orchestra there's a kind of completeness that composers and performers far in the future would find dazzling.

It wasn't always appreciated at the time. The prince for whom he wrote the six 'Brandenburg' concertos – he rejoiced in the title of the Margrave of Brandenburg – seems never to have paid him for his work, and the surviving manuscripts suggest that in their original form the Duke never had them played. Yet they remain some of the finest examples of the style ever written, rather more familiar to us today than they seem to have been to the man who commissioned them.

These sounds have become part of our tradition – with the keyboard music we call the 'Goldberg' Variations (written for the harpsichord), the *Christmas Oratorio*, the organ fugues, the simple progressions of the early preludes from *The Well-Tempered Clavier*, the solo cello suites that are so precious to any player of that instrument, with their simple power. How odd it is to think of Bach in Leipzig, complaining about the cost of living and the petty arguments of his civic employers, arguing about the quality of singers and players available to him and stopping writing religious music for a time around 1730 because of some passing unhappiness, knowing throughout these vexations that he was seen by many people as a jobbing composer and not as an international figure like some of the names that travellers carried back from France and Italy.

Instead, there was the patient mastery demonstrated in the two books of *The Well-Tempered Clavier*, written twenty years apart, the first begun in 1722 and not published in full until half a century after his death. The title page explains precisely what he intended to do: 'Preludes and Fugues through all the tones and semitones . . . for the use and profit of the musical youth desirous of learning'. It adds, reflecting the technical demands made by some of the pieces, that they might also prove useful 'as a pastime of those already skilled in this study'. So he starts to work his way through the keys, beginning with C major.

The pianist and conductor Daniel Barenboim says that when he reaches the last work in the first book (the B minor fugue, in the last key before the player returns to C major) he feels that he has heard all the music there has been and all the music that is to come. He even claims he can hear the radicalism of Arnold Schoenberg, stirring up Vienna with his atonal experiments at the beginning of the twentieth century. This is a striking assertion, not because it is a practical piece of analysis – it is an emotional response rather than a description of the piece – but because it reveals how these two books have come to represent something monumental in music-making. They seem to reveal music's nervous system, the way it functions.

These volumes are still used to teach the essentials of musical construction – how the scales work, how harmony happens, how composition requires craft as well as imagination. Much of this came about through the efforts of the Leipzig school of the nineteenth century, championed by Felix Mendelssohn and Robert Schumann, who both had a distinct and quite rigid view of what should constitute the Germanic tradition, and for both of whom Bach was the master.

The Well-Tempered Clavier (a title which has spawned many still-active academic disputes about whether it was a reference to the tuning of the keyboards, and whether 'equal-tempered' might be a more appropriate description) is a telling Bach memorial, because it illustrates the way that his reputation among modern musicians differs so markedly from his own conception of his work, and indeed from the acclaim he was accorded in his lifetime. He was respected, sometimes revered, but there was never for him the flaming popularity that followed the boy Mozart across Europe a generation later or the grandeur that would attach itself to Joseph Haydn when he reached his maturity.

He worked on the project at a difficult period when he was employed by Prince Leopold of Köthen, who had taken a wife quite ignorant about music. Her arrival appears to have convinced Bach that he should move on, and he applied for the Leipzig post. In starting the preludes and fugues in the 1720s, he was producing keyboard pieces (for the harpsichord) that would act as an education tool, pairs of preludes and fugues that would ascend through the chromatic scale and reveal something of the structure of music in the way they explored harmony as they advanced. The later adoption of the two books by musicians as near-sacred texts is a development that would have astonished Bach. It was only the devotion of his pupils and admirers that caused them to be published complete early in the nineteenth century, and they were given a posthumous weight that had not been consciously produced. They had simply been written for purposes of instruction.

The two books are, of course, a straightforward progression through the keys, and demonstrate Bach's remarkable interest in order and precision. In the thirty-two pieces that make up the 'Goldberg' Variations, published in 1741, the first melody is followed by thirty variations before it returns at the end. They are all built on a thirty-two-note ground bass, and there is a deliberate symmetry between the first sixteen and the second; and in the nine written in canon form (spaced out equally through the variations) the two parts of each canon go up by one note from one to the next. Whether or not this was a reflection of Bach's belief in a settled world – a fixed universe – connected with an ordered and meticulously worked-out faith, it was a feature of his work.

As with the six cello suites, written in the six years after 1717 before he went to Leipzig, Bach produces a dazzling mixture of simplicity and complexity. That is one of the reasons why so many jazz musicians are drawn to him. The Modern Jazz Quartet, founded in 1952, used to improvise on Bach fugues and blend their solos with passages of adapted Baroque counterpoint; in the 1960s, the Jacques Loussier Trio introduced a new generation to the rhythms and harmonies of his music, translated into a contemporary and beguiling idiom.

Part of the appeal is Bach's flawless technical confidence, which suggests a foundation on which almost anything can be built. Another attraction is the spiritual dimension of so much of his music. His own explanation for that would be clear: his celebration of Christian commitment in the oratorios, for example, or in the sublime Mass in B minor (started in 1733 and finished at the end of his life when he was already blind) was bound to be powerful if he had accurately represented the message. But of course many people with different faiths, or none at all, have found Bach uplifting in a way that opens up a spiritual realm.

When BBC Radio 3 broadcast its bold season of all his works at Christmas 2006 – a hugely successful enterprise – the Archbishop of Canterbury, Dr Rowan Williams, said this about Bach and faith:

> It's very difficult to know how you would characterise Bach as a religious composer – he's not just a composer who sets religious texts, he's a composer who sees all his music as a kind of spiritual exercise. Although performers and listeners may not share his confessional convictions, it's difficult to listen to Bach without that sense that you are being invited to change your life . . . something in Bach prompts you to re-evaluate who you are, that re-evaluation of your feelings and your thoughts.

The Archbishop recognised that although Bach's devotion was Christian – rigidly so – his music produced an effect which was much more than an invitation to contemplate and celebrate a particular 'truth'. This was characteristic of music in previous ages, as we've seen – William Byrd in England and Claudio Monteverdi in Italy, for example – which might be written for use in church but could arouse profound feelings in some who might not share the faith. Bach, however, reached a new and higher plain: his exploration of human frailty in the *St John Passion*, for example, is a musical progress even for those who do not feel personally involved in the journey that is the course of the Passion, from the Last Supper through the Garden of Gethsemane to Calvary.

In German his name means a brook or a fountain and you can see him as a source of gushing sound, bubbling out of him in immense quantities, promising never to end – perfect craftsmanship and instinct together. Above all, he was the voice for a way of thinking about music that would become a tradition. Under all the arguments was high seriousness. Bach brought delicacy and robustness together in composition. He fed a hunger for music in Leipzig and elsewhere, and, who knows, perhaps if he hadn't collided with the institutions and the people around him – lived with frustration as well as inspiration – it might not have happened like this. As it was, he slipped from sight for a time, before resuming his place as one of the fathers of European music, the man whom Beethoven would call 'the immortal God of harmony'.

Great music transcends its time, and throws off the shackles. You forget the reasons for it, the composer's sweat and his storms, the fashions of the day. It survives by itself. Take Bach's *St Matthew Passion*, the first version of which was performed in 1727. It was revised nine years later, for bigger orchestral and vocal forces. The version we know today was written for two choirs, two orchestras and probably two sets of soloists, as well as for an extra boy's choir which sang from a 'crow's nest' high up in the church. The oratorio is an example of how Bach could imbue a traditional form – using some well-known tunes from long ago – with new life.

The oratorio had developed in the seventeenth century, when Lutherans began to give more artistic continuity to the Catholic settings of the story, which had choral settings interspersed with sections of plainchant. By the beginning of the eighteenth century a hint of operatic technique had been imported, with a narrative being sung by soloists who could carry the story forward, with the chorus sometimes acting as interpreter or commentator, giving weight and context to the story.

The *St Matthew Passion* shows Bach transforming the familiar. First of all, he used melody from the past. The central chorale, which returns in five different forms, is a tune which would have been known in Leipzig a century before as a dance tune. The chorale – we would now call it simply a hymn – 'O Haupt voll Blut und Wunden' (O bloody, wounded head) is a direct link with Luther, who, as well as writing music himself, deliberately brought familiar secular music into church on the ground that congregations should participate in the music rather than just receive inspiration as passive participants. When Bach's *Passion* was used on Good Friday, the most solemn day in the Christian year, the worshippers would expect to join in. This was no performance to be admired from a distance; Bach would say that it was music that involved the people as well as God. It is formal church music with the grip of operatic tension. At the beginning, there seem to be footsteps, a rhythm that can't be stilled. From the start, this is drama. Bach never wrote an opera, but turned this text, from two chapters of St Matthew's Gospel, into music drama.

He wrote it over two years in the 1720s, and it's curious that there was no great stir when it was first performed. Like his *St John Passion*, which it's thought had only four performances in his lifetime and was changed slightly for each one, this was, in a way, functional music: to be played and sung at a service (though it's about three hours long) and taking its place as part of something bigger. Yet into it Bach introduces subtlety and passion of a sort that had been rare in this form before he came along. In the arias, in which a soloist reflects on the story after it has been told by the chorus, he writes with the suppleness of an operatic composer. The limitations of the church setting slip away.

At the soprano aria 'Blute nur, du liebes Herz!' (Bleed now, dear heart!) the story is infused with an intensely personal note at the moment of Christ's betrayal by Judas Iscariot and the choir's ensuing question – Has thunder and lightning vanished in the clouds? – possesses enormous power. This music never appears to be formulaic. Instead, the characters take on human form. They aren't stock figures illustrating a well-known story, but people with feelings, which is why the *St Matthew Passion* is a turning point. Bach gave the story a humanity of a sort that many of his contemporaries who were trying to satisfy the public demand for Baroque opera couldn't manage.

It doesn't simply proceed from one aria to the next, with the tenor Evangelist taking us through the story, and the chorus providing a background. Bach builds an arch from the opening chorus that rises as the story develops and seems, at the end, to keep everything connected. One of the ways in which this is done is by making the moment of Peter's denial of Christ – after the cock crew three times – as powerful as the crucifixion itself, perhaps even the emotional heart of the music. The aria 'Erbarme dich' (Have mercy), placed near the beginning of the second part of the *Passion*, is a sublime piece of writing for solo voice and violin. The repeated chorale, in different keys with different harmonies, acts as a reference point; at each stage of the story the music seems to echo an earlier mood or phrase. The tread of those footsteps at the start is impossible to avoid, the eventual destination inescapable.

The musical tension, established at the start and never slackening, is accompanied by especially expressive recitative – the solos which are sung to give the feeling of speech. In Bach's hands they're fused with the formal choruses and solos, so that the story seems to move without a break. When the Evangelist describes what happens after the crucifixion, the earthquake and the consequent fear of the Roman soldiers – with a cello trembling underneath his voice – the chorus sings, 'Truly, this was the son of God,' and Bach's ability to create finality in the line with the weight and measure of the music is typical of the way in which he moulds the drama.

As a firm believer, Bach invested the utmost importance in this music, an account of the Christian story. It seemed that he cared a great deal about this *Passion*: when the manuscript was damaged he painstakingly pieced it together, pasting new bits of paper over the old, making sure that it was in good shape. It was written with particular clarity – the solo and choral parts in different colours, the bar lines solid, all the notes clear. Composers in those days (including Bach) often produced manuscripts that were a muddle, scribbles that spoke of a rush of blood, a quick harmonic fix. This was different. The Mass in B minor, revered in our time and showing Bach in sublime mode, wouldn't be completed for twenty years or more (and he may never have heard it performed). Much was to come, but the *St Matthew Passion* was an extraordinary achievement.

On this journey we've travelled from the monasteries of the dark ages to medieval cathedrals and courts and on to the long opening up of the Renaissance; to Florence and to Venice; to the purlieus of the Sun King and Elizabethan England. Now with Bach, and with this oratorio, we reach a high pinnacle from which you can look back, and forward. The careful musicianship of the Baroque period attains something close to perfection: the new instruments, the techniques that had been polished through the seventeenth century, the confidence in blending tunes into complicated fugues, the easy fusion of choir and solo voice. Above all, you hear the understanding of how expressing the greatest emotion is also a matter of the subtlest technical skill.

Bach pulls it all together. The *Passion* is better than anything that had been written before in this form. It surpasses much of the crude opera of its time. The balancing of the voices shows an almost unconscious feeling for the way a tenor or an alto or a counter-tenor or a bass would want a musical line to be written. For the crowd, listening in the pews and perhaps singing in the chorale, it is uplifting. The *St Matthew Passion*, however, was not performed consistently in the years to come. It didn't disappear (like the *St Mark* version Bach wrote, pieced together later, or the rumoured version of *St Luke*), but it passed from general use. The congregations in Leipzig thought of it as part of their lives more than as a precious piece of art, though it became a pillar of our aural history.

This piece reveals so much – Bach's roots in a particular society, wanting its own kind of music; his genius in bringing inspiration to bear on a tradition that he knew, and could transform; his place in the world as a composer, driven by the politics and outlook of those around him, as well as by his inner beliefs and talents. When the composer Felix Mendelssohn was given a copy nearly a century later, and realised that it spoke to the Romantic heart as powerfully as to a Baroque sensibility, he saw that it reached far beyond its time. 'If life had taken faith and hope from me,' he said of one passage, 'this chorus would restore all.'

And when the public gazed on it again, this work became one of the foundation stones of a whole tradition of music-making, the choral surge in the nineteenth century that still sweeps so many people along today, and brings so many amateur enthusiasts through the door. The *St Matthew Passion* was one of the most outstanding achievements of the whole Baroque era, which stretched over more than a century; and an illustration of how genius can take the potions and elements that others play with in the laboratory, and turn them into something startling and permanent.

Bach's Evangelist in this story tells of betrayal, tragedy and coming redemption, and the composer himself reveals a transforming power of his own. Bach died exactly at the middle point of the eighteenth century, in 1750. The cleverness and power of this *Passion* are evidence of the heights European music had begun to reach, and of how far it might go – though there are parts of Bach's accomplishment that have never been surpassed.

8

Father and Son

Haydn and Mozart

~

A N OLD *New Yorker* cartoon says almost everything about Mozart, without a single musical reference. The conductor Sir Colin Davis hung it on his wall, as a daily reminder. It shows nothing but a desolate landscape with mist and a lowering darkness over a couple of shadowy, unwelcoming hills on the horizon. The foreground is almost bare, a picture of emptiness: there is a scrunched-up tin can, a discarded pencil, an old rubber tyre, an empty bottle, a few stones on a parched moonscape. The bleak caption by the cartoonist, Mick Dennis, reads: 'Life without Mozart'.

No composer seems more life giving, so consistently effervescent. For all the effort and the pain, and the frequent chaos in his life, music poured from him in a stream that was rich and full and never stopped. He was inspiring in every mood – in the *Requiem*, the only one he wrote, which lay unfinished beside his deathbed, in his setting of *Ave Verum Corpus* written in the summer of 1791, about six months before he died, aged thirty-five, in the unfinished Mass in C minor (K 427) from 1782–3, in any one of half a dozen of the piano concertos from the 1780s, in the concerto for flute and harp, or for clarinet, or the wind quintet (K 452) from 1784 which he thought at the time was the best thing he had written, in the three operas he wrote with the librettist Lorenzo da Ponte which take you to other worlds. This is transcendent music, lifting up anyone who opens their ears to it. When the fragment of the 'Lacrimosa' in the *Requiem* breaks off after a mere eight bars, it marks a life cut short, but you feel a certain completeness nonetheless. A journey is over, a summit conquered. Mozart was the genius craftsman, the prodigy and boy wonder who became the master – often worried, beaten down and poor – but always in command.

In his time, he represented a peak of achievement. That was recognised by the composer who, more than any other, was the rainbow bridge that led from the Baroque period to the Classical, Joseph Haydn. The labels for these ages of music are inadequate, even a little confusing, because there is no clean break and no divide to be healed, but in the course of the eighteenth century music did begin to use forms that invited a contrast with the glories of the past: the string quartet, established by Haydn, was a conduit for chamber music that was 'modern' and inviting in a new way, and the symphony became the vehicle for orchestras that grew bigger, fuller in sound, and laid the foundations for the Romantic composers and for the full flowering of the symphony orchestra in the nineteenth century.

Haydn was the father of the string quartet, bringing it to maturity. He did not invent the symphony, which was well established before he began to compose as a teenager in the 1740s, but he was its most brilliant innovator, writing more than a hundred of them and giving the century one of its most characteristic sounds. A Haydn symphony – crisp, tender, firm but delicate in construction – is unmistakable. He and Mozart are naturally linked in this story, one the master of a tradition that he saw being passed on and enriched by a genius who understood its power, the other an anxious student, hungry for every morsel of inspiration, as well as an impatient inventor.

They met (probably) in 1781 in Vienna. The Irish actor and singer Michael Kelly described in his *Reminiscences* a quartet party that he attended in the winter of that year at the home of Stephen Storace, a member of the Anglicised Italian family who played such an important part in English musical life in the late eighteenth century and whose sister Nancy sang in Mozart's operas in Vienna. Kelly, who created the roles of Don Curzio and Basilio in *Le nozze di Figaro*, alongside Nancy, wrote this of the quartet, apparently with an attempt at humour:

> The players were tolerable; not one of them excelled in the instrument he played; but there was a science among them, which I dare say may be acknowledged when I name them – the first violin, Haydn; second violin, Baron Dittersdorf [a prominent operatic and symphonic composer]; violincello, Vanhall; tenor [viola], Mozart. The poets Casti and

Paisiello formed part of the audience. I was there, and a greater treat or a more remarkable one cannot be imagined.

The picture of Haydn and Mozart playing together is alluring. By this time, Haydn was approaching fifty and on these visits to Vienna from the Hungarian plains, where he was composer and music director for his patrons, the Esterházy family, he was celebrated as the greatest of established composers. Mozart was the fiery, brilliant performer who had first charmed rich families with his talent as a child and then startled his elders with invention. In the mid-1780s, Haydn told Mozart's father Leopold that he was the greatest composer he knew, alive or dead.

These two, one roughly half the age of the other when they met, also reveal in their careers the way the life of a composer was changing. Haydn worked for many years for patrons on whose employment he depended. Though he profited from his tours at the height of his celebrity (notably to London), he was contracted as a musician who had to perform tasks as if he were any other member of the ducal household, administrator as well as creator. Mozart needed his patrons too – an archbishop and an emperor famously among them – but much of his last decade in Vienna was spent in what we would now call a freelance life. Private patronage (or the blessing of the Church) was still the essential pillar of a composer's life – Beethoven might be described as the first of the great composers who made his own way – and these two illustrate the change that was round the corner, helped by easier access to printed music, more travel, prosperity that was beginning (very slowly) to broaden the audience for music, and a certain excitement in cities like Vienna and London that allowed composers to become more than talented vassals to the powerful.

When Mozart began to reveal his brilliance as a child, however, it was in a world that did not seem to be changing fast. He played for the Emperor in Vienna, and enthralled the noble houses and royal courts of Europe when his father brought him to play. The boy capered with Marie Antoinette, did tricks in royal drawing rooms, where he played the piano with mesmerising dexterity and accuracy with a cloth draped over his hands, entertained the court of Louis XV of France. He was an infant phenomenon. In Soho in London there is a blue plaque in Frith Street marking the spot where he and his family lodged for some months in 1764 and 1765 in the course of a long European tour. It says that he 'lived, played and composed' there. He was eight years old.

He wrote the first of his forty-one symphonies on that visit to London and when his father Leopold fell ill he and his sister gave daily concerts for a week at the Swan and Harp tavern near St Paul's to help to pay the bills. By 1766, after a visit to Holland, the family was back in Salzburg, the city of his birth, and by this time his name was known in the capitals of Europe. He was commissioned to write his first opera, *Apollo and Hyacinth* (K 38), first performed in Salzburg in 1767, and in Vienna (where he contracted smallpox in 1768) he was already the Emperor's favourite. It was a remarkable progress already, but those fund-raising recitals in a London tavern were telling indications of how life would always be. More than two decades later, despite all his celebrity and the status accorded him by so many musicians, including a humbled Haydn himself, he found it difficult to get subscribers to publish his latest string quintets in Vienna, because the first night of his opera *Don Giovanni*, the second of the operas written with da Ponte, had not been as successful as he had hoped in its first performance in Prague in 1787 (though it took off in Vienna the following year).

The disordered and sometimes even perilous course of Mozart's life as a musician reflects a combination of instinctive brilliance with the necessary effort of a musician who had to make his way. At the time of his birth in Salzburg, composers needed patrons. Unless they were successful in opera, which could attract a paying audience, the Church and the princely courts were required as employers and their loyalty might make the difference between reasonable comfort and penury. In the last ten years of his life he held only one salaried post, writing dance music for the Emperor's court entertainments in Vienna. Everything else was commissioned individually.

That decade produced works of luminous brilliance. Take the piano concertos, of which he'd written ten before entering his last decade. He moulded the form to something like perfection. Listening to the last, No. 27 in B flat (K 595), which he played for the first time in public in the year of his death, 1791, having probably started it three years earlier, you hear an intense voice, its colour and expressiveness revealed in the intimate bonding of piano and orchestra. It's sometimes called (fancifully) his farewell to music; and it seems to have running through it the sparkle and vigour that were Mozart's lifelong characteristics, with a tenderness that suggests a comprehension of sadness. By this stage, he was weaving together six or seven thematic ideas in the course of a couple of movements, seeming to take the straightforward structures of the early concertos and transforming them into something quite different. His last composition for solo instrument and orchestra was the Clarinet Concerto in A major (K 622) which, like the concertos for horn, bassoon and jointly for flute and harp, sprang from an infatuation with an instrument and its possibilities, a vision of what might be done that hadn't been done before.

Nonetheless these works, even at this sublime level, didn't simply pour out unbidden. During the 1780s when his popularity waxed and waned in Vienna, he was producing concertos at a rate determined in part by demand. It was a difficult life, though not as miserable as the one pictured by future generations of admirers who would paint him as a tragic figure, burning with a fever of inspiration and victimised by a heartless world that drove him to a pauper's grave. The picture was one that suited the conception of the Romantic artist as doomed even at the moment of his greatest triumph, the shrivelling of a consumptive or depressed hero. It wasn't quite as simple as that.

Mozart was caught up in a world that was evolving fast, for musicians as for everyone else. The tide of Enlightenment thinking was encouraging a European bourgeoisie to sense its power, and the idea of a composer or performer as a mere servant – a sycophant at court, elegant though he might be – was now being questioned. One patron, for example, insisted on an agreement that his court composers shouldn't marry. That kind of feudal relationship was starting to pass away, slowly.

Composers were not as lucky as singers, who were commanding substantial fees for public performances. The famous castrato Francesco Ceccarelli was earning about double Mozart's income in the early 1780s, around 800 florins (about 150 gold ducats). How many know of him now? So when Mozart went to Vienna, where he would spend his last decade, he seems to have thought that he would make most of his money as a virtuoso performer. He found that he could also harness his inspiration to the demands of those who wanted to commission him.

By the time he was in his early thirties he is thought to have been earning enough money to allow him to live quite comfortably – perhaps three to six thousand florins a year – though he made regular appeals to friends, often fellow Freemasons, to help him through arid patches.

You can see Mozart's life in part as a struggle between the impulse to let his imagination run free and the need to write what people wanted. His letters reveal that he was often short of money (and they show how disorganised he was). Sometimes he is basking in the sunshine of an emperor's adulation, or playing one of his dazzling concerts in front of the young Ludwig van Beethoven, and sometimes he is a pained and driven craftsman who seems incapable of balancing successfully his spirit and the weary demands of life.

There was no calm. And out of the torment came brilliance. He would write with rampant inspiration for the early pianos that were starting to supersede the harpsichord; for the voice, for the orchestra and the choir in church; and also for a player he admired, or for an instrument that captivated him. As in the wind quintet, or the final string quartets written in his last three years, music is being pushed forward.

Nothing quite like it had been heard before. His life was one of invention. Blessed by the chance arrival of an emperor, Joseph II, who wanted to encourage music, a Vienna in which the aristocracy had a keen appetite, and a bourgeoisie that was growing in power, he seems – with the distance of years – to have been an instrument of transition, one that he couldn't have imagined in his own time. Take, for example, the Emperor's request for more German culture, the demand that caused him to write the *Singspiel* (literally, the song-play) called *Die Entführung aus dem Serail* (The Abduction from the Harem). This was the opera that produced the Emperor's famous remark that for Viennese ears it had, perhaps, too many notes. No, said Mozart, just exactly as many as were required.

The singing of German in opera houses was the start of something extraordinary. An emperor who was one of the last of the true autocrats was nonetheless the agent of a development that was important in helping Vienna to become home to a particular kind of Germanic culture in the early nineteenth century – a culture of which Beethoven was the shining star but which also fed the confidence of musicians in Leipzig, Prague and far beyond.

Mozart was able to write with such originality, for the keyboard, the orchestra, and the voice, that it sometimes seems effortless, despite what we know of the pressures and the uncertainties that beset him. In the three operas he wrote with the astonishing dramatist da Ponte, he produced, again and again, passages that shimmer long after the curtain has fallen. Imagine being in the Burgtheater in Vienna in 1790 and hearing *Così fan tutte* performed for the first time. Act I is a masterpiece on its own. Mozart wrote it as a commission for the Emperor at a time when things were difficult, though he was writing with spellbinding confidence. Subscriptions for concerts in Vienna were falling, and in a letter in June 1790 he complained about the fate of his last three string quartets: 'Now I am forced to give away my quartets – this laborious work! – for a trifling sum, just to get some money in hand.'

Music historians who study the scores from this period argue that in the last phase of his life Mozart was beginning to experiment, in part as a result of shifts in public taste as well as because of his own maturity. There is little point in speculating about what might have happened had he lived: he didn't. This is the period of the great concertos, the opera *Die Zauberflöte* and the last, inventive piano sonatas. At the end came the *Requiem*.

Mozart's genius was shaped by his age, as well as by the inexplicable fertility of his imagination. He began to enjoy a freedom that composers in earlier times didn't have – though it was precarious, and fickle in its effect on his life. Fame and the occasional bursts of comfort were undermined by persistent anxiety. His experience had features that would have been familiar to the music masters of previous generations; it also anticipated a time when composers valued freedom, and were able to have it, without the shackles that had constrained even some of genius in the past. That freedom is especially obvious, and powerful, in the greatest of his operas.

Così suffered neglect in the nineteenth century because its central conceit – the propensity of women to put instant pleasure above loyalty in love – was thought to be offensive. Translating the title itself has always been a bit of a problem. Literally, it could be rendered as 'All women are like that', though the subtitle *The School for Lovers* has often been preferred, and great ingenuity has been expended in trying to come up with some acceptable phrase that has some meaning in English. The opera's passing from fashion, however, was a spectacular misunderstanding of Mozart's subtlety.

Far from falling for a simplistic cliché and indulging in the conventional artificiality of the comic *opera buffa*, Mozart exploited the conventions to illustrate how it was possible to escape from them. In the 1990s, when Jonathan Miller directed a celebrated production at the Royal Opera House, Covent Garden, with the men dressed by Giorgio Armani, he said that its formal artificiality was part of its essential mechanism: 'It demonstrates reality without slavishly representing it. It is an argument as opposed to a report; an epigram rather than a memo.' Like other directors, Miller understood that that very artificiality helped the opera become more serious, not less, because Mozart and da Ponte were able to use the mechanical symmetry of the two pairs of lovers to reveal contrasting attitudes and emotions. Far from being a constraint, the structure allows the music and the drama to produce intimacy and clarity.

Of all the operas in which nothing is what it seems, *Così* may stand alone. Opera-goers are used to plots that have to be swallowed like medicine before the enjoyment can come, or characters whose texture seems to emerge only when they are singing, and sometimes it is all worth while. *Così*, though it uses the familiar conventions of Mozart's time that an audience would have expected and enjoyed, is different. Here the artifice is itself an elaborate joke, taken by Mozart and turned into something serious. We're expected to believe that this is a witty commentary on fickleness and the conventions of love, but it is also a piece of defiance about opera itself. Audiences in the 1790s would not have missed the point. In this last of the three operas with da Ponte, Mozart was making fun of the hack composers who become slaves to the pattern of mistaken identities and crossed love which were the staple fare of an earlier age.

From the beginning, the opera feels singular. In the overture itself, after the robust chords which establish the rhythm of the score, the oboe manages to sound mischievous and melancholy at the same time, winding its way through the music and somehow suggesting the sinuous pattern of the story that's about to unfold. But from the very first bars this is obviously no romp. There are hints of darkness everywhere, a sense of longing rather than of farce.

Musicologists can try to capture the magic of Mozart in meticulous deconstructions of the score, discovering the patterns that give the music its shape, but that old description of his achievement as 'divine simplicity' is still the best one. Like the first hour of *Le nozze di Figaro*, the opening act of *Così* feels almost perfect. The characters are delineated clearly, their relationships are established with bold strokes and vivid colours, and the whole progress of the story takes on a kind of symmetry that gives it perfect balance. This is partly a matter of plot, and partly the creation of a musical character for the opera that is so clear and so distinctive that, by the time the curtain falls for the first time, you are feeling not so much that this is a story which is gradually picking up pace but that you have lived with these people for a long time and have a feeling for their dilemmas as if they're your own.

This, of course, is absurd. Men are going off to foreign wars in support of causes of which we know nothing; they're planning disguises to play a trick on the two women they're leaving behind that wouldn't fool a child at a pantomime; their cynical manipulator Don Alfonso is arranging a game so ridiculous that its outcome seems laughably implausible. Will the women be fooled by the real lovers coming back in disguise and swapping roles? Unlikely, you may think.

But remember that Don Alfonso is billed as a 'philosopher', a word which had a much more flexible meaning in Mozart's age. Never mind that in the course of the opera his interest is apparently in who is making love with whom, and how people react to the deceptions of love. He represents something that's deeper than a cardboard character who's engaged in producing a fake doctor with a magnetising machine (a jokey contemporary reference that a Viennese audience would have understood well) and a fake notary to simulate a wedding ceremony. Everything is acceptable because underneath there are real feelings which are touched by an understanding of the world's woes.

When the beautiful trio begins in Act I, in which Dorabella, Fiordiligi and Don Alfonso appear to pray for the safety of the men off to war ('Soave sia il vento') – the manipulator being well aware of the nonsense he's creating – the music becomes so beguiling that everything else passes away. There are few opening acts in all opera that have a greater capacity to transcend the awkward stage business that, especially when comic business is involved, can threaten to undermine proceedings.

There is no point in pretending that *Così*, for all its genius, is easy to stage. It is not. Audiences have seen men's disguises sent up, overdone, underdone – even imagined, like a non-appearing ghost in *Hamlet* – and have watched productions on rock-strewn landscapes, in draped rooms that seem like Turkish bordellos, on board ship, on darkened stages where nothing seems to move for three hours, as well as in the setpiece eighteenth-century drawing rooms that are so often used as backdrops for every opera written between about 1650 and 1800, and seldom give anything to a production but a sense of dusty antiquity. They have this in common, however – that they work as opera when the emphasis falls on the current of sadness that flows just under the surface. When the froth overwhelms everything, everyone on the stage is likely to die a death. Audiences usually take the cue.

Don Alfonso's philosophising may seem to amount only to the ruminations of a roguish roué, but it touches on the most sensitive feelings: the precarious business of young love, the fragility of courtship rituals, the ease with which passion can turn into rage. Each of the four lovers has a character that is distinct from the others, though those of the men don't properly become clear until they are in disguise. When Fiordiligi sings of her rock-like determination in Act I, for example, she's not only showing that she's the one who will argue that they should support their men, but demonstrating that she has a weakness for self-aggrandisement or at least a histrionic streak. It's therefore more poignant later in the opera when her defences melt away.

The power of *Così* isn't just in its hijacking of comic-opera conventions for high purposes, but in the way that it allows the characters to be transformed in the course of the story into more complicated figures that the plot would seem to allow. In the second act, they have all become much older, though no time has passed. Indeed, through all the machinations of the deceptions and the bogus weddings the music speaks of the feelings that swim around underneath. At the end, the women, who have been led such a merry dance by their two lovers and by Don Alfonso, are driven to apologise for their own behaviour. Everyone's defences, like their disguises, have been stripped away.

The three da Ponte operas are surely among the most robust pieces of music theatre that we know. Everyone has closed an eye at a grim production from time to time – usually when *Così* or *Figaro* is staged with no melancholy or no menace, or when *Don Giovanni* is done in the dark (why does that happen so often?) – without feeling the need to walk away from these monumental achievements. Mozart was approaching the end when this opera was written, and for many years it was neglected (even suffering the indignity of performances throughout the nineteenth century with new libretti to restore some 'dignity' to the women). Its rediscovery was in itself an escape from the misunderstanding that had dogged its early years and a recognition of the subtlety and, above all, the truth of its observations.

Like *Così*, *Le nozze di Figaro* reveals the boldness of Mozart's innovation. The composer who had mastered orchestration in his teens, who understood instinctively how to write different music for the violin or the clarinet, whose mastery of the keyboard seemed complete, was able to produce, with da Ponte's perfect dramatic touch, an opera that can sometimes feel for three hours or so to be the greatest of them all. The overture, heard for the first time in the Burgtheater in Vienna on 1 May 1786, introduced the audience to a masterpiece. Mozart had finished it only two days before, scribbling right to the end. Yet this opera has very few rough edges. Its construction feels meticulous – each piece fitted together, balanced, elegant in design – and the music seems to bubble up with an energy of its own, the illusion created by a composer of genius. If *Figaro* drags or creaks, takes a wrong turning, it is the fault of a clumsy director or a heavy-handed conductor.

The opera encapsulates a moment in history and in the history of music: when the stylistic conventions of eighteenth-century opera were transformed, and when the darkness and noise of the world outside were allowed their dramatic entry on to the stage. Europe was shaking. France was on the brink of revolution, and in Austria the aristocracy felt the tremors. The play on which *Figaro* was based, by Beaumarchais, had been banned in its original form by Louis XVI in France and by Joseph II, his brother-in-law, in Austria. The story of a licentious count being humiliated and exposed by an underling servant, Figaro, wasn't only uncomfortable but dangerous too.

This was the first of the three da Ponte operas with Mozart, and it demonstrates how opera was maturing – picturing a world that audiences knew, and turning characters from the stereotypes of an earlier age into living, breathing beings who shared feelings with the audience, and seemed to speak to them.

Take the start of the second act. In Act I Mozart creates an extraordinary scene, giving characters musical identities, letting them sing alone and together in ways that were subtle and dramatic – and, to the audience of his day, modern and daring. He and da Ponte weave a complicated story of deceit and anger through the comic conventions that opera-goers knew. Then he has to introduce the Countess, longing for her husband's love, trapped by her position and the expectations directed at her, and revealing her pain. The curtain rises for Act II, and for this he produces, in 'Porgi amor', one of the most glorious short arias ever written for the female voice. Such moments are precious. Everything on the stage is still, and with that aria a window opens on to a world *inside* – beyond what we see to what we know. Technically, Mozart does it with such ease that he can bring every character to life. From nothing, Mozart produces delicacy, wit and an understanding of pain. These are characters whose psychology is laid bare, in an opera that looks forward to the music dramas of the future.

The plot unfolds in the course of one bizarre day – the wedding day of Figaro and Susannah. The Count wants his wicked way with Susannah, insisting on his seignorial right to have what he wants, the servant Figaro wants to humiliate him and preserve his own self-respect, the Countess longs for real love, and they become swept up in a story of deceit and misunderstanding in which they all learn something. From the first scene, where Figaro is measuring out the room he'll share with Susannah after the wedding, there is sexual tension, because it's a box room next to the Count's, where he hopes he'll entertain Susannah. The simmering jealousies are infused with a different kind of anger: Figaro's hatred of the power under which he has to live. Few operas have a richer mix of darkness and light; it is comedy that becomes deadly serious and emotionally draining.

This is not the place to go through the plot scene by scene. In any case, it's remarkable how many people who know the opera well would find it hard to explain all the twists and turns off the top of their heads (especially in the right order). The point is the exposure of frailty, and not always when you would expect it. Everyone is brought down to earth. When Figaro rails against the perfidy of women – he has discovered that his new wife has made an assignation with the Count in the garden – he's expressing real anger, but the audience knows something he doesn't: Susannah's encounter is only part of the plan hatched by Susannah and the Countess to trap the Count and make him confront his own behaviour. So Figaro's genuine cry of pain is the product of deceit. Such moments are the heart of the opera.

Susannah sings a perfect aria. In the dark, in the garden, with thunder in the air, where nothing is as it seems, she calls on her secret lover to one of Mozart's most sinuous melodies ('Deh vieni, non tardar'). Figaro think she's singing to the Count, and meaning it. But we know that she's well aware that Figaro is watching her from the bushes. The beauty of the moment is lyrical, but it's the dramatic irony that gives it weight. At times like this in opera, you realise how the marriage of music and drama can create unforgettable scenes – confrontations, revelations, powerful portraits.

A couple of nights after *Figaro* opened in Vienna the Emperor decreed that no encores should be allowed: there had been so much cheering that the repeats were keeping the audience there too far into the night. An opera that had taken on a risky subject was an instant success. Da Ponte had to persuaded Joseph that he had removed the most radical thoughts from the Beaumarchais play, and they only just got away with it. But Vienna was ready.

The story of *Figaro* reveals a great deal. We have reached a point in the story of music-making when opera has blossomed. There had been good tunes for the stage for nearly two centuries and an understanding of how drama that told the ancient stories could be adorned by music. In Italy, and in England when Handel swept to fame in the 1720s, opera became an entertainment for the crowds and an opportunity for the virtuosity of a tunesmith. Handel could write for the popular taste – though such a phrase would have been quite foreign to him – and yet create tableaux of exquisite grace and tenderness with his music. In eighteenth-century France, Rameau and others were trying to use opera as a vehicle for philosophy, searching for a tragic voice.

Now Mozart produced an opera (his seventeenth, if you count the fragments) that seemed to do it all. He used familiar forms – farcical misunderstandings, disguise and deceit, a woman singing a man's part, even the discovery of his long-lost mother by Figaro himself, all the comic apparatus that audiences brought up with the Italian *opera buffa* would understand and expect. An audience turning up in its finery and getting anything less would feel short-changed. In his hands the music transformed these conventions, as if characters who had been seen in black and white were now in vivid colour. They shone and sparkled; and exposed their distress. Take the Countess, who wants to reveal her husband to himself but, even more, longs for his love. At her entry at the start of Act II, Mozart gives her the glorious aria 'Porgi amor', and later, in Act III, while she's wondering if the plan she has concocted with Susannah will work, she asks: can a lost love be recovered? Where am I? The aria 'Dove sono' brings spontaneity and refinement together. Nothing seems forced, though everything is flawlessly crafted.

Le nozze di Figaro revealed to those first audiences in Vienna what opera could achieve. The door was open to the nineteenth-century composers who would turn it into a playground for the Romantic imagination. Mozart took a great leap out of the stylised world of Italian opera, in which he had been brought up, carrying his audience with him. The confusion in the garden, and its ultimate resolution, that brings *Figaro* to an end was a familiar device. As predictably as in a pantomime, the audiences would get a traditional working out of the story. But Mozart gave them something new. His characters revealed themselves directly. When they sang together they would each tell their own stories, speak from a distinct point of view – they would demonstrate in their trios and quartets how emotions work.

In an age of political uncertainty and coming revolution in which poets and painters were beginning to delve inside themselves for inspiration, letting their emotions speak, opera was evolving too. When the story is almost over, and we know the Count is going to improve his ways, he asks for forgiveness from his wife, and the principals celebrate and reflect. As the curtain falls, we hear more than the satisfying end of a story neatly finished. We hear opera transformed.

Mozart's achievement is the dazzling climax of his own century, and it is important to recognise that his genius was working in a tradition without which the shape of his achievement would have been quite different, or might not have happened at all. Haydn's influence was vast, and the impact of his music on Mozart profound. To listen to the eight string quartets in his Opus 76 and 77, written in the 1790s, is to hear that form in the hands of the master: no one had done it better. His story is intertwined with Mozart's, partly because of the obvious debt which was picked up and repaid, and also because of the way in which he appeared to be Mozart's musical father. The one learned from and grew with the other until he was ready to fly free.

In the long story of patronage in music – from the Church to kings and queens, to aristocrats and rich traders, to the state – there are very few accomplishments to compare with what was done by the Esterházys of Hungary. By their sponsorship of one musician in Haydn, they had a hand in the birth of music in the Classical period, through the symphony and the string quartet. That adopted child – whom they paid for and encouraged – became the friend of Mozart, the teacher of Beethoven and the father of the music that came after the Baroque. His hand is in the symphonic tradition that dominated the nineteenth century; those string quartets were the first great attainments of chamber music; his orchestral techniques were the foundations of the music that followed him.

We cannot know what would have happened without the patronage of one family, but Haydn himself said this of the arrangement: 'I was cut off from the world. There was no one to confuse or torment me, and I was forced to become original . . .' He certainly couldn't have worked as he did without patronage, wouldn't have produced the body of work that includes 104 symphonies, more than 80 string quartets and a huge number of piano sonatas in the new form that he had established.

His involvement with the Esterházys happened by chance. He was born in 1732 in a community of peasants, the son of a wheelwright who happened to be a natural musician. The father sent his son to learn to sing and he became a choirboy at St Stephen's Cathedral in Vienna. Eventually he was taken on by a Bohemian count as his *Kapellmeister*, and one day he was seen conducting by Prince Paul Anton Esterházy, a member of one of Hungary's most powerful and richest families. Before long he was taken on as the Esterházys' vice-*Kapellmeister* and would spend most of his musical life in their service.

The consequence was a period of amazing fertility. Haydn produced music at a dizzying rate, at a time when he had onerous duties as the Esterházys' director of music: the Haydn scholar H. C. Robbins Landon estimates that in one decade he conducted more than a thousand Italian operas for his patrons. Imagine the musical director of an opera house today, with all the resources at his command, keeping up that sort of pace. The work was hard. Each morning he would turn up in full court livery and wig to get his instructions; as staff composer all his music belonged to the Prince; he was manager of the court musicians, settling all their disputes.

He settled one in a way that has become a musical standing joke. The 'Farewell' Symphony was written to make a point. The orchestra hated the Esterházys' winter palace, dank and cold and out on the marshes. The family compared it to Versailles; the musicians didn't. So Haydn wrote a symphony in F sharp during which the players left one by one, each blowing out a candle as he went. Only one musician and Haydn – directing from the violin, as he always did – remained at the end, in the dark. The Prince got the point. The orchestra were given permission to leave for a furlough.

That episode reveals something of Haydn's personality, which was famously sunny. Musicians liked him and he turned that to remarkable effect. He built around himself the first symphony orchestra. In the Baroque period, lasting roughly until the middle of the eighteenth century, the orchestra was small. The highly decorative but direct music of that time was written for small ensembles: that was its nature. It had been conceived when clarity was everything. With Haydn we hear the first rumbles of what became the symphony orchestra, that sounding board for Classical music – the conduit for high Germanic seriousness in the next century, the Romantic spirit in music that was to come, through to the tumult of the early twentieth century. With Haydn as composer and conductor, it began to take shape.

He didn't invent the form; he gave it a character. The Esterházy court had all kinds of musicians – not just the string players, but also the drummers and horn-players who went out with the hunt, and the trumpeters who played fanfares for visiting grandees. Haydn pulled them all on board for his symphonies. Everyone got a chance, and the sound changed. From the fine curlicues of the Baroque there emerged a fuller, rounder tone. The symphony existed before Haydn's time, but it was he who fashioned it and made it gleam with possibility, bringing it from infancy to maturity. He embedded the standard four-movement form. He would take a theme and build layers of music on it, understanding how to construct an arch in the music so that when the symphony ended you felt that it had a shape and a natural design that held together. These were the principles that would be handed down to the successor generations.

Haydn's fame spread quickly. The Empress Maria Theresa of Austria-Hungary came to visit in 1769. He had written a celebratory symphony for her, No. 48 in C major, and an opera was staged in her honour (*L'infedeltà delusa*). The party went on until dawn. Then they started dinner, and they were still partying the next afternoon. 'When I want to hear a good opera,' the Empress said afterwards, 'I go to Esterházy.'

Haydn wasn't permanently marooned in the Hungarian outback, where the Esterházys boasted that they had a palace to match any in Europe. It was Prince Nikolaus who gave Haydn his glory years there, a music-lover who sported a diamond-studded jacket and who cared passionately about the culture of his court. When his less musical son succeeded in 1790, the atmosphere changed – with the one happy effect that Haydn, now nearly sixty, was freer to travel. One particular trip was important – to London, where he knew that there was a lively musical scene.

He had a triumph there, where concerts were now the fashion. He was a star, complete with his own impresario, Johann Salomon, who ensured that the concerts were a great success. There were two long visits in the early 1790s, so enjoyable and profitable that he thought of settling there. And prolific as ever, he wrote twelve symphonies while he was in England. In them, you hear the mature Haydn, who by this stage was so much in command of the symphonic style that he was able to introduce popular elements – folk tunes for example – and make them seem perfectly natural. Above all, his symphonies were popular. He played for the royal family in London. Crowds wanted to watch him direct an orchestra (he never conducted, but directed from the front row as he played the violin). You can see him on the high curve of the Classical period – rising towards its zenith.

The result was that when Haydn returned to Vienna from London he was the most celebrated composer in Europe. He gave some lessons to Beethoven, whom he'd met, aged twenty, en route to London for the first time. It wasn't an entirely happy experience, despite the high regard each had for the other. Haydn's comment that some of the piano trios needed more work seems to have been a mistake. Beethoven never publicly acknowledged the debt to Haydn that is obviously there in his symphonies and string quartets.

That debt runs through all of the nineteenth century. Haydn was the bridge from the world of Bach and Handel to the opening of the Romantic era. Listening to some of the string quartets is to be taken forward in time to the work of composers who wanted to write for the heart: in the fine description by M. H. Abrams, to turn the mirror that in the Classical age was supposed to reflect nature in all its perfection into the lamp that could illuminate the soul. His hand is everywhere. Though Beethoven didn't wish to give him his full due, you can hear the homage being paid, for example, at the end of his Ninth Symphony, pinnacle of his orchestral writing. There is a clear echo from Haydn's 'Le Midi', written long before. A shared feeling, a common motif, reverberates between them.

Haydn had the happy fortune to live to a good age, and to have the temperament to work with vigour for most of his life. He is the perfect example of a musician who, given an opportunity, turns it to the service of his skill. The Esterházys were patrons who might have been sent from above. In their employ, for all its demands, he could grow and flourish. Out it poured, across Europe – music that was both technically daring and popular; secure in its construction, but touched by magic. In the Germanic tradition that mingled high seriousness with determined boldness he was an inspired builder.

In the year that he died, 1809, Napoleon was firing his guns at Vienna. The more settled and apparently more predictable age in which he'd been born in the 1730s had given way to revolution and war, and a struggle of great ideas. Patronage of the sort that he'd enjoyed was passing away and a new kind of culture was coming. He was one of the last adornments of the Augustan age, and his mark was on all the Romantics who followed.

Haydn and Mozart are the heroes of one of the most glorious chapters in the story of music, an age of confidence and adventure.

When Haydn died, Beethoven was in the middle of his symphonies, opera in Italy was entering a period of brilliant invention, the piano was starting to appear in bourgeois drawing rooms, and music was an expression of the Romantic imagination that was producing a revolutionary tide of poetry. Mozart, dead eighteen years before, saw little of that. He and Haydn are, however, the dual voice of that electric era, one the master who had learned the lessons of his elders and J. S. Bach, and the other the offspring ready to take wing alone.

They spoke for the last time on 15 December 1790 when Haydn left Vienna for London. He wondered whether he would ever see his young friend again, but it was his own ripe age that raised the question. One of his biographers reports that Mozart said to him: 'We are probably saying our last adieu in this life.' Was he, too, wondering whether Haydn would return? A year later he himself was dead, aged only thirty-five. When Haydn came home, it was to Beethoven that he turned, and to the future.

9

Beethoven the Revolutionary
From the Bastille to Vienna

~

E VEN IN HIS quiet moments, Beethoven always seems to be on fire.
In the string quartets, all of the symphonies, the piano sonatas, his
energy is explosive. When he is skittish he still manages to inject a shaft
of troubling seriousness and sometimes of menace. The conductor Sir
Thomas Beecham said he thought him responsible for all the wrath that
was to come in music, and the image of the composer transmitted to
later generations is that of a restless spirit, all flowing hair and creased
brow – difficult, angry and driven. It is therefore natural to see him as
the musical manifestation of a European revolution.

He was in his twenties at the climax of the French Revolution, when
William Wordsworth said it was 'very heaven' to be young, and the
Vienna where he lived and worked for most of his adult life was first
invaded by Napoleon and then became the scene of the Congress that
reordered Europe (temporarily) after the French defeat and Bonaparte's
exile. Beethoven lived at the beginning of the age that would discover
democracy, learn some of the lessons from the New World which had
thrown off the shackles of European ways, and celebrate the Romantic
spirit. He cannot be separated from it.

Yet it is misleading to think of a musician, especially Beethoven, as a
mere offshoot of some social upheaval. That view is nonsensical. The
fallacy of placing his works so firmly in the context of the time that they
lose their own character and originality is a temptation, because it seems
such an obvious thing to do. Beethoven, above all, deserves more. His
passions were influenced by events, and his life was affected practically
by the ideas and changes that were swirling around him, but they were
his passions still. For example, one of the last of his sixteen string
quartets, written in the mid-1820s, is not a commentary on his time nor

even a reflection on what has passed, but an abstract meditation filled with all the residue of that experience. Its tenderness and anger, its hypnotic complexity, are at one remove from the world, creating a place of its own.

Finding dubious effects for causes is too easy. Beethoven's genius was not produced by the turmoil of his time, though it confronted the questions that troubled artists, thinkers and some of the men in power. His was a parallel force, a spirit released that was on the loose at a point when every foundation seemed about to tremble. He can neither be caricatured as a creation of his age nor pulled out of it. His inspiration is bound up in it, yet free to have its way.

Ludwig van Beethoven was born in Bonn, in a house that still stands, in December 1770. He was not an especially gifted child at school, except in music. When he was eleven he was given Bach's *Well-Tempered Clavier* to learn for the harpsichord, or perhaps an early piano (we would now call it a fortepiano), which had much less subtlety and range than the instruments for which he would be able to write later, and so made it difficult to give the notes much brilliance. His father and grandfather had been court musicians, employed by the Elector of Bonn, but his talent seemed nonetheless out of the ordinary. When he was fourteen he was appointed assistant to the court organist, and three years later he was off to Vienna for the first time, where he met Mozart, though the anxiety to make connections between them has since been understandably so great that perhaps the level of intimacy has been exaggerated. Mozart is often quoted, however, as having said: 'Keep your eyes on him; some day he will give the world something to talk about.' This was despite having remarked that his piano playing seemed to him a little too studied, though pretty. No doubt he did say something like that; Beethoven was evidently already a startling character.

By the time he was twenty, Beethoven had succeeded his father in charge of the choir of the Elector of Bonn and he was playing the viola in the opera orchestra. He had been writing music for five or six years. Now, having met Mozart, he encountered Haydn. The great triumvirate was established. The grand old man (aged around sixty by now) was happy to act as teacher to the young composer, but he seems to have misjudged Beethoven's temperament. Whether or not it was because of Haydn's critical approach, Beethoven was subsequently mean-minded in his acknowledgement of the debt, as we have seen, though it is obvious in his music. There was no doubt about it – through the great arch built by Haydn, and then finished by Mozart, Beethoven found his pathway.

He inherited the tradition they had established, and he also understood the legacy of J. S. Bach. There were practical changes, too. Orchestras were expanding (they had bigger string sections, better woodwind and a weight that distinguished them from the smaller Baroque ensembles) and pianos were starting to be built. In London, the firm of John Broadwood began making more pianos than harpsichords in the 1780s, first the 'square' piano and then the grand. Uprights were still a long way off. It was a Broadwood grand that was sent as a gift to Beethoven in Vienna in 1818, which he was delighted to receive. The makers had every right to be proud that after its long journey the piano arrived more or less in tune.

His other inheritance was the rampant political excitement of the time. Events in France in the 1780s and 1790s were provoking astonishment across Europe, and Bonn was close to the French border. At the first climax of the Revolution in July 1789, even *The Times* in London could hardly control itself. The paper presented itself as new, having changed its title from the *Daily Universal Register* the previous year, and some of its reports from Paris were extraordinary. On 23 July 1789, having informed readers of the fall of the Bastille the previous day, more than a week after the event, its (anonymous) correspondent insisted that no one could doubt that political good must come of it. He said this of Spain: 'Look to your Inquisition – to your racks – to your tortures – and to your religious tyranny, O Spain, for the day of your emancipation cannot be at a very great distance – the right hand of your tyranny is cut off, and Freedom approaches to place her standard on the wall of your Inquisition.'

Although *The Times* would sober up (in the course of the next month it reported the beheading of the Mayor of Paris for allegedly embezzling corn with the observation that 'there have been enough of sanguinary sights in Paris without this'), that first whoop of glee is characteristic of the surge of excitement, and the accompanying fear, that sped across the continent. The world was being remoulded.

Enlightenment ideas had elevated reason among thinking people to be the highest goal, and Beethoven's creative life unfolded with that feeling of liberty embedded in it. Rationality – free-thinking – was the mechanism by which the human spirit could be released.

It is worth leaving Beethoven's Bonn briefly to try to catch something of the atmosphere of France at that time, because it was from there that so much poured out. Haydn and Mozart might have been in Vienna far to the east, but from Paris there came music that spoke of the feeling in the streets. These were sounds that weren't confined to salons or court, but that appealed to the people. The most famous song of all emerged from a difficult moment in the revolutionary struggle.

One spring night in 1792, a young French captain in Strasbourg spent the night writing a marching tune, under instructions to produce something inspiring. Austrian and Prussian troops were in Paris trying to protect the institutions that had been overturned. The French defenders of the Revolution, which had been rolling on for nearly three years, needed a shot of adrenalin. By morning, the song was finished. At first, it was simply called 'A Song for the Army of the Rhine'. Military bands started to play it and liked it, and volunteers sang it when they streamed into Paris throughout the summer to support the Revolution against the foreign invader. Soon, 'La Marseillaise' was the unofficial national anthem and was sung by order of the authorities before the curtain went up in theatres. It was a tune that spoke of the tumult of the time – an expression of vigour and determination in music.

But the continuing story of 'La Marseillaise' is less straightforward. When Napoleon came along as first consul in 1799, declaring that order had to be imposed on the Revolution if it was to be saved, he banned the song. Something about the ferment it aroused, its effect on the crowd, was dangerous. Inspiration was fine, but it had to be kept under control. Street music had by now become important and powerful. One estimate is that there were more than a thousand songs that were written or arranged in the last decade of the eighteenth century in France. Crowds sang them, and that popular outpouring carried on its wave the spirit of the time.

It is certainly true that there had never been an event of the magnitude of the French Revolution that had such a soundtrack.

The preceding century had been a rich enough one in France – Rameau and his colleagues were writing 'new' opera, Baroque Italian opera was popular, instrumental music was ubiquitous, and both Haydn and Mozart had composed symphonies for Paris. Now, certain strands of music took on a popular tone. The aims of the revolutionaries were reflected as much in culture – high and low, you might say – as in the politics of the state.

Composers rallied to the cause. Etienne-Nicolas Méhul (1763–1817) was in his thirties when he wrote the 'Chant du départ' in 1794, first heard on the fifth anniversary of the Revolution and soon to be one of the most popular republican hymns. These songs were played and sung all over France, in theatres before performances and on the huge military parade grounds that were being built in Paris and other cities. Quite often arranged for large bands, dominated by wind instruments, they had an intensity and boldness that were meant to echo the heavy task the Revolution had set itself. Music in those days was no distraction: it had to speak of the obligations of the people. That, at least, was the idea. Pieces like 'Chant du 14 juillet' by François-Joseph Gossec (a composer whose operas were acclaimed and who was the best French symphonist of his time) pleased the crowds, and they were also incorporated into stage works that were supposed to celebrate the New Age. Gossec's opera *Hymn to Liberty* was especially popular.

The atmosphere changed when the Consulate, dominated by Napoleon, took power ten years after the fall of the Bastille, at a time when this music was being played at the revolutionary festivals that were being held all over France. Like Robespierre's wonderfully named Festival of the Supreme Being in 1794, they were great public gatherings and spectacles celebrating the scale of what the revolutionaries believed they had achieved. Many of them were stage-managed by the painter Jacques-Louis David, who also designed uniforms, triumphal arches and much of the physical paraphernalia of victory. His traces in stone and cloth still tell the story of revolutionary France and give those years a style. Though he seems to have worried about the betrayal of the ideals early on – his painting of *The Death of Marat* is a poem to the founding revolutionary spirit, after all – he went on to paint Napoleon again and again (fairly obsessively) as an heroic figure, giving him the stature and demeanour that he wanted after he declared himself emperor in 1804 and draped himself in purple.

For revolutionaries like David, music was a natural means of expressing political will. As well as spectacle there was sound, and Napoleon, when he came to mould the new France to his own purpose, understood how powerful it was. He was a music-lover himself. He had listened to a great deal of Italian opera – indeed he was said to prefer it to French opera, a latterday echo of the bizarre trauma of the War of the Buffoons that had engulfed the opera house and the Paris intelligentsia in the 1750s. Méhul, for one, was so irritated by Napoleon's taste that he wrote an opera in Italian under a false name and fooled him with the performance, only revealing himself as the composer at the end.

It was a dangerous game, because the First Consul was all-powerful after 1799, but it is a reminder of how prominent and how important music had become. Napoleon wasn't retreating to some private salon to hear this: the opera was public, popular, talked about. Revolutionary operas were attended not just as a matter of duty by some politically correct class of functionaries (though many were in that category, no doubt) but as popular entertainment. The tunes were on people's lips, the hymns were sung in the theatre and in the square at the parade. Arias and songs were in wide circulation, even among those who couldn't go to the opera house.

After he won the Battle of Marengo in 1800, his imperial ambitions now well matured, Napoleon commissioned from Méhul a work of celebration. He got the 'Chant national du 14 juillet 1800' which was performed under the vast dome of Les Invalides in Paris in June 1800 with two orchestras, two choirs and an extra group of singers to use all the space to hand, in the place where Napoleon would eventually lie in his tomb. Years later Hector Berlioz's *Requiem* was written to be performed in the same building and you can hear in Méhul the beginning of the style that Berlioz would make his own, as he became the greatest French composer of the nineteenth century.

Berlioz, who was born in 1803, was taught by Jean-François Lesueur, one of the most prominent French musicians of the revolutionary years. He was the author of an operatic version of the stories of the supposed Celtic bard Ossian, fabricated by the brilliant and imaginative poet–faker James Macpherson on the subject of the Irish mythical hero Fingal, which became massively popular across Europe, and proved fascinating to Napoleon himself. It is striking that Berlioz balanced his gratitude to Lesueur with criticism of his 'antediluvian theories . . . and antique flavour' as if even such a revered composer had not been able to understand that music should now be looking forward instead of back. From the middle of the nineteenth century Berlioz could see how important the Revolution had been.

Music was released, and in practical ways it established a modern French tradition. For example, the popularity of wind instruments in the bands that played for the festivals and parades was one of the inspirations for the setting up of the Paris Conservatoire, which became the centre of study and music-teaching for generations of French composers. Berlioz himself wrote a famous setting of 'La Marseillaise' in 1830 for choir, soloists and orchestra which established it as the unchallenged national anthem. His magnificent orchestral works, and the sweep of his writing for the voice – especially in his operatic masterwork *Les Troyens* (1856–8) – owe a great deal to the excitement of music in the revolutionary era, whose stimulus survived into his childhood and youth.

The pulse of events is in the music, on the street and in the theatre. It burst out in part because the old sources were no more. The King's court, where so many composers had prospered and so much had been commissioned, had gone. The Catholic Church was also a victim of the Revolution. Though it would make its peace with Napoleon after a fashion, its centrality in French life would never be quite restored.

The music that had flowed through the *ancien régime* had to be replaced. And the new France needed reassurance. As well as fostering a sense of community, the bravado of much of the music of the revolutionary period is designed to stiffen the sinews: in a time of violence and war, disorder and uncertainty, music was something to depend upon for sustenance. The sort of song they loved was 'Le Reveil du peuple' (The People's Awakening) by Pierre Gaveaux, which was so popular that it provoked riots and was eventually banned.

Napoleon's own tastes took him away from the raw passion of 'La Marseillaise', which he banned from public performance. The new state, which had in effect become a commissioner of music in the way that the King had once been, was no longer in need of songs to help the streets rise up: it was, Napoleon thought, more mature than that. Just as he wanted David and Antoine-Jean Gros and others to demonstrate in painting an heroic image of France (and of his own person), bestriding the world, spreading light across Europe and the seas beyond, so in music, too, he was searching for a new patriotism.

It was inescapable that music was now public business. It had given energy to the Revolution, prompted a stirring patriotism, offered succour to those about to march to war. In the past, the sound of a band or a little orchestra was remote from the streets, sequestered in a royal court or a great house. Those days were gone. There seemed less of a gap between a popular song and high culture than once there had been. Opera was popular; you didn't have to go to church to join in fine singing; the supply of composers who would pursue new ideas in music was as prolific as ever. The ideas of the Revolution were as one, in art and on the streets. The subjects that artists chose were the politics of the day. Poets weren't writing about the past, but about the future. When Wordsworth said that it was bliss to be alive in the dawn of the Revolution, and very heaven to be young, it was because the imagination and the turmoil of the world seemed – for a brief moment – to have come together. This is what he wrote in lines entitled 'The French Revolution, as it appeared to enthusiasts at its commencement . . .':

> Now was it that both found, the meek and lofty
> Did both find, helpers to their heart's desire,
> And stuff at hand, plastic as they could wish;
> Were called upon to exercise their skill,
> Not in Utopia, subterranean fields,
> Or some secreted island, Heaven knows where!
> But in the very world, which is the world
> Of all of us, – the place where in the end
> We find our happiness, or not at all!

Though that thrilling optimism didn't survive the Napoleonic era, in the crucible of France many ideas were forged that would inspire Romantic artists – poets, musicians, painters. At the height of revolutionary fervour, and the turning upside-down of Europe that had started in Paris, music, like poetry, spoke of the turmoil. It reflected the ambitions and the agony, and demonstrated how the old sources of patronage and control were changing. Above all, it showed how what we've come to call the Classical tradition in Europe had become a central strand in public discourse.

Great events demanded great melodies, vivid settings of songs and a fine noise. Depth of national feeling and political passion demanded music with the strength and weight to match the moment. In the 'Hymn to the Pantheon' by Luigi Cherubini, the operatic star in Paris during the Revolution, you can hear the throb of that commitment. His operas would become famous, and his hymns were sung by everyone.

By chance, there is a direct link between Pierre Gaveaux, the Revolution's favourite composer, and Beethoven. It was Gaveaux who wrote a successful *drame lyrique* called *Léonore*, with a libretto by the playwright Jean-Nicolas Bouilly, which provided Beethoven with the subject of his only opera, *Fidelio*. That opera, an astonishing blast of originality and passion, reveals how Beethoven's musical personality was shaped by the political and intellectual arguments around him. The revised version that we know was first performed in 1814 (with the seventeen-year-old Franz Schubert in the audience), and the delegates to the Congress of Vienna a year later were able to hear it as they tried as best they could to reorder the Europe that had been thrown up in the air by the Revolution and the Napoleonic years. It takes us back to the world of Beethoven, who had moved to Vienna in 1792, probably as a result of the patronage of Count Waldstein, the man who had financed the first visit, five years before, during which he had met Mozart.

Near the end of the first act of that opera, the prisoners who've been kept in the dark, far underground, get a short glimpse of the sun and a sweet breath of air. Their freedom does not last for long, which gives their moment a trembling power. 'How pure and bright,' they sing. 'The air is light around us.' The scene in which they emerge – blinking, shuffling, incredulous – is among the most moving in an opera that has freedom as its theme, their soft chorus growing into a hymn of hope. A cruel regime is brought down by love. The heroine Leonore finds her lover Florestan in the depths of the prison where he's been hidden away and they're reunited by her persistence and faithfulness. A familiar enough plot, you might think, but *Fidelio* is an opera that seems to stand on its own. Somehow, it's different.

Beethoven wrote no other opera, and although the plot and structure has traditional elements, its passions and its seriousness set it apart. By the time the trumpet-call announces from the castle ramparts that liberation is at hand – in a good production, the moment is a dramatic sunburst – the audience has been taken to the depths of despair and waits to be lifted out, like the prisoners. When the first version was staged in Vienna in 1805, there were officers from the occupying French army in the audience. No wonder it was an uncomfortable evening.

Fidelio reveals Beethoven's forcefulness. From the moment his teacher realised that the way the boy played Bach spoke of a precious talent, he began to exude a power that went far beyond technical brilliance. In the piano sonatas, the string quartets, the symphonies, you feel a concentration of emotion and belief. One composer and pianist said that you had to have suffered greatly yourself even to attempt to play the F sharp minor adagio from the 'Hammerklavier' Sonata. That sonata, Opus 106, No. 29, shows how, with Beethoven, there is always drama. You are off on a tempestuous journey to who-knows-where and you cannot escape the force.

Beethoven's confidence speaks of a change that made him a different kind of composer. Mozart existed (often uncomfortably) for part of his life on individual, paid commissions, but by Beethoven's time things had moved further: he never held a salaried post. Though he had patrons who championed him like Count Waldstein (to whom he dedicated one of his greatest pieces for piano, the Sonata No. 21 in C major, written in 1803), and gave him regular work, he was probably the first important composer to control his own destiny.

That fitted with his own commitments. When one of his patrons wanted him to play for the occupying French, Beethoven is claimed to have told him that while he, the patron, was a prince by an accident of birth *he* was a composer who was what he was by his own efforts: there had been, and would be, he said, thousands of princes – but only one Beethoven. We can't be certain that they were his precise words, but the sentiment rings true and they fit the man. He was an Enlightenment figure, in thrall neither to the Church nor to kings and princes. And he was passionate – often angry, frustrated by his ill health and progressive deafness, no sufferer of fools. That intensity is stamped on his scores.

The great Hungarian-born pianist András Schiff once explained to me, when he was about to record all the thirty-two sonatas for the first time, how Beethoven had always been the mountain that stood back waiting to be tackled even after Bach, Mozart, Haydn and Schubert had been conquered. Schiff, having just turned fifty, said: 'I am only now ready to play Beethoven. There is more going on in his head than with any other great composer. I wanted to be ready for it. Of all the great composers he is the hardest to typecast, maybe the hardest to understand. It's very fulfilling because it's so very serious.'

Serious, and personal. Beethoven was not writing to go with a fashion, or to turn a trick. There's a famous story about the rehearsals for the first of the quartets written for Count Andreas Kyrillovich Razumovsky, Russian Ambassador in Vienna, when the distinguished leader of the group who would play them said that the quartets 'weren't music'. Beethoven exploded with anger. They weren't written for the likes of him, he said, but for a future age.

If you take the 'Razumovsky' Quartet in F major, Opus 59, No. 1 (1806), Beethoven reveals himself as a composer who is about to conquer new territory. Listening to these middle quartets you sense a composer breaking free, anxious to inhabit his own world. In a literal sense, of course, Beethoven was beginning to be cut off, because the deafness that he'd first spoken about at the turn of the century when he was about thirty was creeping up on him. By the time he was in his middle forties – with about ten years to live – he could hear almost nothing at all.

These pieces – as the violinist faced with the 'Razumovsky' Quartets understood – took Beethoven on a new path, one laid on the foundations of Haydn and Mozart, whose chamber music he revered, but leading upwards and away. They were the sounds of a composer who was defining his own kind of freedom in music. It wasn't a commentary on the politics and ideas of his time – he was making a musical world, writing in a language that had a meaning of its own – but his inspiration was connected to the change in the role of the artist in what we call the Romantic era, when he might become, in the poet

Percy Bysshe Shelley's great phrase, one of the 'unacknowledged legislators of the world'.

He was committed absolutely to that change, and perhaps it was part of the anger. The poet Goethe, whom Beethoven thought far too fond of the trappings of court, said this about him when they met in 1812:

> His talent amazed me; altogether he is an utterly untamed personality, who is not altogether in the wrong in holding the world to be detestable but who surely does not make it any the more enjoyable either for himself or for others by his attitude. He is easily excused, on the other hand, and much to be pitied, as his hearing is leaving him, which perhaps mars the musical part of his nature less than the social.

Beethoven believed in his music – in a later age he might have been described as having a mission, though the notion of such inappropriate zealotry would have seemed ridiculous at the time – and he was suspicious of popular pressure. During rehearsals for *Fidelio* he's said to have shouted at someone: 'I don't write for the galleries.' If they didn't understand him, so be it. Beethoven described music as being a higher revelation than all wisdom and philosophy. He once said that it was the wine of a new procreation and he, as Bacchus, was pressing the grapes. A nice thought.

In that distillation you find tenderness, exquisite sadness, and gentleness – and volcanic passion. His alleged description of the drumbeat opening of the Fifth Symphony as 'fate knocking on the door' is almost certainly apocryphal, but you can see why it would be believed and why it has stuck to the symphony as a simple encapsulation of its spirit, as compressed and clear as the 'V for victory' signal borrowed from its opening bars as an uplifting radio call-sign in the Second World War. It is his spirit.

In the first decade of the nineteenth century, with his hearing deteriorating, Beethoven's music began to take on a quality which is often described as heroic. It speaks of struggle. Towards the end of his life, he embarked on another phase in which, by the standards of his time, he was writing experimentally. Take the extraordinary 'Grosse Fuge' in B flat – a one-movement piece for string quartet – written after he had lost his hearing entirely and finished in 1825. It's introspective, complicated, challenging for musicians, and it was unpopular at first because it seemed strange, perhaps unworldly. It was never popular in the nineteenth century but Igor Stravinsky said at the beginning of the twentieth that it would be 'forever contemporary'.

Beethoven was a musical visionary. Born in the embrace of Haydn and Mozart, he was a poet of the new age. His music was written in a world that was changing fast; he surmounted it and spoke in an original language of his own. The language is deep, sometimes mysterious, but often luminous and direct. When the Society of London (later the Royal Philharmonic Society) commissioned his ninth and last symphony, he blended voices and orchestra in the last movement in a way that hadn't been done before. Embellishing the words of the poet Schiller he gave his own idea of brotherhood and humanity an unforgettable form. At the beginning of the climax, the tenor cries out to his friends:

O Freunde, nicht diese Töne!
Sondern lasst uns angenehmere anstimmen und freudenvollere!

Let's be joyful. Beethoven himself said that he would seize fate by the throat and live a thousand times over. At the end of the Choral Symphony in D minor this complex, angry, restless genius refines everything, his own beliefs and the world churning wildly around him, into a transforming hymn of simplicity about freedom – which, for him, was music.

Since the age of recording began, generations who have hardly entered a concert hall have grown up to the sound of Beethoven symphonies, and can hear in their heads the beginning of that great chorus: 'Freude, schöner Götterfunken, Tochter aus Elysium'. For many people such moments are the very core of what we call classical music, the rhythms and themes the most familiar of all. We sometimes forget what a shock they once were.

In trying to place Beethoven in his time, and capture his originality, one of the symphonies in particular is a natural place to start. When he wrote his Third Symphony, the 'Eroica', he was challenging convention and shaking his audience in their seats. A radical was at work, and deploying formidable power. Remember that when Berlioz heard it for the first time he said he was seized by 'an antique sadness'. It begins with two hammer-blow chords and a few bars in which he plays with a trio of notes in the home key of E♭. Then the cellos come in with an unexpected C sharp. He has established a sense of urgency and anticipation in these first moments. A disturbing passion is going to have its way: there will be no stopping him. To audiences more familiar with Haydn or Mozart, and who knew Beethoven's first two symphonies, this was going to be a journey.

The theme wouldn't grow predictably, from the foundations of a structure deliberately laid for the development to come. They were given a promise of something else: a harmonic adventure, a certain disturbance in the air, a dramatic pulse in the orchestra. The opening has a sense of the unexpected. When the sforzando chords − to be played with special emphasis − come along early in the first movement, Beethoven is announcing himself. Something about this symphony will make music irreversible: what composer, having heard it, would try to imitate an eighteenth-century symphony?

In looking at how music was made, we've been tracing the influences that composers absorbed, and the events with which they lived; seeing how music was shaped and how, in turn, it became a mirror in which that world could see itself. Now and again it's worth pausing to look at one work. The 'Eroica' is a natural stopping place because in it you can hear something new. A composer of genius is taking us, with a great musical sweep, into another age with different ideas and new horizons. Emotions are going to be let loose. And the artist himself has become the hero. No other single piece from the early nineteenth century speaks so clearly of that transition. The symphony is exuberant and painful, at the same time optimistic and anxious. It's also a piece that may mark Beethoven's disillusion with the ability of those who aspire to power to remain uncorrupted.

He had originally dedicated it to Napoleon, before the First Consul decided in 1804 to have himself crowned emperor in Notre Dame in Paris. On the score of 'Eroica' the name Bonaparte has been scratched off the title page so roughly (it's assumed by the composer's hand) that there's a hole in the manuscript. Some say that there was an element of political calculation at work: the Austrians were fearful of Napoleon, and Beethoven had a history of being careful of revealing his opinions.

But a symphony that was certainly intended at first to be dedicated to Napoleon had his name removed.

Though scholars are still trying to unravel the details of the story, there's no doubt that Beethoven's admiration had soured. To see why, look at the painting of the Emperor's coronation by Jacques-Louis David and you see lavish obeisance that any king would have treasured. The Pope himself had been summoned from Rome as a mere witness, and saw Notre Dame hung with the trappings of temporal power. The Emperor-to-be was dressed in purple, and wore a wreath of gold laurel leaves on his head.

Like so many artists, Beethoven had been moved by the challenge of the French Revolution, and had supported Napoleon's rescue of it from the Reign of Terror with the establishment of the Consulate triumvirate in 1799. But he was infuriated by the sight of heroism being turned into the very kind of display that so many had wanted to see expunged by the Revolution. The 'Eroica' isn't an attack on that coronation; it's an exposition of the feelings that it aroused.

The funeral march that opens the second movement must have sounded very odd to the audience when Beethoven conducted the first public performance in 1805. It wasn't the usual way to write the slow movement that the audience would have expected after the first pause. But it's so assured, so measured, that it flows naturally and gives the 'Eroica' an elegiac quality at its heart. The listener is taken from the vigour of the first movement to the quiet sadness of the second with great ease.

Where the symphony had once been thought of as a satisfying construction, the movements adding up to a suitably whole en-tertainment, the 'Eroica' demands more of the listener. Here is how Berlioz, many years later, spoke of the end of that second movement. He described how the slow march theme from the opening comes back, but in a fragmented form, with only three plucked notes underneath it in the double basses. He added: 'When these tatters of the sad melody, left on their own – bare, broken and lifeless – have collapsed one after the other into the tonic [chord], the wind instruments utter a final cry, the last farewell of the warriors to their companion in arms, and the whole orchestra fades away on a pianissimo pause.'

This is music that echoes the great funeral marches for revolutionary heroes that had been heard in France, but also offers much more. The hero is gone. The one who is left is the artist, whose heroic impulse isn't destroyed by the ways of the world: at his best the musician or the poet is incorruptible, with an inextinguishable fire. The Romantic agony lay in the knowledge that the artist was the possessor of real power – inside himself – but was also alone. When the poet Byron watched Napoleon's assumption of imperial power he reflected on ambition being 'less than littleness', and asked this:

> Is this the man of thousand thrones
> That strew'd our earth with hostile bones
> And can he thus survive?

Bonaparte aside, Beethoven wrote this symphony as a farewell and a beginning. It marked the opening of a phase in his life when he seemed to become engrossed in the idea of struggle. He was already seriously deaf, prone to rages and dyspepsia, and in the music that followed the 'Eroica' that discomfort with the world is expressed in piano sonatas, string quartets, the middle symphonies and *Fidelio*. In that latter work he dealt directly with liberty, the argument being played out in the violence of his time. His symphonies draw pictures of struggles that can be resolved; the string quartets are meticulously crafted journeys into the emotions; but *Fidelio* looks outwards. It's a celebration of freedom – a story of political repression and the resilience of the human spirit against it. A lost love is restored, a wrong is confronted, the prisoners emerge into the sunlight from the depths. In the 'Eroica', that's the theme he'd begun to explore. Take the third movement, which his audience in Vienna would have expected to be lively. That was the form. But Beethoven gave this one a more sombre wash, colouring it with melancholy even as the symphony drives on.

The evidence is that his first public performance of the symphony was more disturbing to his listeners than exciting. There was a lot of grumbling. It was about twice as long as the symphonies they were used to, and invited them to enter a different kind of sound world from the one they knew. The harmonies were different, the dissonances quite defiant, the orchestration full of the unexpected. One reviewer said it was a 'tremendously expanded, daring and wild fantasia' which often lost itself in 'lawlessness'.

You cannot pinpoint a moment when the clean lines of the Classical age were moulded into something new by the Romantic spirit, but in this symphony you hear the urge that caused it to happen. Sometimes driven by philosophy or politics, energised by revolution or war, artists were exploring inside themselves to find a way of facing the world. Haydn and Mozart had established the symphony. Now Beethoven was using it to give a voice to the generations that would follow in music. By the time he came to write his last five or six string quartets – the most profound body of chamber music that anyone knows – and the Choral Symphony, the Ninth and last, he was a new kind of composer: the heroic artist on a quest to the deepest places.

Conductors know the Beethoven symphonies backwards. They're the spine of the orchestral repertoire. But knowing the notes is only the start. Speak even to some of the greatest conductors and they'll admit to approaching the 'Eroica' with trembling respect after half a lifetime on the podium. Such is its eloquence, the force of its passions, its completeness, that for a moment it seems to say everything. Yet when he finished it in 1805 Beethoven was only setting out on the rest of his journey. His greatest and most radical work was yet to come.

When he died, in 1827, the streets of Vienna were filled with tens of thousands of people. The oration written by Franz Grillparzer said that the mourners stood before the broken strings of an instrument now stilled. Reading out his words, the actor concluded thus: 'Return to your homes, then, distressed but composed. And whenever, during your lives, the power of his works overwhelms you like a coming storm; when your rapture pours out in the midst of a generation yet unborn; then remember this hour and think: we were there when they buried him, and when he died we wept!'

10

Pain and Confidence

Romantics, the Virtuosi and the Masses

~

N O COMPOSER IS a better exemplar of the troubled Romantic than
Franz Schubert. He was one of the greatest tunesmiths who ever
lived, with a strand of genius in his music, who found little but trouble
in the world. Famous and sometimes fashionable, but frequently poor
and disappointed, he died at the age of thirty-one, racked by typhoid
and probably syphilis too. On his deathbed, he said he wanted to be
buried alongside Beethoven.

Though he lived in Vienna, and had watched Beethoven conduct
and play the piano, the two never communicated, Schubert having to
be happy with a couple of sightings in a coffee house. His hero-worship
was doomed to operate at a distance, laced with the social humiliation
which was often his lot. Schubert was the artist whose life involved
suffering for his music; the freedom that his generation was beginning
to feel brought him down in the end. He died in the same decade as the
young John Keats succumbed to a fever in Rome, Percy Bysshe Shelley
drowned in the Mediterranean and Lord Byron was killed, also by a
fever, during the fight for Greek independence. With them, he seems
to represent the spectacularly broken ambitions of youth, for all their
brilliance, leaving a legacy that will always have pain and disappointment running through it.

When Schubert reached his maturity as a composer, Beethoven had
not yet finished his symphonies, nor the late quartets, and it was as if he
was taking off on his own, inspired by the master but not weighed
down by his final achievements: the pianist, symphonist and writer of
songs was one of the first shooting stars in the Romantic firmament,
tracing his own path. Beethoven had built on the achievements of
Haydn and Mozart, working out his powerful passions in his own way,

and Schubert was different again. His gift was for graceful melody, and for the brilliant liquidity that you hear in the string quartets which he began to write in his teens, and it made him an original. He was the composer who brought the German lied, the art song, to a pitch of near-perfection.

In Schubert you can sense the excitement and sheen of Viennese music-making in the 1820s and he introduces an age in which composers were released from the conventions of the past. Aristocratic patronage was less dominant in the aftermath of the French Revolution, and the Church was no longer so powerful as an arbiter of musical development. There was a certain freedom, though it was dangerous. And growing bourgeois prosperity meant that musical taste was more varied, perhaps more fickle, simply because music was more available. The stage was set for the virtuosi who would introduce an element of circus to serious performance. In Schubert's Vienna, the world was on the move.

If you listen, for example, to his 'Wanderer-Fantasie' in C major, written in 1822, it is easy to think of it as a picture of imagination released – speeding away with an energy that seems unstoppable. Schubert was in a city that thought of itself, with good reason, as the centre of the musical world, and he was the living vision of the restless, wandering artist who represented the Romantic spirit, free to take the Classical mirror that was held up to nature and turn it towards himself. Alongside him, you see a piano. As the violin had given the age of the Baroque its sound, so the piano announced the nineteenth century. Schubert, writing for the keyboard, and then bringing the voice and the piano together, gave it a delicacy – a personality – that revealed what could be done with these ivory keys and the new iron frames that transformed the cruder sounds that Haydn and Mozart had tamed and refined in the early instruments of their time.

The piano had grown up, and was rolling into the drawing rooms of Europe. In Schubert's Vienna, where the Biedermeier style had given the classical lines of music and architecture a new look and the city an elegance of its own, that instrument was the voice. Biedermeier was the fictional name of a worthy Austrian citizen and was applied to the elegant and heavy style that is familiar in the city to this day. The furniture was solid, dark and well turned, there were rich, deep colours and intricate needlework in the fabrics, and the home succumbed to the cult of the drawing room, in the centre of which stood a piano. They would play pieces like Schubert's 'Marche militaire', whose thumping rhythms have remained familiar to generations of reluctant young pianists, and the composer himself would write alongside them piano music that had little to do with family soirées but revealed his own insights, and his pain. The F minor 'Fantaisie' for piano duet (1828), for example, was on a different plane, a journey into feelings that left cosiness far behind.

The well-to-do families of Vienna would come to call an evening round the piano a *Schubertiad*, in remembrance of those days when Schubert began to write his sparkling music and was sometimes a star guest. It was the respectable pastime of the day. A bourgeois home saw music as the most enlightened pursuit. After a generation of revolution and war, the authorities were disbanding many of the public societies – the clubs and lodges – that might pose trouble. The home was everything. It was safe, for those with enough money it could be elegant, and domestic music-making could be improving. High seriousness had invaded the drawing room.

In this atmosphere, Schubert's short life was like an electric storm. As Beethoven had transformed the symphony, and given chamber music a depth of passion and complexity that no one had heard before, so Schubert turned the piano into an instrument for the voice. German lieder, the songs that he could write seemingly at will (he is said to have produced seven in a single day), were his gift to the city. He felt the piano, the voice and the poetry working on each other in a new way.

Though he and Beethoven died only a year apart, they seem now to have inhabited different eras. When Schubert carried a torch at the master's funeral in 1827, as when he'd sold schoolbooks to pay for a ticket to the première of the revised version of *Fidelio*, he was celebrating something that was passing away. Beethoven was honoured by the aristocracy, gave great concerts and had a famously fiery personality. Schubert was shy and ill paid and his world was that of the emerging middle class. The social consciousness of music was changing, and Schubert rode the tide. Yet he heard few performances of his eight completed symphonies in his lifetime, and his twelve operas were no great success, to his immense disappointment. By 1824 he could write to a friend that he was the most unhappy creature in the world:

> Picture a man whose health will never entirely recover and who in his despair about it makes matters worse and worse instead of better – picture, I say, a man whose brightest hopes have come to nothing, to whom the joys of love and friendship can offer only the greatest pain, whose enthusiasm for beauty is in danger of dying away, and ask yourself if he is not a wretched, unhappy creature.

His cherishing of a Romantic spirit brought the pain that Shelley said was an inevitable companion of a beauty that could 'humanise and harmonise the strain'. In his poetic meditation on the painting of the Medusa in the Uffizi Gallery in Florence, which he thought (like everyone else at that time) was by Leonardo da Vinci, he described a fusion of beauty and horror that he thought divine:

> Upon its lips and eyelids seems to lie
>   Loveliness like a shadow, from which shine,
> Fiery and lurid, struggling underneath,
> The agonies of anguish and of death.

That conception of the Romantic understanding seems etched on Schubert's life. His piano music, and his songs, became the lifeblood of a different kind of music-making. Yet he didn't get the benefits in his own lifetime. He made little money, and when he died there was no fanfare. It was all in his legacy, which injected a touch of genius into the society around him. This unspectacular figure – only about five feet tall and podgy – found a method of expression that would give to the Viennese, then to all German-speakers, and eventually to the world, a musical miracle. He wrote musical settings of more than 700 songs and in the process brought poetry and music together with a modern power.

Accompanied songs were old, carried by travelling musicians over the centuries and passed on. Later, they'd bred brilliant writing for the lute, the harpsichord and the early pianos. Schubert did something different. He used the piano as a partner for the voice, and wrote for them as if they'd always meant to be intimates, each knowing everything about the other. A wide vista opened up. Forget the confines of the drawing room; he was writing about the depth of an experience that was in the world beyond. He conjured up landscapes and the feelings they stirred, spoke of the rawest emotions. Borrowing from the folk traditions everyone knew, his output was a bubbling stream.

Take the one year of 1815. In the course of it, he wrote two symphonies, four piano sonatas, a dozen dances, piano variations, two masses, a 'Stabat Mater', some dramatic pieces for voice and orchestra – *Singspiele* – and no fewer than 146 songs. He was eighteen years old. That profusion inevitably produced much that was routine. He was able to conjure up an original tune so easily that he could write songs to order in no time at all. His output also included song cycles that were recognised (though not until after his death) as being on their own: not simply humane and touching, like so many of his individual songs, but profound. He wrote the twenty songs in *Die schöne Müllerin* in 1823 and four years later produced *Winterreise* (A Winter's Journey), twenty-four songs which are a meditation on suffering. The singer wanders through the snow and ice, gripped by the melancholy of lost love. They are dark, but produce light.

Schubert understood the intimacy that could now be discovered between the voice and the piano. They move together, entwined. The pulse is human. Whereas the Classical form that had been passed on from the eighteenth century strove for instrumental perfection, Schubert always seemed to be driven by the voice itself and its moods. He bridged the world of the colloquial song, which would be played and sung by young ladies in Viennese drawing rooms, and high art – a distilled understanding of the deepest emotions. He died in the year that Wordsworth and Coleridge made their journey up the Rhine – 1828 – and he epitomised the Romantic quest which drew them on, reaching inside himself to find ways of expressing sadness, love, loss.

He was therefore part of a profound change in music-making. It had a practical as well as an aesthetic effect. Schubert's writing for the piano helped the instrument come of age. Across Europe, factories were trying to satisfy a rampant demand. In London, John Broadwood – claiming to be the first piano manufacturer in the world, the firm which sent that grand piano to Beethoven – had a business that was growing fast. By 1840 they would be making 2,500 a year. As the century began the harpsichords that had made up the bulk of their output two decades earlier were slipping into history with the early box-like 'square' pianos that Haydn and Mozart knew. They were now being replaced by the grand, and much later there would be the 'cottage piano' – the upright that would sit in so many Victorian drawing rooms, and which the pre-Raphaelite artist Edward Burne-Jones would celebrate as 'the very altar of the home'.

In Schubert's time a six-octave grand in London (of the sort that Beethoven was given by Broadwoods) would cost about £40 – a little under half the annual salary of one of the company's skilled craftsmen. The price had come down by about half in a few years. More and more were being sold. The mechanisms very quickly became more refined and more robust. They were easier to keep in tune. The wood, the pins, the hammers, were improved, steel wire and the iron frame arrived – the piano was part of the modernising of music. One of the consequences was that amateur music-making become easier and more popular. Another was that the piano's peculiar powers inspired composers: they were offered a range of sound, delicacy, opportunities for rich harmonies and limpid simplicity that had been much more of a struggle for their predecessors, and beyond the reach of the harpsichord and the first successor instruments on which the strings weren't plucked but hit by a hammer.

In Vienna, Beethoven was writing for strings and piano in a way that no one could have managed in the eighteenth century. His genius was to be able to exploit the instrument and summon up unknown voices that had lain hidden. And Schubert, a man who always seemed to have a new tune in his head, understood instinctively how it could be a singer's companion and soulmate. In his song cycle *Schwanengesang* (Swansong), for example, written a few months before he died, it seems impossible to separate the voice from the accompaniment, so interwoven have they become. In his hands, the keyboard could also speak on its own. The impromptus for piano written in his last year (in which he also produced his C major symphony, 'The Great', and his intoxicating String Quintet in C) are a torrent of invention, sparkle and pain.

Schubert's career was an adventure, though often an unhappy one. He was one of the true explorers, plunging into music with a flashing eye and a taste for experiment. Though he revered Beethoven above all, and drew from his inheritance, he was a creative force with his own unmistakable character. Like two slightly later composers in the Germanic-speaking world, Robert Schumann (1810–56) and Felix Mendelssohn (1809–47), he shaped a sound world with new dimensions and character.

It was Mendelssohn who was anxious to direct the Romantics back to the works of J. S. Bach, whom he saw as the source of musical 'truth' that modern masters might turn to their own purposes. Not all Romantic composers took the same view. In France, his rough contemporary Berlioz (1803–69) had none of that misty reverence for Bach, and thought Handel's music almost unspeakable. But the common thread was their blazing commitment to music as the highest art – greater than poetry, for example – through which they could explore and celebrate the complexities of human emotions. They would draw on myth and fable from the past, write directly for the emotions, try to invent their own kind of magic in music. So song and opera were especially important, despite the excitement of writing for the modern piano and the ever-expanding symphony orchestra. In Italy, this was the era in which grand opera came into its own. But that is another story.

In Germany, one composer produced an opera that more than any other was a beacon of Romanticism, and summed up the way in which an art that was supposed to exist for its own purposes, set apart from the dreary doings of the contemporary world, was also crafted to appeal viscerally to the senses, to leave no heartstring unplucked. The composer was Carl Maria von Weber, and the opera was *Der Freischütz*.

At its climax, you can imagine the moonlight stealing across a lake, an owl swooping from the trees as our hero crouches in the Wolf's Glen, making magic bullets with the help of the Devil himself. From the moment the overture began for the first time on 18 June 1821, the opera was a roaring success, and an anthem to German Romanticism.

Der Freischütz gave audiences a glimpse of a realm they would like to think they might inhabit – where the imagination ran wild, the senses were sharpened, and fantasy infected the natural world. Opera, which could break all the rules, could deliver that thrill. On the first night in Berlin the audience were so excited when they heard the overture – full of fire and melting melody – that they demanded an encore before the action even started on the stage.

Storms and disasters, ghosts and roaring wild beasts, and blood. Like the Gothic novels which were pouring out of the travelling libraries in Britain, Weber's opera was feeding a taste for the exotic and the untamed. Melodramatic plots with supernatural twists and heroes with magic powers were the agents of a craze that, in Germany, spoke of something more than a passing fad. With Weber, audiences grasped, even in the fantasy of *Der Freischütz*, a spirit that they thought was their own. The characters used folk tunes on the stage. They sang about the beauties of nature. They walked by lakes and forests and, as in the fairy tales, they usually lived happily ever after. The landscape and the people were familiar – and they were singing in German. The unification of the country under Bismarck was still a generation away – but in this opera, with its folklore and adventure, Germans found something that brought them together.

How curious that it was done by such means. Yet Weber's music reveals how Romanticism was changing the way that listeners saw the world, even as it seemed to be offering an escape from it. He was not of Schubert's generation, and was closer to Beethoven, whom he pre-deceased by a year. Yet he was of the age that was looking forward, away from the eighteenth century, and trying to create a new sensibility.

The story of *Der Freischütz* is an appeal to the imagination. In the Wolf's Glen, the young huntsman Max gets the Devil's help with the magic bullets to win a shooting competition and, as a result, the love of the heroine. All the musical craft, and its power, is turned unashamedly on the emotions: make them laugh, make them cry, and scare them a little bit along the way. Weber was the cornerstone of a particular kind of Romanticism in Germany that became one of the most important strains in the European tradition. This is what Richard Wagner, a beneficiary of his work, said about Weber:

Freischütz . . . because of its spooky plot, affected my imagination with characteristic intensity. The excitement of horror and fear of ghosts constitute a singular factor in the development of my emotional life . . . I tried with playmates to imitate performances of *Freischütz* and devoted myself with great zeal to the production of costumes and masks through grotesque painting . . . Nothing moved me more strongly than the music of *Freischütz* . . . and I tried in many ways to reproduce the effect it had on me . . . the swelling C of the *Freischütz* overture announced to me that I had stepped with both feet into the magic realm of awe. Anyone observing me at the time could hardly fail to see what the nature of my case was . . . despite my dismal piano playing.

Intensity was the thing. As with the Romantic poets, for whom directness of feeling was all, the musicians in Germany who would follow Weber saw music as a force that could fire the imagination, and give it unstoppable power. Who cared if an opera plot was implausible or thin? If the emotions were strong and vivid enough, and true to the heart, what else mattered?

Outside the opera house, an orchestral sound would capture this Romanticism, with unequivocal depth of feeling. Wagner himself, Gustav Mahler, Anton Bruckner towards the end of the nineteenth century and Richard Strauss in the twentieth were the great heirs to the tradition. In their music there is an echo of the horns that you hear in *Der Freischütz*. It is the call of the *Waldhorn*, from the hunter in the forest, but associated in Germany too with a mysticism about nature that reached deep into the past. The Romantics were no longer in thrall to the established religion in which most of their artistic ancestors had lived and worked (just as they broke with the artistic rules of Classicism). Instead, they turned to a love of nature that was almost pantheistic. Nature was itself a sort of temple, in which there was redemption – as well as danger, excitement and love.

Just as Wordsworth had written about a power that he found almost indescribable but real in nature – 'A presence that disturbs me with the joy / Of elevated thoughts; a sense sublime / Of something far more deeply interfused . . . that . . . rolls through all things' ('Lines written a Few Miles Above Tintern Abbey', 1798) – so composers were trying to describe an inner world, which you could penetrate only through music and by surrendering your emotional defences. They often turned to the past for inspiration.

In the early nineteenth century the novels of Sir Walter Scott, so neglected in our own time, were entrancing all of Europe. His long, rich descriptions of a lost Scotland in his historical novels spoke of an heroic past. There were great deeds, bloody adventures, surging love stories. Italian operatic composers like Donizetti and Bellini loved the spirit of his books because they allowed feeling to conquer everything, and audiences relished the stories when they were turned into opera. Though Weber had no use for the Italianate style, hypnotic though it was, and wanted to develop a distinctive German sensibility, he was stirred by the same feeling.

Myth was important. Real life was pictured as having a supernatural element. In the darkness of a forest, or the fading light of a sunset, you would find magic and the inexplicable. Truth was somewhere beyond the solid contours of the here-and-now. Painters like the German Caspar David Friedrich tried to find it in moonlit scenes with ruined buildings that held memories of the past, on dark pathways through a forest. Friedrich said of one misty outlook in a painting that it 'enriches the imagination and intensifies expectation – like a girl wearing a veil'. One of his most famous pictures is called *Wanderer above the Sea of Fog*. We can't see the wanderer's face. He could be anyone, and is every-man. He has his back to us, his frock-coat billowing out behind him in the wind, and he's looking out from the top of a craggy mountain. But the landscape, which we assume is vast and beautiful, is hidden by the fog. Can he see through it? What's hidden there? Where will he go? Nature is mysterious and compelling: the wanderer will be drawn to what lies beyond.

Romantic artists were indeed wanderers, pulled on by their instincts and feelings. By the time Weber was writing in the 1820s it was as if the eighteenth century was long, long gone. As it happens, his first cousin Constanze had married Mozart, but the world from which Mozart had been threatening to burst free towards the end of his life (only thirty years before) seemed distant to the artists and composers who were growing up around Weber. Across Europe, the shock and turmoil of revolution and war were harbingers of a new age. Industry was coming, empires were spreading, democratic ideas were flourishing in the New

World across the Atlantic and coursing sporadically through the politics of Europe. Poets had huge audiences and epitomised the spirit of their time. While *Der Freischütz* was becoming the talk of Germany, Byron was heading off to Greece to fight for independence and the poems of his Romantic contemporaries were electrifying Europe.

Music, especially in Germany, was set on a new path. It was the sound of nationhood and history, and because it was beautiful it represented truth. The Romantic philosopher Friedrich Wilhelm Schelling described architecture as 'frozen music', as if the sounds themselves, shaped by a composer's imagination, were the source of all the highest feelings and insights. Whether in popular operas or the concerts that were becoming available to more and more people, in the piano music that was played in family drawing rooms, or in the art songs that came to define a certain kind of feeling, an era had begun in which the inheritance from the eighteenth-century masters was turned into something new. Beethoven, who had straddled the ages of high Classicism and the Romantic, had laid foundations on which the musicians of the nineteenth century were building their castles and their follies, places where their imaginations could be free.

Schubert and Weber were two of the figures who illustrate the character of the Romantic age, which took many forms. An urge to reveal the emotions and to indulge in painful introspection was part of its musical manifestation, together with the taste for the melodramatic, the ancient and the bizarre. Alongside that imaginative revolution came profound social changes. In Vienna, Schubert was serving a prosperous middle class where Beethoven had once survived on aristocratic patronage (because he had no choice). With increasing prosperity came audiences, and all over Europe they began to enjoy the phenomenon of the concert in a way that previous generations could not. Halls and theatres were bigger, the prices were such that the middle class was enticed out of its drawing rooms, and performers were beginning to enjoy the celebrity that was encouraged by the excitement of musical life. One of the consequences was the rise of the outrageous performer.

When Nicolò Paganini came to play his violin it was as if a circus had rolled into town. He presented a remarkable, even sinister spectacle, his hands zipping with bewildering speed across the strings. He bowed so low and with such gestures to his audiences that it was said of him that he 'bowed like a camel and grinned like a goblin'. The pianist and composer Franz Liszt (1811–86) left a memorable description:

> Here was an apparition to match the wildest excesses of the Romantic imagination. Dressed from head to foot in black, here, surely, was Mephistopheles himself: the fleshless tortured body, even now ravaged by the tubercular disease that finally killed him, the aquiline nose, the haunted eyes, the powerful forehead, the long lank mass of raven-black hair, the brittle-thin fingers on the violin. And when he played it seemed as though the devil was dancing on his bow. The unearthly tones of his harmonics, the double trills, the thirds, the sixths, the octaves and tenths, the shimmering arpeggios, the cascades of glissandi, the bowed chords combined with a dancing pizzicato from the left hand . . . If a string should break, no matter, for he would continue on the remaining three – indeed a favourite trick was, after breaking the middle strings, to play a love duet on the two outer ones. No one else played such music, for no one else could. And Paganini was careful to preserve his secrets. At rehearsals of a concerto his habit was to omit the cadenza so that any rival among the violins of the orchestra would hear it only once – at the public concert.

Liszt himself knew about performance. He organised duels with 'opponents' – in 1837, for example, challenging the pianist Sigismond Thalberg to three rounds of competition, hiring the opera house in Paris for the second round, where the two played for an audience of 4,000. The climax came in round three held at the salon of the Princess Belgiojoso, where seats were sold for forty francs each – the profits on that occasion going to charity. Liszt won. The pianists appeared as they wanted to, like twentieth-century celebrities (Liszt often wore diamonds for his public concerts) and they were comfortable with the idea of the public challenge, free of intellectual abstraction. In the 1820s and 1830s, more and more people were able to go to concerts and recitals and these virtuosi – the players of exceptionally athletic skill and endless energy – were the physical manifestation of that popular explosion.

Liszt's description of Paganini catches the flavour. The violinist was born in Genoa in northern Italy in 1782. He was a prodigy, and in his early twenties became musician to Napoleon's sister, but even then he was already touring, because he loved the crowds. By the 1820s his fame had travelled far and in 1831 he conquered Paris and London. By the time Beethoven was nearing the end of his life in the middle of the 1820s, the Romantic movement to which he'd given such intellectual weight was revolutionising public taste. Music seemed to be everywhere, and the virtuosi could fill theatres as if they were music-hall stars of a later era. Paganini sometimes played his fiddle behind his back to amuse the crowd, and he would pluck the strings for long pizzicato passages. Yet his tricks never seemed to interfere with his ability to produce a beautiful sound. 'What a man, what a violin, what an artist!' said Liszt. 'God – what suffering, torture and agony in those four strings.' That description was a strangely loving one.

Everywhere Paganini went, stories followed him. As happened in the world of the blues a century later, people peddled tales of him going to a crossroads at midnight to sell his soul to the Devil in exchange for a special talent. He made and lost at least one fortune, drank and gambled to spectacular excess, and one of his world tours lasted more than six years, taking him to many towns and cities on its long British leg. Halls were filled in places from Edinburgh to Blackburn and Manchester, from Birmingham to London, to hear him play. Though his sunken cheeks and unusually long fingers were striking, and he played with great theatricality, Paganini was no technical freak. He simply embodied the idea of the performer as magician. Just as composers were now thought to be in touch with an inner, hidden world, so the great soloists – the artists of the musical stage – were held to be the transmitters of music's special secret.

Public concerts were big business. They made Paganini rich enough to try (unsuccessfully) to open a casino in Paris, and they turned musicians into stars. When Liszt began to tour – in what he called 'my travelling circus life' – he said he wanted to do for the piano what Paganini had done for the violin. The composer Felix Mendelssohn spoke wearily of these 'tomfool pranks' on stage, accusing him of lamentable misdemeanours in his playing, but Liszt's showmanship was extraordinarily popular. Mendelssohn was comfortable at home giving

Sunday-morning concerts in his Berlin home with his pianist sister Fanny and another sister and brother. For Liszt, the crowd mattered more and he thrived on the atmosphere that could be whipped up in a great gathering.

A favourite piece at the climax of a concert was his own 'Grand Galop Chromatique', which was pure style, an opportunity for virtuosity with no pretence at profundity. His wizardry was indeed a circus act. Though he was a serious character – a deeply religious Catholic – he rode the wave of popularity with relish. His American pupil Amy Fay said that he knew very well the effect he had on his audience. 'He always fixes his eye on one of us when he plays, and I believe he tries to wring our hearts.' He played with such ferocity that some of his pianos couldn't take the strain: he often had two of them on the stage so that if one was bashed out of tune, he could switch to the other. Women in the front rows at his concerts sometimes clutched at his legs as he played. He would toss cigar butts and gloves into the crowd, to be fought over by fans and carried off as souvenirs.

Liszt, however, was much more than a dazzling performer. He became a serious composer and in the ten years he spent as director of music at the court of Weimar, from the late 1840s, he produced many innovative works. He is credited, in particular, with the invention of the 'symphonic poem' which was a form that became important in the development of many later composers, deliberately setting out to paint a picture of the world – a feeling, a scene, a narrative – that was meant to be a contrast with the notion of music as an intellectual creation entire in itself, subject only to its own rules and inhabiting an abstract sphere.

His music was popular, delighting the crowds who enjoyed spectacle in performance. He was probably the first musician to use the word 'recital' to describe a solo performance, in 1840. He also decided to place the piano at right angles to the audience, and established the arrangement on the platform that became so familiar. Liszt's career shows how the popularisation of music went hand in hand with innovation in composition. He was daring, and the object of scorn from more conservative musicians. Brahms was one of them, fulfilling his lifetime role as the suspicious critic of all things dangerously new. He attacked Liszt for what he thought his lack of seriousness, formlessness and even lack of musicality. But his critics failed to puncture his popularity.

The pianists whom he taught fanned out across Europe, imitating his style and playing his pieces. They remained popular and had a considerable impact on public taste: his daring harmonies, with their cascades of chords across the keyboard and their torrential climaxes were instantly recognisable. Brahms might complain that Classical purity was being besmirched. Audiences didn't mind. Liszt's friend Frédéric Chopin watched these performances in amazement: 'I am not fit to give concerts: the crowd intimidates me and I feel asphyxiated by its eager breath, paralysed by its inquisitive stare, silenced by its alien faces; but you, you are made for it. For when you cannot captivate your audience you at least have the power to stun it.'

Chopin's power was of a different sort, as he realised, but it was also profound. He was born the year before Liszt, in 1810, and was introduced by him to the love of his life, George Sand, the pseudonym of Mme Amandine Dudevant, the novelist and early feminist. Chopin, too, was a virtuoso–composer but gave far fewer concerts than Liszt and died a much younger man, at the age of thirty-nine. But Chopin epitomised the hypnotic power of the pianist–composer, with the ability, as the conductor Sir Charles Hallé put it, to take you to dreamland.

There was drama in his music – many of the études and fantasies are festivals of notes – but also an exquisite gentleness. No one in the Romantic era produced solo piano works that had a more melancholy beauty. His musical world, of course, was rooted in his native Poland and he adapted the dance rhythms he knew from his youth, and the sounds of traditional music that he'd heard as a boy, into an utterly recognisable style. His mazurkas and nocturnes are his alone; you only need to hear a couple of bars to feel his presence and the memory of Warsaw. Chopin was shy, unlike Liszt, and there clung to him the pallor of the artist stricken by weakness. He always seemed a figure who was struggling against the world to get his music out: he liked subdued lighting and didn't enjoy crowds, and he liked to play softly.

When he toured, he preferred the salons of great houses to the concert hall, though he didn't always warm to his 'generous' patrons.

Writing from London to his friend Albert Grzymala in July 1848, he wondered whether he would travel to Scotland again (where he had charged the Duchess of Sutherland twenty guineas to play for her guests). 'My Scots women are kind and affectionate, but they bore me to death at times . . .' he said. Chopin had no illusions about their taste, nor indeed about the seriousness of patrons elsewhere:

> As for the fashionable world which travels, it is haughty but civil, and has very good judgement when it chooses to exercise it; but it is so much distracted by a thousand matters, so closely hemmed in by tedious conventions and etiquette, that it no longer cares whether music is good or bad – hearing it from morning to night. There is not a flower show without music, not a dinner without music, not a charity bazaar without music. There are as many Savoyards and Czechs and colleagues of my own as there are dogs, and they are all mingled pell-mell . . .

For all his discomfort, he and Liszt were bound together with the other virtuosi like Paganini in making the case for music as a cry from the heart. In this period, integrity of personal expression was everything. It poured in torrents from Liszt, seeming to possess him in the course of a performance. And from Chopin there was endless lyricism – an ability to capture again and again in memorable phrases moments of sadness and despair, and flashes of excitement. Extraordinary performers had always been valued. The young Mozart was carried across Europe by his father to play the part of 'child prodigy' in front of kings and queens. The era of the nineteenth-century virtuosi, however, established the solo performance as a vital conduit for new music, for invention, for stylistic innovation. Chopin wrote for pianists whom he expected to apply their own emotions to his music, letting it breathe for them in different ways without worrying about metronome timings. It was more important to strive for authenticity in expression. He didn't expect everyone to play like him.

Chopin was what we would now call a cult figure, at least in high society. Paris couldn't get enough of him, and Liszt continued to tour into old age, inspiring fanatical devotion among those who wanted pyrotechnics on the keyboards. Paganini was magnetic. Brahms might think it vulgar, and some of Paganini's capers certainly were, but the effect of these performances was profound. Long before the age of recording came along, these were musicians who could inspire huge crowds and set the fashion. They were emotional and dangerous. All you could predict was the excitement. The musician had become the object of fame and wonder. The Romantics wanted to bare themselves, and performance itself became a vehicle for self-expression. Musical invention – originality in composition – was important; and so was the ability to invest it with emotion. With their style and precision, and their respect for the musical idea, these musicians established, too, the value of the quality that turned these attributes to gold in helping to bring them to a wider public – sheer brilliance in performance.

In their era, the Romantic composers were able to speak to listeners whose equivalents a century before would have found it more difficult to hear musicians at work. Public concerts had begun in London in the late seventeenth century, and in the course of the next century those musical societies had sprung up in Bath, Oxford, Edinburgh and other cities while London theatres and gardens were becoming popular places of musical entertainment. But in the nineteenth century that movement became quicker. The symphonies of the Romantic composers, the profusion of chamber music built on the masterpieces of Haydn and then Beethoven, German lieder and the flood of inspired composition for the solo piano all meant that public concerts grew in number and popularity.

This was happening across Europe, and there is no clearer picture than in London at the mid-point of the century. It was a city that was outward looking and confident, optimistic and even a little brash, although in a Victorian fashion. The Crystal Palace built in Hyde Park for the Great Exhibition was an expression of bravado and style. The Exhibition itself was a blazing statement of the Victorian belief in progress. It opened on 1 May 1851 to the sound of Handel's 'Hallelujah' chorus from *Messiah* sung by a choir of nearly a thousand voices. It was thought to be the Queen's favourite (as it had been of Handel's last king, George III). The palace of glass and iron that she declared open was a showcase of modernity to the world: the fruits of the industrial revolution were on display and the promise was of more invention, more trade, more prosperity.

It has been claimed that six million people – a third of the population – saw some aspect of the Exhibition (a figure that surely involves some gentle exaggeration). They could listen to the biggest organ in the world, see machines making steel, inspect iron cookers that were going to transform household kitchens and wonder at gadgets of all sorts. The showman and trapeze artist Blondin fried eggs above the crowds as he walked along his tightrope. There was circus, and there was music.

The confidence that the Exhibition represented – like Sir Charles Barry's new Palace of Westminster, built to house the Lords and the Commons, which opened the following year – was a cultural boast. Progress and the spread of Empire were held to place London at the centre of the world. Moreover, the crowds that travelled to Hyde Park were evidence that, by comparison with the world in which their parents had lived, they were part of an age of participation. Parliamentary democracy was still limited, the labouring classes lived hard lives and had ambitions shackled by a heavy hand – Dickens was writing *Bleak House* during the Exhibition and *Hard Times* would follow soon – but there seemed to be hope.

Part of the evidence lies in the way people were claiming music for themselves. Choirs were springing up in every town and city. A few (very few) enlightened employers – like the Cadburys in Bourneville – were even organising singing classes for the workforce. Music was part of the democratisation that was in progress. They rediscovered Handel, whose oratorios could give an amateur choir such pleasure, and that same urge prompted the commission in Birmingham, in 1846, to Mendelssohn to produce *Elijah* for the choral festival. The audience in Birmingham Town Hall for the first performance brought the composer back again and again for further ovations. *The Times* reported that he was 'evidently overpowered' and its critic said there had never been a more complete triumph – 'never a more thorough and speedy recognition of a great work of art'.

That word 'speedy' is interesting. At this time, music was spreading very fast. The piano was a fixture in many homes. Popular songs were everywhere, and the sheet music for drawing-room ballads poked out from under the lid of every piano stool. Orchestras were starting to form – Britain's first fully professional one, the Hallé, began life in

Manchester in 1858. The Crystal Palace was taken off to south London to a new home, but in that part of London where it was originally erected there is still physical evidence of what happened there. The centrepiece is the Royal Albert Hall, opened in 1871 twenty years after the Great Exhibition and springing from the same confidence. It was modelled on a Greek amphitheatre, to hold about 8,000 people, and was meant to become a kind of permanent exhibition encased in lasting grandeur. Just across the road, on the edge of Hyde Park, is the Albert Memorial, a gleaming gold-leafed monument to its age and to the Prince Consort who made a hefty contribution to the tradition that's still alive there. After the Great Exhibition, he supported the idea of a Royal College of Music round the corner; and it was because of him that the museums that cluster round that part of London were established – the Victoria and Albert, the Science Museum, the Natural History Museum. They called Kensington 'Albertopolis'.

It was an age of deference, and the social order was rigid, but in these places you can see how music was indeed spreading fast. It has sometimes been argued that Albert's 'meritocracy' was an illusion, a trick to help to keep things calm, yet there was certainly an element of liberation at work. A musical culture was available. Like evening classes and free museums – and the public libraries that were opening their doors in every town now – music was there for those who wanted it. More people than ever before were exposed to it, and absorbing it. Not only were the public concert halls full, and the opera popular, but the Victorians could join a choir just as they might enjoy the drawing-room songs round the piano at home.

You can understand why it was that around the centenary of Handel's death, in 1859, they started an annual Handel Festival in the Crystal Palace, featuring choirs that seemed to get bigger and bigger. When George Bernard Shaw, as a young music critic, attended one of them much later in 1877, he spotted quite clearly what was going on when he heard 4,000 people singing. Sharp tongue in cheek, he said that maybe it was time to add another thousand to the choir, in the interests of 'a more sensational attraction'. Because, he said, the aims of those who put on the Festival were 'firstly, commercial; secondly, phenomenal and lastly, artistic'. It was true, of course. The Royal Albert Hall was always home to the bizarre and the spectacular as well as to the refined (as it still is). It wasn't even a great place in which to hear music, the old joke being that the echo was so bad that it was the only hall in which a composer could be guaranteed to hear his work played twice. That particular problem was only solved properly in the late twentieth century, and even today no one would claim that it is a hall in which an orchestra is likely to sound its best.

Music in the Victorian era was blousy and loud as well as delicate. That building represents it all – a commitment to the history of music (the frieze that goes around the outside, just under the dome, shows the classical muses) and an unquenchable enthusiasm for the power of music to enthral and entertain. Each summer at the BBC Proms thousands come each night for a remarkable festival that keeps that tradition alive. They don't dress up – and never wear funny hats or ridiculous costumes as some do on the Last Night in September, that oddest of occasions which repels at least as many people as it attracts. The audiences for the six dozen and more concerts are an advertisement for the power of music to cross boundaries, held together not by background or wealth or intellectual weight but simply by the desire to experience the visceral thrill of live performance, and to spend two or three hours giving themselves up to it.

It is instructive to look at the concert programmes for the regular Saturday performances at the Crystal Palace after its transfer and rebuilding in south London. There were first performances of many of the great works of the continental composers who gave the nine-teenth century its orchestral sound – Schubert and Schumann alongside Beethoven, Mendelssohn, Liszt and Berlioz.

A piece like the 'Symphonie fantastique' by Hector Berlioz was exactly the kind of nineteenth-century Romantic symphony that seems written for places like that and for the crowds who wanted to hear the grand and exotic as well as the intimate. Over a period of thirty years or so the Crystal Palace was the home of exciting performance and innovation. As it happens, Berlioz had come to the Great Exhibition from France on a rather testing mission from the Minister of Agri-culture and Trade in Paris. His job was to pick the winners in a competition for musical instruments from around the world, category by category. It was a wearisome business. 'There are days when I am quite overcome with despondency,' he said of his 'dreadful chore'. He was about to fall asleep at the Exhibition one morning, he said, when a colleague tapped him on the shoulder and said: 'Take heart. Today we have thirty-two musical snuffboxes, twenty-four accordions and thirteen bombardons [newly invented tubas] to examine.'

But Berlioz was lifted up by a London that he found intoxicating. He heard 6,500 children singing in St Paul's, walked the streets all night afterwards and came back to the Great Exhibition in early morning when the hall was empty, feeling that all things were holding 'a mysterious conversation together, in this strange language that can be heard with the ear of the mind'. That 'ear of the mind' was alert, and everywhere there was sound. Choirs were singing, orchestras were playing; in Italy and Germany and France the era of grand opera was at its height. Schubert songs were played at the piano alongside drawing-room ballads. Liszt was enthralling massive crowds with his playing and Chopin had brought a gentle melancholy to Romantic piano music which was fixed in the public mind and would never fade. The great symphonies – of the eighteenth century and of Beethoven – were finding new audiences all the time, in new places.

The excitement of live music was public property. These concerts in London were entertaining and inspiring. Young Edward Elgar, born in 1857, began to travel from Worcestershire to attend them on Saturdays, sometimes to hear an orchestra conducted by Sir Arthur Sullivan, the great hope of British music of his day. The young man who would become, unquestionably, the most eloquent voice of English music in the period immediately before the Great War a generation ahead was part of a population that had, at last, the opportunity to draw from the well of European music with relative ease. It had never been so before; and the change was irreversible. From the excitement and the pain of the Romantic age came music whose power was growing ever wider.

If crowds in London were beginning to take to concert-going (and more people were finding it affordable), in Italy there was a different enthusiasm. While in Germany and Austria symphonic and piano music was the most characteristic product of the Romantic era – an apparently simple song like Schubert's 'An die Musik' (To Music) or Beethoven's later symphonies seeming to express best its appeal to the emotions – in Italy it was in the opera house that music was most popular.

Nineteenth-century Italian opera is glorious and, though it is sometimes cheap and melodramatic, there is nothing else like it. To this day, sitting in the Teatro alla Scala in Milan, you can revel in some of the pretension and theatricality of an audience that thinks of the opera, in part, as a spectator sport, but you can also enjoy the confidence of a tradition embedded in Italian life.

11

Viva Verdi!

The Italian Love Affair with Opera

~

GIUSEPPE VERDI LIVED a long life that began in the age of
Napoleon and ended in the twentieth century. No other composer of opera has swept a wider path through his times, and almost
none has achieved his breadth of popularity. His first operas were a
rousing accompaniment to an age of change and revolution, the last of
them a glimpse into the future. Verdi was melodist, master of music
drama and political hero. In the glittering story of opera no one's star
gleams more brightly.

The popularisation of music in the nineteenth century had a
distinctive character in Italy. There, the crowds preferred the opera
to the symphony. That was their first love and Verdi's life reveals it all.
When he was born in the village of Le Roncole near Parma in 1813,
the *bel canto* era was about to begin in Italy under the batons of
Giaocchino Rossini (1792–1868) and his two greatest compatriots,
Gaetano Donizetti (1797–1848) and Vincenzo Bellini (1801–35). Verdi
imbibed the spirit of the time, then set his own course. His late works
encompass the epic spirit of the grand opera that blossomed in Paris in
his youth – but without any of the heavy-handedness that weighed it
down – and by 1893, when he wrote *Falstaff*, his last work for the stage,
he had travelled into new realms. The simply structured arias and
muscular choruses of the first operas were an age away. He was writing
with the whisper of modernism in his ear, and producing music drama
that would have startled, puzzled and almost certainly bored the
audiences he'd first known and served in Milan as a young composer.

Verdi began to write at the moment when Italy was consummating
its love affair with opera. Since the Florentines and Claudio Monteverdi
at the beginning of the seventeenth century there had been many

heroes who made the Italian style the envy of Europe. It invaded France and inspired the young Handel, who wrote his first successful opera in Rome in 1709 (*Agrippina*) before he took the style to England with him. With Rossini, born in the last decade of the eighteenth century, Italy discovered that Romantic expressiveness, the appeal to emotion and love of history, myth and distant lands were the natural vehicles for opera. Within half a century it was established as the most popular form of music-making there, with a character that seemed to reflect the politics and texture of the country as it performed its melodramatic and frequently chaotic transition from a collection of competing states to nationhood.

This excitement was different from the Romantic experience in Germany. In Weber's operas, and in the music of Schubert – springing directly from the intensity of Beethoven's late works – you hear a longing for escape, a sensuousness that might open up new worlds. Though it was often expressed through Germany's own history and the myths of northern Europe – and the landscapes of artists' imaginations were close and familiar – that urge was driven in part by a feeling for the warmth and colour that was associated with the south, something like the intoxication that Keats described in 'dance, and Provençal song, and sunburnt mirth'. The gleam in the eye was not jealousy – that would be to over-simplify the feeling to the point of absurdity – but there was longing built into it. The Romantic spirit was adventurous and out-ward looking, even in its concern for the inner thoughts and senses.

The focus of Italian Romanticism was different. Germanic musicians were dominating the symphonic world, and they were the instrumental innovators of the early nineteenth century. The Italians' own property was their attraction to opera, and it became their special musical language in the Romantic era. Though composers shared their fascin-ation with the internationally popular novels and poems of the day (both Rossini and Schubert, for example, found inspiration in Sir Walter Scott's dreamy poem of mythical fantasy, *The Lady of the Lake*) they established a style that was emphatically Italian, home grown and built with the special sounds and cadences of their own language.

Imagine life in Naples in the 1820s. Opera-going was one of the most important strands in city life. People would be seen at the theatre four or five nights each week, and its sounds would flow into the streets so that up every alleyway you could hear someone singing or whistling a tune from the latest show. The beggars on every corner – the *lazzaroni* – would know what was on, and all of the bustle of the place sometimes seemed centred on the theatre. There was none of the sometimes false reverence that later generations introduced; crowds would swirl around the foyers and salons as if they were in the market-place, smoking, drinking, gambling. Indeed, the Teatro San Carlo in Naples was rebuilt on the proceeds of the casino that operated inside the front doors.

Inside, you could smell the food from the more expensive tiers, where the wealthy would bring their servants to cook for them in adjoining rooms behind the boxes which they bought or rented. In some theatres there were metal grilles through which the cooks and waiters could peek down to the stage after their work was done. The smell of woodsmoke hung in the air, from the fires that heated the place. Crowds flowed constantly through the passageways: there was a picnic atmosphere. The boxes had curtains which could be pulled shut to allow who-knows-what to go on (as it seems to have done a great deal, quite naturally) and then parted again to allow the occupants to see the opera, and to be seen by the hoi-polloi down below. Seats were priced to admit an audience that wasn't entirely made up of people who wanted to parade their wealth and power, and though some of the patrons prized the exclusivity of their seats it was an audience far broader than those, for example, which had gathered in the theatres of Vienna and Prague to hear the early performances of Mozart's operas or thirty years later to hear Beethoven's symphonies.

Performances were noisy. Approving cries of 'Bravo!' were encouraged, shouts of 'Basta, basta!' for a cracked high note or a fumbled duet were part of the experience, as they still are in Italy (one very famous soprano of recent times still recalls a demented cry of 'Strega!' – witch – from the balcony after one aria had gone a little awry). The theatre was never entirely dark and one of the reasons that composers wrote overtures with tremendous force and pace was that they were useful ways of imposing some order on proceedings, which were always threatening to get out of hand. The Irish novelist Lady Morgan, whose vivid pictures of Italian life were much admired by Byron, described a performance in Rome in 1820 during which 'the prompter, with his head popped over the stage-lights, talked to the girls in the pit, the cello flirted with a beautiful townswoman in the boxes, and a lady in the stage-box blew out the lamplighter's candle as often as he attempted to light it, to the infinite amusement of the audience . . .' And if they were amused, they laughed out loud.

Theatres were places of social spectacle, but though the glitter and drama of the opera encouraged ostentation, as it always has, Italian music at this time had a rough humanity too. It was intimate rather than remote, and the stories of heroic deeds in distant lands or tales of untouchable love seemed real despite the improbability of most of the plots. They offered a life of the imagination that everyone could lead, or at least experience for a few hours with the thrill of discovery.

The evidence is in the place that opera made for itself in society. The French novelist Stendhal (Marie-Henri Beyle) described, in his biography of Rossini published in 1824, the 'peculiar kind of life' in Italian theatres and among its audiences for which he saw no parallel in France. Stendhal's fascination was almost as great as his enthusiasm. He recounted how Rossini would travel through Italy spending two or three months in a town at a time, fêted wherever he went, and showered almost nightly with new plots and even completed libretti in the hope that he might pick them up and turn them into gold. This is Stendhal's account of the approach to a first night:

the work of the ensemble is being discussed everywhere in the town, in the expectation of the pleasure or the annoyance to come during the most brilliant month of the year, the success or the downfall of the new opera. A small town, at this stage of intoxication, forgets the existence of the rest of the world. It is during this period of uncertainty that the impresario has really the time of his life, being the king of the castle . . .

The decisive night has arrived at last. The maestro sits at the piano in the orchestra. The theatre is as full as can be. People have come from a distance of twenty miles around; curious visitors are camping in their carriages on the road; all the inns have been crowded out since the day before. All work has stopped. When the performance starts, the town has become a desert. All the passion, all the uncertainty, all the life of the population is concentrated in the theatre.

The performance begins. One could hear a pin drop. The overture being over, a terrific hubbub starts. One extols it to the clouds, or one hisses it and howls it down without mercy. And after every piece of the new opera, after hushed silence, the same noise starts all over again. The roar of the stormy sea would offer an imperfect comparison.

This was the world of Rossini, and later of Verdi. Opera is often caricatured as music drama that takes you out of the world, as if it is an artificial means of escape. When it became the most popular entertainment in Italy, the opposite was true. Opera energised life itself. The commitment of composers was matched by a boiling enthusiasm among audiences who would direct all their passions towards the stage, turning the manufactured world of the opera plot into an uplifting portrait of their own feelings. The operatic music of the period is, above all, a thing of vigour: it trumpets the emotions and paints life in rich hues. The triumph of Rossini and, more especially, of Verdi was to take that energy and invest it with musical and dramatic insight and weight so that it acquired a memorable power that lasted long after their time.

Rossini was the pioneer. Imagine him in Milan in 1817, preparing for the first night of *La gazza ladra* (The Thieving Magpie), an opera with all the passion and verve that the audience would expect. On the afternoon of the performance, the overture was still not written. So he was 'imprisoned' – his own word – in the attic of the Teatro alla Scala by four stage carpenters who had instructions from the manager that he shouldn't be allowed out until he had finished it. The pages were passed one by one out of the window to the copyists down below who were writing out the orchestral parts and handing them on in turn to the musicians – who were no doubt a little anxious but not at all surprised. It is one of Rossini's great overtures, sparkling like a piece of polished glass (rather more attractively than the opera as a whole), and that picture at La Scala catches it all. Opera was quick, effervescent, alive.

Rossini, Donizetti and Bellini were the three composers who perfected the *bel canto* style – literally, beautiful singing – and made it wildly popular, in the streets as in the theatres. Everywhere you could hear the cries of distraught lovers, weeping fathers, heroic avengers, heroines driven to madness, though in the beginning Rossini's comedy was his most obvious skill. His ability to write with delicacy and verve, and to turn out beautifully embellished scores, made him famous.

Within a few months of the first of his great operas, *Tancredi* (1813), he produced *L'Italiana in Algieri* for the opera house in Venice, La Fenice (he had written it in less than four weeks) and it was an instant success. Dozens of composers were churning out work for the opera stage but Rossini, aged only twenty-one, was already streaking ahead of the pack.

He was original. One of the problems for composers in Italy was that there were strict assumptions about operatic form. An *opera seria* (dealing with a tragic or high-minded story, unlike the comic *opera buffa*) was expected to have two acts, the first much longer than the other. The ballets which were traditionally inserted as interludes were often impediments, especially those which were an hour long. The singers didn't help. They ruled the roost in the theatres, making demands which would seem extravagant even to the harassed opera managers of today who have had to deal with the more highly strung or grasping of the breed (or both). The famous castrato Luigi Marchesi sometimes demanded that his first entrance should be on horseback on a hilltop – just because he fancied that style of entrance – and he would insist on wearing a plumed helmet with white feathers several feet long, whatever the part he was singing in whatever plot. There were also conventions about the placing, the length and the style of arias that audiences treasured. Woe betide the composer and librettist who broke them.

Rossini was able to surmount such difficulties by sheer brilliance. He could produce music easily. Composing was 'nothing' – he said that it was the rehearsals and the disfigurement of his operas by second-rate singers that brought on his darkest moments. By the time he produced *The Barber of Seville* in 1816 – though it had one of those sticky first nights in Rome – he was in command of his musical voice, though he was still in his mid-twenties. That opera is a masterwork of the comic form of the time, but in the machinations of the guardian Bartolo and the sly Basilio (both stock figures whom the audiences knew intimately) Rossini's music produces a hint of darkness. The froth of the comedy is carried by music that bubbles with mirth, but he adds a layer of understanding that can be heard throughout the capering.

Donizetti and Bellini were born in the decade after Rossini, and the operas of these three composers – more than a hundred of them altogether – were the backbone of the Italian repertoire until Verdi

approached his peak in the 1840s. They had a brilliant polish and
effortless melodic energy. The Sicilian Bellini, though he died when he
was only thirty-three, could write with an ear for a memorable tune and
an instinct for performer and orchestra that allowed singers their
cherished, unforgettable moments. No wonder he was popular with
singers, despite a strong streak of vanity. Verdi was a little snooty about
Bellini's technical skills, saying he was best at the things he couldn't
have learned in the conservatoire and worst at the things he should have
been taught there, but no one could ignore his tuneful invention. In his
last opera, *I puritani* (first performed in Paris in 1835) he displayed his
genius for vocal writing, but it was against the background of an
orchestration that had little of the subtlety that Verdi would introduce.
Bellini's brilliance was in capturing a moment of emotion – anyone
who treasures the recordings of Maria Callas early in her career singing
'Casta diva' from his *Norma* understands how he could write naturally
for any singer with a feeling for hypnotic drama – and he had the ability
to produce a simple melodic line that would hang in the air and stay in
the memory. Rossini was the master of the decorative style; Bellini
treasured clarity.

He was also aware of what his audiences wanted. Though he
wrote only eleven operas, he had an utter certainty about his task. To
one of his librettists, he wrote: 'Carve this in your head in letters of
brass – an opera must draw tears, cause horror, bring death by means
of song. Poetry and music, to make their effect, must be true to
nature, and that is all: anyone who forgets this is lost and will end by
producing a dull, heavy work which can only please the pedants.'
This was not an era for pedantry, at least in the theatre. Opera was
entertainment.

The third member of the gifted trio, Donizetti, was the most prolific.
He wrote more than seventy operas, and he is the link between Rossini
and Bellini, the most dominating of the Italian composers in the 1830s
and 1840s. Much of his work has slipped away, bundled together with
the operas that poured out of lesser composers who were great names in
their day but who have long since been forgotten by all but enthusiasts
for the period. But Donizetti was a giant. Is there anything better in its
style than his *Don Pasquale*, the *opera buffa* first performed in the
Théâtre-Italien in Paris in 1843? The familiar figures of the comic

plot are turned by his music into flesh and blood; their ensembles and duets have a lightness of touch that is magical.

Few of his early operas are heard these days, although the ebb and flow of fashion will no doubt bring them back (it was only in the 1980s that twentieth-century audiences began to become reacquainted with early Verdi, long dismissed as musically too crude for modern perform-ance). Donizetti wrote forty operas before he was thirty-five, often producing three or four a year in Rome, Venice, Palermo, Milan. He had a touch for popular taste. *Anna Bolena*, about Henry VIII's second wife, became a favourite throughout Europe (including London); his comedies, like *L'elisir d'amore*, which has survived in the repertoire, had a touch of elegance and a show-off role for any tenor; and, of course, in a few operas, like *Lucia di Lammermoor*, he produced unforgettable work.

Lucia epitomises much of the operatic spirit of the time. It was first performed at the Teatro San Carlo in Naples in 1834, the year before Bellini died. The plot came from Walter Scott's novel *The Bride of Lammermoor* which had precisely the kind of setting and story that appealed to opera audiences, and gave a composer opportunities. A great family broken by rivalry in love and a lost inheritance, a heroine who is driven to madness and death by the conflict of love and loyalty, a hero who dies at the moment of revenge – this was the stuff that audiences wanted, and it allowed Donizetti to write from the heart. Mad scenes were familiar components of Italian opera: Lucia's is probably the finest of them all. The flute obbligato that accompanies her descent through agony and delusion to death is an unforgettable description of loss; the writing for a soprano with the decorative and coloured vocal style that the Italians now called *coloratura* is majestic. Throughout the score, Donizetti seems able to transform conventional scenes into pieces of high originality. The sextet at the end of Act II in which all the principal characters express first individually and then together their feelings of love, regret and anger is one of the finest setpieces in all nineteenth-century Italian opera.

More than a quarter of a century after Joan Sutherland gave the performance as Lucia at the Royal Opera House, Covent Garden, that established her overnight as an operatic star, she returned to sing the part in the mid-1980s with one of the greatest masters of the *bel canto* tenor repertoire, Carlo Bergonzi, as her lover Edgar. By this time she was nearly sixty; and Bergonzi had left that landmark far behind (the precise date being lost in the traditional mist that singers like to inhabit). Watching them, and to hear an elderly member of audience sobbing regularly throughout the opera (it turned out that she had been present at Sutherland's famous first night in 1959, which shimmered for her still) was to realise how Donizetti's music was the perfect expression of the feelings that opera in Italy was *supposed* to engender. Emotions would be brought to the surface, as they should be.

In 1953, early in the career of Maria Callas, the conductor Herbert von Karajan was given a fragment of tape – with only about three minutes of music – from a recording session with Callas, Tito Gobbi and Giuseppe di Stefano who were producing a disc of *Lucia* under the direction of the maestro of EMI recordings in those days, Walter Legge. Karajan was in Milan, listened to it once and immediately rang La Scala, demanding that a full score should be sent round to his hotel. He then contacted Callas to say to her – perhaps to demand of her – that he would stage and conduct a new production at La Scala, with her singing Lucia. The result was extraordinary. Even for musicians like Karajan whose natural métier was not *bel canto*, the power remained alluring.

There was no heavy pedantry in their operas, and many tears. The young Verdi grew up to this sound, which was the Italians' interpretation of the Romantic spirit, turning stories from the past and familiar historical scenes into contemporary form. The subjects may often have been antique, but opera was talking to its audiences about feelings that were their own. In the bustle and tumble of Italian opera houses – and some remnants of the wild days still survive there – these composers fashioned magic. It might produce a torrent of ecstasy, or a riot, but it would always matter. Rossini said that the people who were putting on the show would be 'tearing out their hair in handfuls' before an opening night. Throughout his professional years in Italy, he said, he noticed that every impresario was bald by the age of thirty.

From this great trio of Italian composers, it was Rossini who made the most important connection abroad, though its immediate consequences were controversial. He went to Paris in 1822, where he was already considered the leading composer of the day, taking with him the wife of the manager of the San Carlo theatre in Naples with whom he'd been having an affair. There, he took over the management of the Théâtre-Italien. Gradually, the idiom so popular across Europe was fused with a French style. The result was even more spectacle and musical richness. It came to be known as grand opera.

When Rossini wrote *Guillaume Tell*, first heard in Paris in 1829 and to a French libretto, it would be his last work for the stage. Remarkably, he never wrote another opera in his remaining forty years or so and his musical output dried up. But this final opera, from the familiar Swiss story of William Tell, the boy, the apple and the arrow, was to influence a generation of French composers. It didn't, however, stop the greatest of them all, Hector Berlioz, from being catty. He said that the overture was a work of enormous talent, so much like genius that it might easily be mistaken for it. Whether or not they thought they were making a mistake, many French composers too saw *Guillaume Tell* as a model of orchestral writing for the stage.

The Italian style had long been popular in France – Luigi Cherubini had dazzled France with *Medea* in the 1790s – and eventually the two styles began to merge. Italians working in Paris discovered that the audiences wanted more spectacle, magnificent sets, rich orchestration and length. It was impossible, it seemed, to go over the top.

Guillaume Tell was suitably long (to the extent that it is often thought by modern opera houses to be a very risky part of the repertoire), but Rossini's writing for the voice was as fresh as ever, and out of the marriage of French and Italian styles came a lusty offspring – opera that was epic in scale and also musically daring. Curiously enough, it was a German who took advantage of it. The Jewish Berliner with the cross-cultural name of Giacomo Meyerbeer (1791–1864) was in Paris at the same time as Rossini (he was almost the same age) and his opera *Robert le diable* announced a new regime at the opera house. It looked forward to epics like *Les Troyens* of Berlioz and further ahead to Verdi's later work, and Meyerbeer's own *Les Huguenots*. Though Wagner couldn't stand Meyerbeer – his operas drove him into a fury because they seemed empty of ideas – he could hardly deny that he himself was influenced by him too.

In Paris there was little of the cacophony of Italy's opera houses where everyone would know the tunes and where the music seemed to flow easily across social divides, down every alleyway (though the popularisation was partly engineered by the managements who encouraged the practice of employing *claques*, the paid bands of spectators given precise instructions about whom to boo and whom to cheer – and when, and how often – the slightly depressing but also comic habit that persists in some Italian theatres to this day). France thought opera should be grander – more serious in some ways – but it needed the spark that came from Italy. That was how the torch was passed on.

Meyerbeer was intoxicated by Rossini in Italy and began by imitating him, but when French taste began to influence him he started to produce opera that despite its stylistic provenance and despite its scale has often been condemned as vacuous and backward-looking. His tableaux were huge, his five-act scores long and heavy, the intervening ballets often irritating in the way that they interrupted the plot, and his obsession with the epic scene often ridiculous. In *Le Prophète*, for example, he gave his audience a ballet on skates, a full coronation with all the trimmings and a gigantic explosion (sparing them the underwater ballet from *Les Huguenots*). In *L'Africaine* he wanted the wreck of Vasco da Gama's ship to be portrayed as realistically as possible on the stage. He was popular, however, and from this style there developed remarkable works – it is likely that without it Berlioz would not have produced his ambitious and stunning opera inspired by Virgil, *Les Troyens* (the second part of which was performed first in 1863, and the earlier part not until after the composer's death).

By the time Meyerbeer's *Le Prophète* was staged in Paris, at the height of his fame in 1849, Verdi was conquering audiences in Italy and entering his prime. The first version of *Macbeth* (1847) was behind him and, from his early operas, *Nabucco* (1842) was established as a favourite. It seemed that every Italian knew the inspiring anthem he wrote for the Hebrew slaves in Act III ('Va, pensiero'), with words drawn from Psalm 137, which was associated with the nationalist sentiment that was sweeping the country in the 1840s. Though Verdi drew on the operatic explosions in Paris – he discussed them with Rossini, whom he regarded as a father-figure – he was already on a path that was his own, which would lead him towards uplands that eluded Meyerbeer and his fellow 'grand' composer in Paris, Jacques Halévy.

Verdi had started to compose for the organ as a boy. He was refused entry to the Milan conservatoire – a blot that still casts a shadow over it – but by the time he was in his mid-twenties he had managed to sell some songs and the opera *Oberto* (1839) to La Scala. The association with that theatre would last for more than sixty years and make their names inseparable. The Via Verdi runs past the theatre today. His early career had ups and downs and it took *Nabucco* to carry his name abroad. But in the decade afterwards he became the master of the musical stage.

In the early 1850s the intermittent successes of his early life turned into a blaze of glory. In two years he produced *Rigoletto* (1851), *Il Trovatore* (1853) and *La Traviata* (1853), three operas that sustain opera-house seasons round the world to this day. The first two were more or less immediate successes, but *Traviata* had to endure one of those peculiarly Italian experiences when it was first staged in Venice. The preparations had been undermined by Verdi's difficulties with some of the singers, and his forebodings proved accurate. Throughout its run (after a first night at which it had been booed) it attracted thin houses and the baritone who sang the part of Germont *père*, the father of Alfredo, Violetta's lover, was just as much of an irritant as Verdi had predicted. He noted that at one performance there was no applause at all after Act III (an observation that is very hard to believe) but a curtain call for the composer, perhaps because he was known to be leaving Venice the next day.

It did not take long, however, for *Traviata* to become loved. Its vivid orchestration, a heroine's role that gives the singer the opportunity to create a different aspect of Violetta's character in each of the three acts and a supply of memorable melody soon gave the story of the tragic courtesan its proper place. With Rigoletto himself, Violetta is a Verdian character with a texture that pointed the way forward to his later operas in which he was able to write in a manner that seemed quite different from the simpler, more familiar figures of his earlier work, and from most of the operas written by even such gifted composers as Donizetti.

Verdi was making his own way. When he went to Paris in the year of *Traviata's* first performance he was still not regarded in the same way as Meyerbeer, whose works were the staple diet of the opera houses, and he had to work hard. When he wrote *Aida* to celebrate the opening of the Suez Canal a few years later – the first performance was in 1871 – there was still that sense of pageantry and procession. The formality of the victory parades is an important part of the architecture of the opera. Yet it combines that with intimacy, which is set against the pageantry of wars, victories and divided loyalties. When the lovers Aida and Radames are entombed in the last scene, their fate sealed in stone, it's the end of a drama that has been intensely personal from the beginning, the characters emerging from a score that is seductively sinuous as well as grand. And with *Otello*, finished in 1886, Verdi attained a new level of subtlety. As when the cellos introduce the great love duet at the end of Act I, and Otello and Desdemona are gripped by the love that will destroy them both, Verdi produces a certain magic for the stage; Iago's own description of his jealous and vengeful nature is a baritone's dream.

Verdi journeyed from the heroism and the brilliant vigour of the choruses of his early operas to a sensitivity that seemed entirely his own. By now Richard Wagner was staging his Ring, having been striving for a different kind of opera for nearly four decades, and Verdi understood. After the première of *Aida*, he wrote that he was pleased that the success of the opera was, as he put it, 'frank and decided – not poisoned by ifs and buts and dreadful talk about Wagnerism, The Future, The Art of Melody etc. The audience surrendered to its impressions and applauded. That's all!'

Verdi was looking to the future in his own way, and in his last opera – *Falstaff* – he went out in a blaze of glory. It was one of only two comedies that Verdi composed. There are no setpiece arias; the orchestra and the voices are fused with the effervescence and lightness that were his most brilliant characteristics. He wrote duets, trios and sextets with vitality and ease – and managed to give the slapstick of Shakespeare's *Merry Wives of Windsor*, from which his librettist Boito fashioned the plot, a dash of melancholy as well as fun. At the climax, the principals sing a fugue to words of benign wisdom – a kind of farewell to the operatic stage by one of its greatest masters.

Verdi had long worked on ideas for an operatic version of *King Lear*, though he never started it in earnest. His reverence for Shakespeare was important to him, because he understood the purpose of opera to be to create on the stage a texture that was as rich as the work of the best dramatists. *Falstaff*'s brilliance lies in its many-layered understanding of character. The sad buffoon himself is as full and rounded as Shakespeare's own conception in *Henry IV*, with a personality in music that catches the sadness beneath the fun. As Verdi worked on it, he wrote in a letter to his publisher, Giulio Ricordi – rather ridiculously – that he was doing it 'to while away the time'. That was far from the truth; he was working on an homage to Shakespeare that had been in the making for nearly fifty years and doing so in an idiom that looked forward, not back.

Verdi's attitude to his inheritance and the particular spirit of Italy is revealed in a letter he wrote to an admirer (unnamed) in 1878, between *Aida* and *Otello*. He's despairing about the fashion for the vocal quartet – a craze at the time – which he thinks might be the ruin of opera. He goes on:

> We cannot, I would even say we should not, write like the Germans, or the Germans like us. If the Germans sometimes borrow certain of our qualities, as Haydn and Mozart did in their day, while still remaining faithful to the quartet; if Rossini even took over certain forms from Mozart, while still remaining a melodist – all well and good; but to give up our qualities to suit the fashion, out of a mania for novelty or the affectation of learning – to renounce our art, our instinct, our sure, spontaneous, natural sensitive way of doing things, our bright sparkle, is absurd and foolish . . .

Falstaff wasn't following fashion, but was an original conception. It reminds audiences of how far Verdi had come, from the straightforward stand-and-sing arias of his early operas, with their magnificent choral backdrops, to a pattern of inspired and complicated musical needle-work. The picture is always clear, but the detail is rich and compelling. They were his last notes for the operatic stage. He died in 1901 in the same week as Queen Victoria, after a stroke in the Grand Hotel, Milan, a composer who started to write in the age of Rossini and was still producing opera long after his exact contemporary Wagner was dead. He was a genius of the theatre, reflecting the turbulence of his time in Italy and stirring the passions of those who were caught in the heart of it. Verdi showed how opera can create its own world – beautiful, touching, heroic, intimate – and be a mirror of the world beyond the theatre doors, capturing the 'still, sad music of humanity' as well as its glory.

When he died, they filled the streets of Milan around La Scala, which had been temple and playground for his music for so long; and, as his coffin passed, the crowd sang, unprompted, the chorus that had anchored him in the life of his country, 'Va, pensiero' from *Nabucco*. He grew up in an Italy which was a collection of warring states, lived through the battles between them and the campaigns of Garibaldi and Cavour to pull them together, saw Victor Emmanuel crowned king of a more or less united country and survived into a century when the Italian Republic, though plagued by melodramatic politics and a flash of fascism, would celebrate a common cultural legacy.

Around him, in his last year, Italy was enjoying the fashion of *verismo*, which was a natural offspring of the opera. Verdi was already ahead of it, more subtle and forward looking in his musical imagination, but it was the popular form that was helping to introduce new generations to music on stage. The style was the rage of the last few years of the nineteenth century in Italy, a *fin de siècle* fashion for rustics, ruffians and raw emotion. As if in preparation for the movies a generation later, operas began to deal with the grainy messiness of life, presenting their characters as flesh-and-blood people we might know ourselves.

The wellspring of *verismo* was a little Sicilian short story by Giovanni Verga which inspired Mascagni to produce *Cavalleria rusticana*. Later came Leoncavallo's *Pagliacci*, its inseparable partner for life – they're still yanked together in the repertoire – and they remain the essential evidence of what the *verismo* style produced, an unashamed simplicity that revelled in its emotional directness. Verdi, moving towards the end of his life, liked *Cavalleria rusticana*, saying that Mascagni had invented 'a most effective genre – short operas without pointless longueurs'. Leaving aside the fact that there are plenty of short operas from the turn of the century that still incorporate longueurs, and lots of pointlessness (brevity being no guarantee of taste or genius), Verdi understood that there was something in the speed and the cut of these plots that gave the operas a certain energy.

Take Umberto Giordano's best-known opera, *Andrea Chénier*. Though it uses older conventions to build its plot, set in the French Revolution – aristocrats and poets, the sound of great events that are shaking the world beyond the windows – it has the style that was becoming so popular, and tries to deal with emotions in a way that somehow seemed more personal than would have been the case a generation earlier. The problem has been that sometimes the *verismo* composers, in trying to maintain musical concentration, seem to jump rather too fast without the sustaining theme that carries you through. In *Chénier*, Giordano is saved by his last act, in which Chénier the poet at least seems truly poetic and has the chance to carry off as nicely turned an aria as a tenor can come across. Plácido Domingo, for example, has given it many outings, understanding the opportunity it provides. The hero's duet with Maddalena, the Countess's daughter who has decided to die with him, is a worthy climax. So it is an opera that does not fade; it blooms. This is what distinguishes it from *Fedora*, the only other of Giordano's operas still fairly well known, which acts as a reasonable vehicle for a decent tenor but is somehow an opera without guts.

The *verismo* operas are natural crowd-pullers if they are played with verve. They were meant to be played for lively audiences, spilling across the floor in some small-town theatre, who might join in a familiar chorus or chuck a vegetable at a tenor who cracked on a high note. They were supposed to deal with emotions that the audience recognised in themselves. Even if the setting was remote, and the events historical, they would be people who seemed real. That was the conceit of the style; it allowed directness.

The result was therefore often an almost naive construction. In *Chénier*, for example, the scene is set for an exploration of the feelings that might boil up between the servants in the Countess's home and her aristocratic friends, with the arrival of the dashing poet an unexpected and unpredictable catalyst. Yet the story remains one-dimensional. Think of the subtleties Beaumarchais gave da Ponte and Mozart for their *Figaro* in his play, and how deep the layers become as the twenty-four hours of festivities, tricks and deceits unfold. Such operas as *Andrea Chénier* exist on a humbler plane. Yet if there is little genius, there is plenty of theatrical flair.

Chénier was spotted by the publisher Sonzongo as the kind of opera with which he could put one over on his rival Ricordi, and when it was first seen at La Scala in 1896 it was duly a hit. It zipped round Europe in the next decade, arriving in Manchester in 1903 and in London two years later. In New York, especially, it has been an exceptionally popular piece and many of the great tenors have kept it in their

repertoire as a sure standby. It was a particular favourite of Beniamino
Gigli, one of the twentieth century's most celebrated lyric tenors. They
enjoyed it, of course, because it gave them an opportunity for a grand
flourish in the last act, under the shadow of the guillotine, and there was
a certain crudity built into the style. One of the critics who admired
Giordano said of his (little-seen) opera *Mala vita*, dealing with street life
in Naples, that 'in its merciless truthfulness to life it is both gripping and
revolting at the same time, like most of these realistic pieces'.

The German Romantics were the real bridge to the twentieth
century, but there was something in *verismo* that also led forward –
away from the distant and remote world of kings and emperors, strange
potentates and their exotic retinues, to the world around, which turned
out to be just as suitable a subject for serious opera. If it had not been for
the popularity of *verismo*, would we have got Puccini?

There is a photograph of Giacomo Puccini in his villa at Torre del
Lago in Tuscany, sitting at his (upright) piano, in which he has the air of
a slightly louche American in the late 1920s. He sits back with his hat at
a rakish angle, an electric light on the table beside him, the scene
distinctly twentieth century, and a jumble around him that seems to
have little to do with the previous century. It's often said of him that if
he had lived for another decade he would have been the master of the
cinema score, something which he would not have spurned. As it was,
he died in 1924, aged sixty-three, but as well as stretching back to the
era of Verdi in his prime, Puccini was a modern figure. In the score of
his opera set in the Wild West, *La fanciulla del West* – first heard at the
Metropolitan Opera in New York in 1910 – you hear a composer who
had the gift of compression and drama in a modern idiom.

He could sprinkle the *verismo* form with magic dust and become a
natural composer for a twentieth-century audience that understood
how a story might be told on celluloid, at great speed with scene
changes so fast that you hardly noticed them. A series of images of the
characters could be placed on top of one another in minutes, so that a
composite picture sprang out, with many dimensions. In music,
Puccini understood that skill. Lesser characters like Giordano lacked
the capacity for such brilliant alchemy, though they had pushed opera
forward. Theirs were enormously popular pieces, for the good reason
that they were touching and full blooded and they gave you what you

had come for, a good night in the theatre. But they needed a Puccini to blaze a new trail.

Verdi was able to soar above the *verismo* composers who came into vogue in his later years, but they shared an understanding of how opera on the stage has to work through its ruthless exploitation of the moment. Puccini inherited the gift. A heartbreak, a deceit, a tragic understanding of betrayal or loss – they are the points of the compass for the composer who must turn a complicated emotional pattern into the linear story which has to move across the stage and carry the audience with it. Keep it moving, keep fingertip control of the pace, time the climaxes – the secrets of so much operatic writing, even if you take 'realism' to a new level like Leoš Janáček or are concerned above all with an intellectual argument like Richard Strauss.

At the end of a century in which Italian audiences had luxuriated in the brilliance of Rossini, Bellini, Donizetti and then Verdi himself, they were ready for rather different kinds of heroes. These were just as majestic in their way, and certainly as much the mesmerising focus of attention, as their predecessors were in the opera of earlier days. But they seemed to have a different kind of encounter with their audiences, something more direct and gritty than had once been the fashion.

Puccini took naturally to that style. *Tosca* (1900) is a *verismo* opera – his most obvious inheritance from the style – but one that rises far above the throng. Though it was famously described as a shabby little shocker on its first outing, its resilience has a simple explanation, a score that combines brilliant melodic originality with a pace and depth that avoids any of those longueurs. Bernard Shaw saw *Manon Lescaut* in London in 1894 and hailed Puccini as Verdi's natural successor; with *La Bohème* two years later, he was established as the master of the lyric score; and after *Tosca*, he moved away from the *verismo* style which he'd taken on and perfected in that piece and reached forward, combining his life-long fascination with the consequences of intense love affairs with a fascination for the exotic.

His last opera, unfinished, was *Turandot*. At the first performance at La Scala, the conductor, Arturo Toscanini, decided not to play the ending that had been added by the composer Franco Alfano, pieced together from Puccini's musical sketches for the climax to the story, to make the point that a life had been cut short. Instead, it ended with the death of Liu, the girl who loves the hero Calaf and whose tragedy is entwined with that of the Ice Princess, Turandot. Only on the next night was the completed version performed.

Puccini was Verdi's heir, and the inheritor of the rich tradition of nineteenth-century Italian opera. It was lusty enough to survive throughout the new century, and though some Italians complain that the generation of today has lost the natural affection for the melodrama and the melodies of Donizetti or Verdi – no longer do the beggars of Naples, still there in vast numbers, whistle an aria from Rossini – there is a legacy that hasn't yet been squandered in its entirety.

Audiences at La Scala still behave badly, and still know their opera. Callas and her successors in the second half of the twentieth century still perpetuated the sometimes infuriating but often uplifting tradition of the singer who gives up a life for the stage, like Tosca herself. From the rough cheerfulness of the open-air audiences in the Roman arena in Verona, where all the leading singers have performed to the thousands who cluster through the summer under the stars, to the glitzy socialites at La Scala or La Fenice the memory of one of Italy's greatest loves is still celebrated. In the history of music-making, that infatuation and the brilliance it spawned in singers and conductors, as well as composers, is a surviving jewel that continues to sparkle, a treasure that is Italy's own.

12

Wagner the Revolutionary

The Battle for Ideas in Music

~

ON A MODEST green hill outside a little town in Franconia, north-east of Nuremberg, there stands a theatre that looks now much as it did when it opened in 1876. The auditorium has a distinctive keystone shape – it is a Greek amphitheatre deep in Germany – so that its whole vast stage can be seen from every seat and the orchestra pit is hooded and sinks so low that the players and conductor are invisible to the audience. The auditorium was constructed so that the sound, especially from the brass, has a full, blooming quality that is uniquely its own.

It is now a place treated with reverence by many opera-goers, as if they were on a pilgrimage and drawn to a shrine. Richard Wagner intended nothing less. His opera *Parsifal*, composed with the acoustics of the theatre in mind, was described by him as a Stage-Consecrating Festival-Play, meant to produce an experience that was like a religious transformation. In his theatre at Bayreuth, crafted meticulously for his own purposes, he was fomenting a revolution.

You could say that he has been causing trouble ever since. No composer's name evokes the same potent mix of adoration and distaste. He was a dominating force and a contrary spirit whose shadow and profile – that aquiline nose, the flowing wave of hair – are stamped on the musical story that followed him, because of what he did. It was as if he represented the energy of the Germany that was coming together, forged in the fire of the nationalism that was sweeping across Europe, victorious in the Franco-Prussian war of 1870–1, supremely confident by the time the theatre opened.

It hardly looked like a revolution on that first night in August 1876, when Kaiser Wilhelm I was part of the crowd that came up the hill to hear the first complete performance of the cycle of operas that had consumed twenty-six years of Wagner's life, his Ring of the Nibelung which he'd begun more than three decades before. Bayreuth was the summation of Wagner's strivings; he wanted it to represent the sacred place of art. This was opera that would rise above the commercial and the trite – bold, all consuming, music and drama fused together, displaying the work that Wagner had been producing since the 1840s. It would cement the purposes and the style of a Germany only recently unified and victorious in war – confident, majestic, universal in its vision. The celebration, however, also had a subversive purpose. The works of Wagner which would be heard there were about change, the arrival of a different style, and about the composer as philosopher – the argument that he'd been making for half his life, embodied in the extraordinary boldness of an early opera like *Tannhäuser* (1845) and then *Tristan und Isolde* (1859), quite apart from the Ring cycle itself.

The theatre was designed to help the audience to have a different experience. Performances would begin in utter darkness, the hood over the orchestra preventing even a flicker of light from a musician's stand to enter the auditorium. Then, they might hear the first low E flat of *Das Rheingold*, the opera which Wagner had finished in 1854, and be drawn immediately into the waters of the Rhine by these opening siren sounds and the entreaties of the Rhine maidens guarding their horde of magic gold. Wagner said the start of the opera came to him in a dream, and his purpose was to create a different universe in which the Ring saga would unfold, untroubled by the contemporary, where gods of war and fire and thunder would tangle with dwarves and giants and the power of magic gold, to work out a human story of greed, ambition and lost love. Over four days, and more than fifteen hours of music, they would be transported into the realm of ideas and higher things, leaving all else behind. So he thought.

That was why Wagner was revolutionary. Composers for the next couple of generations would bear his mark. He wrote for bigger opera orchestras than anyone before him and made demands on singers that meant only the strong could survive. It was as if he were laying down a challenge to all who would follow him: it's only on this scale that music should be heard. When *Die Meistersinger* was first performed in 1868 it was a sounding board for throbbing German nationalism, and a vast celebration of how art is sustained and nurtured by innovation and originality – which was the composer's obsession. No one exceeded him in his enthusiasm for taking himself, and his mission, seriously. In one letter to the composer Franz Liszt, whose daughter, Cosima, Wagner would marry, he described his own attitude to his craft: 'I cannot live like a dog. I cannot bed in straw or satisfy my soul with gin. Mine is a highly susceptible, intense, voracious yet uncommonly sensitive and fastidious sensuality, which must somehow or other be flattered if my mind is to accomplish the agonising labour of calling a non-existent world into being.'

From an early age – he was born in Leipzig in 1813 – he searched for the truth about art through philosophy, believing that he was no 'mere' composer but a thinker who would find a method for the transmission of his ideas through music. His orchestral work is limited, most of his energy going into opera because he felt it was his task in life to reinvent music drama. His early opera *Rienzi* (1840) sounded conventional, and its popularity used to irritate him. He wanted to dig deeper. With *Tannhäuser* (1845) he began to expand his horizons and *Lohengrin* (1848) was the opera that preceded the writing of two parts of the Ring. He had found his territory, where love, religion and fate might mingle.

Die Meistersinger (1867) is the only one of Wagner's operas that uses humour, but it is a significant work – an enormous, glowing canvas which taxes any opera company that tries to roll it out. The story is of inspiration, craftsmanship and achievement. The hero, Walter, becomes the pride of Nuremberg with his prize song that wins admiration as well as the heroine. Art is revealed as the highest craft of all. Yet the opera is more than a celebration of the new Germany (the good cobbler Hans Sachs singing at the end about the need to protect the nation against foreign invaders). The Meistersinger themselves, the masters of the craft guilds, are bogged down in their traditions – pointed up by the pernickety and infuriating clerk, Beckmesser – and Walter, who is an aristocratic outsider, is in part a challenger to their settled ways, much as Wagner saw himself as a revolutionary force who could release powers that had lain hidden. On to the background of an admirable and robust German culture, Wagner projects some awkward thoughts.

He saw himself as being on a crusade. He had joined the European revolutions on the barricades in Dresden – in 1849, a year after they'd begun in France – raging against the old order, and when he came back from a Swiss exile to write at the court of Ludwig II in Bavaria, Bismarck was trying to unite Germany. Bavaria was not yet a part of it. The Iron Chancellor wanted to give the new nation a voice, an aspiration which Wagner shared. But it was a struggle. After Bayreuth opened, Bismarck stayed away. He couldn't stand Wagner.

For Wagner, there always seemed to be disdain as well as praise. For everyone who cherished him there was someone who would complain. Tchaikovsky said the Ring was 'endlessly and wearisomely spun out'. From the very start there were those who found the physical effort too much and began the series of jokes about the length of the operas that goes on still – you know a Wagner opera because it starts at five o clock, you sit in the dark for an hour and a half, look at your watch and it's ten past five.

These are not simply modern insults, hurled back down the years. The philosopher Friedrich Nietzsche, writing in 1888, said that he refused to hide behind aesthetic formulae in explaining his objections to Wagner's music. They were physiological: '. . . I breathe with difficulty as soon as Wagner's music begins to act upon me. I say that my foot gets annoyed and rebels against the music; my foot wants rhythm, dancing, marching. The rhythm of Wagner's *Kaisermarsch* keeps even the young emperor from marching in time with it.' He then complains about the state of his stomach, his throat and even his bowels. Enough said.

Wagner's demands were immense, on singers as well as audiences. The great soprano Birgit Nilsson – with Kirsten Flagstad, one of the towering Brünnhildes of the modern era – was once asked what was required of a singer in *Tristan und Isolde*, and replied, 'A pair of comfortable shoes.'

Yet, from the first, Wagner cast a spell. In the darkness of the Bayreuth theatre he demanded concentration. An audience for the Ring was expected to treat it as it might a religious festival. There were long intervals for rest and contemplation between acts; the performances were timed to avoid late-night restlessness. By the time Brünnhilde was engulfed in flames at the end of *Götterdämmerung*, with the destruction of Valhalla and of the rule of the gods, Wagner intended all of life to be laid bare and, especially, the consequences of greed and betrayal to be explained at least as clearly as they would in the course of a religious service.

The Ring, its story rooted in Norse and German mythology, tells the story of the disintegration of the power of the gods as a result of greed. *Das Rheingold* opens with the theft of the all-powerful gold from the Rhine by Alberich, who is happy to renounce love in exchange for its power, forging the omnipotent ring and cursing it when it is taken by Wotan, chief of the gods. Through the four operas a saga develops that is universal – dealing with the enduring themes of love and greed, frailty and deceit. It is also a drama that has a strange intimacy despite the grandeur of its subject and a setting that encompasses the world of the gods as well as that of men (and many generations of them too). At one level, it is a family drama; at another a struggle for universal power. The first act of *Die Walküre*, the second opera, is one of the most erotic conceptions in music history – presenting the meeting, and incestuous falling in love, of a brother and sister who don't know each other; the death of the hero Siegfried is a scene of monumental power; Brünn-hilde's immolation at the end of *Götterdämmerung* is one of the great climaxes of all opera. The libretto may be dense (it was written by Wagner himself) but the force of the story and its musical realisation are incomparable.

His influence on composers who followed him was prodigious, and he became the transition between the Romantics who followed Beethoven and the music that would announce the opening of the next century. As a character, of course, he was a mixture of high seriousness and emotionalism. Though he was fastidious in many respects, he had a voracious sensuality – enjoying several affairs at once, living high on the hog's back when he could, swinging from poverty and obscurity in his youth to fame and notoriety after he succeeded as a conductor in the 1840s and began, as a self-taught composer, to try to reinvent opera (as he put it himself).

And just as Bismarck tried to stamp the spirit of Prussia on the new Germany, Wagner turned himself into the Composer Who Couldn't Be Ignored. Every philosopher, musician, artist wanted to come to Bayreuth, to sit in the dark and hear the different texture of sound that Wagner seemed to have conjured up for himself from the depths of the Rhine, where, he appeared to suggest, German myth and legend lay ready for reawakening. As Brünnhilde dies in the flames, and the gods' power is dissolved at the end of the Ring – every theme, the leitmotifs that accompany characters and their possessions through the story, seems to recur and resolve itself in the merciless light of the fire.

The power of that music is intoxicating, and Wagner's genius lies in the grip he can exert. But it's proved a dangerous power, almost as if emotions at that intensity are too much. Nietzsche, who for part of his life was in thrall to Wagner before his feet, his stomach and the rest of him started to complain, said that artists and intellectuals should always be wary of attracting disciples. Wagner has been Exhibit Number 1 in the ranks of those who have suffered at the hands of posthumous admirers. Where philosophers and kings once climbed the hill at Bayreuth, Nazis would later revere him, almost as an alternative deity, with Hitler leading the obeisance and the celebration of a mystic national power that was thought to flow from the scores of his operas.

The excuse – the glib justification – was Wagner's anti-Semitism, about which there can be no argument. As early as 1850 he wrote, in his essay *Judaism in Music*, that it was not possible for Jewish artists to be other than shallow and artificial. They had no connection with the wellsprings of true German culture. He imbibed with relish the nineteenth-century prejudices that turned the Jew into the interloper, the destructive force, the enemy. It is not hard, either, to find traces of that instinct in the Ring. Many people sensitive to the caricature of the Jew find it hard to look squarely at Alberich, the ugly dwarf who steals the gold from the Rhine maidens, renouncing love to get the power and eventually wreaking destruction on everything. For many it has poisoned his music. When Daniel Barenboim insisted that it be played in a concert he conducted in Israel – breaking a custom that had nearly the force of law – he found deep resistance to the idea that the music had a greatness beyond the narrowness of Wagner's anti-Jewish prejudice. The association with those who'd marched to the rallies at Nuremberg to the sound of his music has been difficult to break.

Photographs from 1939 show Hitler at Bayreuth a few weeks before the invasion of Poland, with the ambitions of the Third Reich well advanced and the persecution of the Jews under way, celebrating the healthiness of German culture by listening to Wagner. He sports a fedora, receives flowers from blonde, pink-faced girls as he leads a party to his box. He would have ranked no composer higher, and the Wagner family were part of the circle that rejoiced in the association between the composer's nationalism and the 'new' Germany of the 1930s. It is a miserable story.

Yet put Wagner in his surroundings, think of the Germany that was being born – which seemed to him good and devoted to the highest purposes – and you rediscover a musician who wanted to prove that in sweet sounds there could be ideas; that music could fulfil its destiny and elevate those who heard it. This wasn't relaxation or escape, it was absorption in the essence of things – when you heard Tristan and Isolde confronting the serpentine knot of love and death, or Wotan, the chief of the gods, discovering that even the greatest power can be broken by greed, you were made to think. Wagner would want everyone going to one of his operas today to have in mind his volumes on philosophy, artistic theory and politics (there are dozens of them). Almost no one does, because the truth is that Wagner was right: he could say it best in sound. At the beginning of *Tristan und Isolde* there is a famous chord – it is built on the notes F, B D sharp and G sharp – which creates the atmosphere of longing that is the theme of the opera.

The chord is not resolved as the ear might expect – its dissonances are left hanging in a gentle torment. The philosophy of Schopenhauer, which greatly attracted Wagner, embraces the idea of eternal frustration, the longing for something that can't be had. At the heart of the opera is the *Liebestod* – literally, love and death – a fusion of the emotions that grip the lovers, a climactic passage treasured by many who would not risk spending a whole evening in his company – though Wagner has the capacity to exert a surprisingly strong hold over some of those who first approach him with scepticism.

Tristan is an opera that seems miraculous. The atmosphere produced by the opening chord, which Wagner turns into a musical backdrop, is never broken. The characters are few, the action long drawn out, but in a sensitive production, in which a conductor produces the texture in the orchestra that illuminates every emotion and every glance, it is as absorbing as some all-action drama. Giuseppe Verdi said that he stood in 'wonder and terror' before *Tristan* and even the composer Grieg, who'd complained about 'ceaseless modulations and wearying chromaticism' in Wagner's music, said after he heard the Ring that he'd come 'face to face with the greatest that the music drama of this century has given us'. He said Liszt was right when he spoke of Wagner as 'a Mont Blanc above all the other Alps'.

That mountain has often proved a hard climb. Like everything worth while, it takes time and effort. Wagner was remarkable in making that challenge on an epic scale. He matured in the ferment of mid-nineteenth-century Europe in which the stirrings of nationalism were the weft and weave of the time. The climax he engineered in his own place – that small town of Bayreuth, chosen in part because it wasn't grand or important – was meant to be a surprise, because it would (he hoped) transform that story into a new kind of art on the stage.

Wagner himself referred to the final scene in *Tristan* not as the *Liebestod*, but as the *Verklärung*, which means transfiguration. He envisaged the obstructions of the world passing away and some transcendent power taking over. In Isolde's last phrases, the chord that established unease in the prelude and whose dissonance gave the opera its musical character is resolved at last. It comes in the final bars. Isolde sings two F sharps an octave apart, the oboe plays D sharp, which gives the phrase a certain sweetness, and the orchestra brings the opera to an end on the chord of B major, which was lurking in the prelude itself, waiting to be reached and casting an aural shadow over the opera. Everything has been a struggle, and now it is over.

Wagner's boldness on the stage was revolutionary and magisterial. No one had heard operas on such a scale before. The lumbering acts of Meyerbeer or Halévy had none of the concentration or daring of Wagner: where they would turn to spectacle for effect, and punctuate the opera with diversions to gratify the audience, he would have none of it. In *Lohengrin* or *Parsifal* he was brave enough to ask an audience to watch a stage for long periods in which almost nothing happens at all. The action takes place in the music.

In the Ring he dispensed with nearly all the conventions for telling an operatic story. Instead of duets, trios and large ensembles with chorus he gave his characters a score in which each is an individual narrator. They seldom sing together, though when they do it therefore carries special weight. Instead each carries the story on: Wotan greedy for power just as Alberich lusts for wealth when he steals the gold;

Siegfried, the hero born of incest, who finds love with Brünnhilde but seals it with the ring that bears the curse of the man who abandoned love to get it; above all Brünnhilde herself, whose immolation at the end of the fourth opera is an act of sacrifice that frees the world of its shadows because she has taken the sins of the gods upon herself.

The monumental arch of the operas, like the rainbow bridge that leads the gods to their new lair in Valhalla at the end of *Das Rheingold*, has its foundations in the orchestra. Nervous opera-goers who approach the Ring for the first time are often given the (wise) advice by old-timers to let the music speak and think of the characters almost as parts of the orchestra. It is the most obvious truth about Wagner, that in his construction of these music dramas he was determined to abandon the familiar pattern in which emphasis shifts between singer and orchestra. Although there are moments of soaring drama on stage – Wotan's farewell to Brünnhilde in *Die Walküre*, Siegfried's death in *Götterdämmerung* – they are inseparable from the music emerging from the pit, music which has at no stage been a brilliant accompaniment, but is always part of the action. At the deaths of Brünnhilde and Siegfried, or when Wotan takes his leave, Wagner's fusion of the characters' leitmotifs – their very personalities – with the sweep of their fate produces an orchestral richness that has hardly any rivals in the story of opera.

It is easy to argue about the text in the Ring, weighed down by obscure and dense references and archaic style, or to complain about the difficulty of giving the action a proper setting that can fit Wagner's conception (which leads to so many productions that leave audiences puzzled or seething), but it's a majestic creation – huge and intimate at the same time, and constantly perplexing, challenging, revealing. What more can you want in music?

When the French director Patrice Chéreau took on the Ring at Bayreuth in 1976, with the modernist Pierre Boulez as conductor, he produced one of the most famous settings of recent times, and a first night to remember. Traditionalists at Bayreuth – more comfortable with gods clad in horned helmets standing on rocky promontories with rivers running by and great clouds behind – were appalled by the modernist setting (with all the references to the early industrial age in which Wagner was writing) and by a reading of the operas that emphasised human feelings of love and jealousy among gods and men alike – interpreting the drama as a story that worked best when it came down to earth. To make matters worse, Boulez worked with a smaller orchestra than Bayreuth audiences expected. The festival director Wolfgang Wagner, the composer's grandson, was at the centre of a demonstration by those who hated it and those who loved it, a demonstration so lively that his new wife had her dress ripped and another woman with him had an earring ripped off (complete, it's said, with earlobe). At Bayreuth, the Ring was not to be tampered with.

But of course it survived. The truth about these operas is that, although they are capable of being diminished and cheapened by a messy production, they respond if care is taken with them. By the time Chéreau's cycle had its last run at Bayreuth in 1980 it had become a pillar of modern opera production, the model for the next generation. Since that time almost no opera house in the world has for a moment considered returning to the mouldy wigs and breastplates of yesteryear. On the last night of that Bayreuth *Götterdämmerung* there was a ninety-minute standing ovation and someone counted 110 curtain calls for the cast. Wagner's conception and the vastness of his musical landscape invite adventure.

You can only think of him as someone who was riding the tide of a new Germany. In *Die Meistersinger*, the benign and commanding Sachs sings this:

> Beware! Dangerous times now threaten all;
> If we Germans should ever fall
> In thrall to any foreign land,
> No prince will understand his people
> And foreign mists will blind our eyes . . .

Sachs is a good man, but he sees the enemy at the gate. So did Wagner. His wife Cosima recorded in her diary that he saw the humiliation of the French in the Franco-Prussian war of 1870–1 as a dream, like his happiness with her and his son. These were times when even those who spoke of music as the highest calling did so against the background of a scramble for national ascendancy, and struggle for pride.

You hear there the voice of her husband, who conjured up spirits from the vasty deep, set stages and orchestra pits that were bigger than anyone had known, and insisted on only the widest canvases for the ideas that he wanted to translate into music. He would have a continuous stream of music, all evening long. And he would create something that was at least in part the culmination of the turmoil that he'd known all his life, since he was born in the twilight of the Napoleonic age.

Wagner, whose reputation nurtures such conservatism, was a revolutionary spirit: and when he laid the first stone at Bayreuth on a wet and windy night in 1872 and the building of his temple began, he was inaugurating a quest – and an adventure – that has gone on ever since and should be celebrated without recourse to the simplistic and unfair straw man of Hitler. It was as if he'd discovered a new piece of territory in the age of empire – wild, uncolonised, ripe for conquest. Moved by the same forces that were shaping a new country around him, and giving it ambitions for power and glory, he set a course for composers – and for music – from Gustav Mahler to Claude Debussy to Dmitri Shostakovich to Britten, that none could ignore. From the strange world of Valhalla, the gods' home high in the mountains, they heard the mournful but inspiring message of Siegfried's funeral music when a hero was laid to rest, and found, as they were meant to, that it couldn't be resisted or forgotten.

Wagner, accused of high treason after joining the 1849 uprising, was a radical and an innovator. His idea of music as all encompassing, art that might encircle the world, was an effort to carry the story forward; he was restless and ambitious. In Germany, where the debate about the place of music was at its most passionate and where the symphonic tradition was taking root most deeply, it is inevitable that he should be seen as being the opposite of one of the other giants of his age, Johannes Brahms. Their relationship is much more complex, but the contrast is not entirely unfair. First of all, Brahms didn't like Wagner's music. He was a musician who gave the impression of not having to struggle, though that was an illusion. Technically, he was commanding. His friend Robert Schumann said of him in admiration that he had arrived 'fully armed, like Athena from the head of Zeus'.

Brahms was born in Hamburg in northern Germany in 1833 and though he left school at fifteen he quickly established himself as a musician of rare talent. However, when he was introduced to Liszt, and to the progressive musicians around him at the court of Weimar, he felt uncomfortable. He was only twenty when he travelled to Düsseldorf on the advice of the concert-master at the Weimar court to visit Robert Schumann, who was then in his early forties. Schumann lived with his wife, Clara (Wieck), the famous pianist who was the daughter of his first teacher and whom he had met when she was only fifteen. Brahms became something of a protégé, Schumann writing an article declaring that the younger man was the true representative of the best of the coming generation.

The music they championed came, of course, from the same roots as Wagner. Their inspiration flowed in the same way, but whereas Wagner – and Liszt – wanted to build something new on those foundations, Brahms was more concerned with gilding the legacy. He was one of the first composers to develop a thorough knowledge of the history of music, collecting manuscripts and studying works by the masters, back to Handel. The fact that he produced only four symphonies in a full life (he died in 1897) was maybe one of the indications of how hard he toiled at his orchestral pieces, working on the intricacies and design over long periods, despite his ability to write memorably with an easy simplicity. He did not produce his first until he was past forty, but all four have an imposing architecture and a melodic drive that made them immediately popular.

As in his Variations on a Theme of Haydn ('St Anthony's Chorale'), Brahms demonstrated a technique that seemed the natural product of the Romantic tradition. There was none of the innovation that Wagner was producing – those chords beginning to strain at the conventions of tonality – and Brahms appeared to be the composer who was cementing all that had been achieved rather than trying to build anew. Arnold Schoenberg wrote an essay on him at the start of the twentieth century called 'Brahms the Progressive' in which he tried to demonstrate how radical he was. It was not how he was seen in his lifetime. One of the reasons was the determination of Wagner – and Liszt – to argue the philosophical case for music as a more powerful transforming force than had been supposed. Nothing was more serious; nothing promised so much for the human spirit.

Though for much of his life Brahms was seen as a more conservative force, he too was influenced by the age of change. After Schumann's death in 1856 he was unsettled in Germany, and in the early 1860s he moved to Vienna. Although it was an imperial city of confidence and style – its architecture spoke of wealth and power – the Habsburg capital was a magnet for Hungarians and Bohemians, and the conservative establishment around the court was being challenged by a new bourgeoisie, rich and relatively liberal. All across Europe, alongside the confidence – the optimism of Victorian Britain, for example – there was upheaval. Nationalist movements were bubbling up everywhere; transport and technology were opening up new horizons; and in music there was the sound of experiment and anger as well as the perfect expression of an established symphonic transition.

Brahms's fate was to be cast as the representative of the past; others looked to the future. His antithesis is Wagner. In 1849, following the Year of Revolution in Europe, which started in Paris and spread eastwards, Wagner was taking to the barricades in Dresden while the teenager Brahms was trying to keep himself out of trouble. Musically, Wagner was just as rebellious. By the 1850s he was working his way out of the pattern that Brahms was representing as he reached his maturity. They shared a debt to the giants of the past, from Haydn to Beethoven, but interpreted the inheritance in quite different ways. Brahms did bring his originality to bear on the symphony, but it was because he wanted to be true to a tradition. Wagner wanted to escape from it.

One wanted to match the achievements of the past by echoing them; the other to use them as a springboard to something new. Brahms referred contemptuously to the 'so-called music of the future', by which he meant the new Romanticism of Wagner, and Wagner excoriated his conservatism. By the time he wrote the chord that opened *Tristan und Isolde* in the late 1850s Wagner had developed ideas about the fusion of music and drama that were taking him into new territory. Twenty-five years later Brahms would still be writing symphonies which, powerful and beautiful though they were, would resolutely resist such obvious departures. Their architecture was still the one Beethoven had used. Compare the music heard at the first season at Bayreuth and the first symphony which Brahms (at the age of forty-three) had just completed.

However, it is too easy to listen to, say, the first movement of that symphony and the end of *Götterdämmerung*, compare them and declare the two composers opposites. They weren't. Brahms, as Schoenberg pointed out, was an innovator; he just was not interested in Wagner's ideas about the drama, and Wagner wasn't much interested in any musicians' ideas but his own.

Along our journey we've encountered many periods like this. It's nonsense to think of music as a stream that flows placidly forward, sometimes picking up a little speed, then slowing down, but always proceeding in the same direction. Sometimes it's a circular movement; often there is a pause. Contradictory movements take off at the same time. Music is used for adornment and celebration – and for argument and protest. We've traced the story through the excitement of the Renaissance and the turmoil of the sixteenth century, through to the zenith of the Classical age in the second half of the eighteenth century and into an age of revolution, after which came the Romantics. Now, in a Europe where bigger audiences were able to hear music, where orchestras and famous conductors were proliferating, we've reached a period of passionate argument about what music was *for*.

Liszt, the composer, pianist and father-in-law of Wagner, said he wanted to 'hurl a musical lance as far as possible into the boundless realm of the future'. He was on the cusp of change and was one of its most important instigators, revering the past and the masters from whom he'd learned all he knew, but determined to be an innovator too. He invented the idea of the symphonic poem, a form that Brahms couldn't abide.

The kind of programme music that Liszt championed was part of the revolution that Wagner was fomenting, and from which Brahms felt distant. Wagner believed in music as a means of expression that was complete in itself, needing no references to the objective world beyond, of the sort that Liszt was championing in his symphonic poems and that composers like Hector Berlioz had pursued in France. Wagner, of course, believed in the idea of the *Gesamtkunstwerk* – the total work of art which he said was the only thing that could satisfy man as artist. It had to be all embracing. 'In every individualisation of his artistic capacities he is unfree, not wholly that which he can be – in the collective art work he is free, wholly that which he can be.' Hence, for

Wagner, the necessity to turn music and drama into one on the stage, inseparable from each other.

Nothing human stands still, said Liszt. 'Cult, custom, law, government, science, taste and mode of enjoyment – all change, all are constantly coming and passing away, without rest, without respite . . . Art moves on, strides on, increases and develops, obeying unknown laws . . .' The change with which he and Wagner are associated is one that closes the Romantic chapter. It began with the artists whose imaginations ran wild in the era after the French Revolution and produced the poets who lit up the 1820s, the composers who believed that inner feelings were the secret of great music, the writers and painters who delved into the past to find stories and images that could fire the imagination. Their conception of beauty was one that encompassed pain and longing. Goethe's Faust, when he sees a pale young girl at the witches' Sabbath with Mephistopheles, admires her eyes – in Shelley's translation – 'like the eyes of a fresh corpse'.

> Oh, what delight! What woe! I cannot turn
> My looks from her sweet piteous countenance.
> How strangely does a single blood-red line,
> Not broader than the sharp edge of a knife,
> Adorn her lovely neck!

In music, Robert Schumann, so important to the young Brahms, was maybe the last of the first Romantics. His piano works from the 1820s and 1830s are perfect examples of Romantic music, some of his song settings rivalling those of the master, Franz Schubert. Schumann's life, his marriage to Clara, his mental collapse and his death from syphilis paint a familiar picture of the Romantic artist. He was inventive, original, full of ideas, and his music, like Schubert's or that of his friend and contemporary Mendelssohn, seems now to describe his time: a listener today will know that this is a disciple of Beethoven and a Romantic at work.

He was important as a writer about music (founding the *Neue Zeitschrift für Musik* which became a forum for contemporary criticism) and his gifts for writing for the piano and voice were in full flood. His songs in *Liederkreis* and *Dichterliebe* in 1840 are particularly treasured by singers. His four symphonies, the piano concerto and the violin concerto are all staples of the concert programme, although they have tended to find a place at the top of the second rank rather than in the first. Yet Schumann, in his songs, or, for example in the Piano Quintet in E flat (1842), is a composer who scales vertiginous heights.

Brahms and Schumann (the latter encouraged his much younger friend in a way that perhaps made an important difference to his flowering as an artist) can be seen as representing the end of the Romantic story that began in the era of the young Beethoven. The new Romantics, to whom Liszt was a kind of bridge, would be different. While Brahms was still writing with a solid attachment to the tradition he'd discovered as a boy – and he didn't write his Fourth and last Symphony until 1884 – Wagner was engineering the shock of the new. As early as 1860 Brahms and some of his friends were on the attack, signing a petition against those around Wagner, and saying they would have nothing to do with futuristic music. Their petition declared that they had deplored and condemned 'the productions of the leaders and disciples of the so-called New German school, which . . . lead to the advancing of new and unheard-of theories, to the detriment of the intrinsic nature of music'. But what, precisely, is its intrinsic nature? Liszt said that art obeyed 'unknown laws' and was always changing without rest or respite. Brahms would have found nothing in those words themselves with which he would disagree. He had simply chosen a different path.

An age of confidence and optimism was also a time of intellectual turmoil and artistic experiment. In England, John Ruskin was arguing that the medieval spirituality represented in the Gothic was wholesome and modern industrialisation ugly and inferior. As we'll see, that argument – about the weight of the past and the promise of the future – was being played out among musicians with great passion. For some, a tradition seemed to be threatened; for others it was time to move on. As we've discovered earlier in this journey it's an argument that's always there, and never ends.

Composers in the mid-nineteenth century who found themselves pitted against each other in arguing about the place and character of music were no inhabitants of different planets. Brahms and Wagner shared a ceaseless urge to innovate, to discover new harmonies, to work on the opportunities in the orchestras of their time, to find new inspiration. Yet they show, too, how profound the public argument about the place of music had become.

Disputes could flare up in journals and newspapers. The critics – Schumann combined reviewing with composition for a time – were influential, and in at least some sections of society, interested in new music, there was a debate about its function. Wagner made his view clear on stage (for those who hadn't spent hours immersed in his philosophy) and so did Brahms. Between them they represent music at the flood – at a time when the symphony was at its height, with Brahms's contemporary Anton Bruckner (1824–96) producing his mighty nine. In opera, Wagner was defining a new Romanticism that would influence two generations of composers. Brahms might look to the future with foreboding, fearing for much that he cherished in music. But nothing is static, nothing frozen in time. Music-makers have always celebrated the past, because it bequeaths works of genius and ideas that stay alive, but they have also been the innovators and explorers. They are driven to be adventurers, though sometimes they travel down different paths.

13

Nations Everywhere

On the Neva, the Vltava and the Seine

~

THE NATIONALIST BANNERS that were part of Verdi's inspiration in Italy in the 1840s, which rose in different hands with different colours across the continent in the decades afterwards, were the signals of movements that together shaped the second half of the nineteenth century. Their characters were distinct, their objectives differed like the nature of their political arguments, but inescapably the first stirrings of popular democracy and the growth of a more open Europe – in travel, the speed of news, the liveliness of intellectual exchange across borders – meant that the sense of country was stronger. Nationalism was the vehicle for power, and also a means of recovering a sense of history. Paradoxically, the more open the continent became, the more it became aware of the special quality of its constituent parts.

Wagner's argument for the centrality of music was, in some measure, a statement of his commitment to the ideal of a Germany that he felt he could summon up in his scores. It was happening in Italy and away out on the uneasy ramparts of the Habsburg Empire, and it was even happening in Russia. Where else to begin but in the city that looks east and west, St Petersburg, as it was then and is now, despite interregnums as Petrograd and Leningrad. Russian music, as it developed in the nineteenth century and as most people think of it today, is a product of that nationalist feeling and in its depths you can hear the power of the idea and also experience something of its ambiguity.

In the prologue to Modest Musorgsky's opera *Boris Godunov*, the bells peal and the coronation of the Tsar begins. Boris Feodorovich Godunov stands at the foot of the red staircase that leads to the Tsar's apartments. The cathedrals, of the Assumption and the Archangel, flank the new Tsar. He asks everyone to pray at the tombs of the rulers who have gone before him. The crowd sings his praise, but he is tormented by guilt. The power is only his because he murdered the heir to the Tsar (son of Ivan the Terrible), his half-brother. The guilt weighs heavily on him. Needless to say the censors had a fine time before the more or less complete opera was seen in 1874, excerpts from it having been staged the year before.

Boris Godunov is an opera of great spectacle and foaming emotion, and it is notable for another reason. When Musorgsky (1839–81) finished the first version it was a time of introspection and anxiety in Russia (hence his trouble with the authorities, who did not take lightly the subject of a poisoned succession, in exactly the same way as the Neapolitan bureaucrats had tried to stop Verdi staging *Un ballo in maschera* with an Italian plot). He had chosen an episode from the late sixteenth century for a reason. He was searching for the essence of his country, its heart. Defeat in the Crimean war in the 1850s had undermined Russian power and sapped the national mood. The country that had seen off Napoleon after his disastrous march on Moscow in 1812 seemed now to be in retreat. Nationalism was the theme, and the arguments it produced were heard in the Russian music that Europe has since adopted as the authentic voice of that country in the nineteenth century.

Musorgsky was looking for a Russian identity, perhaps even a Russian soul. The assumption was that one did exist – it just had to be found, and cherished. He and his friends thought that they could find musical inspiration in Russia's history or perhaps from the people in whose language and customs, even in day-to-day conversation, they might discover something 'true'. In writing about the new Tsar, about his approaching the throne despite his crime and his guilt, Musorgsky was also writing about the crowd, whose presence in the opera from that prologue onwards is a vital part of the drama. In a letter to his friend the realist painter Ilya Repin, the composer wrote:

> It is the people I want to depict, sleeping or working or drinking. I have them constantly in my mind's eye – again and again they rise before me in all their reality – huge, unvarnished, with no tinsel trappings! How rich a treasure awaits the composer in the speech of the people – so long,

that is, as any corner of the land remains to which the railway has not penetrated.

As with nationalist movements to the west in Europe, many artists in Russia were trying to reflect in their work the distinctiveness of their own country. In this respect Musorgsky inherited the mantle of the composer Mikhail Glinka, who died in 1857, and who had championed what he considered to be 'Russianness' in his music, rejecting a westward-looking fashion. Northerners, he once said, responded to things differently. And, by way of example: 'I came to detest fashionable Italian music.' That sums it up.

However, it was a battle, as these things always are. Set against that nationalist movement in music was an effort – or at least an impulse – in the other direction. In St Petersburg, the Russian Musical Society opened its doors in 1859. The first piece the audience heard was the overture to the opera *Ruslan and Ludmilla* by Glinka himself, the composer thought of as the father of Russian music. Yet it was rather a misleading choice, because the purpose of the Society was not quite what Glinka would have decreed. The pianist and composer Anton Rubinstein certainly wanted to turn it into a creative cauldron – eventually it would become the St Petersburg conservatoire – but the principal objective was to professionalise Russian music by bringing to that city and to Moscow a new professionalism in music. To him it seemed natural and progressive; to those who celebrated a Slavic culture and wanted a Russia unpolluted by European habits and taste it was anathema.

Rubinstein and his brother (his partner in the enterprise) complained that Russia didn't have choirs, orchestras or music-teaching like Germany; they bemoaned the fact that the Tsar's government was interested in painting and sculpture but not in music. The solution, obviously, was to look outwards.

But what of the soul of Russia that composers like Musorgsky believed in, and sought? When Leo Tolstoy published *War and Peace* in instalments in the late 1860s, his picture of life in the Napoleonic era in Russia was a rich version of the same quest. There's a scene in which Natasha Rostov, the girl at the start of the story who grows up to be one of its pillars, is visiting a man she calls 'Uncle' in his cabin

in the forest. To the simple tune of a peasant's balalaika she begins
to dance:

> Where, how, and when had this young countess, educated by an *émigré*
> French governess, imbibed that spirit from the Russian air she breathed,
> and obtained that manner which the *pas de châle* would, one would have
> supposed, long ago have effaced? But the spirit and the movements
> were those inimitable and unteachable Russian ones that 'Uncle' had
> expected of her. As soon as she had struck her pose and smiled
> triumphantly, proudly, and with sly merriment, the fear that had at
> first seized Nicholas and the others that she might not do the right thing
> was at an end, and they were already admiring her.
>
> She did the right thing with such precision, such complete precision,
> that Anisya Fëdorovna, who had at once handed her the handkerchief
> she needed for the dance, had tears in her eyes, though she laughed as
> she watched this slim, graceful countess, reared in silks and velvets and so
> different from herself, who yet was able to understand all that was in
> Anisya and in Anisya's father and mother and aunt, and in every Russian
> man and woman.

The idea that 'in every Russian man and woman' that same spirit
welled up from the same sources was the inspiration for composers
like Musorgsky, Alexander Borodin (1833–87) and Nicolai Rimsky-
Korsakov (1844–1908). Their works combined an affection for folk
song with an idea of Mother Russia and a celebration of the peasant
class (though the Tsar's 'liberation' of the serfs in 1861 had left many of
them worse off, and huge numbers were on the edge of starvation).
Towards the end of the nineteenth century the style these composers
established was notable for its mystical quality – influencing the strange
work of Alexander Skryabin among others, in his journey towards
abstraction. They did, however, establish a Russian musical voice.

We hear it still in the music of Peter Ilyich Tchaikovsky (1840–93).
When the oboe picks up a folk tune at the beginning of his Second
Symphony, written in 1872, his passion appears to be the same as
Musorgsky's. But he did not share the feelings and the urgency of the
nationalist composers. He said of them: 'Realism undoubtedly implies a
certain narrow-mindedness, an ability to satisfy very easily and cheaply

the thirst for a knowledge of truth . . . The realist is sceptical towards those who seek reconciliation with life in a religion, in philosophy, in art.'

He was saying that if there was a 'realist' school, he was not part of it. He yielded to no one in his patriotism, he could be as ardent as Musorgsky – and listening to much of his music you can't miss the importance to him of the same sources that were energising the 'realist' nationalists – but he was also able to look westwards with a confidence that it did not involve the surrender of his Russian soul. He was horrified when Tolstoy himself – who'd become something of a crank, dressing in peasant clothes and arguing a fiercely nationalist case, told him that he thought Beethoven was inept.

Tchaikovsky thought himself part of a musical tradition that stretched far beyond the borders of Russia, and it was his purpose to let his national identity shine through it, not separate itself. His triumph was in establishing in the mind of the world outside that successful music could come from Russia. In the next generation, music from the likes of Musorgsky would have just as big an impact – on Claude Debussy in France, for example – and these composers were vital in the development of national music in other Slavic countries. But Tchaikovsky would remain one of Russia's most important exports.

There's an irony in the way he was later cherished by the Soviet Union, since it involved suppressing the fact of his (illegal) homosexuality (as he'd had to do himself – acknowledging it privately, though never in public). His marriage was a short-lived disaster and his emotional life was conducted instead through an extraordinary twelve-year correspondence he carried on with Nadezhda von Meck, a rich and eccentric widowed patron, who guaranteed him an allowance and became his confessor. 'Every note which comes from my pen is dedicated to you!' he wrote in 1877 after their strange relationship began. They agreed never to meet – though they encountered each other once or twice by accident on her estates. She was the recipient of his most intimate reflections, and they seemed to give him confidence, the completion of his Fourth Symphony in 1878 being a cathartic moment for him, as is clear in his letters. Around the same time he finished the violin concerto and the opera *Eugene Onegin*. He wrote his

'Manfred' Symphony – based on Byron's dramatic poem – in the mid-1880s and soon afterwards the greatest of his ballet scores, *The Sleeping Beauty*. The period of his protection by Mme von Meck, financial and sexual, was fertile.

Tchaikovsky's gifts were celebrated far beyond Russia. By the time he began to write his magnificent opera *The Queen of Spades* in Italy in 1890 he'd achieved popularity across Europe and in the United States, where he wrote the music for his ballet *The Nutcracker*. He said he had never before experienced anything like the enthusiasm that greeted the performance of the first piano concerto in New York in the concert hall that would later become Carnegie Hall. His international fame, however, is linked to something more important – the development, maybe the creation, of Russian music at home. Tchaikovsky didn't see himself as part of the nationalist group of composers, despite his passion for Russia, and particularly in his operas *Onegin* and *The Queen of Spades* he's writing in a style that is recognisably European. *Boris Godunov*, by contrast, seems more rooted in Russian culture. Yet his story – with its heavy personal sadness – is part of the rediscovery of Russian music, or perhaps the finding of it for the first time.

As would be clear when later generations of Russians, and the Soviet regime, celebrated his music, especially the Fifth and Sixth symphonies and the most famous ballet scores for *Sleeping Beauty* and *Swan Lake*, Tchaikovsky was still felt to be embedded in Russia rather than Europe. The spirit of that bond is heard in his symphonic masterpiece, the 'Pathétique', No. 6, finished in 1893, completed only about three weeks before his death. He conducted the first performance; the second was a memorial to him.

Despite the argument about the meaning of Russian nationalism – whether it involved an outward-looking confidence or more of an introspective concern for native traditions – the music bore the imprint of a shared devotion. You find it eloquently expressed in Musorgsky's *Pictures at an Exhibition*, written in 1874. The composer's perambulation at the gallery is the conceit for the piece and when he reaches the last work on display, Musorgsky turns the taps on full. The tenth and last picture by the artist and architect Viktor Hartmann is his design for the Great Gate at Kiev. At the end of a piece that draws on folk song, with a distinctive character – using melodies that aren't chromatic and have uneven bar lengths – Musorgsky summons up a picture of pre-Muscovite Russia, perhaps the true Russia that lies in the past but that he believes is still alive among the people. It's unmistakably Russian, which is what, more than anything else, he wanted.

However, nationalism is sometimes at its most powerful when the country it celebrates doesn't exist. In eastern Europe, a Slavic spirit was working itself out in a way that was simpler than the argument in Russia. Bedřich Smetana's cycle *Má Vlast* (My Country) is a hymn to territory that is utterly recognisable and the object of the composer's political devotion as well as his emotional loyalty. The first symphonic poem in the cycle evokes the sight of the Vltava river and the Vysehrad castle high above it which was the seat of the early Bohemian kings in the eighth century, dreamlike and stirring at the same time. The cycle was an expression of his own patriotism, a way of separating himself from the German culture of the Habsburg Empire in which, as a young man in Bohemia, he'd been prevented from speaking or writing in Czech.

For Smetana (1824–84), music was a voice for his nationalist, political feelings which had taken him to the barricades in Prague in 1848, the Year of Revolution across Europe, when he was twenty-four. He was a virtuoso pianist who wanted to open his own conservatoire for students; and in the end he put his talent at the service of his politics. His home was a mere part of the Austrian Empire, the Czech language a reminder of an ancient country that was no more. Smetana was musically progressive – in shorthand, he was a disciple of Wagner and thought that Brahms was the voice of the past – and for him the urge to compose in a modern style was inseparable from the desire to revive his national culture and give it a home.

The composer Robert Schumann once said that Chopin's music, with rhythms and roots that were unmistakably Polish, sounded 'like cannons hidden in roses'. At the beginning of the second half of the nineteenth century, a great deal of European music – in Italy with Verdi and in Germany with Wagner – was no abstraction, but a stream that was part of national life, a strand of the argument about how the old empires should be carved up, how democracy could be nurtured. A composer like Smetana didn't, of course, turn deliberately to music for that purpose. He was gifted, so he played the piano and wrote. That was the natural way. He told his diary with all the naive pretentiousness of youth, when he was seventeen: 'I wish to become a Mozart in composition and a Liszt in technique.' But as he honed his talent he found that it was naturally channelled into his nationalism, first fired in 1848, and rekindled when he returned to Prague in 1861, after five years in Sweden.

There was nothing crude about it. In the opera for which he's probably now best known, *The Bartered Bride*, first performed in 1866, the power which Czechs would cherish came from subtlety. Rather than using Czech folk tunes themselves he created a folk idiom of his own in his tale set in the Bohemian countryside, and the score – despite its sparkle and the everyday bucolic subject of the story – was seen by some critics at the time as displaying a dark Wagnerian influence. Much more important than any debt to Wagner was Smetana's ability to express in music what Czechs longed for: an identity that was more than a language they were told not to speak and a past represented by the ancient castles and churches they saw on the outcrops high above the Vltava river.

Prince Metternich, the diplomatic star of the Congress of Vienna at the end of the Napoleonic age and thereafter the evangelist for a 'balance of power' in the warring continent, said that when France sneezed all Europe caught a cold. It was true that the upheavals of 1848, which started in Paris, meant that national movements were unleashed in the Habsburg Empire, of which it was often said that it was held together by the mutual dislike among its peoples. Music after the Romantic age reflected those feelings; its expressiveness meant that national sentiment was a natural subject, the proper concern of serious composers. That was less true in France and in Britain, where prosperity and the successful spread of empire produced confidence. Elsewhere, cultural identity sometimes seemed everything. In *Má Vlast* Smetana described how the Vltava river came from two streams in the mountains, broadened and quickened as it passed through Prague and flowed west and north until it joined the Elbe. The music placed Bohemia at the heart of Europe, the river flowing like an artery.

Smetana wrote this music after he went deaf as a result of syphilis in 1874. It didn't stop him. He wrote five operas afterwards as well as *Má Vlast*, first heard complete in 1882, and demonstrated how a particular national feeling could be captured in music. The identity between Czech nationalism and Smetana's music has always been close. To this day, when a Czech Airlines flight prepares to land in Prague, you usually hear *Má Vlast* squawking out of the sound system: Smetana still speaks of something that's all around in middle Europe. Antonin Dvořák, his successor, whose productivity was greater and who took the sound of middle-European music to America at the very beginning of the twentieth century, was in the same tradition.

It hardly needs to be said that music with that character couldn't have come from anywhere else. Behind the magnificent frontage of the Romantic symphony, which crossed borders and sometimes seemed to come close to creating an international language, there were many mansions, in which composers found ways of expressing their own national instincts. Metternich once said, grandly, that Italy was no more than a geographical expression. He was wrong. And though Czecho-slovakia would only be put together – very ineptly – in the messy aftermath of the First World War, and dismantled into its natural constituent parts only in our own time at the end of the Cold War, Smetana and Dvořák are evidence of how music reveals a 'geographical expression' to be something deeper: a feeling that, for better or for worse, pulls people together.

You can find evidence throughout our musical tradition. In northern Europe, Jean Sibelius is the exemplar. Though he lived until 1957, he was born when Smetana was at his peak in Prague in 1865. No Finnish composer has achieved an international stature close to his, and in his symphonies and songs especially you feel a power that's rather like the influence that Smetana wielded. When he wrote the tone poem *Finlandia* at the end of the nineteenth century, in a country that was still a Russian duchy, it was considered inflammatory and banned by the authorities. No one could doubt that its deep stirrings were a reflection of people's desire for something different. It was music that spoke clearly, without a word being said.

Sibelius, whose music has had such a renaissance in recent years, was, first, a composer of brilliance and depth; he was also a sounding board for nationalism, giving it energy and style. Music of this sort isn't a translation of a raucous street-cry; it's a depiction of tradition and mood that reaches above the here-and-now to something that a community, a country, a people can recognise and claim for themselves. The orchestral music of Sibelius is the perfect illustration of how it's done. Within it, of course, is a dangerous power, as dangerous as the magic of the orator with a purpose. It can corrupt and it can destroy. The power is real, and no illusion. Composers in the nineteenth century, especially, had an inheritance which valued feeling and the importance of personal expression, and lived in a world shifting under their feet. It was therefore natural that the medium of music could be made to speak more simply – and more profoundly – than many speeches or pamphlets.

Who can listen to a Smetana opera, or a Dvořák symphony, or a Sibelius song-setting and turn them into an argument, piece by piece? You can't; that isn't the point. They speak in a different way; but it is meant to be just as forceful. Smetana wrote to a friend in 1880:

> I hope that if I have not yet reached the goal I set myself I am at least approaching it. And that goal is to prove that we Czechs are not mere practising musicians as other nations nickname us, saying that our talent lies only in our fingers but not in our brains, but that we are also endowed with creative force – yes, that we have our own and characteristic music. How far I have succeeded in this hitherto, not I but the world will judge . . .

The fulfilment of Smetana's dream didn't come until the twentieth century, with the disintegration of the Habsburg Empire. By that time the battle he'd fought was being carried on by two composers both of whom would become important figures – the Hungarian Béla Bartók (1881–1945) and Leoš Janáček (1854–1928).

Like Smetana, Janáček had grown up in a country where the Czech language was discouraged, but by the early 1880s there was a Czech national theatre – producing plays in the language of the people – in Prague. Alongside his nationalism, he developed music which reflected the rhythms he knew from that language. But his nationalism wasn't narrow. He was an admirer of Russia, which he saw as the only independent Slavic nation and two of his great works, the searing opera *Ka'ta Kabanova* and *From the House of the Dead*, had stories taken from Russian literature. Like Bartók, Janáček became a modernist composer in his time. The two men produced some of the masterpieces of the early twentieth century, and both took inspiration from the streets and the fields. In one of his essays, Bartók described the experience:

> Collecting folk music is not easy. One should search for them among the simplest and poorest people, inhabiting regions as far removed from the 'iron horse' as possible, if the object is to find the purest forms, as yet undistorted by city influence. It must be admitted, however, that the folk living in these 'virgin' lands are most suspicious of strangers knocking on their doors. Attempts to explain the reasons for collecting their forgotten songs are useless. They find it hard to believe the gentleman from the 'big city' is willing to forsake the comforts of his life just to listen to their old peasant songs. Many of them are convinced that the purpose of his visit is to burden them with another tax, this time a tax on – music!

Like Janáček, Bartók managed to turn a modern ear to the old melodies and speech patterns that he heard. Both men were dipping into the thriving folk tradition for inspiration and were forward looking in their writing. Janáček, though born before the start of the Crimean war in the middle of the nineteenth century, is unmistakably a twentieth-century composer. When he died, in 1928, his music didn't sound part of a vanished world, but was quite contemporary – maybe because the edgy tonality that he employed fitted the spirit of his time, when composers were pushing at the conventions and, in some cases, deliberately dismantling them. Bartók (born thirty years after Janáček), who was taught the piano by a pupil of Liszt, was similarly trying to build on the foundations laid by Liszt and Wagner for a 'modern' Romanticism, and as a young man he was most influenced by the music of Claude Debussy and Richard Strauss – both of whom were masters of atmospherics, the creation in an orchestra of sound patterns that seemed to be a break with the past. By the time Janáček's late work appeared, Bartók was already an established modernist.

Bartók's enthusiasm for folk music, far from running against that instinct, fitted it perfectly. He used a harmonic freedom that was 'modern' but imbued with a spirit that he recognised deep in the Hungarian plains where he went with his recording machine. He showed how the use of nationalist elements in composition need not be restrictive but can open doors. His loyalty to his country made him an internationalist, and there's no paradox there. He understood from the start that traditions cross borders and that oral culture has been carried across Europe for generations. Different styles and languages can be geographically identifiable; more often it was the similarities between them that were arresting and intriguing.

When Janáček started out, nationalism arose out of an angry resentment of power exercised from Vienna; when Bartók was producing his vast output alongside him, it had moved on. By then, cultural richness was valued for its own sake – though, as we'll hear, Bartók was fated to endure a period of unhappy exile, and a nationalist anger of his own, when Germany occupied Hungary in the Second World War.

He was fascinated by folk music because it gave him the opportunity to replicate its 'simplicity' by using dense textures and richly layered harmonies not usually associated with it, producing something that was fresh. No matter how great the complications on the page – the meticulous detail of the orchestration for chamber group, for example – they would produce a sound that even with its 'modern' character would reflect the purity of the tunes he'd heard in the fields. Bartók, who lived most of his life in the twentieth century, was a modern composer, challenging conventions and searching out new sound patterns. In his dissonances can be heard the experiences of an artist who lived through the two world wars which wreaked unimaginable damage across the globe.

The desire of Janáček and Bartók to break away from German domination was reflected in the style and spirit of their music, which was meant to describe in its intricacy and subtlety a simple feeling. Bartók believed in its authenticity. He thought that the peasant melodies had a kind of unconscious perfection – showing how musical thoughts could be expressed in an ideal way with the simplest means.

Smetana equated his creative gifts with the passion he developed for his people and their ways. He seemed to ask – Why else write music? Many composers after him would take a quite different view of the musician's purpose, but he represents that part of our tradition that sees a symphonic poem or a string quartet as a voice for feelings that must have abstract expression.

Such instincts were prevalent across Europe in the second half of the century. In France, there was no nationalism of the sort that Smetana, Janáček and Bartók would embrace, because there was no need. But there was an effort to find ways of expressing a national distinctiveness, so say something which would be indubitably *French*. Claude Debussy (1862–1918) became the master of a particular style not simply because he was impatient, or talented, but because he found it natural to search for something new that would not be his but would belong to France.

When Debussy went to the Paris Exhibition of 1889 he heard something wonderful. It was a gamelan – an assembly of instruments from Indonesia using tuned percussion instruments like bamboo xylophones, wooden and metal chimes, and gongs. The composer had never heard them before. Nor had almost anyone else in France. They went to the exhibition mainly to marvel at the Eiffel Tower, built to mark the centenary of the Revolution in 1789, and to celebrate French achievements, but Debussy (who was twenty-seven years old) found the most intoxicating experience the hours he spent in the mock-up of a Javanese village, a *kampong*, listening to the rhythmic patterns of the gamelan-players. He was transported, imagining them turning into sorcerers, nymphs and fairies before his eyes.

One of the reasons why he was mesmerised by the sound, and its possibilities, was that he felt trapped by tradition. He's said to have called Beethoven an old bore – *quelle horreur!* – and it was to Wagner's innovations and ideas about the purpose of serious music that he felt more drawn. Yet he wanted to be French not German. This wasn't a musical 'nationalism' of the sort that was sweeping the Czech-speaking lands, or in Russia, or in Italy, but something deliberately outward looking.

Debussy thought that the way to express his Frenchness was to respond in a fresh way to nature, as the Impressionists said they were doing in painting, looking at their surroundings through a different lens, and giving the scene new life in colour by conjuring up natural effects on canvas. Their techniques with the brush were meant to present the world in quite a different way – to persuade those who looked at the pictures that their surroundings were being given more meaning. Debussy spoke in the same way about music:

> Music is a free art – a spontaneous, open-air art commensurate with the elements – wind, sea, sky. It is a mistake to turn it into a closed, scholastic song . . . I loathe doctrines and their impertinences. That is why I wish to write my musical dream with complete detachment from myself. I want to sing my interior landscape with the native candour of a child. That will always shock those who prefer artifice and lies . . . Music is precisely the art which is nearest Nature.

It's easy to link Debussy with the Impressionist painters, whose high point of influence was in the 1870s, but it's slightly misleading. He and they were certainly devoted to the idea of representing nature and their feelings about it in a new way, but Debussy was probably closer to the Symbolist painters and writers. They disliked the obsession (as they saw it) of Monet, Renoir, Sisley, Cézanne and the others with the physical world around them, despite their effort to represent it the form of feeling and not as objective reality. Symbolists wanted to concentrate on ideas, even dreams – the inner life itself.

When he heard the gamelan, Debussy heard a different way of using sound. The players didn't use the eight-note western scale, but the pentatonic version with five notes, scales without the familiar western semi-tones. They produced a new atmosphere, one which Debussy said expressed every shade of meaning.

From that time on, he began to experiment. In the extraordinary String Quartet in G minor, written in 1893, for example, the rhythms and colours catch something of the spirit of the gamelan. He had just turned thirty when he wrote it and he was already in his own sound world, with harmonic patterns. In that same year he saw Maurice Maeterlinck's play *Pelléas et Mélisande* and decided that its story of doomed love would make the opera he wanted to write, though it would be nearly a decade before it would be ready for the stage.

Debussy was breaking away. He was heavily influenced by the German Romanticism of Wagner, but described him as 'a beautiful sunset mistaken for a dawn'. He was looking for a different kind of sound that would take music on from the sensuality of Wagner which he admired so much. His work was one of the most important transitions from the musical ideas that dominated the nineteenth century, though much of his piano music, many of his songs, have a simplicity – a perfect naivety – that seems to belie the idea of radical transformation. The conductor and composer Pierre Boulez, probably the most important French figure in music after the Second World War, said that modern music began with Debussy's setting of a poem by Stéphane Mallarmé, *Prélude à l'après-midi d'un faune*.

He wrote it between 1892 and 1894 and it shows how Debussy, not yet halfway through his career, was turning into a great innovator, whose work would be an important influence at the start of the next century. In setting the poem, he wasn't writing the kind of programme music developed by Liszt – in other words, following the sequence of the verse – but instead producing a set of images. He wrote it for an orchestra much smaller than the one favoured by late-Romantic composers. The poem is the description of a fawn dreaming in the sun, memories and desires mingling together. You're invited at the start of the piece to luxuriate in voluptuous sound, a flute coloured by harps joining it and then by cymbals, which leads you through the experience of the fawn on a simple sunny afternoon.

Pieces like these illustrate how Debussy was producing new effects, and it's fascinating that although they were original – daring – they seemed to be accepted immediately by audiences, although at that stage in his career he wasn't at all well known. The conductor at the first performance, Gustave Doret, said that he was only familiar to connoisseurs of the modern music of the day. But Paris at the *belle époque* was confident and when the first-night audience heard the piece – which Doret said had entranced and seduced the orchestra during rehearsals – they fell in love with it on the spot.

> The hour of the great test duly arrived, Debussy pressing my hands and hiding his anxiety behind a grin that I had come to recognize. There was a vast silence in the hall as I ascended the podium and our splendid flautist, Barrère, unfolded his opening line. All at once I felt behind me, as some conductors can, an audience that was totally spellbound. It was a complete triumph and I had no hesitation in breaking the rule forbidding encores.

The composer Camille Saint-Saëns thought it was pretty but lacking in style: the conservative instincts of some musicians (never mind audiences) can always be relied upon to resist the new. But it was the harbinger of more than two decades of work by Debussy that would shape the minds of many twentieth-century composers, like his fellow Frenchman Maurice Ravel.

At about the same time he was starting to adapt *Pelléas et Mélisande*, in which Mélisande's love for her husband's brother kills them both. Its music is ethereal, mysterious and erotic. The singing is conversational, the orchestra ever present and the atmosphere unique. The noted soprano Mary Garden sang on the first night (despite the reservations of some in the Paris audience about her pronounced Scottish accent). She was very close to Debussy and said this of him:

> Debussy's the most difficult because you have to sing him as he writes – not as you want to. Everything that he wrote, every word of Mélisande or the other characters, has the right music tone. And they mustn't sing *their* way; they must sing his way. Because everything that she does, or her husband did, or Pelléas – it was perfectly human, and you had to make it that way.

Debussy lets a phrase hang, then pulls it away, brings in another thought, then another – so that the effect is of a series of layers that reveal the plot. It is more of a picture than a narrative, and he invented a new musical language. Like painters who were rejecting the naturalistic forms of most of the nineteenth century, he was moving away not only from the patterns of the composers whom Wagner wanted to supersede, but beyond Wagner too. Apart from his natural desire to write with a French accent and not simply to add something to German Romanticism, he was a composer who responded boldly to the modernisation of the world around him, and drank deep from the potions of *fin de siècle* Paris.

He heard sounds from abroad and responded to them, absorbed the thinking of visual artists who wanted to escape from traditional representation, and searched for harmonies that were startling, disturbing, haunting. At the end of *L'Après-midi d'un faune* he deliberately avoids a climax that suggests we've reached the conclusion of a story that has a beginning, a middle and an end. It has been a dream, a playing with memory and desire, and the music hasn't developed on a simple timeline. Instead – just as he did in piano music, in such treasured orchestral works as 'La Mer' and in *Pelléas* – Debussy paints an atmosphere in his own colours, and then lets it fade, naturally. The great iron tower that rose over the exhibition where he first heard the gamelan was supposed to be temporary. Instead, it changed the skyline for ever. Debussy the moderniser did the same. Like nationalists elsewhere in Europe who were driven by political objectives, he was able to give his own country a sound and a sensibility that was his own, but his country's as well.

14

The Century of Wars

Vienna, Paris and the Trenches

~

IF YOU WANTED to go back in time and hear the nineteenth century
turn into the twentieth, Vienna would be the best destination. This
city, where music was held to have a special importance, embraced the
best of the Classical tradition and throbbed with intellectual radicalism;
it illustrated, too, the precarious state of the fast-crumbling world of old
empires that would soon spectacularly pass away. The composers who
worked there, and the musicians who drank at their well, were
confident but restless. Something new was coming.

At the time when Gustav Mahler was writing his Fourth Symphony
in the last years of the century, built on the foundations he'd inherited
from the nineteenth-century Romantic masters, the young Arnold
Schoenberg was setting out on his mission to dismantle the settled
forms of music and recreate the primitive thrill of sound in a different
way, on a template that no one had used before. Theirs were the faces
of Janus, connected by a shared consciousness of the past and excitement about the future, but gazing outwards in different directions.
Vienna, where Sigmund Freud was dissecting dreams and Friedrich
Nietzsche's gloomy introspection was the fashion of the young, was as
inspiring as it had been when Beethoven and Schubert were in the
coffee houses in the same streets eighty years before.

There was a clash of sounds as well as of ideas. Even in the first pieces
he wrote as a young man before the turn of the century, Schoenberg
was giving signals of what might come. His string sextet 'Verklärte
Nacht' (1899) marked out new territory, and although it would be
more than a decade before he abandoned tonality and dispensed with
the traditional musical keys to foment a revolution in sound, he was
already striking out. Mahler's journey into a century of new sensibilities

was different. His fate would be the accusation, which would persist for two generations, that he had succumbed to easy emotion in his own search for the hidden layers, and only after two world wars would his achievement be recognised across Europe. But, like Schoenberg, he was plunging into the depths all the same.

These two figures capture the character of the opening of the new century, boldness on the surface and fear lurking underneath. Mahler's symphonies, along with the nine of Anton Bruckner who died in 1896, were like a mountain landscape – a collection of peaks that towered over everything, though their true height wasn't recognised at the time, almost as if they were shrouded in mist. They were, however, the summits of achievement in the Romantic symphony. Alongside them, Schoenberg was mapping out a different way, drawing his inspiration from the same sources. He said that he had heard each of Wagner's operas twenty-five or thirty times by the time he was twenty-five, in the last year of the old century. Bruckner himself couldn't have made a prouder boast, and certainly couldn't have exceeded the stamina.

Vienna was at the dawn of great change. The Habsburg Empire was in its last phase – politically self-deluded, complacent and weak. Austro-Hungary was creaking at its borders and couldn't survive for long, with nationalism the predominant political force in much of Europe. Yet Vienna remained in large part a confident, comfortable city, cradling its warm cultural memories and maintaining a remarkable devotion to music, as well as the tradition of wine, women and song – perhaps summed up in the chocolate-box elegance and reassuring pulses of the waltz.

Johann Strauss the younger, from the family that gave Vienna its distinctive polish, died in 1899, in the same year that Schoenberg wrote 'Verklärte Nacht'. The city of the waltz was changing. The Emperor Franz Joseph gazed back rather than forward (he always refused to acknowledge the invention of the telephone, though he knew it, irritatingly, to be a fact) and Vienna was gripped by the conflict between tradition and the desire of intellectuals and artists who'd imbibed its spirit to create something that would give it a new life. Schoenberg's music wasn't at all popular at first – audiences complained that he was muddled and hard to understand – but, with a determination as great as Freud's when he published his *Interpretation of Dreams* in the city in 1900, he was unstoppable.

He and Mahler together mark an important transition in music, at the same time as Freud was coining the word 'psychoanalysis' and Nietzsche was working on what he thought was a post-Christian philosophy. Why should it have anything to do with the turn of the century? That was an accident of the calendar, and no more, but the decade falling on either side of that date was one of adventure and surprise. The two centuries seemed to meet at a point where there was an argument to be settled.

Mahler bridged the old world and the new. He converted to Roman Catholicism when in 1897 he became director of the Vienna Court Opera (later the State Opera) because his Jewishness was a problem – there was rampant and vicious anti-Semitism in Vienna – and although he drew heavily on the same legacy of German Romanticism that had helped to inspire Bruckner in his symphonic writing, he was aware of Wagner's notorious belief that Jews could not be truly original artists because they were 'synthesisers' of other styles, doomed to be musical magpies and no more. So although he prospered as a conductor (much more than as a composer, in which role he was hardly celebrated at all at that time) he had to bear the scars of his background. And in his symphonies – which he said had to 'embrace everything, like the world' – he managed to write simultaneously with an echo of Wagner and Bruckner and with an edge that cut through the cosiness of Viennese *Gemütlichkeit*, that near-untranslatable word that combines conviviality with a certain smugness, and perhaps the feeling of having had too many cream cakes and too much white wine.

Enthusiastic acceptance of his achievement would only come in Vienna half a century later, despite the reverence accorded him as a conductor. Indeed, concert programmers across Europe remained sniffy about Mahler until some post-war conductors – notably his own pupil Bruno Walter and then Leonard Bernstein – began to champion the symphonies and popularise them.

Vienna in the few years around 1900 was a fiery crucible. New ideas in philosophy and science were bubbling up, painters like Gustav Klimt were 'seceding' – their own word – from historical and naturalistic styles, and one particular experiment in music was beginning. Each of these elements seemed to work on the others – the shock or the liberation of Freud and Nietzsche (who died in the first year of the century) had an important influence, for example, on Mahler, who thought of calling his Third Symphony 'The Joyful Science' in imitation of one of Nietzsche's works, not that joyful is an adjective with which that philosopher has often been paired. Freud's ideas about dreams were being promulgated at the same time and were a daring challenge to settled ideas about human consciousness and the operation of reason. This is what he said in 1900:

> Dreams are disconnected; they accept the most violent contradictions without the least objection, they admit impossibilities, they disregard knowledge which carries great weight with us in the daytime, they reveal us as ethical and moral imbeciles. Anyone who when he was awake behaved in the sort of way that is shown in situations in dreams would be considered insane.

Vienna was not a place where the idea of the human being as a moral imbecile was commonly contemplated. The dramatist August Strindberg, who published *A Dream Play* in the same year, said this in his author's note:

> Everything can happen, everything is possible and probable. Time and place do not exist; on an insignificant basis of reality the imagination spins, weaving new patterns; a mixture of memories, experiences, free fancies, incongruities and improvisations. The characters split, double, multiply, evaporate, condense, disperse, assemble. But one consciousness rules over them all, that of the dreamer. For him there are no secrets, no illogicalities, no scruples, no laws. He neither acquits nor condemns, but merely relates; and just as a dream is more often painful than happy, so an undertone of melancholy and of pity for all mortal beings accompanies this flickering tale.

This was heady stuff. In music, young Schoenberg was fascinated by the power of the dream and the unconscious. He turned Wagnerian Romanticism, which he adored, into a belief in 'unconscious form-making', arguing that art belonged to the inner self, unaffected by external influences or knowledge, or even skill. So he began to consider abandoning the structures on which music was built. Within a few years of the turn of the century he was writing music that was atonal, discarding the system of keys that everyone's ears were used to. He asked a disturbing question. Why should music return in familiar cadences to its starting point? That was the signal of music that relied on the conscious mind; the unconscious would take it to new places.

So Schoenberg eventually opened the door to serialism, an arrangement of notes that had little to do with the cherished masterpieces Vienna loved, nor indeed with any music that it knew. It began with his twelve-note system but can be applied to any compositional form imposing an ordered arrangement on the notes which doesn't spring from the scales that all composers before him had used. Mathematics – or perhaps an attraction to physical order – was superseding the ear. A serial piece of music pays no attention to the 'natural' course of music to which our ears have become accustomed, and instead of a tonal structure attempts to give the music meaning by creating a different pattern.

His early works, 'Verklärte Nacht' among them, had been radical enough. Adjudicators at a competition in which that string sextet was entered denounced it for containing harmonies that couldn't be rationalised by the textbook rules of music. It was therefore expunged from the record. Schoenberg said afterwards that they must have discovered a chord that didn't exist, so it was obvious that there had been no performance. How could you play a piece that didn't exist? You can imagine the debate among the Viennese music examiners asked to consider that question, and their temper. Schoenberg believed the piece would prosper, as it did.

He would continue to experiment for other ears, and was off on a journey that would influence a generation of composers and take him to America. Much later in life, when the Nazis came to power in 1933, he left his work in Berlin in good time for the United States, for the simple and depressingly obvious reason that he was a Jew. It was in the early years in Vienna, the city that was still breathing the atmosphere of the nineteenth century, the sweet intoxicating air of the *fin de siècle* before the skies got dark, that he glimpsed the path he wanted to take. Sometimes a cultural atmosphere is generated – or comes about by chance – that becomes exotic and transforming. That is what happened in the city of Schoenberg and Mahler at the start of the twentieth century.

German Romanticism reached its summit there – Wagner's legacy was turned by Bruckner, particularly, into symphonic glory. His symphonies were perfectly sculpted monuments to a tradition as well as living things with their own complicated nervous systems. Twentieth-century composers would feed on them as voraciously as Bruckner had on the music of Wagner, but they would remain the finest examples of the great nineteenth-century symphony since Beethoven.

With Mahler, Bruckner brought one age to an end and opened the way to another. He was born in upper Austria in 1824 and developed his musicianship as an organist, having something of an epiphany when he met Wagner at the first performance of *Tristan und Isolde* in Munich in 1865. Three years later he conducted the first performance of the last act of *Die Meistersinger* with the Linz Choral Society. Wagner's conception of music moved him; deep in the majestic sweep of his orchestration and imagination, etched on the arches of these mighty constructions, he was striving for something new, too. Schoenberg, and slightly more conventionally Richard Strauss, were ready to take the journey on.

Freud's exploration of the dream and Schoenberg's argument for the 'unconscious' nature of musical creation – despite his meticulous and agonised technical experiments – were a release. In one city in the course of a decade on either side of 1900 a vista opened up that allowed composers, like the painters alongside them, to glimpse a tantalising future. Vienna is still a city that protects its style jealously and cherishes its conservatism; yet in that period it was the arena in which serious music was feisty and radical as well as familiar and comforting.

The end of its time as an imperial capital was close, but the Europe that was about to sink into the war-to-end-all-wars could hear in Vienna a transition that would carry forward the best of the tradition that had been nurtured in the city for a century and more and feed into it the sounds and thoughts that were new, disturbing and impossible to ignore.

Across the continent, new sounds were being heard. In Hungary, Béla Bartók was adapting the rhythms and tones of the folk songs he knew to break away from what he called 'the tyranny of the major–minor system', bringing the dance patterns that he'd known as a boy to turn a 'nationalist' sensibility – understanding the unique qualities of a country, or a territory – into something which flowed across borders. Bartók, who died unhappy in America at the end of the Second World War, was evidence of how national styles were mingling together in the closer, busier world that was developing. It was also a world that was about to fall apart.

It's tempting to search for a date in which the shock of the new century can be captured for a moment. In truth, there is not much competition. The day is Thursday, 29 May 1913. You might say that, musically, the century arrived a little late, but the night of the first performance of Igor Stravinsky's *The Rite of Spring* has every claim to be the opening of a new chapter.

It had hardly begun when the trouble started. The ballet score was accompanied by dancing which shocked supposedly unshockable Paris – despite its reputation as the sexiest city in Europe at that time, as well as the one with the highest and most impregnable notion of its intellectual superiority. The audience began to boo when the first semi-naked dancers appeared; there were calls for a doctor, and when one dancer pressed her hand against her cheek someone screamed 'Get a dentist!' Some members of the audience were apparently enraptured from the start; others were not. They continued to boo, making life almost impossible for the conductor, Pierre Monteux, and even worse for the world's most famous dancer, Vaslav Nijinsky, who was trying from the wings to shout the instructions for his choreography to the Ballets Russes company doing its best on the stage, with Stravinsky holding his coat for part of the performance to try to keep him steady as he stood on a chair and yelled to the dancers, trying to help them count their way through the music in the din. It may have been the best riot in the history of European music. The impresario Serge Diaghilev tried switching the lights on and off to get some order; the police were called. The composer Camille Saint-Saëns said afterwards that he had never before been at a performance where he felt he was being deliberately insulted.

When one critic said that never had 'the system and the cult of the wrong note [been] practised with such industry' he had got the point, however reluctantly. Stravinsky was breaking with the recent past – particularly his own, in Russia – and using primitivism to express the new. Pounding rhythms and disturbing chords – from a huge orchestra with an expanded percussion section – gave the music an urgency, and a feeling of uncontrolled lust on stage broke with convention as dramatically as Picasso was doing on canvas in that same city; and as T. S. Eliot and Ezra Pound would do in poetry in the course of the next decade. If there were artistic conventions, they were breaking down.

To many in that first-night audience, it was a noise without form or purpose. They were wrong, of course. Stravinsky's construction was meticulous: after the sacrificial dance came into his head, and he knew he had found the climax, he laboured long at the piano, sitting in Switzerland, to find a way of expressing it aloud. His method was to break with the idea of music that moved naturally from one development to the next – growing organically phrase by phrase, movement by movement. Instead, repeated notes and musical ideas would be superimposed, so that the hypnotic texture was startling and deep. It made the audience work for their money. Some loved it; others hated every note.

Stravinsky was exploiting the bravado of a city that was the most culturally stylish in Europe, and the brilliance of the Ballets Russes and Diaghilev, who were one of its great boasts. The Russians were there because they spoke the language and they thought Paris the intellectual capital of Europe. The best painters were exhibiting there; ground-breaking drama was filling the theatres; it was at peace, and having fun.

Diaghilev had brought Stravinsky to Paris four years earlier, and the composer was already celebrated. Paris loved him; musical episodes like the infernal dance from his *Firebird* suite (1910) gave audiences the thrill they wanted. And Stravinsky wanted more – the idea of violent release and an ancient urge let loose – to turn a primitive subject and fascination into a contemporary statement. In his autobiography he wrote: 'I saw in imagination a solemn pagan rite: sage elders, seated in a circle, watched a young girl dance herself to death. They were sacrificing her to propitiate the god of spring.'

That fascination with the primitive was not at all new; nor even was it strange in Paris at that time. Matisse had been painting ritualistic scenes set far away from the avenues of Paris since 1905; Picasso's startling painting *Les Demoiselles d'Avignon*, painted in 1907, was based on African sculptures which had caught his eye and was an attempt to capture the atmosphere of sexual freedom in a brothel, though it also explored a fourth dimension in the way that he pictured the faces on his giant canvas. He always called the picture *Le Bordel* (The Brothel) and it wasn't shown until the year *The Rite of Spring* was first heard, and that was in New York. Stravinsky's expression of that fascination in sound would be another way of breaking deliberately with the past; both his music and Picasso's painting were eventually seen as cultural milestones.

He'd grown up in Russia under the influence of composers like Tchaikovsky and Borodin. His father was a bass at the opera in St Petersburg, singing with the company in the Mariinsky Theatre. Rimsky-Korsakov and Musorgsky visited the family as friends, and the shining exoticism of so much Russian music of the time inspired him. There were magic themes, fairy stories, flights of the imagination to carry you off. Yet the effect was going to work on him in a different way. Instead of sticking with a tradition that absorbed folk melodies and a fascination with the remote and mysterious, turning them into something rich and usually reassuring, he would disturb.

You can hear it in the orchestration of his *Fireworks* orchestral scherzo, for example, first performed in 1909. Diaghilev's presence in the audience would change Stravinsky's life. Only twenty-seven years old at the time, he was still writing as a Russian composer, steeped in the sound world of the Romantic music that he'd inhaled in his youth. Rimsky-Korsakov became his tutor when he was in his early twenties and Stravinsky's early music glistens with the shimmering sounds that were Rimsky's own, for example at the end of his opera *The Invisible City of Kitezh*, in which the whole city rises miraculously into the air.

That was the kind of music which Stravinsky would feed on, and then abandon. His break was not as sharp as that of Schoenberg, who was beginning to dismantle the scale in favour of his twelve-note system and dispense entirely with the keys that gave music its shape and familiar contours. His argument was about the nature of music itself, about the falseness that he felt in the need for a tonic key at its heart. Stravinsky's rebellion was in moving towards music that didn't express personal feelings and was therefore 'objective', referring only to itself and nothing else. His predecessors and teachers would take a different view. Rimsky was a conservative in a Russia that was turning in on itself under Nicholas II, the last of the tsars, and where Symbolist poets, for example, were being denounced as decadents. Diaghilev liked ballet, mysticism, sexual liberation, the rhythms of folk music much more than Rimsky did.

In Paris there seemed to be little of the stultifying atmosphere of Moscow or even of St Petersburg. Stravinsky enjoyed the intoxication of the city, where there was an air of discovery. Audiences loved the Russian spirit of Diaghilev's company, and they were ready – they thought – for experiment. Stravinsky's *Firebird* was a great success and it was in that year that he began to plan *The Rite of Spring*. He had come under the influence of a Russian painter and archaeologist called Nicholas Roerich who was absorbed, almost mystically, in ideas from Russia's Slavic past, fascinated by prehistoric religious life and ritual. In part, *The Rite* was his idea. He had a vision for a piece with the title 'The Great Sacrifice'.

Stravinsky was able to take it on because he was now popular. After the *Firebird* he'd written the *Petroushka* suite and Paris was at his feet. He wasn't yet thirty, and was ready to break out. Living for much of the year in Switzerland, he began, with Roerich, to plan the ballet. Roerich recounted: 'The first set should transport us to the foot of a sacred hill, in a lush plain, where Slavonic tribes are gathered together to celebrate the spring rites. In the scene there is an old witch, who predicts the future, a marriage by capture, and round dances.'

The choreography was being done by Nijinsky, and the truth is that in the first rehearsals composer and dancer didn't really understand each other – at least according to Stravinsky. Long afterwards he described the collaboration:

> The dancers knew what they were doing, at least, even though what they were doing often had nothing to do with the music. 'I will count to forty while you play,' Nijinksy would say, 'and we will see where we come out.' He could not understand that although we might at some point come out together, this did not mean we had been together along the way.

From the beginning, it was obvious that it would be difficult. In Stravinsky's head, everything was clear. The music seemed to have found a 'natural' form; it made sense to him – although when the conductor, Monteux, first heard him banging it out on the piano he said he thought he'd gone a little mad. Diaghilev suspected there was a *succès de scandale* in the making (he wouldn't be disappointed), but when the first rumbles of protest broke into a roar at the appearance of the dancers after a couple of minutes, Stravinsky left for the wings, furious and apparently uncomprehending. When the performance was over he was still livid: 'I left the hall in a rage. I was sitting on the right near the orchestra and I remember slamming the door. I have never again been that angry. The music was *so* familiar to me. I loved it, and could not understand why people who had not yet heard it wanted to protest in advance.'

But of course he had indeed produced a masterpiece, cherished by orchestras and audiences ever since and recognised as a departure more immediately comprehensible than the highly intellectual – almost mathematical – arguments of Schoenberg in Vienna. It was a matter of feeling. Just as artists were using primitive images, and the Cubists new ways of seeing, to represent something contemporary, Stravinsky produced music that, for all its subtlety, still sounded raw. Its spirit survived the scandal, and the audience who booed, the critics who moaned, missed the point. This was music that seemed to them to lay waste a glorious past, to destroy, but it did not. *The Rite of Spring* was one of the building blocks of the twentieth century.

Oddly enough, Walt Disney got the point. When he wanted to give the volcanoes a voice in *Fantasia*, he turned to Stravinsky, who had produced one of the great musical eruptions. No volcano has ever sounded so elegant.

Stravinsky's experience in Paris was part of a wider struggle between established art and the avant-garde which was going on among painters too. The intellectual atmosphere in the city in the years before the First World War was electric: it was not only the Russians who were drawn there, because it seemed the epicentre of Europe, but everyone interest in fashion and ideas. Paris had poise, style and daring. The period in London before the formal end of the Edwardian era in 1910 with the death of the King was less fevered. Indeed, the first two symphonies of Edward Elgar (1908 and 1911) and his Violin Concerto (1910) can be seen as the last pre-war flowering of a special kind of English confidence. Their lyricism and passion were deep, but somehow untroubled. The mysterious questing energy of his 'Enigma' Variations written a decade before (1898–9) seemed to have been calmed. The symphonies were multi-layered and complex in their thematic structure but did not suggest unease or a break with the past. They were summations (he would leave only sketches for the Third Symphony, and that much later in 1933, the year before his death at the age of seventy-six). After the war was over, the Cello Concerto of 1919 – his last important work – revealed a disturbing shadow that had not been there before.

Elgar was remarkable. He is still thought to define 'Englishness', though it's not as easy as it seems to explain why. 'Nimrod' from 'Enigma' has become a solemn anthem for great events; the tune from the first 'Pomp and Circumstance' March is England's second national anthem; and the figure of Elgar himself, the countryman with a white moustache and a dog at his heel, seems the quintessence of English stock. Yet there is much more to it than that. The texture of his music has a pastoral calm and confidence which is invaded by a shaft of sadness. There's no fevered, youthful nationalism here, more an understanding of what there is to be lost.

Elgar was forty before his reputation made him a national figure, a birthday that fell in the year of Queen Victoria's Diamond Jubilee in 1897. The British Empire was at its zenith, covering nearly a quarter of the land-mass of the world, and about a quarter of its people, perhaps 370 million. On the day of the Jubilee parade – when 50,000 troops marched by – the Queen pressed a button at the central telegraph office off Trafalgar Square and a Morse code message of 'thanks to her people' was sent to the four corners of the earth.

Elgar's 'Imperial' March for the Jubilee was popular and, after years of teaching and conducting without much fame, he entered the period in which he wrote two of the works that would establish him, 'Enigma' in 1899 and, a year later, *The Dream of Gerontius*. *Gerontius*, that choral setting of a poem by Cardinal Newman, who'd sought the reunion of the Church of England with Rome, is a Catholic meditation on death and immortality. Elgar's mother was a convert to Catholicism and though he wasn't raised strictly in that faith as a boy it became important to him. Even at the turn of the twentieth century, however, it was still natural for Catholics to feel outsiders. Emancipation and formal acceptance of the Church had come less than a century before. Feelings of belonging in his music are touched, unmistakably, with irony. His father was a piano-tuner, who taught young Elgar the organ. Elgar then taught himself the violin and demonstrated his urge to learn.

> I am self-taught in the matter of harmony, counterpoint, form, and in short the whole of the 'mystery' of music . . . when I resolved to become a musician and found that the exigencies of life would prevent me from getting any tuition, the only thing to do was to teach myself. I read everything, played everything and heard everything I possibly could.

The influences were, naturally, the late Romantics like Wagner and Bruckner, and Debussy too. Elgar understood how to colour music to his own taste, giving it a characteristic that his friend the critic Ernest Newman called its 'sunset' quality, with harmonies and cadences that evoked a dying light. In the First Symphony and the Violin Concerto – written two years apart – there is expressive writing that seems to have longing in it. By the time the Concerto was first heard in 1910 he had a great body of work behind him. There were early choral pieces that he'd conducted in Worcester and Malvern (the cradle of his music), work for piano, violin and orchestra – but only one symphony. He did say that it was the highest form of art, towards which he strove, yet a career as a symphonist eluded him. His second, in 1911, wasn't a popular success and he left only sketches for his third. It was completed, to considerable acclaim, by the composer Anthony Payne in 1998, and has become a posthumous and popular part of the concert repertoire.

In that particular sense, Elgar's life as a composer was unfulfilled. Yet he is a musician whose stature and influence were secured by something different – a breadth that encompassed his time. He sits, of course, at a turning point in the history of his country. The swagger of the Edwardian era – prosperous, expansive, even self-indulgent – would pass away quickly. With the First World War came a shrivelling of the glory, as Sir Edward Grey looked from his room in the Foreign Office across St James's Park in the summer of 1914 and saw the lamps going out all over Europe. All the old empires began to shrink. One of the reasons why Elgar's music speaks so powerfully of his country is that it reflects that story – the heady jubilation of Empire at its peak, the confidence of a country whose cities were expanding and whose rural heart still beat strong, and then the coming of war.

His early music exudes a comfortable security. Whether in the delicacy of a lovely tune like the one everyone knows in 'Salut d'amour', or in the snap of a march, Elgar's melodic flow never stops. He was a tunesmith. In writing for the voice, for example, he could bring to mind an unforgettable scene or a dart of sadness, a flash of light on the hills, a rushing of clouds. His five *Sea Pictures*, written in 1899, are perfect miniatures. His instinct for the voice was sure, and so was his feeling for the orchestra. In his Introduction and Allegro for Strings (1905) – a brilliant piece of short orchestral writing – he manages to produce abstract music that mirrors his listeners' emotions. He had become the English late Romantic.

That piece is in one movement, and quite short, scored for string quartet and orchestra (it was written for the newly formed London Symphony Orchestra) and it reveals Elgar's mastery as an orchestral writer, bringing us back to the mystery of the symphonies. Where are they? The success of his first in 1908 – which had nearly a hundred performances in the season after it was written – was never repeated. It's surely not fanciful to ascribe some of the change in Elgar to the darkening landscape across which he walked. He was a man of great sensitivity, who seemed to pick up the vibrations of everything around him – whether from the friends who are sketched out in 'Enigma' or the memories that are embroidered in the 'Wand of Youth' suite. After 1910 and the death of Edward VII the ground he knew began to buckle and crack.

One of the most touching pictures of the last year before the war is Elgar's symphonic study (as he called it), *Falstaff*. There's no more English character, of course, than this jovial mixture of buffoonery and rough wisdom. He spoke of Shakespeare, fun, a larger-than-life appetite for women and drink, and a certain benign *permanence*. Yet Falstaff is also a figure who experiences loneliness. His stupid pranks lose him friends; and he feels the touch of humiliation. Elgar, who had that shadow of the outsider on him, despite his place in public life and despite his brilliance, had a feeling for Falstaff. When the old man is in Gloucestershire we're travelling through Elgar's England too and at the end, when Falstaff dies, and Prince Hal rises – 'the man of stern reality' as Elgar calls him – you're in no doubt about where Elgar's sympathy lies, and the sense he feels for an oak brought to the ground. It was first heard at the Leeds Festival in the last year before the war began. Something of England is lost in Falstaff's death, and Elgar was writing with passion for that which was slipping away. The bombast now was left to the songs that the troops would sing to raise their spirits, or to enjoin their families to 'keep the home fires burning'.

Though he lived until he was seventy-six, dying in 1934, only one great work came after that war was over. It was the Cello Concerto, which he finished in 1919. Everything about Elgar is in it. It has strong sinews and vivacity, but a comprehension of sadness. The critic Neville Cardus in the *Guardian* called it 'a swan-song of rare and vanishing beauty'. The reason for its popularity is surely that it is unmistakably Elgarian and English – a gently painful depiction of sadness. Elgar always had hope, from his faith, but he understood darkness. His triumph was to turn music to the service of that vision. In doing so he was able to speak with a subtlety that few of his British contemporaries would ever match. In the splintered Europe that he came to experience, the British story was a special one, taking a country from a notion of untrammelled glory to the reality of a broken generation and poverty. On the first part of that journey, Elgar is the best guide.

In the Cello Concerto, completed after the Armistice, the vision of his early choral works and the first two symphonies is overlaid with a wandering melancholy, as if the cello itself is seeking rest and resolution. Its voice is passionate – troubled but true – and seems to have been let loose in a world that has lost its bearings. The composer's brilliance is in delineating with perfect clarity the shape of that disordered place. After the war, what else could be said?

He leads into a time when musicians tried to speak in notes of a world that was bewildering. For all the diplomatic jousting among the great powers in the first decade of the twentieth century, the obvious weakness of Austro-Hungary and German expansionism, the warm glow that survived the death of the old Queen was hard to dispel. The optimism of the immediate post-Victorian era, which in Britain saw widening prosperity, some political reform and modernisation, darkened late. Artists trying to reflect the world – to explain and describe it – were faced with a dramatic and painful change with the outbreak of war. Even in that first summer the patriotic tub-thumping in Britain was accompanied by the insistent promise that the fighting would end soon. That feeble deception soon gave way to horror. By 1916, two years after the war began, the whole country knew that its young men were being slaughtered and that the world had changed.

Composers throughout Europe were affected individually. Many were drafted themselves. Schoenberg was called up to the Austro-Hungarian army reserves in 1915, and his pupil Alban Berg was called up too. In France, Maurice Ravel was one of many musicians who served, he as an ambulance driver on the western front. Ravel dedicated his 'Tombeau de Couperin' to his friends killed in battle. Berg based the barrack-room scenes in his opera *Wozzeck* (1925) on his wartime experiences, and it became one of the most vivid pictures of the shattering effect of the war and the inhumanity that seeps into a soldier's life and spreads far beyond the battlefield, to the community at large.

One British musician in particular is worth special attention. Ivor Gurney (1890–1937) was a talented student at the Royal College of Music. Sir Charles Villiers Stanford, the celebrated Irish composer who had written and taught in Britain for decades, ranked him high, predicting that he might even outshine other pupils like Ralph Vaughan Williams, Frank Bridge and Arthur Bliss. Gurney was called up and went to France as a private. It was the making of his art, and the destruction of his life.

He was wounded in 1917 but not before he had written poetry and set songs that caught the bleakness and pain of life in the trenches with exceptional poignancy. Like so many others he'd gone to the front reasonably cheerfully; the poet Rupert Brooke said at first that the war was a condemnation of 'a world grown old and cold and weary'. In August 1915, Gurney wrote to his friend Marion Scott: 'Well, here I am, a soldier of the King, the best thing for me at present. I feel that nowhere could I be happier than where I am . . . so the experience may be called a success . . . It is a better way to die; with these men, in such a cause.' A year letter he was telling her by letter that 'death would be preferable to such a life'.

By this time Gurney was already getting a reputation as a poet and as a setter of songs. In one of his best-known songs, 'In Flanders', he set a poem by F. W. Harvey imagining a soldier looking round at the alien flatness of Flanders and dreaming of English hills.

> I'm homesick for my fields again –
> My hills again!
> To see above the Severn plain
> Unscabbarded against the sky
> The blue high blade of Cotswold lie;
> The giant clouds go royally
> By jagged Malvern with a train
> Of shadows. Where the land is low
> Like a huge imprisoning O
> I hear a heart that's sound and high
> I hear the heart within me cry:
> 'I'm homesick for my hills again –
> My hills again!
> Cotswold or Malvern, sun or rain!
> My hills again!'

As in so much English music of the war years, a nostalgia for home takes on a deeper resonance, becoming an elegy for a pastoral, settled England that was already passing away, even before the war began. It was as if its loss wasn't fully understood until the guns opened up in Flanders; the realisation was not that it had been destroyed by some assault by the Kaiser but that it had been poisoned in a way that couldn't be explained. Gurney captured in his songs a longing for what was lost, expressing a feeling of mystery as well as loss.

The effect of the war on music went far beyond the recording of personal experiences. Music was an argument in itself, an assertion of a set of values that was different to the other side's. Naturally enough, popular music played at the piano and sung in the pub was a straightforward appeal to patriotism, unmistakably home grown, familiar and reassuring. But art music – for want of a better description – wasn't so easy to co-opt, for the good reason that there was a heavy German influence on much of British serious music. The reason why Elgar's orchestral works were so popular in Germany before the war is that they sounded agreeably familiar; they could be taken as Brahmsian symphonies with an English accent. This was all very awkward when Germanophobia became rife before the war – spies were thought to be everywhere – and, when the guns began to fire, there were efforts to ban German music. At one Promenade concert in August 1914, at the very outbreak of war, Richard Strauss was replaced by Tchaikovsky. He couldn't be tolerated.

It was difficult for musicians, because many of them shared the views of Sir Hubert Parry on Germans and German music: 'I owed too much to their music and their philosophers of former times to believe it possible that the nation at large could be imbued with the teaching of a few advocates of mere brutal violence and material aggression. We know now that it is the hideous militarism of the Prussians that has poisoned the wells of the spirit throughout Germany.'

That generosity of spirit towards many Germans wasn't echoed in France, where the sight of Prussian soldiers marching down the Champs-Elysées in the 1870s during the occupation in the course of the Franco-Prussian war was still remembered by the older generation. France's distinctive musical tradition had to be reinterpreted as embodying the virtues of a classical Mediterranean culture, as opposed to German culture – what the writer Jean Cocteau would sneer at after the war as 'Teutonic fog'.

The reactionary monarchical writer Charles Maurras identified Classicism as 'natural' and opposed it to the sickness and degeneration of Symbolism and Romanticism. The great ogre to those of his view was, of course, the old bogeyman himself, Richard Wagner, accused of being the fount of all that was sick in French culture, from Baudelaire to Proust. So there was a crusade to reinvigorate national values in French music. On 15 December 1915 Jacques Fouché, director of the recently reopened Paris Opera, presented a spectacle entitled *La Mademoiselle de Nantes*, in which musicians in costume on stage presented a concert of Lully and Charpentier to the imagined daughters of Mme de Montespan. The previous November, the 'Matinées Nationales' were launched at the Sorbonne. The conductors at these concerts were dressed in patriotic blue, like French soldiers at the front.

One composer who threw himself into this musical offensive was Claude Debussy himself. He contributed a preface to a series of lectures given in Lyons for a group called Les Amis de la Musique Française, where he wrote that French music suffered from too many 'importations singuliers', and in a strikingly aggressive image added: 'It is a matter of pulling out the weeds without mercy, just as a surgeon cuts away a gangrened leg.' Debussy had always mocked German music for what he called its 'administrative musical forms': 'Let us recover our liberty, our forms: having invented them for the most part, it is right that we conserve them; there are none more beautiful. Let us no longer exert ourselves in writing symphonies, for which we stretch our muscles without an appreciable result . . . let us prefer the operetta.' Debussy represented his view in music. His last three sonatas are signed on the title page with a flourish, 'Musicien Français', and compared to his earlier impressionism they have a new clarity, with subtle hints of the great French composers of the Baroque.

In Germany itself, of course, there was a quite different tone. Its most brilliant composer, Richard Strauss, spoke of superiority, both military and musical. To composers like Strauss, German and Austrian pre-eminence in music seemed to be matched by those countries' industrial and military might. It was the way of things. He was a composer at the top of his game. *Salome* (1905) and *Elektra* (1909) were extraordinarily bold pieces of opera in the first decade of the century, crashing cymbals of change, followed by his brilliant simultaneous evocation of the fun and darkness of Vienna in *Der Rosenkavalier* (1910). At the outbreak of war he was working on a new opera, *Die Frau ohne Schatten* (The Woman without a Shadow), in one of his regular collaborations with the Symbolist poet Hugo von Hofmannsthal, and he sounded confident about everything. He wrote to Hofmannsthal in October 1914 saying 'we're bound to win, of course', and, just after finishing the opera, said to the poet's wife: 'These are great and glorious times . . . one feels exalted, knowing that this land and this people stand at the beginning of a great development, that they must and will assume the leadership of Europe.'

The point about these sentiments is that they were the common currency among patriotic Germans – because Strauss was no war-monger. He refused to sign a petition in favour of the war, which already bore the signatures of many luminaries of German culture, explaining that 'declarations about things concerning war and politics were not fitting for an artist'. Declarations might have been 'not fitting' but no one of sensitivity could remain unaffected by the war, or avoid being scarred by it. Musical idioms strengthened in its flames – neo-Classicism in France and the pastoral melancholy in England – would be important elements in establishing the mood of the post-war world.

When the war began Strauss was established as the inheritor of German Romanticism who had given it life for a new century. By the time *Der Rosenkavalier* was first performed in 1911 he was probably the most famous living composer in the world. In the opera, a comedy of manners and love, he summons up all the effervescence of Vienna, both eighteenth-century and contemporary – its love of the waltz, the empty vigour of its high society, and the importance of tradition, especially in the presentation of the silver rose as a token of love. But Strauss was not a composer dazzled by surface glitter; he was making his reputation as a musician who was willing to plunge into the dark.

Though his roots were in Mozart and Wagner, his music was his own. In the first decade of the twentieth century his two operas *Elektra* and *Salome* shocked their audiences, though they sprang directly from the tradition that Wagner had established, using large orchestras to produce textures of sound that allowed a world of dissonance to coexist with sweetly expressed emotion. When *Salome* was heard for the first time, in New York in 1905, the audience found its music hard and its subject matter – from Oscar Wilde's play – unpalatable. It closed after one performance. But in Europe it thrived from the start.

In *Salome*, Strauss took motifs and themes and seemed to wind them round each other so that in the climactic dance of the seven veils – which leads to death, like the sacrificial dance in Stravinsky's *Rite of Spring* – there is an explosion of energy. Strauss's debt to Wagner is obvious in the recurring themes, but so is the originality of the opera: an audience two decades before wouldn't have been ready for this. In Germany it was popular, and with *Elektra* four years later Strauss was established as a master who could summon up almost uncontrollable passion on the stage through brilliant orchestration, vivid harmonies and memorable melodies. The opera, from Sophocles' play of the same name, is the story of Elektra's hatred for her mother Klytemnestra, who had murdered her father Agamemnon and taken a new lover. Elektra waits anxiously for her brother Orestes to avenge their father's death. This done, the opera ends in her terrifying exultation in the gory revenge and she dies in a blood frenzy after Orestes has killed both his mother and her lover, the guilty pair. There is no darker story, and the dense chromaticism of Strauss's score produces an overwhelming effect.

Where could he go from there? Elizabeth Schumann-Heink, who created the role of Klytemnestra in the first *Elektra*, said that she would never sing the role again, because she thought Strauss had exceeded Wagner, who had already taken the human voice to the limit. 'It was frightful,' she said. 'We were a set of mad women. There is nothing beyond *Elektra*.' It was Strauss's fourth opera (there would be eleven more) and his first collaboration with von Hofmannsthal. Although now recognised as a master, he is an example of how musical styles can move on, more quickly than you might think. For the truth is that, after the First World War, Strauss – like a number of other composers – seemed to be part of the past, for all the shock of *Salome* and *Elektra* and the polished brilliance of *Der Rosenkavalier*. *Die Frau ohne Schatten* fell flat at the Vienna State Opera, not least because its Symbolist plot was hard to grasp. After the war tastes would change quickly, as if everything that had contributed to the cataclysm should be forgotten.

In France, while the first influences of jazz crept across the Atlantic and the style and vigour of the 1920s started to give contours to a landscape flattened by war, the neo-Classicist movement would begin. Composers looked to the European past – to Bach and Haydn – for inspiration that would take them away from what they thought was the suffocating grip of German Romanticism, and even from the expressive music that had come from Debussy and those inspired by him. It would not prevent Ravel sounding French, nor Igor Stravinsky moving on from neo-Classicism to quite different music, but for a time in the 1920s the fashion shifted. Strauss had been a giant before the war; afterwards he would find that he was diminished. Nothing in his talent had altered – his operas *Ariadne auf Naxos* and *Capriccio* were yet to come and he would still be sounding a Romantic voice in the year before his death, 1948, with his *Four Last Songs*. But the war had changed everything.

Nationalism, of course, was still important. Empires collapsed in the war, and one of the curious results was that millions of Europeans found themselves living in their own countries for the first time. Finland became a republic, with the three Baltic states, Lithuania having flirted briefly with monarchy; Hungary became a monarchy. Czechoslovakia became a nation under Masaryk. Germany and Austria reincarnated themselves as democracies after 1918. Russia was reconstituting itself – and pulling in many outlying republics – as the Soviet Union. In western Europe change was afoot – two constitutional monarchies, Britain and Italy, widened their electorates (reluctantly) to include all adult males. Some women got the vote in 1918 in Britain, and the rest of them ten years later. The flower of youth was shed; and societies were reordered too.

The intellectual turmoil that had characterised Vienna and Paris around the turn of the century was now electrified by the physical horror of the war itself and the destruction of the architecture of the old Europe. Berg's *Wozzeck* was probably the most profound operatic meditation on the effects of war on life at home as well as on the battlefield, and remains almost unsurpassed in its period for the bleakness of its vision. Artists reacted in different ways: Dadaism was a means for some of them, though others thought its nihilism was simply an escape. Neo-Classicism, the last flowering of German Romanticism and pastoralism were all different consequences of the war and had a long sunset glow ahead of them.

Alongside, a new primitivism would arise in music, which would take much inspiration from jazz. In much of the music of the early 1920s there was a strange absurdist, almost Dadaist spirit, expressed in an odd mechanical quality, suggesting perhaps that the savages of war had lost their souls. You can hear something of that quality in the first of the 'Mouvements Perpetuels' written in 1919 by the young Francis Poulenc. It was a common response to the tragedy of war, as everything had to be stripped back to its principles, the foundations rebuilt.

How could music written after the First World War fail to reflect the depth of its horror? In Ivor Gurney's evocation of England, in songs like 'Severn Meadows' or 'Nine of the Clock', there is a haunting understanding of the permanence of the change: all was gone. To the generation growing up after 1918 they spoke of darkness. Gurney himself was a broken victim of war. The depression from which he'd suffered as a student became a curse and soon after he came back from

France, wounded and gassed, he began a steep decline. He was never able to recover, and his greatest work was behind him, though he was still young. Stanford's prediction about what he might have achieved was never tested; yet in his work we can still feel the power of the wartime experience on the artist, and see the contours of the country which he thought changed for ever.

W. B. Yeats said that Elgar had an heroic melancholy in his music; and Gurney captured with exquisite simplicity the plangent understanding of a world splintered and shattered, and a generation betrayed. In the modern music of war, these songs are as permanent as any memorial in stone.

15

From War to War

Leningrad, Hollywood and the Diaspora

~

IF YOU DROPPED into the Splendid Palace cinema in Leningrad on
an afternoon in 1925 the chances are that you would see a film with
improvised piano accompaniment played live. A grumpy-looking
young man would be devising rhythms and melodies to add some
lustre to the first feature. It might be *The Extraordinary Adventures of Mr
West in the Land of the Bolsheviks* directed by Lev Kuleshov, or one of his
earlier films, *On the Red Front*. He was the fashionable director of the
day. The pianist would be smoking, almost certainly, and he would
probably be Dmitri Shostakovich.

The picture is alluring. A man who would become one of the giants
of twentieth-century music – if not its greatest all-round composer,
then a contender for the crown – was earning about 100 roubles a
month to help his family while he was studying at the Leningrad
conservatoire. In front of him was the flickering screen that would
revolutionise popular entertainment around the world, even in the
Soviet Union, until Joseph Stalin came along. He would be improvis-
ing new sounds, maybe even introducing a few hints at jazz, of which
news was beginning to spread from New York. He would be playing to
an audience that still retained some of the optimism of the revolutionaries who had been in the streets of Leningrad a few years before.
It's a useful snapshot of the beginning of the 1920s.

It was the decade of hope and hedonism, and then of depression –
the age in which Europe reshaped itself after the Great War and
America began to race ahead. Film-makers were beginning to understand the possibilities of the camera and musicians were starting to try to
build on the foundations that had been laid before the war by
composers who had sensed the start of a new era. Whether from

246

Stravinsky or Schoenberg, Debussy or Ravel, the message was exciting. And there was Shostakovich playing for the movies, perhaps learning how slick narrative continuity can be in film, how effectively a director can flash backwards and forwards with images to imprint a thought or make an impact. These were the techniques that, married to his prodigious originality, would give much of his music its drive and power.

The danger, of course, is getting carried away with the thought. The Shostakovich at the piano was probably fed up. He'd left the Bright Reel cinema the year before because they were slow in paying him his agreed fee, and he resented the whole business:

> The cinema has finished me off. Because I am somewhat sensitive, when I arrive home the cinema music is still ringing in my ears and the dreadful heroes still appearing before my eyes. As a result, I'm unable to fall asleep for ages. I finally get to sleep but not earlier than 4 or 5 a.m. So in the morning I get up very late and in a foul mood. All sorts of ugly thoughts creep into my head – such as that I've sold myself to Sevzapkino for 134 roubles, or that I've become a movie-pianist. By then it's time to dash off to the conservatoire. After that I come home, have lunch and fly off to the Splendid Palace.

Shostakovich the movie-pianist introduces the decade with an appropriate flourish, despite his despair. His city and his country would become a strangely confused musical world, first exciting then repressive and depressing; and the films he watched would multiply and improve. Soon, pianists wouldn't be necessary, because they had soundtracks of their own. And that sound would introduce to many audiences, at least outside the Soviet Union, America's gift to the world – jazz.

The music that gave the twentieth century its own rhythm turned improvisation – inspired invention – into a principle. It bubbled up from the streets and the fields, drew on the singing of spirituals and the early blues in the American South, and opened a new chapter in the story of music. Before long, with the first recordings and the radio, the jazz bands in the dancehalls were speaking in a musical language that became international, and irresistible. At the start of the

1920s these sounds were the lifeblood of entertainment and represented a break with the past. The Great War was over, and for a few years there was untrammelled optimism, despite the memory of destruction. Never mind that the soul of jazz was rooted in the misery of slaves and the downtrodden, and that it washed the world with tuneful melancholy – it was fresh, with all the energy of a country that was building skyscrapers and making fortunes, at least in its big cities. It had the appeal of the primitive; and in these songs and these rhythms the point of all the artistry was in finding something untamed and raw.

When Adelaide Hall recorded 'Creole Love Call' with Duke Ellington in 1927 she was the portrait of the age. She would still be singing in the 1990s as an old lady in Britain (where she married) and still carried the legend of those days. When she sang with Ellington on that disc she was twenty-six, New York born, and the recording – a song without words, just sounds that echo the jazzmen's instruments – still crackles with the atmosphere of New York.

F. Scott Fitzgerald wrote, after the Wall Street Crash of 1929 when the depression came and the skies darkened again, that sometimes he could still hear 'a ghostly rumble among the drums, an asthmatic whisper in the trombones' that swept him back in an instant to the early 1920s when it seemed as if all the world was young, before the days when he imagined watching a friend in Wall Street jump from his window and crawl back to the Princeton Club to die. The spirit of jazz drew you back to the start of the Roaring Twenties when it seemed as if the roar would never stop. Never had music become so popular so quickly. A generation was entranced; if you could play or sing there was an audience waiting. You could easily be persuaded that nothing could stop you.

We've been following music-makers down the centuries, from early singers through Baroque and Classical masters to the Romantics, listening to composers who had craft and intellect, and who brought profound thinking to music in expressing their originality. In the twentieth century that tradition – call it Classical, if you will – met the thundering torrent of jazz. At first they seem quite remote. Jazz spoke of a world with different rules, treasured improvisation and free form, and celebrated music from the gut.

But of course it's not as simple as that. They are different streams – as in some ancient Biblical family tree, those composers who thought of themselves as serious artists and those who embraced popular culture seemed to sprawl off in different directions, breeding different families. But they are related. The descendants of jazz – be-bop, swing, rock 'n' roll, the intricacies and high refinement of modern jazz – are part of another story for another day. They would take us into different territory. But when it all began, many of the composers who were the inheritors of the European tradition were enthralled. They couldn't ignore these sounds, and didn't.

When Igor Stravinsky wrote his Ragtime for Eleven Instruments in 1918 he was excited by the possibilities. Composers like Erik Satie, Paul Hindemith and Darius Milhaud would all plunder the same barrel. How could they resist? Stravinsky first learned of jazz from piano arrangements brought back from the United States by a conductor friend and, like Debussy and Satie who'd written cakewalks, he was drawn instantly to the idiom. Picasso drew a picture of two jazzmen (in one continuous, wonderfully fluid line) for the cover of the piano transcription of that Stravinsky piece. Paris, the home of the new, was excited. When Josephine Baker arrived from America in 1925 with her Revue Nègre she was a sensation, even there. She would dance wearing only a few spare feathers, simulating sex with her partner on stage, and the dance critic André Levinson said that the origins of her act lay 'in the primeval forest as rhythmic orgies, induced by a panic terror of the demons who inhabit the night'. She was a star. Smart Parisian women bought special make-up to darken their skin; Matisse sculpted her in cut-out cardboard.

The sounds were chic. Francis Poulenc wrote a ballet in 1925, *Les Biches*, that was infused with jazz; Maurice Ravel, the heir to Debussy, was incorporating the new rhythms. His two piano concertos, written in the three years after his successful tour of the United States in 1928, have the stamp of jazz on them, as well as the influence of the European tradition from which he sprang. In America, where he had imitators who carried on the back-and-forth traffic of musical ideas across the Atlantic, Ravel was surprised to find some of those who came to his concerts (at which he said he was received more enthusiastically than sometimes he was in Paris) dismissive and also a little fearful of jazz. It was threatening; and it was black. These were early days and urban America, for all its devotion to progress, wasn't sure. In Paris, musicians were happy to open their ears to it. That was even more true in Berlin.

Christopher Isherwood's account of a tour of the brothels of Berlin in the early 1930s – in *Goodbye to Berlin* – gives an elegiac account that breathes with longing for the wildest days of the Weimar Republic in the strange chaos after the war, written in the years leading up to the outbreak of its successor. That Berlin was edgy and thrilling. There was violence in the streets, fun in the nightclubs, where you couldn't always be sure who was a man and who a woman. Sometimes you weren't supposed to be able to tell. You can hear something of that fusion of darkness and frantic hedonism in the early music of Paul Hindemith (1895–1963), who'd become a pillar of serious German music but in the 1920s was dangerous. Most of all you feel it in Kurt Weill (1900–50). His first important collaboration with the playwright Bertolt Brecht was in *The Threepenny Opera*, first performed in Berlin in 1928, a piece of music theatre that gave a musical signature to its time.

The lead role of Macheath was written for a well-known tenor of the day (Harald Paulsen), Lotte Lenya, whom Weill would marry, was also in the first-night cast, and the musical found a popular nerve. The year before, the Austrian composer Ernst Krenek had written an opera called *Jonny Spielt auf* (Jonny Strikes Up the Band) in which the lead character was a black American jazz musician. It played in forty-two opera houses across Europe for more than 400 performances in its first year. The plot has the jazz violinist winning over a self-doubting European composer to the ways of the New World where all is excitement and innovation. That message and that style were infectious; they were almost established already.

As Ravel had noticed, in the United States the association of jazz with the black underclass meant that institutional prejudice was bound to keep it at bay – at least until white musicians began to play. Europeans might find raw primitivism exciting; in America it smouldered with a threat, or so they thought. One of those who spanned the gap wasn't a real jazz man at all – though he styled himself the King of Jazz – Paul Whiteman. With his improbably appropriate name, he used his dance band to try to bring jazz and established music together. In 1924 he conceived the idea of a piece that might take its place on the concert platform – at the Aeolian Hall in New York – but would bring with it the heady odour of the dancehall and the speakeasy (this was the era of Prohibition).

Whiteman wanted to bring the popular and the highbrow together. He decided to commission a piece from a young composer – he was only twenty-five – who shared his view. 'There had been so much chatter about the limitations of jazz, not to speak of the manifest misunderstandings of its function. Jazz, they said, had to be in strict time. It had to cling to dance rhythms. I resolved, if possible, to kill that misconception with one sturdy blow.' The young composer was George Gershwin (1898–1937), and he had an idea for the piece: 'I heard it as a sort of musical kaleidoscope of America – of our vast melting pot, of our unduplicated national pep, of our blues, our metropolitan madness.'

He called his composition 'Rhapsody in Blue'. The first performance was in February 1924, in a programme of songs by Irving Berlin, Victor Herbert and Jerome Kern, and – as a bizarre companion piece – one of Elgar's 'Pomp and Circumstance' marches. The programme called it 'an experiment in modern music', and in the audience that heard the opening wail of the clarinet for the first time were musical luminaries including the violinists Fritz Kreisler and Jascha Heifitz, the composer Sergei Rachmaninov and the conductor Leopold Stokowski.

The *New York Times* said the next day that Gershwin might yet succeed in taking jazz out of the kitchen. He certainly made a lot of money. A million recordings were sold and with the sheet-music sales he became a very rich man. In one conversation with Rável, in which Gershwin was asking for advice, Ravel asked him how much he earned. The answer was somewhere between a hundred and two hundred thousands dollars a year. 'It is you who should teach me how to compose,' said Ravel. Jazz and the music or the concert hall or the academy have gone on separate paths, perhaps divided by money, race, tradition. Yet they've borrowed one from the other throughout the twentieth century and beyond. No serious composer since the 1930s has been unaffected by the sound revolution that came to New York with the first jazz bands from the South in the same year as the Great War ended, and by the 1960s many modern composers were engaged in precisely the same kinds of explorations as the high priests of modern jazz, like John Coltrane. They often marched apart, but sometimes in step.

In the 1920s and 1930s the two streams encountered each other – one from a tradition that saw it as the highest art, another from the streets and fields where it was the people's voice and nothing more. They would go their separate ways again – the recording studio and the explosion of popular culture would see to that – but not without remembering each other.

Jazz was music's unruly offspring – full of life, originality and a restless passion. It is refreshing and energising, leaving its mark on everything it has touched. With film, it made a heavenly match. Sooner or later, music would arrive on the screen and the labouring figure of Shostakovich would be allowed to leave the dark of the cinema pit and his piano. It happened, of course, in Hollywood. The first 'talkie' was *The Jazz Singer* with Al Jolson in 1927, with a few synchronised songs, but a year earlier the same director, Alan Crosland, had produced *Don Juan*, which had a full score.

So Hollywood began to use music, inevitably at first in a popular idiom. But in the first days of film – in the early days of the century – the piano accompaniment in the cinema (later a small band might play) was usually a classical medley. In 1915 D. W. Griffith's film *Birth of a Nation* had a piano accompaniment that borrowed from Grieg, Tchaikovsky and Wagner. It wasn't long before composers began to sense the potential. Gottfried Huppertz wrote the score for Fritz Lang's *Metropolis* in 1926.

With the arrival of recorded sound in the 1920s, composers began to look towards the silver screen. In Hollywood, Erich Korngold and Max Steiner wrote successful scores, Steiner producing the music for the first *King Kong* in 1933 and Korngold writing the music that accompanied Errol Flynn on several of his adventures. Both composers had come from Vienna, influenced by a musical culture that embraced the experiments of Arnold Schoenberg and the light lyricism of Franz Lehar. Steiner was the grandson of a theatre manager in Vienna (and the godson of Richard Strauss) and had conducted operetta there in his teens. He left London for the United States at the outbreak of war in 1914 rather than face deportation home to Austria.

After working in music theatre in New York – with George Gershwin and Jerome Kern among others – he became one of the most successful writers of film music in Hollywood history, producing about eight scores a year from 1936, including *Casablanca* in 1942 and, perhaps most famously, *Gone with the Wind* in 1939. 'Music should be felt and not heard,' he said. His style was to have emotion on the surface and never to let it flag. He became a master of cinematic leitmotifs so that characters would carry a musical phrase with them wherever they went – hardly Wagnerian in style but perhaps in inspiration. There were two trends at work in Hollywood. The first was a straightforwardly commercial impulse to produce attractive, tuneful music that might lift a film as easily as possible. Much of it is forgettable. Indeed some of it is meant to be, no more than a bit of packaging around the action. But there were also composers who thought of themselves as 'serious' writers who were immediately attracted to the medium and recognised what possibilities it offered.

The American composer Aaron Copland was one of them, Virgil Thomson another. Thomson was a composer and film critic for the *New York Herald Tribune* who was excited by the beginning of documentary-making, encouraged in those far-off days by the American federal government. In 1936 he wrote the score for a film called *The Plow That Broke the Plains*, a publicly funded film that was meant to help bring Americans together. Its narration began: 'This is a record of a land, of soil rather than people . . . the four hundred million acres of wind-swept grasslands that spread from the Texas panhandle to Canada.' Thomson's score is memorable – reassuring and plaintive, a portrayal of a community told through its surroundings and remarkably free of cheap sentiment.

It would be a generation before Hollywood started to take more seriously the opportunities for music that matched the boldness of film. You only have to hear the start of Bernard Herrmann's score for Alfred Hitchcock's *Psycho* in 1960 – or his later eerie, experimental music for *The Birds* – to realise what possibilities were (mostly) missed in the early days of American cinema.

Though Hollywood was where the movies were creating stars and millionaires, and attracting a vast audience, it was in Europe where film music was bolder, earlier. In France – where the Lumière brothers could claim to have invented cinema in the 1890s – Camille Saint-Saëns and Satie were writing film scores and when the French film industry took off in the 1920s the neo-Classical composers known as 'Les Six' were in the vanguard. One of them, Georges Auric, worked closely with Jean Cocteau, who eventually turned to film-making himself. Cocteau said he saw film as a powerful weapon for the projection of thought – even, as he put it, into a crowd unwilling to accept it. He didn't want a simple accompaniment; the music had to breathe even more life into the images by what he called 'accidental synchronisation' rather than slavish obedience to the editor's cuts. Auric wrote the score for his film *La Belle et la bête* (Beauty and the Beast).

In France music for film was taken seriously. Cocteau's idea that even an unwilling audience had to be made to understand certain things wasn't Hollywood's way, of course. There it was a question of satisfying whatever taste was the fashion of the moment. In the Soviet Union, there was a similar seriousness. When Sergei Eisenstein produced his film *Alexander Nevsky* (1939) he engaged Sergei Prokofiev to write the music, and it was cinema that maintained Prokofiev's position as the Soviet 'national composer' in the 1940s until his denunciation by Stalin along with Shostakovich for the usual artistic 'deviations'.

From the beginning of the history of cinema there were opportunities. It is still true in the modern cinema that it's easier for a director to reach for 'The Ride of the Valkyries' or a Brandenburg concerto or some dreamy Debussy to make a point than to encourage original composition. Max Steiner said bitterly in 1966 that composition for film was now dominated by 'young men who can only hum a tune'. But a modern composer like Philip Glass did write a memorable score for *The Hours* and in Britain musicians like Michael Nyman, Carl Davis, John Williams and others have written many original scores. Even from the early days there are reminders of how composers of what bears the often unhelpful title of serious music (though their artistry was unquestionably serious) were drawn to film.

Sir William Walton wrote more than a dozen film scores – and was maybe the British composer who brought to the screen the best of the originality he expressed elsewhere. In the music for Laurence Olivier's *Henry V* in 1944, intended as a patriotic rallying cry towards the end of the Second World War, he demonstrated how effective the medium can be. Across Europe many composers have written powerful scores, yet it remains true that many haven't dealt with film at all. Perhaps it's because they're repelled by easy emotion – like the young Shostakovich who had nightmares about those heroes – and by the slick world of Hollywood. But back in the origins of cinema, when the movies were primitive things, music of originality was being developed. Even with the profusion of memorable film scores, perhaps the question is: why not more?

Jazz and film were the liberating forces of the 1920s, riding the tide in a world that, in western Europe and the United States, seemed to be free of the shadow of war. The illusion persisted for a few years, but the Wall Street Crash of 1929, the subsequent worldwide depression, and the rise of Hitler to power in Germany in 1933 marked its formal disappearance. Between the wars, music and musicians were influenced by the pace of popular culture; their lives were also changed by persecution.

The persecuted of Europe came to a country where there were democratic freedoms but, in the 1930s, rampant poverty. The depression was a collision of optimism and despair. President Franklin D. Roosevelt said in his first inaugural address in 1932 that the only thing Americans need fear was fear itself, but it was also a time of wretchedness for many people, in cities and on the land, an era whose contrasts and whose sounds left an indelible mark on the American folk memory. Cole Porter was in his prime, jazz was giving birth to swing and the big bands, and American composers who straddled the worlds of popular music and the classical tradition were developing a strain that was recognisably of the New World, in a voice that sounded less and less European.

Despite the aftermath of the Wall Street Crash, the fortunes and the jobs lost, the truth is that the cultural adventure didn't stop. Although record sales fell like the stock market – by more than 90 per cent, from 100 million in 1927 to only 6 million in 1932 – music was booming. The radio was reaching millions of homes, jazz was now part of the country's musical patois and the big bands were on the way. The bands were a paradoxical consequence of the depression: unemployed jazz musicians found that getting together in groups made more sense and they had a chance of finding an audience. So away from the dustbowls and soup kitchens, there was life in music. Virgil Thomson summed up the unquenchable spirit: 'The way to write American music is simple. All you have to do is be American and write any kind of music you wish.' Duke Ellington's definition was expressed in one of his most successful songs – 'It Don't Mean a Thing If It Ain't Got That Swing'.

The stream that produced American composers like Copland (1900–90) and Samuel Barber (1910–81) was one in which the Duke also swam. You couldn't ignore jazz, or later swing, because they were everywhere. With them came a revival of interest in the traditional song – collectors like Alan and John Lomax and Charles Seeger were starting to catalogue and then later put on tape the songs and tunes they heard in the Appalachians and the South, from the hobos along the tracks and the drifters in the fields. From the slave culture and from the rural songs that had crossed from Europe – especially Scotland and Ireland – a colourful tapestry was woven, and it nurtured singers like Woody Guthrie who influenced two generations of singers, including those who shaped the tradition of American folk-rock. When Thomson spoke of writing anything you liked, he meant that the influences were so rich and diverse – and so close to anyone interested in music – that they opened up the world. There was much less division between 'high' and 'low' culture in America than there was in the Old World.

Nothing written in the 1930s illustrates the point better than one of George Gershwin's masterworks, *Porgy and Bess*. It turns up in the repertoire of the world's opera houses now, but when it was written was it a musical, an opera or something different? The question troubled no one, though in some quarters it was pigeonholed a little too crudely; it was not until the 1980s that the Metropolitan Opera, New York, mounted a production. In 1935 it demonstrated how an artist like Gershwin could produce a score for music drama that drew on the traditions of opera (Porgy, after all, uses leitmotifs just as the disciples of Wagner were taught to) with the style of popular music. A generation later, in the era of the civil rights movement, it would be criticised for its treatment of the blacks in Charleston whose story it is – and at the time Duke Ellington grumbled about Gershwin's 'lampblack' characters. But it was good enough to survive that controversy.

In the first production on Broadway, the cast were classically trained black singers telling the story of the inhabitants of Catfish Row and painting a picture of a life of poverty, the shadow of disease and drugs

('the happy dust'), the elusive hope of a new existence in the big city –
and the certainty of death that comes too soon. Gershwin was able to
evoke an experience that in those days was strange to most Americans
who went to the theatre: outside the South, eyes were averted from
streets like Catfish Row, and in the South, that was just the way things
were, unchanged and unchanging.

Gershwin's achievement was to take the popular song – and in that
genre he stands shoulder to shoulder with Porter, Irving Berlin and
Richard Rodgers – and weave it into the best music drama of its time in
America. He was a synthesiser, and so was Aaron Copland, who
worked in the classical tradition but had that same ability to transcend
divisions, cross boundaries in music. He'd been in Paris in the 1920s,
where he studied with Nadia Boulanger – high priestess of the neo-
Classicists – and like so many Americans who made the trip he was
intoxicated: 'The sheer glamour of the period exerts a magic spell. The
very word "modern" was exciting. The air was charged with talk of
new tendencies, and the password was originality – anything was
possible.'

Copland was a fine example of the paradox of neo-Classicism in its
conjunction of old and new, and the New York to which he returned
was intoxicating too – the first skyscrapers were climbing high (the art
deco architecture that would become the fashion and produce the
Chrysler Building, for example, was a spectacular take on neo-
Classicism) – and music was pouring out of him. Although there
was great poverty, America was the powerhouse. As Europe slid
towards war, Roosevelt's New Deal was putting people to work;
New York had the greatest man-made skyline in the world and the talk
was of prosperity. Not for nothing was Roosevelt's permanent campaign song 'Happy Days are Here Again'.

In the mid-1930s Americans were singing 'Anything Goes' in the
clubs, Wallace Stevens was producing startling poetry in *The Man with
the Blue Guitar*, Frank Lloyd Wright built his classic of home design in
Fallingwater and the radio was creating a reassuring, homely culture
with Jack Benny, George Burns and Gracie Allen, and cosy fireside
chats from the White House when people wanted something more
serious. After the dark days that followed the Crash – when average
family incomes dropped 40 per cent in three years – the sun was

peeping through: the United States was a country on the turn. It wasn't a steady progress towards prosperity – a terrible dip in 1937 cost four million jobs in six months – but Americans' resilience was remarkable, and you can hear it and see it in their culture.

Hundreds of swing bands were on the road, the recording industry was back in big business and Hollywood was transforming entertainment for ordinary families. With such energy, and such a fountain of talent, composers like Copland became voices for a culture that was new, feeding on jazz and the blues, the folk songs that Americans had taken from Europe and made their own, and the ways of life peculiar to a country that never seemed to stop expanding westwards in search of another frontier.

It came together for Copland in a ballet score in 1936, in surprising circumstances. Lincoln Kirstein started a company called Ballet Caravan. He was a leftist who supported the Popular Front – an unusual political organisation whose slogan was 'Communism is Americanism of the 20th Century' (work that one out). Kirstein sent Copland some cowboy songs because he wanted him to adapt them for his new ballet, *Billy the Kid*. Copland wasn't keen. 'I have never been particularly impressed with the musical beauties of the cowboy song as such,' he said. The tunes were 'often less than exciting'. But he was gripped by the story of the boy who saw his mother die in a brawl, killed her murderer and went on the run. He began to use the melodies, trying to give them what he called 'fresh and unconventional harmonies' without losing the naturalness of the tunes themselves.

He wrote with a feeling for the spirit of the plains and the dustbowls, the train tracks and the life of the city, catching something of the loneliness that can invade even the most populous places and that is part of America. At the end of the ballet, Billy's funeral procession mingles with some wandering pioneers who are heading inexorably west. It is melancholy but hopeful, the sound of a country always striving, always wondering, always pressing on – and a country that in the depths of the depression was developing a culture that would remain resolutely its own.

That confidence was in contrast with the despair felt in a Europe that was tipping into the second war in a generation. While America, even in depression, was forging a modern culture, the problem in Europe was that the old one was under attack. Many European musicians emigrated, either because they faced brutality, arrest and worse, or because their consciences told them they couldn't watch the spread of Hitlerism – a creed that was peculiarly painful for artists because it claimed to spring from a cultural source.

When Hitler watched *Lohengrin* or went to see the Ring cycle in Wagner's own theatre at Bayreuth – heard those horns, listened to the music of the Rhine – he was, he said, honouring his nation. He was, of course, engaged in a great betrayal. In Germany, and in Austria, where European music had flowered and prospered more spectacularly than anywhere else in the previous two centuries, and where it was especially cherished and taught, people were being hunted down in its name. Jewish musicians were in flight. In Germany, they couldn't play in orchestras. The Nazi Brownshirts organised riots against composers deemed to be depraved (almost always for a Jewish connection or an imagined one). In Austria, after the Anschluss in 1938, Nazi taste dictated everything and dissent was unacceptable. In the countries invaded by Hitler, the poison spread. Artists who simply couldn't bear to live under fascism got away.

The sound of it is still with us. At the beginning of the fourth movement of Béla Bartók's Concerto for Orchestra written in New York, the composer wrote a mournful oboe solo that winds through the orchestra and carries with it the authentic spirit of Hungarian folk song. It speaks of history. Bartók was exiled (very unhappily) in the United States at the end of his life after the German takeover of his country in 1944, and in that concerto he travelled home. Bartók said he'd lost all confidence in people, in countries, in everything. He was the picture of an artist uprooted, disconnected and searching. Thousands like him – composers and players – felt the same. There was a mass exodus and a musical diaspora.

Players left orchestras because they sensed the tide of hostility that was on the way. Then they were stopped from playing, and when the purges in Germany got worse in the late 1930s many fled for their lives. German-Jewish composers who sailed for America included Schoenberg, Hindemith, Weill and Krenek. The wider politics of Europe also drove away Stravinsky, Milhaud and Bartók. Many more whose names aren't celebrated did the same, for the same reasons.

Nothing like it had happened in Europe before. Musicians had been tossed around by kings and patrons, disowned by the Church or cherished by egomaniacal sponsors, but the systematic artistic purge that was carried out in Germany and its occupied states was new – and given a grotesque twist by the claim that it was part of the defence of a 'true' culture, undefiled. One of the consequences, however, was that the genuine European tradition – unpolluted by Hitler's ideology – thrived elsewhere, and more healthily than it might have done had the Nazis never come.

Several conductors of renown, having got away in time, prospered in the United States. George Szell became the king of Severance Hall in Cleveland and took the orchestra into the world's first rank. Bruno Walter was at the New York Philharmonic, and Otto Klemperer, who left Germany in 1933, at Hitler's advent, went from Los Angeles to New York, then to Philadelphia and on to Pittsburgh. At home he couldn't have survived. Abroad, in the United States and later in Europe – notably in London in the Philharmonia's heyday in the 1950s – he became one of the great conductors of his age, an arbiter of style and insight.

These American orchestras were entering an age of elegance and achievement, and part of the reason was the persecution of musicians in Europe. Exile didn't always produce a natural match. In New York, a German chamber music society called the New Friends of Music was known colloquially as the Old Friends of Schnabel (after Arthur Schnabel, the German pianist), and patronised. Nonetheless, the influence grew. American universities employed many European teachers of music, among them the French-Jewish Darius Milhaud (1892–1974), who was one of those who responded vigorously to his American surroundings.

Schoenberg's experience may have been more typical. He loathed the consumer society that was springing up with such vitality around him. 'I die daily of disgust,' he said, after he saw an advertisement for car insurance that showed a father weeping over the body of his dead child by the side of the road. He refused to rewrite some of his early works, though it would have meant that he would get copyright protection for 'new' music produced in America. When MGM offered him the chance to write a film score, he deliberately set the price so high that

they couldn't accept: an interesting example of the effects of disloca-
tion. He enjoyed his students greatly – though he found them utterly
lacking in any of the cultural background that he might have taken for
granted in Europe in those years – and you sense a weary withering of
his creativity. Bertolt Brecht – Marxist exile – found Hollywood a pain,
too. He didn't produce what the film-makers wanted. He used to drive
out into the desert and up into the hills where, in the Californian sierra,
he could find sparse trees that reminded him of winter in the Europe he
had left behind.

That experience was miserable for some, but the energy that
European exiles brought to America was intense. Stravinsky – you
might describe him as the 'radical chic' figure of Paris before the Great
War – was in fine form. He hadn't come because his life was in danger,
but when he arrived at Harvard to lecture at the start of the Second
World War he decided to stay. He became an American citizen five
years later. He bought a house near Schoenberg's in Hollywood, which
was an odd thing to do because the two old adversaries (who'd never
agreed about the direction of music, and had fought over Stravinsky's
neo-Classicism in France in the 1920s and 1930s) then avoided each
other.

Stravinsky, who lived in the United States from 1939 until his death
in 1971, had the opposite experience from Bartók's. He found the snap
and crackle of America to his taste, and became a citizen in 1945. His
'Ebony' Concerto for the Woody Herman band was an embrace of
jazz; he wrote a polka for the elephant in the Ringling Brothers Circus,
and he tangled with the tango, bringing a subtle darkness to the
dancefloor.

If you look through Stravinsky's output in America you can't but
conclude that it invigorated him and the truth is that – whatever the
experiences of those who found themselves doomed to live abroad, and
didn't like it, and whatever the awful events that caused them to flee in
the first place – the implanting of such European talent and originality
in the United States was hugely important. It helped to build the great
orchestras that still dominate the landscape; it confronted rampant
consumerism with a measure of cultural history; it also inspired a
generation of musicians working in what we call serious music, and
well beyond its assumed boundaries.

There is a British postscript to this story of exile. Many musicians had arrived in Britain in the flood that crossed the Channel from the mid-1930s onwards. One particular consequence proved important. When John Christie set off on his eccentric but determined project to build a first-class opera house on his estate, and established his private theatre at Glyndebourne in the Sussex Downs in 1934, he was committed to excellence above all. He managed it by drawing on the talents of those who were fleeing Nazi Germany and occupied Europe. Fritz Busch was musical director, Carl Ebert the first conductor (he'd run the Städtische Oper in Berlin) and the general director was Rudolf Bing, later to go on to run the Metropolitan Opera in New York and become one of the most influential figures in the musical firmament. All three were exiles from Hitler's Europe. From the first, Glyndebourne was the oddest of successes, something of a musical miracle. The early recordings, especially from the late 1940s, catch the spirit of a place that succeeded in bringing together the discipline of a German opera house with the fresh enthusiasm of a small company which could rehearse happily for weeks in the countryside before the summer audiences arrived with their picnics.

Glyndebourne became one of the most important musical centres in this country. This was despite its size – for nearly sixty years the operas were performed in a shoebox-shaped hall next to the Christie country house which was never intended for the purpose and was a village hall adapted to high art. In the 1990s the Christies raised the money to build a new opera house, one of the finest in Europe and a centre of excellence still. That commitment to great performance and to innovative opera production has been a gift to Britain. Leave aside the arguments about picnics, expense, black ties and the scarcity of tickets: the standards set by Glyndebourne and the young artists (especially) it has encouraged – with the opera directors it has employed – have been a vital part of musical life far beyond its gardens.

It wouldn't have happened in the way that it did without the benefit of those musical refugees. As in the United States they brought discipline, fire, commitment. The conductors drilled and enthused its orchestras, just as a composer like Stravinsky, who remained in the US until his death in the 1970s, adapted to an environment that he came to love. His *Agon*, ballet music written in the mid-1950s for Lincoln Kirstein's New York City Ballet, is a typical postcard to America. It's a cheerful and contented score, speaking of a composer who is at home. The story of those who fled, to a country across the border or across the sea, is a dark affair. It had its genesis in horror and persecution, and in a denial of the liberating force of music. Yet it produced, through the travails that so many suffered, a spreading of musical culture that meant, especially, in America, a vital injection of spirit and skill. We wouldn't be the same – wouldn't hear the same music – without it.

There is another strand to the story of those who fled the Nazis: the repression in the Soviet Union. In a country that began by building the arts into its founding principles, the descent into an atmosphere of cultural brutality – in which artists were hounded indiscriminately for random offences – was rapid. Just as artists found themselves driven from Europe by the Nazis, the Soviet Union created its own stream of cultural refugees as well as a discontented underground at home. The story begins before the First World War.

Russia before the Revolution was unsettled and anxious, a vast country spinning on its axis. It had been humiliated in war by the Japanese, and the Tsar's repression was only intermittently relieved by concessions to his enemies. There was terrible poverty and great anger. Listening to some of the music of that time – to Alexander Skryabin, for example – you feel an otherworldliness. It lets you escape. In *Prometheus: The Poem of Fire*, written in 1910, Skryabin believed his listeners would find ecstasy in the interplay of musical colours: he wanted a white-robed chorus singing music without words. It was the kind of piece that hinted where he might end up, writing a work called 'Mysterium' which he wanted performed in a temple in the Himalayas and which he thought would produce such a thrill and such enlightenment that the whole universe would be reborn. As far as we know, it wasn't.

Skryabin, who died in 1915, was a one-off whose brilliance made him popular in Russia when he came back from Switzerland and years of European touring in 1909. His appeal was connected to the glittering music of composers like Rimsky-Korsakov which often had an air of escapist fantasy. Skryabin suggests something else – the end of one phase of the Russian tradition (carried, you might say, to the point where it dissolves in air) and the start of another.

The atmosphere was potent. Defeat in the Russo-Japanese war in 1905 was not only miserable for Russians, but surprising too. Imagined power was exposed for what it was, and Tsar Nicholas II, destined to be the last of his line, was flailing at his opponents. When more than a hundred thousand protesters marched on the Winter Palace in St Petersburg in 1905 to demand an end to the war (which was depressing their wages and putting prices up), asking for rights for trade unions and progress to universal suffrage, they were massacred. The first, abortive Revolution began. Rimsky-Korsakov said of that day – which was given a name that would reappear years later for another generation – 'Bloody Sunday made me blood red.'

For the next decade and into the First World War, in which Russia with its western European allies fought its old enemies in the Austro-Hungarian and Ottoman empires, as well as the Germans, the country was poor and fractious, the old order crumbling. When food riots and popular anger forced the Tsar to abdicate in February 1917, and the Bolshevik Revolution followed in October, many artists and musicians celebrated. Why not?

Sergei Prokofiev, who was twenty-eight at the time, was in St Petersburg – now in its brief incarnation as Petrograd – in February at the fall of the Tsar when the crowds surrounded the Winter Palace. 'I and my friends welcomed it with open arms,' he said. 'We were out in the streets, hiding behind houses when the shooting got too close.' When he began his 'Visions Fugitives', during the rising, he wanted to express 'the feeling of the crowd rather than the inner essence of the Revolution'. They are simple, optimistic and full of youth. At that time, Prokofiev appeared to have no worries about where events might lead. He was not driven by political ideas, and was not a Bolshevik. But it was freedom, or so it seemed. In the future composers who were more interested in the crowds than in 'the inner essence of the revolution' would find themselves the objects of suspicion of the state and of its unwieldy artistic apparatus. But who could blame him, then, for a certain naivety? He was optimistic, after years of living with a country in decline. When he left Russia in 1917 to tour in the United States he would find such success – there and in

Europe – that he wouldn't live in his homeland again for fifteen years.

In the course of the 1920s, most of which he spent in Europe, he wrote the opera *The Fiery Angel* and his Second and Third symphonies, and found popularity for his opera *The Love for Three Oranges* which, despite his early American success, had gone down badly (that he was fresh out of Russia meant that he was now regarded as suspiciously Bolshevik, though he had only the faintest, passing association with the Leninists). And when he returned to Russia permanently in 1934 after a dozen years touring in Europe, he was able to develop a style that had been avant-garde a decade before into something which the authorities were happy to embrace. His film scores (for example for *Alexander Nevsky* in 1939) and his ballet *Romeo and Juliet* in 1936 had melodic energy and rhythmic life that were popular and – more importantly – officially accepted.

That would end in 1948, by which time he was in his fifties, when he was arraigned for 'formalistic deviations and anti-democratic tendencies' in his music in one of the classic examples of Stalinist mania. From the beginning, just after the Revolution, there was a tension in Soviet Russia that couldn't easily be resolved. First there was a rich musical tradition which meant that Tchaikovsky and his fellow masters would be revered – though it wouldn't do to mention his homosexuality: everyone knew it didn't exist in the Soviet Union, nor among great musicians. If they didn't know, they learned. But alongside there was the establishment of music as the ideology of the state.

To begin with, it was mildly liberating. The People's Commissariat for Public Education (Narkompros for short) had a music division run by a modernist composer, Arthur Lourie. He encouraged the development of the mystical strain that came from Skryabin, who was popular in the early 1920s, alongside the established figures of Tchaikovsky and the ever worshipped Beethoven. In the first phase of Soviet control, innovation was encouraged. Nikolai Roslavets was one of the musicians who took advantage of that freedom. He would let pieces grow out of one six-note chord, as in his violin sonatas, and his music is forward looking and expressive.

But music couldn't be separated from the Revolution, and was caught up in it. Artists who founded the group the Russian Association of Proletarian Musicians began to attack anything they thought lacking in proletarian content and style. The likes of Roslavets didn't meet the test. There's an irony here. A stated desire for a modern 'people's culture' often led the Soviet state backwards instead of forwards – progress in reverse. Yet it was in the Soviet years that the Russian conservatoires nurtured and cherished musicians who gave their lives to the study and performance of the European masterworks, as well as those of Tchaikovsky and the other Russians. Composers who were experimenting, breaking the rules, thinking freely, often found trouble. It takes a genius, as with Dmitri Shostakovich, to survive by appearing to face both directions at once.

V. I. Lenin himself understood that 'the music of the proletariat' was embedded in the bourgeois and even aristocratic past. In his apartment deep inside the Kremlin, where he worked until he left Moscow for the country for the last time in 1924 (and which is seldom opened to the public gaze) you can still see the piano on which his sister would play for him – his favourite piece was apparently Beethoven's 'Appassionata'. He loved music's past. In his tract *New Economic Policy* he wrote:

> Proletarian culture is not something that has sprung from nowhere. It is not an invention of those who call themselves experts in proletarian culture. That is all nonsense. Proletarian culture must be the result of the natural development of the stores of knowledge which mankind has accumulated under the yoke of capitalist society, landlord society and bureaucratic society . . . one can become a Communist only when one enriches one's mind with the knowledge of all the wealth created by mankind.

Working this out was tricky. Operas from the past were performed, but were adapted to give them a revolutionary flavour. Puccini's *Tosca*, which after all had only been written in 1900, was staged as *The Battle for the Commune*, Meyerbeer's *Les Huguenots*, focusing not on French Calvinist refugees but on a group of Russian heroes of the nineteenth century, was turned into *The Decembrists*.

Throughout the 1920s there were arguments between traditionalists who thought proletarian music would develop from the past, as in Lenin's prescription, and modernists who wanted invention, freer thinking, experiment. Shostakovich, an enthusiastic supporter of the Revolution, was uneasy about how it appeared to be turning into an excuse to look backwards. He indulged in some satire, which was unpopular with the increasingly solemn ideologues of the Russian Association of Proletarian Musicians, the kind of people whom Stalin would find useful in the future. Shostakovich was asked to provide incidental music for a satirical play called *The Bed-bug* staged in his theatre by the director Vsevolod Meyerhold, one of the leading sceptics of Socialist Realism who was heading for inevitable persecution under Stalin. Shostakovich obliged with pleasure.

Under the surface of every piece of music there seemed to be argument. Was it celebratory enough of the proletariat? Was it deviant? Did it stray too much into the future without understanding the past? Was it making a point that the People's Commissariat for Public Education might not want to be made? The balancing act was painful, as you can often hear. Poor old Alexander Mossolov wrote a piece called 'Zavod' – it's usually translated as 'The Iron Foundry' – which was meant, of course, to praise hard work and technology. One critic at the time said it was 'a mighty hymn to machine work'. Later, having passed out of fashion, it was called 'a grossly formalistic perversion of a contemporary topic'. It's difficult to listen to. Life was hard.

The best of times, and the worst of times. For musicians, the Russian Revolution produced opportunities – a celebration of the power of their art, a commitment to the tradition they'd inherited and a belief in the place of music in the world. But it also brought censorship and persecution, music ground in bureaucratic millstones, ideological obsession. Stalin supervised it all. One night in January 1936 he went to the opera. He watched the seduction of Katarina by a farmhand in the first act of Shostakovich's only opera *Lady Macbeth of Mtsensk*. The music was dramatic and sensual, the raw sexuality undisguised. Though it had been a riotous success at its première in Leningrad a couple of years before and was already known in Europe, this was not going to be allowed.

Two days later Shostakovich picked up his copy of *Pravda* (Truth – the Party newspaper) and read the editorial, which had the force of a decree:

The listener from the very first minute is stunned by the opera's intentionally inharmonious muddled flow of sounds. Snatches of melody, embryos of musical phrases drown, escape, and once again vanish in rumbling, creaking and squealing. To follow this 'music' is difficult, to remember it impossible . . . 'love' is smeared throughout the opera in the most vulgar form. The predatory merchantess, clawing her way to wealth and power by way of murder, is presented as some 'victim' of bourgeois society. This is music made intentionally inside-out, so that there would be nothing to resemble classical music, nothing in common with symphonic sounds, with simple accessible musical material . . .

Thus Shostakovich was denounced for the first time. It wouldn't be the last. Stalin had his own definition of Socialist Realism – the only acceptable form of art – and it did not include the boldness of this opera, let alone the sex. And Socialist Realism meant what he said it meant, neither more nor less. Literature, proclaimed the founding decree of the Writers' Union (partly drafted by Stalin himself), had to depict historically concrete reality in its revolutionary development. Shosta-kovich had failed. The *Pravda* editorial ended with these words: 'This is playing at things beyond reason that can only end very badly.' Things were ending badly for many people in the Soviet Union at the time. There was starvation and forced labour, the persecution of kulaks and other 'unhelpful' peasants, and over it all loomed a state apparatus that Stalin had set to work on the arts.

The story of Shostakovich is extraordinary. In him you find elements of the loyal Soviet citizen, the clever critic of the regime – the loyalist and the rebel. He lived his artistic life under a regime that often denied essential freedoms yet sometimes championed great music and musi-cians, and he could lay a confident claim to being one of his century's finest composers. Together with Prokofiev's experience, his official disgrace (albeit temporary) revealed how one state – in a way that hadn't been tried by any Church or institution for hundreds of years – had tried to turn music and the other arts to the service of its passing obsessions, whether during Stalin's studied purges of his enemies and the weak, or in the construction of an empire. But a strand of heroism runs through the story. Despite Shostakovich's compromises – which some others found it impossible to make – his survival as an artist produced work that spoke the truth too.

His Seventh Symphony in C major, the 'Leningrad', written during the Second World War siege of that city by the Nazis between 1941 and 1944 in which probably a million people died, was a shattering depiction of emotions drained, giving notice of the symphonic heights he might scale in the future. By that stage in his life Shostakovich was writing with remarkable directness. The intensity of the symphonies – and in a more intimate way the chamber music – has sometimes been criticised as having too much emotion near the surface (he has suffered the same fate as Mahler in that regard), but in the last five of his fifteen symphonies, especially, Shostakovich harnesses a formidable array of forces to make his point – grandeur, intimacy, tragic melancholy, anger – that pushes him into the front rank of symphonists.

The 'Leningrad' was finished early in 1942. The score was flown out of the Soviet Union through Iran to the west. The propaganda value of the score, combined with Shostakovich's picture on the cover of *Time* magazine wearing a fire-fighter's helmet, led to a scrap between the conductors Arturo Toscanini and Serge Koussevitzky as to who should give the first performance in the west. Toscanini won their argument, but they were both pipped at the post by Sir Henry Wood, who conducted it at a Prom concert in June a week after he had broadcast it with the London Philharmonic. The New York performance followed within a fortnight. It was an instant success – and soon afterwards the score was flown by night through the German blockade back to Leningrad, where that city was able to hear it for the first time in August. The radio orchestra in the city had been reduced to fourteen players by war, evacuation and disease, but enough musicians were rounded up for the performance – for which they were given special rations to see them through – and the concert was broadcast on loudspeakers in the streets.

The playwright Alexander Kron who was in the first-night audience said that people 'who no longer knew how to shed tears of sorrow and misery now cried from sheer joy'. That joy was a reaction to the symphony's picture of humanity – reflecting the cruelty, the bravery and the horror of the siege. The revelation of tragedy was uplifting.

Shostakovich had written it quickly. He said: 'I couldn't not write it. War was all around . . . I wanted to create the image of our embattled country, to engrave it in music.' Since music became available to a mass audience through radio and on disc, no symphony has made a more immediate impact in so many countries. With Russia as an ally against Hitler, Shostakovich was a Soviet hero well beyond his country's borders. But many claim to hear in the 'Leningrad' not only a cry against war, but a resumption of the composer's argument with Stalin's regime: a plea for his own freedom, too.

As with Prokofiev, who came home to live in Russia in the same year that Stalin denounced *Lady Macbeth of Mtsensk*, the quality of Shostakovich's music is inseparable from the agony of the Soviet Union at that time. It is indisputable that he signed official documents and petitions that gave succour to censors and bureaucratic bullies. Though he didn't join the Communist Party itself until 1960 (and some members of his family have said that he was in tears at making that final accommodation with the regime), he retained enough loyalty to the ideal, however besmirched, to keep him there.

Prokofiev, on the other hand, back from a long spell in the United States and Europe, was happy to adapt his style for Soviet purposes. He even composed a toast for Stalin's sixtieth birthday. But he did try to use his fame to redefine Socialist Realism, difficult though that was.

The absurdity of it all can be heard in the innocent notes of *Peter and the Wolf*: what could be more straightforward? But read the words of Boris Asay'yev, a critic whose voice in the Soviet Union was close to an official proclamation: 'Every detail of the behaviour of the boy, the duck, the little bird, the cat and the wolf sounds new. One wonders whether elements of the new Soviet symphonic spirit cannot be detected here, liberated now from the intellectual's self-analysis, along with all subjective interpretations of reality.'

You couldn't write anything without it being subjected to a laborious post-mortem examination by the cultural gauleiters whose job it was to purge the state of bourgeois decadence, just as Stalin was ridding it of his enemies. By 1939 it was probably true that more than ten million people in the Soviet Union had been executed, imprisoned or exiled, including most of the generals and anyone in the Party who showed loyalty to anyone or anything other than the Great Leader.

For artists, survival meant some degree of surrender. Shostakovich scholars have spent many long hours trying to find coded protests hidden in his symphonies – messages in a bottle carried away in a sea of music. His bleak Fifth Symphony, written in 1937, followed the humiliation of *Lady Macbeth* (and his decision to withdraw the Fourth Symphony from public performance) and bore on the title page the miserable words: 'A Soviet Artist's Response to Just Criticism'. Yet was the music as grovelling as that makes it sound? The novelist Boris Pasternak said: 'Just think. He went and said everything, and no one did anything to him for it . . .'

Party ideologues could argue themselves into knots as to whether that represented the 'optimistic tragedy' that was meant to be the only outcome of Socialist Realism. To modern ears its darkness seems to cloak a humanity that is set against crude judgements such as that. Shostakovich, in spending his whole life in the Soviet Union, was doomed to a double life – one in which his honesty as a musician (and a humanitarian) would be tested and judged by those around him whose interest wasn't in the transcendent capacity of the symphony or the string quartet but in the prevailing ideological climate or the next Politburo reshuffle and purge.

Shostakovich and Prokofiev each collected Stalin prizes during the war – known in the Soviet Union as the Great Patriotic War – for their music. At a time of peril they were heroes of the cause. But it couldn't last. In 1948 they discovered that they had become pariahs. The cause was an opera by one Vano Muradeli called *The Great Friendship* which attracted the unhappy attentions of the chairman of the ideological department of the Central Committee of the Party, Andrei Zhdanov. He said that recent 'warnings' – he might have said purges – had evidently not done their job, because works like this opera were 'formalist' and alien to the people and were still, unaccountably, being written.

Lumped together with Muradeli were Shostakovich and Prokofiev; the latter was broken by the experience. Soon after his public rebuke, Prokofiev's Spanish-born wife was sentenced to twenty years' hard labour in Siberia for spying. He wrote a pathetic letter of contrition and apology to the Central Committee, thanking the Party for its wisdom. He never recovered, and died two years later – on the same day as Stalin (and with much less fanfare). His wife was released later after the unravelling began of some of the excesses of the Stalin era, and spent the rest of her long life in the west.

Shostakovich recovered, as he'd done after his first denunciation in 1936. In the year of Prokofiev's death – 1953 – he wrote the Tenth Symphony, which suggested a musician becoming more not less determined and powerful. The five symphonies which would follow in the next two decades were vast canvases on which his feelings seemed laid out, works that it's impossible to hear without being drawn into the struggle between patriotism and humanity, which was the course of his life. The Eleventh and Twelfth were celebrated in the Soviet Union as a triumph of socialist art – but in all the later works, maybe especially the last chamber music in the 1960s and early 1970s, you feel the presence of an individual, not the representative of a creed.

Judging Shostakovich as a man is difficult. He displays vividly the tragedy that can befall a musician who is caught between warring loyalties. He valued the Russian musical tradition and felt the obligation for creative honesty in himself. But he was caught in a world where the exercise of that will involved a collision with a way of thinking that represented, to him, an ideology gone wrong. No one should be surprised that there is agony in this music. Without it, would he have become the artist that he was? Inspiration in those years between the wars was shaped by the freedoms that were opening up, and by repression too.

When the Second World War itself came, Russian artists would suffer. They had little choice but to stay in the Soviet Union. And in Europe, though some artists had fled before the war began, many of those who were left behind, or couldn't get away, endured terrible privations.

The Nazis' pursuit of 'decadent' music and of those who wrote it meant that Jewish musicians in Germany and in German-occupied countries had to remain silent or suffer. Many of them chose the latter course. The Czech composer Hans Krása was a German-speaking Jew who had studied with Alexander Zemlinsky in Schoenberg's circle and he became a supporter of the Czech nationalists who were trying to resist German suppression. His children's opera *Brundibár* (Bumblebee) is a Hansel-and-Gretel story of children who are rescued from evil, in the form of a sinister organ-grinder. No audience would miss the character that *he* represented: he wouldn't even have to wear a moustache on stage. But soon after rehearsals for the opera began at the Jewish orphanage in Prague in 1942, Krása was gone. He was sent to the Terezín fortress (the Germans called it Theresienstadt) – a Jewish ghetto which became, in effect, a concentration camp, and a holding prison for deportations to the extermination camps. More than 30,000 people died there in terrible conditions. Yet eventually Krása did mount a production at Terezín and put on fifty-five performances for the prisoners.

Terezín was also home for a time to a remarkable musician called Viktor Ullmann, an Austro-Czech of Jewish origin who'd studied with Schoenberg. For two years in the camp he composed and organised concerts. While he was there he wrote an opera called *The Emperor of Atlantis*, the story of a mad demagogue, who forces humanity to indulge in mass slaughter, and of Death, who refuses to allow people to die. Instead they're condemned to a living hell. The opera wasn't performed: most of the cast, including Ullmann, were sent to Auschwitz, where they perished.

The cellist Anita Lasker-Walfisch credits the women's orchestra in Auschwitz with saving her life. When she arrived at the camp they were short of a cellist and she was recruited; instead of being sent to the gas chamber, she played merry marches and waltzes, often under the baton of Gustav Mahler's niece.

The experiences of composers like Ullmann and Krása are reminders of how much music-making the war cut short. Their efforts were evidence of what might have been. Yet the music that does survive from those experiences tells the story from inside; they are accounts that could not have been written elsewhere. That is true of a remarkable composition by the French composer Olivier Messiaen, who after the war would become one of the most influential European composers and a father-figure to many modernists. He was not Jewish – he was a devout Catholic – but he, too, was imprisoned. He was picked up soon after the German invasion of France in 1940 and ended up in a prisoner-of-war camp in Silesia.

Among the musical friends he made there were a violinist, a cellist and a clarinettist, so he wrote a quartet in which he would play the piano part. It was not music of a sort that most of the inmates had ever heard before. He used birdsong for the first time – it would become the composer's passion – to produce snatches of melody and rhythm. And the quartet has a mystical quality, produced in part by the repeated patterns that sound almost like Indian music. The cellist in the quartet, Etienne Pasquier, said afterwards that the audience of several thousand at one of the regular Saturday-evening concerts in the camp sat spellbound. 'These people, who were completely musically ignorant, sensed this was something exceptional. They sat perfectly still, in awe.' Messiaen called the quartet 'For the End of Time', by which he said he meant 'eternity': he had taken his idea from the vision of the apocalypse in the Book of Revelation.

From the perspective of those affected by the war in quite different ways – persecuted Jews, prisoners of war, pacifists, those anxious to turn to enduring values – the music of those years is a mosaic with patterns that catch, you might say, different colours in the darkness. It was true, too, in Germany. Many musicians had left. But some stayed. Richard Strauss co-operated with Hitler's regime in the early days of 1933 – he has never been forgiven by some – but soon fell out with it. He refused to sever relations with Jewish friends and for the rest of his time under the Third Reich his was an uncomfortable life. Like the conductor Wilhelm Furtwängler he had decided to stay, and the two men watched much of what they most treasured being destroyed around them. There is a recording of Furtwängler conducting Beetho-ven with the Berlin Philharmonic, made at a concert in the German capital towards the end of the war, on which you can hear the distant crump of a bomb falling.

'My beautiful Dresden, Weimar, Munich all gone!' said Strauss. In the misery that overcame him in 1945 he said that until he was called to his gods in Olympus he would keep in mind the truth that, despite everything, Germany had fulfilled 'its last and highest cultural mission with the creation of German music'. But Strauss survived. Others fled, or died. His is a poignant lament, however. He was the last of the German Romantics. His *Four Last Songs*, finished in the year before his death, 1948 (he never heard them performed), is a remnant of the old

Germany, and a defiant echo. When the Americans entered Berlin in 1945, at the end of the war in Europe, they began house-to-house searches across the city. They turned up, unknowing, at the composer's home. Like any German citizen he was challenged. He had his simple identification ready. 'My name is Richard Strauss,' he said. 'I am the composer of *Der Rosenkavalier*.'

16

Out of the Rubble

Different Paths to Modernism

~

A S SO OFTEN on this journey, a chapter in the story of music seems to cling to one particular date. The seventh of June 1945 was a night to remember at Sadler's Wells Theatre. The war was almost over. Next day had been called VE Day, to celebrate Victory in Europe, and battered London was happy. On the eve of the celebrations, however, the opera audience was taken to a darker place.

They were transported into a community that was fearful and vengeful, shown loneliness and isolation. Benjamin Britten's opera *Peter Grimes* is a masterpiece, and spoke to the audience crammed into every corner of the theatre that night of emotions that were sharpened by the experience of war and its deprivations: isolation and the knowledge of violence. There was also an island nation's sense of the power of the sea, how it can represent death and cruel fate. *Peter Grimes* was a spectacular overture to the post-war era, suggesting that a British composer was capable of work at the highest level, taking a familiar subject from surroundings that everyone knew and turning it into a powerful piece of theatre. Britten's achievement ushered in a period of optimism in music, contrasting with the privations of rationing and the slow rebuilding that was needed. Out of the rubble of war, what might come?

Britten's journey to *Grimes* began in the United States, where he was in voluntary exile. As a pacifist he had no wish to remain in Britain during the war. In 1941, in Los Angeles, he read an article in the *Listener* by the novelist E. M. Forster about the Suffolk poet George Crabbe, which aroused his interest in his poem *The Borough*, which relates the story of Peter Grimes, a fisherman accused by his community of murdering his apprentices. Britten told *Time* magazine in 1948 that he was immediately drawn to the story because it dealt with 'a subject very close to my heart – the struggle of the individual against the masses. The more vicious the society, the more vicious the individual.' In his opera, however, he turns Crabbe's ruffian into a more complicated figure, whose guilt is ambiguous.

A commission from the conductor Serge Koussevitzky gave him the opportunity to try to turn the story into an opera. He had written the operetta *Paul Bunyan* in America, but this would be his first full-scale opera. His work on it coincided with his return to England. He and his companion Peter Pears, who'd been living in the circle of W. H. Auden and Christopher Isherwood in New York, were homesick despite the war and were waiting for visas. Britten had a yen for his native Suffolk, all grey horizons, water and reedbeds. In March 1942 they were able to set sail at last. In the course of the voyage Britten completed his 'Hymn to St Cecilia', with words by Auden, and *A Ceremony of Carols*.

He turned the solitary fate of the fishermen Grimes in Crabbe's poem, for crimes against his apprentices, into an evocation of the separation forced by his own homosexuality (which he dealt with more directly in other operas – *Billy Budd* and *Death in Venice*) and the mordant power of a community that could turn in on itself with thoughtless ease. Grimes also reflects the separation that Britten felt as an artist, searching for new knowledge in a hostile world. His antagonism to war was profound.

This dark story was a triumph for him (and his librettist Montagu Slater). The first performance had Pears as Grimes and Joan Cross as Ellen Orford, the schoolmistress, who has an insight into Grimes's plight. Reginald Goodall conducted. At the end of that first performance, during which the composer stalked nervously to and fro at the back of the stalls, the audience sat in one of those rare, telling silences: then there was an explosion of applause and more than a dozen curtain calls for Britten. Everyone knew they had witnessed a phenomenon – an opera soaring above any other written in English in modern times with a contemporary musical character.

There was nothing particularly unusual in the construction of the opera, which was built in a traditional way – solos for the anti-hero at the end of each section were a device that Verdi or even Handel would have recognised. It moved in familiar ways as a drama. The choruses for the townsfolk were woven into the action with great skill. The force of *Grimes* was in part its composer's musical radicalism (critics have identified a gesture towards Stravinsky's neo-Classical phase in the 1920s and 1930s) and in part its sheer theatrical power. In bomb-flattened London, weary in victory, was this the voice of a deeper England that might inspire the arts in an enforced age of austerity? The fact that VE Day was about to dawn may have had something to do with the emotion in the theatre.

The times were changing. The Arts Council was established as a cultural generator in the next year, and the BBC launched the Third Programme. The new Labour government was pursuing the politics of reconstruction in the welfare state and in industry; preparations had started for a Festival of Britain to mark the centenary of the Great Exhibition of 1851; and soon the plans would be laid for a National Theatre. The difficulty came when people talked about how best to invigorate a national culture. Could it be a popular movement, or was it bound to be done by inspiration from the top, high on Mount Olympus? There are seeds of trouble even in the optimistic words of John Maynard Keynes, the economist and social philosopher who'd been the guiding light of the Arts Council's predecessor, the wartime Council for the Encouragement of Music and the Arts: 'Nothing can be more damaging than the excessive prestige of metropolitan standards and fashions. Let every part of Merry England be merry in its own way. Death to Hollywood. But it is also our business to make London a great artistic metropolis, a place to visit and wonder at.'

Hollywood wasn't about to die, of course; nor was popular music in the era of the big band and the profusion of jazz on radio and on records, which were steadily becoming cheaper. The defence of high art – the culture that was dear to intellectuals like Britten in Aldeburgh – was going to be a divisive battle, though he would be, throughout his life, a champion of public, community performance and art. For him, a belief in art did not absolve him of the responsibility of being involved with those around him, despite the sense of separation he felt. But he would man the ramparts in the battle for cultural values, joined by composers like Ralph Vaughan Williams, now alarmed by the nuclear age – like Britten – and shivering in the Cold War, fearful and angry. In

1947, Vaughan Williams's extraordinary Sixth Symphony was a statement of defiance as well as a kind of farewell. Asked to provide a
programme note, he simply quoted from *The Tempest*:

> We are such stuff
> As dreams are made on, and our little life
> Is rounded with a sleep.

Vaughan Williams conducted the première of his own Fifth Symphony at the Proms in 1943 – music that seemed to speak of an
enduring England, a pastoral reflection in the midst of war. In the
symphony he used some themes that had been in his mind for many
years and which later reappeared in his 1951 opera *The Pilgrim's Progress*.
Symbolically, in wartime, he used the material connected with Mr
Valiant-for-Truth, in John Bunyan's *Pilgrim's Progress*, for whom, as he
crossed the river of life, the trumpets sounded on the other side. He had
taken five years to write the symphony, which was dedicated to
Sibelius, and in his response to war (as with the Sixth Symphony
heard in 1948) his anger is merged with an instinct for continuity and
survival. This is not music on the edge; it sustains and restores.

Vaughan Williams wrote with a feeling for permanence, recognising
the power of unchanging principles that would survive war. Some
other composers found it hard to find their own values in the world
around them. For him, writing after the war meant using everything
from his past – particularly perhaps the passion he'd developed for
trying to widen audiences through his Leith Hill festival in the 1930s –
to fashion a musical voice that was appropriate to a world that had been
torn apart by war.

An old man – Vaughan Williams was in his mid-seventies when he
wrote his Sixth Symphony – was sounding a modern note. There
wasn't much accompaniment to it from British music. There were
experimentalists, but most of the ones with the wind in their sails were
elsewhere in Europe. And British composers found that when the Arts
Council tried to settle the question of whether the arts should be
encouraged principally from above – should it be top-down or bottom-
up? – it chose what it thought was the high road.

You could argue that it was not a choice, but it was a strategic decision of real importance. The enlightened part of the establishment, as it would come to be known for the first time in the course of the 1950s, wanted art for the people, but Keynes's 'Merry England' in every town wasn't going to be the way. Intellectual life was lively, painters and philosophers were trying to understand the modern age, but serious music was in danger of becoming marooned in palaces of culture – even if they were as admirable as the private opera house at Glyndebourne, for which the post-war era was a golden age of achievement and adventure. Such money as the Arts Council had would be concentrated on centres of excellence. There would be 'roses, but few', said the secretary-general of the day.

You catch some irony in Benjamin Britten's affection for village life and the simplicities of childhood, because he was also devoted to an ascetic, intellectual musical world from which many people – under the pressure of an increasingly vibrant popular culture – felt remote. When the villagers in his opera *Albert Herring* engrossed themselves in the comedy and small-town disputations surrounding the May Day celebrations they spoke in an idiom that hadn't yet been generally absorbed by those for whom 'democratisation' in the arts was supposed to open doors.

In the 1940s, if an era of artistic progress was to be inaugurated, reform was needed. The 1948 Local Government Act did allow local authorities to levy a rate to support the arts for the first time. The dream of a National Theatre was revived, though after the foundation stone was laid in 1952 there would be two decades of wrangling before the promise was fulfilled. The Festival of Britain itself (planned for 1951) was meant to show that Britain could embrace modern architecture and technology and turn them to good use. 'Let us pray', said the King, George VI, speaking from the steps of St Paul's Cathedral when he opened the Festival, 'that by God's good grace the vast range of modern knowledge which is here shown may be turned from destructive to peaceful ends, so that all people, as the century goes on, may be lifted to greater happiness.'

However, the Festival was as revealing of tension as it was a national celebration. Looking back later in the 1950s, the writer Michael Frayn painted a picture of the argument between 'carnivores' and 'herbivores' in the planning. The herbivores were 'the radical middle-classes – the do-gooders; the readers of the *Guardian* and the *Observer*, the signers of petitions, the backbone of the BBC'. But the carnivores deprecated everything they stood for, objecting to the spending of public money, right-leaning in social outlook, and highly suspicious of the notion of an enlightened elite that was speaking of the arts as if they were a public duty. The division was painful. Hugh Casson, who was responsible for much of the architecture, was a target of that criticism, and couldn't dodge its fire. 'We all had, I suppose, rather naive views that England could be better and was going to be better – that the arts and architecture and music and healthy air and Jaeger underwear and all these things were the keys to some sort of vague Utopia.'

It would not prove so simple. The editor of the Liberal *New Chronicle*, Gerald Barry, was director-general of the Festival and was anxious to put any fun in context. He found it difficult to reconcile the idea of celebration and the higher aim. The purpose was modernisation, he said, a serious business: 'It is intended as an act of national reassessment. It will put on record the fact that we are a nation not only with a great past, but also a great future.'

Artists joined in the cheers. Cecil Beaton enthused about the way 'whole walls of decoration are made of squares of coloured canvas pulled taut in geometric shapes and triangles, to be lit with a variety of colours'. Dylan Thomas looked at the modernist shapes along the river and spoke of 'the shining Skylon, the skygoing nylon, the cylindrical leg-of-the-future jetting'. He was referring to the 300-foot-high aluminium and steel structure outside the Festival Hall, a kind of huge modern spear that had no visible means of support. The new buildings of the South Bank were universally praised by the great and the good.

The effort to raise the sights of the nation was going to be planned and managed by a cosy group which was remarkably homogeneous – the leaders in arts, business, government and the civil service were even closer in background, education and social habits than they are today. The word 'establishment' wasn't coined until much later in the 1950s, but that is what it was and, in practice, the episode itself did little to bridge the class barriers which were such a notable feature of British society at the time, and whose shadow fell over the arts as over everything else.

High culture was to be handed down. This meant that there were many children from unprivileged backgrounds who were given opportunities – by individuals and schools – but it also meant that the inherent stuffiness of British culture wasn't exposed to the air. Artists could paint or compose or write in their rural fastnesses and be protected, but the conventions of a society which often prevented their work from being given its proper place would not change.

Britten's experience with his opera *Gloriana* gives a comic insight into the problem. He was commissioned to write it for the Coronation in 1953, and he chose as a subject the relationship between Elizabeth I and the Earl of Essex, perhaps a slightly sharp-edged one. He went to a great deal of trouble to learn the steps to Elizabethan dances, being determined to fuse them into the score in a reasonably authentic manner. It was a commission he took very seriously. But so did the Lord Chamberlain, whose powers of censorship in the theatre lasted – astonishingly – until the mid-1960s. The Lord Chamberlain's men would tour productions in rehearsal checking that there wasn't an unfortunate word, a partially exposed breast, or – heaven forfend – an unflattering reference to the person of the monarch. In Britten's case, it had been noticed that a chamber pot was due to appear on stage during the production (not that it was meant to be used). It was too much, and the Lord Chamberlain's office believed that since it had been remark-ably lenient in allowing Queen Elizabeth I to be portrayed in one scene without a wig, a line would have to be drawn. The potty was removed.

The critic David Cairns caught the significance of this farce:

> The particular nastiness of the *Gloriana* episode lay in the unholy alliance that was forged between traditional British philistinism, in one of its most reactionary periods, and forces within the musical profession activated by prejudices of a scarcely superior kind. In opposing state-subsidised opera, and Britten as the pampered symbol of it, traditional British philistinism was only acting according to its sad lights.

The establishment, glowing with the urge to do good works, was not about to deal with the arts in a way that would release fully the energy of composers and artists and – perhaps – produce the very 'democra-tisation' which they believed they were encouraging.

This did not mean that the landscape was uniformly bleak. There was a good deal of intellectual ferment, and not simply in the universities.

Britten himself was profoundly committed to community involvement
in the arts. His festival at Aldeburgh and his writing for amateurs,
especially children, was evidence of his belief that the spark of enjoyment (or even inspiration) could be passed on. But there were grand
panjandrums of the day who could not accept that expeditions out of
the temples of high culture could produce anything that wasn't second
rate. In a precursor of the 1990s argument attached to the dread phrase
'dumbing down' (in which the arguments about excellence and
supposed 'elitism' were so often confused), T. S. Eliot, who could
be relied upon to adhere to the most reactionary view available, sailed
into battle. In 1948, he wrote:

> We can assert with some confidence that our own period is one of
> decline; that the standards of culture are lower than they were fifty years
> ago; and that the evidences of this decline are visible in every depart-
> ment of human activity. I see no reason why the decay of culture should
> not proceed much further, and why we may not even anticipate a
> period, of some duration, of which it is possible to say it will have no
> culture.

Instead of celebrating the originality that was at work, the attention
of Eliot and some others was focused on the menacing advance of
popular culture, which they seemed to believe meant that nothing of
value could survive. The consequence was that those who did labour in
the vineyard of serious music (and art) were denied much of the support
they deserved. Throughout the 1950s the argument rolled on, with
serious musicians tending to scramble for what they thought was the
higher ground, because serious art and popular taste were being
portrayed increasingly as polar opposites.

On the stage, there was an effort to cross the divide. By the mid-
1950s, theatre in London was trembling at the advance of the Angry
Young Men led by John Osborne, who wanted to destroy an English
theatre that echoed to little but the cut-glass accents in Terence
Rattigan or Noël Coward: the audiences trembling at the music of
the time were smaller. It was a hint of what was to come in the next
generation, and it's perhaps summed up in Michael Tippett, the twin
giant with Britten of the post-war era.

Tippett had spent a few years in the Communist Party in the 1930s but soon lost faith in its creed, just as he had given up on governments. On the day war broke out in September 1939 he began to write the oratorio *A Child of our Time*, in which, he said, the hero – for whom the music expressed sympathy – was the scapegoat, the one who gets all the blame. He'd been inspired by the story of the Polish Jew Herschel Grynszpan, whose assassination of a German diplomat in Paris in 1938 was one of the causes of Hitler's organised assault on German Jews on Kristallnacht in that year. For Tippett, the persecution that is the subject of the oratorio was the most important emblem of war. In *A Child of our Time* he deals with the question of the outsider, or the group that can't be understood. In the course of the oratorio, searching for a way of expressing that feeling, he reached into the history of the American South, to the spirituals which had been the songs of slaves and often their only source of hope, to find an equivalent for the chorales Bach had used in his Passions. He settled on the old song 'Steal Away' – a most unlikely reference point, you might think. But like Vaughan Williams he was a child of the English tradition.

And, just as Britten was, this lanky, gaunt figure was gay and a pacifist (he was jailed as a conscientious objector during the war for refusing do war work in place of military service). He looked on the teenage culture imported from America with horror, the habits that critics and social thinkers on the left thought of as 'shiny barbarism', to use Richard Hoggart's phrase. And Tippett, from his own English village, surrounded by tradition and thinking radically about music, was withering too:

> I know that my true function within a society that embraces us all is to continue an age-old function – fundamental to our civilization, which goes back to pre-history and will go forward into an unknown future. This tradition is to create images from the depths of the imagination and to give them form whether visual, intellectual or musical. For it is only through images that the inner world communicates at all. Images of the past, shapes of the future. Images of vigour for a decadent period; images of calm for one too violent; images of reconciliation for a world torn by divisions; and in an age of mediocrity and shattered dreams, images of abounding, generous, exuberant beauty.

In his *The Midsummer Marriage*, written over seven years in the 1950s, Tippett emerges as a composer determined never to abandon the high ground on the battlefield, however alluring the trumpets calling him down. He didn't care how long it took his public to tune into his wavelength; his originality was also a matter of duty. The consequence was one that he certainly did not intend. The artistic honesty of figures like Tippett combined in an unhealthy brew with the philistinism in the prevailing culture and the conservatism of the supposedly enlightened establishment to produce little change at all. Those who enjoyed hearing the Philharmonia at its magnificent peak, or Birgit Nilsson at Covent Garden, or admired the fine lines of the Festival Hall were content to celebrate the artistic health of the nation, but not to open the doors wider.

Britten inhabited both worlds. He was an evangelist for original music – for example in the transformation of folk song and church music – and felt that the duty of the lonely artist was to make friends with those whom he might influence. Tippett's music, if not his words, has something of the same spirit. In the course of a very long life it became more experimental and built on all the orchestral brilliance developed in his youth, but there remained a pulse from the past that more radical modernists in the United States and Europe were trying not to hear. It was from them that the real rebellion would come.

In Britain, Tippett's 'true function' for the imaginative artist was destined, among musicians, to be less celebrated than it once had been. Composers with his brilliant gifts or Britten's were cherished and honoured – when Britten died in Aldeburgh in 1976 it was the lead item on BBC radio news, a prominence that might well not be matched today. But they did not live in an era when serious musicians were lifted up. They both lived in small isolated communities – an image that it's hard to ignore.

Peter Grimes expresses understanding, the insight of a glittering emotional imagination and a knowledge of the darkness that comes with violence and fear. It's also a beacon for a British musical culture that, for all its achievements and the commitment of its leaders, was about to dim its lights for a while. The shock of the new would be felt more tellingly elsewhere.

It was natural after the Second World War that European composers should turn away from the past. Everywhere they looked there was ruin. In Europe and the Soviet Union more than twenty-five million people had died; German cities were rubble; the Iron Curtain had fallen and divided the continent in two.

So when someone like Pierre Boulez in France looked at the tradition to which he was drawn as a musician, and to a composer he revered, like Beethoven, he was also driven to use the legacy to do something quite new. His first two piano sonatas, written when he was in his early twenties, took the four-movement sonata form of Beethoven and seemed deliberately to destroy it. Yet Boulez was trying to rediscover fundamental principles, reaching beyond Beethoven to what lay underneath in an act that was not destructive but loyal. Everything that had happened in Europe during his lifetime seemed to have been a disaster. Why not start again?

That impulse among young composers to clear away the debris was very strong. In his 'Structures Book 1' of pieces for two pianos in serial mode, finished in 1952, Boulez used a fragment of music from his teacher, the composer Olivier Messiaen, in order to remove any subjectivity on his part: there was a deliberately mechanical quality to what he was doing. The serial technique involved setting out rows of notes, with no basis in traditional harmonic patterns, no home key, to give the piece a different governing structure. He explained: 'For me this was an exercise in doubt, in Cartesian doubt. I wanted to question everything, to make a tabula rasa of the whole musical inheritance and begin again at degree zero, so as to see how one could arrive at a new way of writing, starting from a phenomenon that lay outside one's own experience.'

Across Europe young composers were thinking in the same way. The Hungarian György Ligeti said that in his early works he, too, was starting again – because he regarded 'all the music he knew and loved as being, for [his] purposes, irrelevant and even invalid'. The important word there is 'love'. Just as Boulez adored Beethoven, Ligeti understood that his absorption of the European tradition had shaped his musical intelligence. And that intelligence demanded originality; that was what he'd admired in the greatest of the composers he knew.

Ligeti, born in 1923, was Jewish and had nearly been killed by the invading Nazis in Hungary. The rest of his close family perished. The experience was shared by many young composers – such as Iannis Xenakis in Greece, who fought in the anti-Nazi resistance as a communist, Hans Werner Henze in Germany, who said that 'everything the fascists hate is beautiful to me', and Karlheinz Stockhausen in Germany, too, whose mother was killed by the Nazis, though his father was a Party member.

Messiaen, who taught Boulez and later Stockhausen, and helped Xenakis, is an important father-figure. He's known to a wide audience for his adoption of birdsong in his music, a brilliant metaphor for his search for a different structure. In 1952 he wrote 'Le Merle Noir' for flute and piano, based entirely on the closely monitored song of the blackbird. The habit of adapting birdsong would remain with him for the rest of his life, and he produced much original (and popular) music using techniques that were entirely his own.

Messiaen, who died in 1992 at the age of eighty-four, was a composer who reached that wide audience with music which is highly coloured and expressive. Among his young students and their friends in the late 1940s, however, popularity wasn't the point. They were engaged, as Boulez said, on an intellectual quest. Quite consciously, they wrote for an elite. It was the only way to safeguard progress. Indeed, the American composer Milton Babbitt went so far as to argue that modern music had reached the stage, like advanced mathematics or physics, at which the public could not be expected to understand it. That, he thought, was no bad thing. He even suggested that composers might withdraw entirely from public performance. Given his cast of mind, why not? 'By so doing, the separation between the domains would be defined beyond any possibility of confusion of categories, and the composer would be free to pursue a private life of professional achievement, as opposed to a public life of unprofessional compromise and exhibitionism.'

That is the extreme view, music as a private activity for those of like mind. Even those European composers in the post-war era who were dedicated to experiment had no desire to cut themselves off completely, like useless limbs; but they were attracted to the idea of abandoning 'exhibitionism and compromise'. In Britain, the approach of Benjamin

Britten and Michael Tippett, in particular, was different. Despite their defence of high art and their commitment to the task, their attempt to develop distinctive voices for a new age was much more closely attuned to prevailing public taste. Britten was passionate about using forms and sound patterns that had roots. Tippett consciously drank from the well of English music and tradition.

By the time he made his own profound statement about war in the *War Requiem* for the dedication of Coventry Cathedral in 1962, with First World War poems by Wilfred Owen incorporated in a setting of the Latin mass, Britten was established as a composer who appeared successfully to bridge the worlds of highly intellectualised art and a broader public taste. He and (especially Tippett) didn't want to be popular for the sake of it, but they did want to communicate.

The severe form of modernism championed by composers like Boulez and Stockhausen was much more ascetic, and seemed at first to have its echo in the United States in the work of the deliberately shocking John Cage. He's perhaps best known now for his famous work of silence, which has an indeterminate length, but whose first performance lasted four minutes thirty-three seconds. He didn't care afterwards how long it look, as long as it was different each time. Cage and Boulez met in Paris in 1949 and though they shared a hatred of convention and wanted to reconstruct music on lines that had nothing to do with key, the traditional means of familiarising the ear – and that started by separating out the elements (rhythm, pitch, density) – they travelled in different directions.

Boulez wanted to take Arnold Schoenberg's twelve-note method on another stage. He still saw himself as the musician who controlled the sound; Cage was much more like an anarchist, almost the anti-composer who would set the music free. Schoenberg, still living in the States, couldn't understand it. 'Why is there no harmony in your works?' he asked Cage. 'Because I'm not interested in harmony,' came the reply. 'Then you will keep coming up against a brick wall.' And Cage said: 'Then I will dedicate my life to beating my head against that wall' (as he has).

Cage's view of the role of the composer was deliberately obtuse. Ideally, he 'feels no responsibility for his work, but out of unconfessed weakness and confusion and the desire for temporary relief, simply throws himself into a puerile mumbo-jumbo . . . In other words, everything happens just as it will, without control (an intentional but not meritorious omission, since there is no alternative), but within a fixed network of probabilities, since even chance must have some sort of outcome.'

It's important to remember, though, that in the 1950s in the United States the most influential composer wasn't someone who embraced modernist ideas, though he was an innovator – Aaron Copland. He was a friend and inspiration to Leonard Bernstein and to young American composers like Marc Blitzstein. In 1948, just as the Young Turks in Europe were trying to dismantle the past, he was writing a clarinet commission from Benny Goodman, star of the big bands of the swing era, that was a characteristic mixture of technical brilliance and native idiom.

As so often, different streams were running alongside each other. Talented American composers like Philip Glass and John Adams (who was born in the year Copland's concerto was written) would draw on the example of composers writing in more traditional forms, like Copland or Samuel Barber, and those who were pushing at the boundaries, or, in John Cage's case, banging his head against every brick wall he could find.

In Europe the avant-gardistes could justifiably claim that they were trying to redefine the music of ideas, though especially in Britain (less so in France) their experiments were regarded with suspicion and considerable hostility outside a small circle of admirers and followers. Boulez and Stockhausen were part of the movement known through the 1950s as the Darmstadt School which was rigorous in pursuing serial music in a way that some other contemporaries, like Hans Werner Henze, found restrictive and counter-productive. Henze was interested in serial technique, creating the arranged rows of notes that replaced the keys as the structure of the piece, usually in a twelve-note pattern of the sort that Schoenberg had used. But although he was a modernist he recognised the danger that those who were most determined to reconstruct music on principles that had never been used before might disappear into abstraction – or separate themselves entirely from a listening public which he was convinced could be introduced into a post-war sound world that had been built from the rubble of the past.

Boulez, whose career embraced a highly successful and popular period as conductor of the BBC Symphony Orchestra, would plead a resounding 'not guilty' to the charge of cutting himself off from the world. And if you listen, for example, to *Le Visage nuptiale*, written when he was in his early twenties just after the war, you hear a master at work. He was setting poems by the Surrealist René Char, and giving them his own colours.

Boulez and fellow Darmstadt composers like Luciano Berio have gained broader audiences over the years. But it was true that under the shadow of war the determination of part of that generation of musicians to break away from traditional sounds produced work that, for a broader musical public, would have to be moderated – and subjected to other influences – before it became acceptable and familiar.

That was one of the great battles of the 1960s, when the explosion of a young popular culture – for the first time – challenged musicians to turn their intellectual commitments, and technical skills, into a language that might travel and be understood. There was an appetite for the new – the word came to embody the spirit of the age – but there was competition. Music of all kinds was everywhere. Establishments and artists might battle about how a national culture could be modernised and sustained, but the persistent question would lie underneath: who would be listening?

17

A Golden Age

Two Visionaries

~

T HE 1950S ARE the most unfairly denigrated of the post-war years. Far from being a weary trudge out of austerity, across a grey landscape, the decade was a time of hope. Houses were being built, clothes were looking brighter and even if the Prime Minister, Harold Macmillan, never did utter the words 'You've never had it so good', towards the end of the decade there was the promise of a fridge in every kitchen and eventually a car in every garage, just as a king had once decreed that he would put a chicken in every pot. Far from being the drab decade that the upheavals of the 1960s made it seem in retrospect, these were years of modest but continuous excitement.

Culturally, while some musicians argued at Darmstadt in Germany or in American colleges about how much of the past should be laid waste, and with what degree of violence, the landscape was shifting under people's feet. The newly identified establishment was just as stuffy, the high priests of the Arts Council no less determined to exercise power from a distance, but sounds were now available in way that had never happened before. In the early 1950s the long-playing record, at a stately 33rpm, was the key to a different world.

It was the golden age of classical recording. Millions of people across Europe had access to quality that had never been theirs before; they could listen to their favourite pieces of music as often as they liked (on machines which were getting better every year) and listen to radio broadcasts that brought orchestras into their living rooms. These were not sounds as delicately engineered as those we know today, but they were a revelation. No longer was concert-going the prerequisite for the enjoyment of live music, and the horizons of the music-lover could be expanded easily.

Compared with the hiss and crackle of shellac at 78rpm on the old gramophones, vinyl recordings offered a clean sound from the moment the long-playing record arrived at the beginning of the 1950s. Never had orchestras, singers, musicians, composers been able to reach bigger audiences. Getting a flavour of the period means thinking of a drawing room or a kitchen as well as the Royal Festival Hall. The record companies were agents of change.

Classical recording began in Germany. The first symphony was recorded on disc in Berlin in the last year before the First World War. Forty players from the Berlin Philharmonic performed Beethoven's Fifth Symphony in a bare room that had few of the accoutrements of a studio. But the conductor, the Hungarian Arthur Nikisch, said the results were 'simply overpowering'. No one had heard such a thing before. For many music-lovers, months or years would pass between performances of even well-known pieces. Now they could be taken off the shelf. The recording was made by the German subsidiary of a British company, the Gramophone Company, called Deutsche Grammophon, which would become one of the most revered names in the industry. The discs were very expensive – forty-eight marks each – and the first set did not reach London until August the following year, a month after the outbreak of war. They were the start of everything.

Looking at the 1950s, two figures illuminate the landscape, though they were quite different characters. Leonard Bernstein was the fabulously talented composer and musician who almost defined post-war stardom, flitting from Carnegie Hall to Broadway to the Musikverein in Vienna and back again, touring the world with its great orchestras, bringing energy and glitz to all he did. The second figure, in contrast, was a shy record producer called Walter Legge, whose name the public barely knew but who managed a revolution in the recording studio, brought the craft of recording within reach of everyone and distilled the genius of a brilliant performance on to a disc. Between them they reveal the glamour and the progress of the 1950s. By the end of that decade Bernstein epitomised the allure that would attach itself to the musicians of the celebrity age, with consequences that would not be as welcome as his own presence on the scene, and Legge was the unlikely representative of the revolution that had brought it about, the lightning spread of recorded music into the home.

In the record business, the two giants who battled it out in Britain were Decca and EMI (the company that was the product of a marriage between HMV and Columbia), and in the heat of their battle they forged some of the best discs ever recorded. EMI had Maria Callas, conductors like Otto Klemperer and Herbert von Karajan (at first; he defected to Decca later), the horn-player Dennis Brain, the violinists David Oistrakh and Yehudi Menuhin, and among orchestras the Philharmonia at its peak.

Decca's principal boast, a proud one, was that it undertook the task of producing the first studio recording of Wagner's Ring cycle under the baton of Sir Georg Solti, which was begun in 1958. The company was slow to attune itself to the growth in the classical market, though it made a brilliant investment when it recruited John Culshaw as a producer in 1946. Over the next twenty-four years he became the company's maestro of the studio, producing the Ring, and bringing the engineering standards of the company to a pitch of perfection so that in the 1960s it was the company to which many classical artists were drawn. Its competitor EMI was almost tempted into its own disastrous mistake in the early 1950s in harbouring suspicions about the coming growth in the LP market but it, too, had a technical wizard on the books. Not only did Legge lead the company to impressive commercial success but he created many of the discs that are most treasured by music-lovers today.

When he was at the height of his fame as a producer – an impresario of the disc – Legge was a figure who wielded enormous power with orchestras, singers, instrumentalists. Yet never did his name appear on an EMI record cover. In the studios, and in the corridors of the concert halls, his name was spoken with awe (and sometimes with a hiss) but his public never knew him. He is one of the stranger figures in our modern music history.

To picture the drama that was attached to this man, imagine one of the world's great orchestras being disbanded, dissolved, on the spot. It nearly happened in London in the early 1960s and Legge was the man who tried to do it. He was strangling his own baby. In 1946, he had created the Philharmonia to serve as a house orchestra for EMI – Sir Thomas Beecham came on board to conduct – and throughout the 1950s he helped to turn it into one of the world's best. It was the equivalent of the London Symphony Orchestra in the closing years of the twentieth century, a band near the top of the first division. The Philharmonia came from nothing to bask in the glory of the 1950s revolution in music-recording, which Legge – more than any other single man – engineered at EMI. It is not, however, simply a technical story. Emotional storms accompanied that achievement, and Legge was caught in his own *Götterdämmerung* when he decided to do away with the orchestra he had created.

The Philharmonia was recording in the Kingsway Hall in London. Some senior players knew what was planned; most did not. Those in the dark were astonished when, on the morning of 10 March 1964, Legge announced that he was winding it up. Even in the febrile world of music, where ego and genius are so often tangled up, the Philharmonia affair was dramatic. One question above all tantalised everyone. Had Legge forewarned the orchestra's principal conductor, Klemperer, a formidable personality who'd come back to European after conquering the United States and was used to getting his own way? There is still dispute about it.

One witness was another formidable figure. The great soprano Elisabeth Schwarzkopf was singing in *Die Zauberflöte*, which was being recorded that day. She was Legge's wife, and for the rest of her life – she died in 2006 – she defended him against the charge of deceit: Klemperer knew what Legge was going to say. The conductor's family hold the opposite view. It will never be settled.

The episode became part of the Legge story, how the man who had inspired musicians in the studio and put his stamp on the recording industry had finally overstepped himself. The conductor Sir Charles Mackerras, then in his early forties, was working with the orchestra at that time and was among those who could hardly believe what was happening. It seemed that Legge – famous for his temper as well as his late-night joviality, and his love of the grand gesture despite his essentially shy nature – had lost any feeling for the players he'd nurtured, among them many of the stars of the orchestral firmament. Mackerras concluded that he didn't care what happened to any of them, while the great edifice that he'd had built, with a reputation that encircled the world and a record catalogue that was the envy of every rival, was being pulled down. It was a decision worthy of a neurotic impresario on Broadway, and perhaps a sign of how strongly the fevered atmosphere of business and celebrity had embraced the classical world.

There followed a wonderful salvo of telegrams between Legge and Klemperer in which each insisted that he never wanted to work with the other again. Klemperer went further, and said he would never conduct the orchestra if Legge were present. He won. The orchestra rebelled, got Klemperer's enthusiastic support, and became a self-governing body that played as the New Philharmonia for thirteen years until it was able to recover the rights to its own name.

The row was the beginning of the end of a puzzling and glittering career. Maria Callas and Herbert von Karajan, Klemperer and George Szell, the greatest German baritone of his age, Dietrich Fischer-Dieskau, the accompanist Gerald Moore, Schwarzkopf herself – these were some of Legge's signings for EMI, a brilliant roster of performers whom he could cajole and inspire and sometimes bully to produce recordings that became treasures of their time and glitter to this day. Which record collection did not have the disc of Brain playing the Mozart horn concertos, or Oistrakh's Beethoven Violin Concerto? Legge's recordings were original creations, yet he never appeared on an honours list, nor even in *Who's Who*, and was never publicly recognised in the country of his birth. He died in 1979 in Switzerland, never having done any of the big jobs – at an opera house or an international festival – that had been predicted as his inheritance when he left EMI fifteen years before.

He was born in a London suburb in 1906. He was half Jewish, with no obvious advantages in life. What he did, he did for himself. Fred Gaisberg, one of the fathers of the recording industry, first spotted him and brought him to a junior position in EMI. Gaisberg understood talent of his sort. He'd recorded Enrico Caruso and knew what the studio was likely to be able to produce with the new technologies that were on the way. He knew how much homework Legge had done and his devotion to the cause. Legge was able to project an enthusiasm for music that was not at all technical. It came from the gut. He once said that he had learned what he knew of music from four people: the tenor John McCormack, the organist and humanitarian Albert Schweitzer, Beecham, and the critic Ernest Newman whose work – especially on the nineteenth-century Austrian composer Hugo Wolf – had inspired him.

He had worked for a time as a junior critic alongside Newman, and began to be drawn towards the recording studio where great things were beginning to happen – but the time was not propitious. The depression was not good for record sales. Legge, however, displayed for the first time the flash of originality that would make his career. He dreamed up a subscription scheme. The recordings were financed by customers who'd agreed to buy the disc in advance. It was revolutionary. And it marked him out. He was still technically in the literary department of EMI, but Gaisberg was so impressed that he let him produce some sessions. There was a second consequence. His beloved Hugo Wolf, who'd inspired him, joined the catalogue for the first time.

There was also a chance partnership with a conductor who would give Legge his big chance. Gaisberg didn't get on with Sir Thomas Beecham, and Legge took him over. The two emotional and irascible characters hit it off, for a while. Their first recording of *Die Zauberflöte* was also Legge's first opera on disc and a milestone in his life for another reason. He met Schwarzkopf, whom he would marry after the Second World War and with whose career his own would be intertwined for the rest of his life.

Everything stopped for the war. Legge was lucky: his bad eyesight kept him out of the forces, so as well as running the classical side of the forces entertainment outfit ENSA he was the man who would oversee any recording sessions that EMI could manage while the war lasted. Here was a stroke of luck. By 1945, he'd been listening to orchestras, hearing musicians, learning the repertoire. In that year he was put in charge of the company's Columbia label.

Yet Legge, bursting with talent, physically awkward, afflicted by his short sight, prone to rage, was never going to escape his middle-class background and sit comfortably with the gentlemen who ran the company in those days, and who were still wearing striped trousers at the beginning of the 1960s. It was one of the themes of his life – a musician who didn't play an instrument, an executive who despised corporate life, a man who loved German culture at a time of war with Hitler. He was always the outsider. In part, it was that difference – that distance – that drove him on.

The key to his success was the Philharmonia, brought together in the year after the war ended. It was perhaps more than any other British orchestra a band of great players with a desire to prove their greatness; it was also one man's dream. He was in charge, and in his pomp and prime. Players like the leader, the violinist Manoug Parikian, still remember those heady days with gratitude despite Legge's erratic behaviour. He personally owned the orchestra for the recordings, his wife was becoming one of the finest singers of the century – thanks in part to his meticulous work with her in the studio – and business was booming. No one worried about conflicts of interest. This was success.

The industry was racing ahead – early tape-recording, better studios, the arrival of the LP as the 1950s began, and then stereo (though Legge himself was strangely late to acknowledge it) meant that customers were renewing their collections much as they would do decades later with the arrival of CD. There was huge demand, and plenty of money.

But with power came responsibility. If Legge was lucky to ride this wave, it's important to remember that his real achievement was in the quality of his work. Legge's recordings of this period were with many of the best performers – with Karajan and Klemperer, Beecham and Sir Adrian Boult, the pianist Dinu Lipatti who died young, Callas, Oistrakh. These records were the mechanism by which many people in Britain first discovered the pieces of music that would remain important to them for the rest of their lives – Schwarzkopf in Strauss's *Der Rosenkavalier* or the *Four Last Songs*, Callas in *Tosca*, Wilhelm Furtwängler conducting an extraordinary performance of Beethoven's Ninth Symphony at Bayreuth in 1951, Klemperer conducting opera.

If the orchestra and the recording company were his, and Karajan his discovery, so was Schwarzkopf, who was willingly shackled to the artistic destiny he saw for her. It remains a controversial and important relationship. He could be rude and demeaning to her in public, and cruel in his work with her. Despite his admiration, he was ruthless – maybe sometimes a little dishonest – in pursuit of his objectives, making a great deal of money owning and employing an orchestra that he often bullied, and driving head office at EMI to distraction with his demands. But among those who knew him well, and who knew his faults, there was admiration, even love.

What happened in the recording studio in the 1950s was like the revelation of what Hollywood could do for the movies. Suddenly, opera was on disc in a quality that could transport the listener to La Scala or the Metropolitan Opera in New York. Legge's work on his home ground of the German orchestral repertoire and lieder and opera was a demonstration of brilliance, and his recordings with Callas touched new heights. He had a genius for music, and for business too. The classical recording business had known nothing like it. Eventually of course, the relationship with Callas collapsed. Maybe it was bound to. As she spent more time with Aristotle Onassis and less time working, the voice was starting to fade. By the early 1960s, the glory days were behind her. Legge thought she wasn't working hard enough, and was wasting her talent. So, as with Beecham and Karajan, in the end he moved away.

The final important discovery of this remarkable career was that of Otto Klemperer, a relationship also doomed. Though the conductor was ageing and in poor health, Legge brought him out of the shadows to record the great Germanic works for the stereo catalogue. It was another act of inspiration. When the break came, on that March day in the Kingsway Hall, the reason may not be as obscure as it first appears.

Perhaps Legge sensed what lay ahead. People had bought their Beethoven symphonies and Mozart concertos. They could listen again and again. The times were changing, and a slow decline in classical recording was perhaps beginning. When he left EMI in 1964 the Beatles had just arrived: the world of recording was being turned upside down, as had happened when he had begun in the industry in the 1930s. EMI brought in Sir Joseph Lockwood to try to make sense of it, and it was the end for Legge. Maybe he wasn't the dinosaur that some critics thought him to be, unable to cope with the demands of new technologies; perhaps instead he was ahead of his time as he had been when he started up his first subscription scheme, rethinking the repertoire, recording Hugo Wolf. He was original and inspiring, and a man who enjoyed life hugely – in the studio, in the concert hall, at the dinner table – but all who knew him sensed a kind of sadness that clung to him, a feeling that there was something missing that he couldn't quite identify. It's in the music that these questions may be resolved, because it's on disc that he lives – his touch sure, his commitment absolute, his nerve firm. To hear Schwarzkopf sing the *Four Last Songs* is to hear Walter Legge too, a man who shaped for so many people the music they came to love.

Only Culshaw's achievements at Decca rival Legge's. The triumph of the Ring recording – its atmosphere caught memorably in Humphrey Burton's landmark documentary for the BBC in 1965 – was Decca's finest classical coup, and after forty years the discs still rank among the best for anyone who wants a close encounter with Wagner. Solti's explosively energetic conducting and the singing of Birgit Nilsson, Hans Hotter, Wolfgang Windgassen and the others (with even Joan Sutherland performing a minor role in *Siegfried*) still evoke the excitement of those sessions.

As decline set in for classical recording, these were the giants that ensured a legacy for anyone who treasured a record collection. Their work lives on. In performance, the best of their recordings are evidence of genius at work. It may be that in the 1950s no one could make an all-round claim to that label with more force (and certainly not with more personality) than Leonard Bernstein. He had a uniquely American glow – the celebrity conductor and composer who embraced the classical and the popular at a time when they seemed about to go their own ways. He commanded the best orchestras steeped in the Germanic symphonic tradition, and wrote maybe the greatest of musicals.

West Side Story, which opened on Broadway in 1957, is a musical that breathes America's oldest narrative – how its immigrants have found ways of surviving – and it pays debts to the country's roots: to jazz, to the New York melting pot, and to the European tradition. Shakespeare's story of the Montagues and Capulets from *Romeo and Juliet* that Bernstein set to music, with lyrics by the young Stephen Sondheim, was no accidental choice. The musical is an homage as well as a confident announcement.

Bernstein was a star. After he died, in 1990 at the age of seventy-two, his funeral procession began on that same Upper West Side where the Jets and Sharks had jousted, from the Dakota building where he lived (like John Lennon, who'd been killed on the front steps in 1980). The cortège wound its long way to Brooklyn through crowds of the sort that might be expected to turn out for a politician of special generosity, or a mafioso. Bernstein got that signal of affection as a musician whose stardom had begun in the concert hall and whose stardust had sprinkled the streets. There was no one quite like him, even in a city filled with personalities, power-brokers and multiple oddballs.

The first flash of fame came by chance. In November 1943, the conductor Bruno Walter fell ill with flu when he was about to conduct the New York Philharmonic at Carnegie Hall, and Bernstein, one of the orchestra's assistants – only twenty-five years old – stepped in. The *New York Times* had him on the front page the next day. As he was to be for much of his life, he was the story.

He was unstoppable. He'd written a first symphony in the year before that first night; and soon he was embracing the American love of music theatre and film. There was *On the Town* in 1944 (with the song that told us that in New York the Bronx was up and the Battery down), *Wonderful Town* in 1953, the film score for *On the Waterfront* with Marlon Brando a year later, *Candide* in 1956 and then *West Side Story*. And all the while his reputation as a classical musician was growing; in the year when the Jets and Sharks were fighting to sell-out crowds on Broadway he was appointed conductor of the New York Philharmonic.

He was intent on repopularising Mahler, as Walter had been, and produced spellbinding performances, in an inimitable style, and an emotional one – though they were not to everyone's taste. Winthrop Sargent in the *New York Times* accused him of indulging in 'fencing and hula-dancing' and of calling on heaven to witness his agonies. Well, said Mr Sargent, he cared about Mahler's agonies, but not one bit about Mr Bernstein's.

This conductor, however, mattered. Quite apart from his first recording of all the symphonies of Mahler (with the enthusiastic support of the composer's widow) – which was a milestone in his rediscovered popularity – Bernstein became an evangelist for live music. People were buying classical discs in vast numbers by the end of the 1950s; the top singers and soloists were hot property. His gift was to bring to recording the atmosphere of the concert hall, the sense that conductor and orchestra were jousting with each other and enjoying every moment. American television viewers were watching him conduct and explain music; he presented himself as part teacher – the father-figure who would tell you what orchestral music was all about – and part sexy maestro, whose commitment told you that music was sensual and exciting.

Mahler was an appropriate enthusiasm. He had suppressed his Jewishness and then converted to Catholicism, when he was conductor at the State Opera in Vienna in the 1890s when it was probably the most anti-Semitic city in Europe. Bernstein, born to a rabbi in Philadelphia, didn't face that same kind of hostility, but his identity (so often the American obsession) was ambiguous.

His First Symphony, written when he was twenty-seven in 1943, was a serious meditation, which he called 'Jeremiah', a lamentation for a Jerusalem pillaged and destroyed – a prophet mourning his people. Was he the contemplative musician, or the poet of the street who could absorb the crackle of the sidewalk? As with his sexuality – he was voracious in pursuit of men and women for most of his life – he faced both ways at once. The spread of a popular culture at breakneck speed meant that he was pulled in different directions. He revered the classical tradition, the lyricism of an American composer like Aaron Copland, Mahler and the concert hall. And he was also able to write in a contemporary idiom that seemed to come from different sources, including jazz and the musical theatre. Maybe Bernstein's greatest triumph was in living with ambiguity.

Jeremiah's lamentations came from the same pen as the overture to *Candide*, which has become a showpiece for orchestras, but which was written at roughly the same time as *West Side Story* was delivered for the musical stage. He described it as a 'Valentine to European music' and used the score to play with polkas, mazurkas, waltzes and even a parody of Schoenberg's twelve-tone music. It wasn't a Broadway hit on the scale he hoped: you'll hear it much more often now in the concert hall. *Candide* shows how Bernstein couldn't resist displaying the showman's touch. In Voltaire's story the ending is meant as a contrast to the silly optimism of Dr Pangloss (who thought that all was for the best in the best of all possible worlds). In Bernstein's musical version he can't resist making an optimistic statement of his own. He was irrepressible.

Bernstein enjoyed lasting celebrity as the creator of *West Side Story* and conducted the classical repertoire around the world – notably with the Vienna Philharmonic, the most conservative of European orchestras in style and habit – and it was inevitable that in the whirlpool and torment of 1960s America he would play his part. Unfortunately his commitment to liberal causes, and his hedonistic enthusiasm for youth movements, led in 1970 to his lampooning in a famous Tom Wolfe essay as the epitome of 'radical chic' after he had thrown an exceptionally smart fund-raising party in New York on behalf of some imprisoned Black Panthers. The *New York Times* described it as a 'piece of elegant slumming that degrades patrons and patronized alike'. Bernstein appeared as a maestro who had gone slightly awry, carried away by his own magic.

His musical life was fused with a changing America in its painful argument about civil rights, its voyage of self-doubt in Vietnam, its attempt to cope with the young revolution. Intriguingly, just as he felt at home in Vienna's Musikverein with the Philharmonic – recording complete sets of Beethoven, Brahms, Schumann and Mahler with them – his later compositions reveal how drawn he was to ritual, as in his Third Symphony (which he called 'Kaddish', after the Jewish prayer) and the moving *Chichester Psalms* written with the Anglican liturgy in mind. But even in maintaining the spiritual drive that had infused his First Symphony he couldn't avoid trouble. When he produced his mass in 1971 (he collaborated with the writer of *Godspell*) the Catholic Archbishop of Cincinnati told his flock not to attend the première. Some were moved, others not. The *New York Times* critic said it was the greatest mélange of styles since the ladies' magazine recipe for steak fried in peanut butter and marshmallow sauce.

But Bernstein was an extraordinary musician. In an age that began to be cursed by celebrity he was able to imprint himself on the public mind by means of his talent. He was larger than life, but he was a conductor of brilliance and power and a composer of originality.

I remember seeing him for the first time, by chance, at Logan Airport, Boston, in the early 1970s. He was wearing a white fur coat, and a retinue was spread out behind him like a prince's train. He seemed imperious, a figure that commanded attention. You expected him to announce that he was going to conduct the passengers, or at least demand of them that they attend his concert that night – a Pied Piper in mink. From Broadway to the concert halls of the world he cast a spell.

Music-makers speak in different ways, but whether in the scores of their own work, or at the piano or on the conductor's rostrum the test is whether they can cast a spell. It may lie in the lure of melody or atmosphere, or in a show of intellectual fireworks, or it may come from spiritual contemplation. Sometimes it is in the stage idiom that Bernstein understood with the instinct of an adopted New Yorker; sometimes in the symphonic repertoire that he did so much to bring to a wider audience in America.

Bernstein thought the two worlds were one. He was a disciplined pianist and conductor who brought life to the classical tradition, and he waltzed on to the stage with the rhythms of jazz in his ears. He brought style to four decades, but he can be remembered above all for lighting up the 1950s.

18

The Sixties and Afterwards
Popular Culture and Confusion

~

THE SOUNDS OF the 1960s were not in the classical tradition. If youth culture had begun with Elvis in the mid-1950s, as a child of jazz and swing that was starting to mature, it became a rampant teenager in London a few years later. With the slow but inexorable death of deference, the rebirth of satire, the ubiquity of television and the falling price of records, the path to a freer, more exciting world was opening up to anyone with a spark of life and youth in their veins. By the time the Beatles and the Rolling Stones began their never-to-be-resolved struggle for dominance, around 1963, a new language in popular music had been invented. The patois became dominant and international within a year or two.

Then a second revolution happened. Within a decade that culture produced inventive rock 'n' roll of the sort that was vanishingly scarce in the early days after the Beatles' first success in 1962. By the early 1970s, rock bands were experimenting, taking risks, energetically exploring (though usually through a self-induced haze) the history of blues and jazz for inspiration and ideas. You could say that Gerry and the Pacemakers became Pink Floyd; Herman's Hermits were now Led Zeppelin. The world had changed twice in a decade.

For composers working in the classical tradition, this had one of two effects. For some, it was a cue to become even more remote, an invitation to trek to the distant mountaintop high in the clouds and stay there. So repugnant was the aggressive marketing of the big record companies, who found themselves making unexpected millions, that the old ivory tower beckoned once more. Some others tried to adapt. The trouble was that the prevailing culture held popularity to be the key, and as part of that process the notion of high art – of music that needed work to bring rewards – became unfashionable and fuddy-duddy. Like jazz aficionados who would gather in secret places to exchange the Masonic handshakes of their obsession, contemporary classical music seemed to be heading into the dungeon. Children of families with a musical tradition would still be plonked at the piano, maybe taken to a concert or encouraged to listen to the 1950s record collection, but the pulse was beating elsewhere.

This was new. Though jazz had begun to take a different path in the 1920s, and Hollywood had encouraged the lightning spread of popular music and the be-bop and big bands in the swing era, nothing so quick or so profound had happened before. At many moments in the course of this journey there have been obvious gulfs between the masses and musical originality and creation, but never had the challenge to those who claimed to be the inheritors of the classical tradition come so suddenly or been so fierce. A middle-aged audience lucky enough to have benefited from some 1950s top-down patronage, and from the commitment in schools to music training, would still be available; but the next generation was going to be a problem. Who would retune its collective ear? What had to be done?

The modernists of the 1950s were, consciously, writing for an audience that was never expected to be huge. Boulez, Stockhausen and the others who trekked to Darmstadt to participate in what Boulez called 'an exercise in Cartesian doubt' were determinedly high minded. Their creativity was fuelled by intellectual curiosity and impatience, not by any desire to please. If an audience responded, perhaps it proved that the experiment had worked; maybe music would take a turn for the better. If it didn't, it just proved that the uneducated were inheriting the earth. The concept of satisfying a paying audience, playing the market, was by its nature abhorrent to them.

The problem thrown up by the 1960s was that competition was beginning to demand compromise by classical artists, slowly but inexorably. Sales were everything. If audiences could be found to fill halls for rock concerts and buy 45rpm records in their hundreds of thousands every week, why should record companies commit themselves to classical music in perpetuity? The answer, from the big companies, was only slowly teased out over the next three decades, but it was in the negative. The standard by which they would judge music-for-sale had changed for ever; the idea that quality was every-thing was on the wane. They would search for the best popular bands, of course, and the dross would be shovelled out of the recording studio. But, in dealing with their classical catalogues, would they take the same risks? The moment when Walter Legge left EMI, after a generation of brilliant, innovative classical recording, was around the time that the Beatles walked in. Unfortunately, the pointless and miserable question was already being answered. In the end it would be either/or, but not both.

One of the consequences was that the work being done by modernists was going to have to confront a popular taste that was already being satisfied. In an effort to break away from conventions that they wanted to destroy, they were facing a potential audience which would almost certainly consist mainly of that (small) section of the existing audience for classical music that was ready to take the plunge and embrace the new, or be swept away by the simple power of popular music, so much of which was exciting, inventive and bound up with the feeling of generation change that was the spirit of the time.

Would someone have to win and someone lose? If so, what is the significance of the appearance on the Beatles' *Sergeant Pepper* album in 1967, in the *galère* of cultural icons assembled for the montage on Peter Blake's memorable cover, of none other than Karlheinz Stockhausen himself? In the 1950s, he had been listening to Schoenberg, trying to apply his principles of serialism to an electronic medium. At that time he was an earnest, radical Catholic with short hair, dressed in a suit. By the mid-1960s he was heading off to consult with Indian mystics, experimenting with drugs, and sporting the appropriate hairstyle of the day, getting shaggier and shaggier. You would hardly know it was him. The serious Darmstadt-goers in Germany, hardline musical radicals but, by a paradox, defenders of a conservative high culture, would have thought it odd (though the album probably passed them by).

But if Stockhausen found a cult following as a result of his experi-ments that took him close to popular music, and involved him in some of the innovations to come, there was still a classical-music establish-ment having to do its best without being drowned out. Shostakovich was writing his last symphonies – better than ever – and Benjamin Britten, entering the final decade of his life, was still writing opera and building on his formidable reputation. He had a public renown which far outstripped that of any other in the art tradition. Though concert audiences at that time still maintained overwhelmingly conservative tastes, the *War Requiem* in Coventry Cathedral in 1962 was a landmark cultural event (and produced a memorable and popular recording), and Britten's distinctly English sound was never drowned out in the land. When the Snape Maltings concert hall near his home in Aldeburgh was opened in 1967, having been converted from old warehouses and malting barns, it quickly established itself as a place of pilgrimage for a legion of music-lovers, and has remained so. Britten, always on the inside track of modern music with a feel for melody and form that could suggest the past as well as the future, was able to retain his reputation as a forward-thinking composer who could appeal beyond the boundaries of what appeared to many to be the impenetrable enclosure of high art. Not least in schools, where his work for children was both appealing and rewarding, he created a taste that without him might never have been encouraged.

There were others who were following paths that seemed to lead somewhere. Peter Maxwell Davies was one of the most restless talents on the London scene, working on serialism as a student and thereafter beginning to demonstrate his capacity for rare originality, which has made such a happy home in Orkney, where his sympathy for landscape and the simple life has found expression in both symphonic and chamber work of distinctive intensity. Who else would have gone to the Antarctic to listen to the silence in order better to incorporate it in a symphony? If anyone had suggested to Max in the 1960s that he would end up as Master of the Queen's Musick, as he did at the turn of the century – a gay, rumbustious challenger of convention – he would have laughed. But it happened.

His experience is instructive. One of his shocking projects (at the time) was to take parts of Handel's *Messiah* – revered by amateur choirs up and down the land – and do to it what Jimi Hendrix did in the same year (1969) with 'The Star Spangled Banner'. It got him into a little less trouble than Hendrix found in the States, but trouble nonetheless. *Eight Songs for a Mad King* was a bold piece of theatre, but found him caught between the majority in a musical establishment who found him too awkward and a broader public who knew little of what he was doing or what he meant. In 1967 he was one of the founders, with Harrison Birtwistle, of the Pierrot Players – later to become the Fires of London – which was a sounding board for new music that had come back from the modernist fringe but was still radical enough to find itself treasured by enthusiasts rather than by a wider audience. In the end, it prospered.

Missionary work was going on. The London Sinfonietta, founded in 1968, had a mission to bring contemporary classical music to a bigger audience and did a great deal to encourage composers who would have found it hard to be championed elsewhere. Founded by Nicholas Snowman (later to run the South Bank in London and – briefly – Glyndebourne), it pressed the case for new music and spread the word about what composers like Steve Reich in America were beginning to do with their minimalist experiments. As time went by, it could claim considerable credit for promoting such luminaries among younger composers as Magnus Lindberg and Thomas Adès, who in 1999 became director of the Aldeburgh Festival, Benjamin Britten's legacy, when he was still in his twenties.

Intriguingly, one of the Sinfonietta's strongest supporters was Sir George Christie, by now patron of his father's family Glyndebourne Opera House in the Sussex Downs, a place financed entirely by audience subscription and sponsorship. His enthusiasm for the promotion of the new was just as fervent as his devotion to making productions of Mozart that were as perfect as they could possibly be. He saw no distinction between the exercise of judgement and taste in new music and that same exercise in respect of the masterworks of the repertoire which the opera house championed. The subscription audience at Glyndebourne, notoriously conservative in taste but containing formidable reserves of knowledge and enthusiasm, deserved to be satisfied because the House could only survive by maintaining its tradition of excellence. But so, he thought, did the audience for music of the sort that at that stage Glyndebourne could not dare to tackle.

It is easy to look back to the 1960s and argue a simplistic case that contemporary composition withered in the face of the popular assault, its musicians cowering in some remote refuge where they could safely communicate with their friends and no one else. It was true in some cases, but the history of music-making should remind everyone that this has always been the way. There is not an age in this whole long story without its forgotten minor figures, no time when taste hasn't operated against some of talent, as well as against those who just haven't made the grade. Diamonds are often surrounded by a coal-heap of dross. The answer is the same as the correct response to the question addressed to English Literature students for at least two generations: 'Is the novel dead?' New music finished? No.

The urge to write serious music – music that sought to challenge the ear and the common assumptions about melody – was un-dimmed. That it was exercised without much imagination by some composers whose works would slip into the dark was hardly a surprise. But in that era, against the odds, there was originality at work that would last. In Britain, the truth is that the groundwork was laid in the 1960s for a generation of composers who are closer to reconnecting with a wide audience than at any time since the war.

Tracing the roots of the change involves a journey eastwards. Perhaps it is best to begin with a composition which has an extra-ordinary history – the Third Symphony of the Polish composer Henryk Górecki (b. 1933), which is the lament of a mother who has lost her son in battle. Written in Poland in 1975, it caused a near-scandal at the Warsaw Festival the following year. The reason was that it wasn't 'modern' enough. The Festival was, ironically for the eastern bloc, allowed by the communist authorities to encourage modernism, but Górecki was a dissenter, trying to recapture something that he thought had been lost. When the symphony became known in the west in the early 1990s it was an unexpected and roaring success. The recording sold a million copies, stayed in the charts for months and became better known, more quickly, to a wider audience than probably any other symphony by a contemporary composer in the post-war era.

The story of Górecki's Third reveals one of the most important strains in modern classical music – how the modernism of the 1960s was translated by some composers into an apparently 'old-fashioned' form of expression but one that struck a loud chord with many of those who'd lost touch with the drift of art music in the excitement of the youth revolution and the dominance of pop and rock.

Górecki began his life as a composer in the avant-garde. He was influenced by Anton Webern and Boulez and studied in Paris, where he produced work that derived from the serialists. But in the early 1970s, back in Poland, something happened. Górecki began to embrace his own brand of Romantic Expressionism. It lost him friends among modernists, who smelt rebellion. The modernist American critic James Wierzbicki said that his material was 'no longer cerebral and sparse – rather it was intensely expressive, persistently rhythmic and often richly coloured in the darkest of orchestral hues'. That, of course, was meant to be a damning critique. Despite resistance from some hardline modernists he was moving on to explore a rapprochement with other musical styles such as minimalism. He was one of those who were broadening the horizons of what could be counted as modernism.

His rebellion – for that's what it was – demonstrated how dissent in east and west was being expressed in different ways. A younger generation, coming to music after the 1990s and unaware of the impact of the Cold War, has to be reminded how much the divide between east and west Europe influenced the way new music was. In the west the youth revolution in the 1960s had made life difficult for composers who believed that they could write for the masses, but were intent on serious, highly intellectual music and on achieving progress by experiment. The masses weren't interested. They were listening to rock music and pop, which by the early 1970s was developing a complexity and richness that – with modern jazz – could sometimes claim to be as challenging as so-called serious music. It was certainly more popular. For those who did lean towards the classical tradition, either exclusively or alongside a liking for popular music, there was a problem: many of them simply didn't like what was being written.

But it was being written for a reason. Artists, as always, were sensitive to the failings of the political system. Many of them rebelled – the most original of them with fire in their bellies. Hans Werner Henze had written at the end of the 1960s with a belief that he might use music successfully as a political force. His *Raft of the Medusa* caused a scandal in 1968. At the première, broadcast by Hamburg Radio, the choir refused to sing because a red flag had been draped across the podium; there were a number of arrests as demonstrations and counter-demonstrations took place inside and outside the hall. The piece was dedicated to the

Latin American revolutionary Che Guevara and was a statement of belief by Henze, a composer utterly committed to political upheaval – he was close to the German student leader Rudi Dutschke (who lived with him in Italy after he fled Germany in the late 1960s, pursued by the authorities).

Like any serious composer, Henze believed that music could educate and elevate – but in the late 1960s he began to believe that music had lost the power to speak of change or revolution:

> The proletariat is, fortunately, far less crippled than we are. It is deliberately kept ill informed, certainly, and bombarded with miserable mass-produced products of the mass media. But in Italy, for example, the workers react in a lively and inquisitive fashion when one takes the trouble to show them things to which they otherwise have no access . . . By joining workers' groups we can protect ourselves to a certain extent from the failure of our attempts at solidarity and in constant conversations and discussions we can hear from our brothers what they need and what they expect from music.

Henze's complaint about the effect of popular culture was voiced by many composers who didn't share his political views, but his vision of what might happen if serious musicians expressed solidarity with 'the workers' was simply a dream. His huge output of opera, ten symphonies and orchestral pieces has brought him bagfuls of awards and honours, but his reputation was made and sustained with an intellectual audience, not with the broader one that he wanted to capture. Few modern composers have a higher reputation for the range and the power of their work, but Henze's quest for a revolution in musical understanding which would release people from the grip of a mass-market, lowest-common-denominator culture hasn't produced the changes that he wished for.

The difficulty on the other side of the Iron Curtain was altogether different. In the Soviet Union, far from the authorities encouraging the kind of radical modernism that Henze, Berio and other leftists in the west were pursuing, they were suppressing it. Western governments didn't think such music was dangerous – most political leaders would listen to very little of it, after all – but the Soviet leaders did. Socialist

Realism, as laid down by Lenin, Stalin and Maxim Gorky, was the state creed, redefined by whoever happened to be holding power at the time: it was a deeply conservative idea, a refusal to contemplate the new. As we've heard, the Soviet Union did champion musical training and performance, and celebrated its young virtuosi (as long as they didn't kick over the traces politically), but the regime wanted safe music, written within the tradition.

Occasional forays from the west were allowed – the avant-garde composer Luigi Nono was allowed into the Soviet Union, though only because he was a convinced communist. But, far more than in the west, musical taste was officially directed, and always towards the glories of the past. Yet there was dissent there, too. It took a very different form from the leftist protests championed in the west by Henze and others. The music of Alfred Schnittke, which was reaching the west, was beginning to make the case for a break with the past.

Maybe it was inevitable that it would be in Poland that it would become most obvious. The tension between that country's deep Catholic tradition and heavy hand of the Soviet Union was stretched to breaking point by the election as Pope John Paul II of the Pole Karol Wojtyła in 1978 and the shipyard rising at Gdansk which gave rise to Solidarity, the most influential political movement in eastern Europe since the Iron Curtain divided the continent after the Second World War. In that atmosphere a composer like Górecki could make statements that mattered – indeed he felt he should do just that. Alongside, rock music from the west was becoming a code for dissent throughout the Soviet sphere, and Górecki's music – like the setting of the 'Beatus vir' that he wrote for John Paul's visit soon after he became pope – was important.

After the 1960s, modernists in western Europe who were excited by dissent and by the prospect of profound political change discovered that they weren't at the heart of the argument in the streets. They had intellectual clout, and especially in Germany and Italy some popular influence, but it was limited. They didn't speak for the masses whom they wanted to represent. In eastern Europe and the Soviet Union, where the system didn't allow an uncontrolled popular musical culture, dissent took a different form – less political, and more spiritual. As the extraordinary popularity in the west of

Górecki's symphony in the early 1990s demonstrated, that was a signal of what was on the way.

In Britain the wave of composers who found a wide audience for the first time, or in their maturity saw that the audience for contemporary music was showing unexpected signs of life, that spirituality – sometimes in the form of mysticism – was an important strain too. It helped to give a distinctive character to music at the end of the century.

Mainstream concert-goers are now likely to encounter Mark-Anthony Turnage (b. 1960) or James MacMillan (b. 1959) or Adès (b. 1971) more regularly than their predecessors; Harrison Birtwistle is a knight of the realm and his 'Panic' made a return appearance at the Proms in 2007; where György Ligeti, Luciano Berio and even Hans Werner Henze have always found it difficult, in Britain, to break down some of the old barriers, a new generation is managing the job with a vigour that is perhaps surprising.

Henze, for example, is an extraordinary orchestrator whose political commitments – the loathing of the Nazis set him on the road to Marxism – have appeared over the years to make his passions seem rather dated. It is a curious fact that in an age when the young have been radicalised to an unexpected degree by world events (and particularly by American policy since its coronation as the only super-power) the post-war seriousness of the high-minded Marxists has come to be seen as out of date. They are the old fuddy-duddy radicals. Like all such drifts, it's a question of fashion as much of ideology, but it is nonetheless a fact. For modern, younger audiences a later generation of composers has more immediate attraction.

Spirituality seems to have played an unexpected part. Two of the more popular contemporary composers – Sir John Tavener and MacMillan – are overtly interested in religious questions, Tavener as a near-mystic and MacMillan as a serious left-wing Catholic. Tavener, born in 1944, was first recorded on the Beatles' Apple label, with his cantata *The Whale* (based on the Biblical story of Jonah), long before he adopted his druid-like posture and became fascinated by chants from the orient and mystical sounds. He joined the Russian Orthodox Church in the 1970s, and has written religious works inside and outside that tradition, including *The Veil of the Temple*, scored for multiple orchestras, choirs and soloists and lasting, in a full performance, for nearly seven hours. His music was heard by a wider audience than he may ever have expected to have when his 'Song for Athene' was played at the funeral of Diana, Princess of Wales in 1997. He was a serious composer in the 1960s who sniffed the air of Carnaby Street (whatever floated on the breeze). He had none of the rhythmic obsessions of pop and rock but he also avoided the intellectual denseness – the multi-layered texture – of the 1960s work of Boulez and of Luciano Berio, which sounded to British ears perhaps too much like an offshoot of the Italian or French film scene, carrying with it a high-art pretentiousness that was assumed to underlie their efforts, however honest they were.

In an age of brittle celebrity in which the bigger recording companies have greatly reduced their commitment to classical music – leaving it to smaller, independent labels to carry the weight (with great enthusiasm and invention) – Tavener managed to stand out from the world of serious music, a world that so often and so misleadingly appears staid to an audience which might otherwise be drawn to it. His height, his air of mystic melancholy, his ascetic distance from anything crude or mass-manufactured, have given him an eminence that perhaps couldn't have been produced by his music alone, but it has led more people to hear it. Tavener is one of a group of British composers, most of them much younger than him, who are probably going to put an indelible stamp on their time – more than any other group since Britten and Tippett were dominating the scene in the 1950s and 1960s.

Like Tavener, MacMillan has a feel for the spiritual power of music, in his case from his own (radical) faith. They both understand how a melodic sense, which comes naturally to them both, can blend with a free-thinking approach to form. The two used to be dangerous companions. Just as John Cage raged against harmony, preferring the thump of the comforting brick wall, so there was suspicion among some of the (generally small) audiences for some of their modernist successors of anything that toyed with a tune. MacMillan was regarded at first with distrust by those who claimed they didn't want to look backwards, but when his extraordinary orchestral evocation of witch-craft and obsession, 'The Confession of Isobel Gowdie', had its première at the BBC Proms in 1990 he immediately swam into the musical mainstream in spite of that early sniffiness. His concerto 'Veni, Veni Emmanuel' (1992), written for the virtuoso percussionist

Evelyn Glennie, quickly became a staple of the contemporary concert programme.

Adès is established as an innovator of rare power – Sir Simon Rattle chose to feature his work alongside Mahler's Fifth Symphony in his first concert as conductor of the Berlin Philharmonic in 2002 – and Mark-Anthony Turnage's work for the stage in *Greek* and *Oedipus the King* suggests that he may yet produce the best new opera in Britain for decades. The succession to the 1960s-reared generation of Birtwistle and Maxwell Davies, Alexander Goehr and Oliver Knussen, seems assured. They are almost certain to have an easier time of it.

That is a remarkable outcome. There will always be many composers doomed to work in obscurity, whose flowers will wither unseen in the desert air, but the diverging streams of the 1960s, which gave such energy to the popular explosion, did not carry away with them the urge to draw from a classical tradition. No composer working today could be uninfluenced by the twists and turns of the popular idiom – inventive as well as sometimes pointless – and the fertilisation of the music scene by the experimenters in rock has been productive. In part because the appetite for adventure among younger audiences has been sharpened in recent years, the gap between what may be stacked on the 'rock' rack of a record store and what is slipped into the 'classical' pile is narrower. Turnage, for example, is a musician with jazz in his being, and gets as much (or more) from Miles Davis as from many in the classical pantheon.

The difficulty has not entirely disappeared. A generation which would sit in the concert hall at a parent's request would now be less willing, to put it politely. Orchestras still appearing in nineteenth-century evening dress appear outdated and stuffy, even when they are devoted to the promotion of new music and adventures in sound. Surely that will change, but until it does there will be a barrier that repels an audience that might be waiting for the spark. It may not be rational and there may be some inverse snobbery involved, but the problem is real.

The dislike of modernists in the early 1960s for the tone and the glitz of emerging popular culture drove them to the high ground (or at least the background); and the conservatism of audiences, for whom Schoenberg was always a trial, persuaded impresarios to play it safe, though there are noble exceptions – the BBC Symphony Orchestra being a shining example. The effect of the two together has been to impede the incorporation of contemporary composition into the mainstream.

Other trends, however, may now be pulling in another direction. The popularity with a younger audience of 'world music' is extra-ordinary. The term is almost laughably inadequate, but listeners know what it means – influences that come from different traditions bringing new rhythms and harmonic patterns, operating in all kinds of genres from dance music to contemplative mysticism, from folk song to electronic abstraction. To western ears, the effect can be as profound as the sound of the gamelans to Claude Debussy at the Paris Exhibition in 1889. The stream is fertile.

The other revolution is in the orient. Why should a Chinese child want to learn the piano and play western music? The question is now redundant. They are doing it, in vast numbers. It is hard to be precise, but by the beginning of 2007 it is likely that somewhere in excess of fifteen million Chinese were learning the piano. The country's largest instrument-maker was producing nearly 300 pianos a day. As happened in Japan a generation ago, when western music was embraced as an exotic and exciting connection with the rest of the world, the change has been eye-watering.

You will now find an annual concerto competition in the southern city of Shenzhen (where Deng Xiaoping established the first of the economic zones in the early 1980s). In 2000, the Warsaw Chopin competition was won by an eighteen-year-old Chinese pianist, Yundi Li, with another Chinese competitor coming fourth. The mayor of Shenzhen now calls it 'piano city', boasting in 2007 that it had more than 93,000 pianos and 13,000 teachers with 150,000 students. Not surprisingly, they managed to assemble 200 pianists – from toddlers to septuagenarians – to play 'Happy Birthday' on what would have been Deng's hundredth. This has been a rapid transformation. As recently as the 1970s, the only piece children were supposed to learn – on a suspiciously western instrument – was the 'Yellow River' Concerto, written by Mme Mao herself, to supersede the pre-revolutionary 'Yellow River' Cantata.

Western artists now tour in China. Travel there is easier for students. Quite soon, there will probably be more capable pianists in China –

many of them playing western music – than in Europe. Who knows where their tastes will take them? They may learn Schubert or Chopin, but what then? It is an inescapable fact that the tradition has been passed on – to be refreshed, reworked, taken apart and put back together again, and pondered. In the summer of 2007, a twenty-three-year-old bass baritone from Shanghai, Shen Yang, became BBC Cardiff Singer of the World. In instrumental and singing competitions around the world, Chinese musicians are on the rise.

European changes have been on a smaller scale, but the collapse of the Soviet Union in 1991 released into the mainstream a number of composers from its former republics who have wielded an influence. Arvo Pärt, an Estonian born in 1935, is probably the best known among westerners, but the Latvian Pēteris Vasks and the Georgian Giya Kancheli have also made homes in the west, finding that their music – perhaps because it carries a touch of exoticism along with it – may be more popular outside their home territory than among their own people.

Pärt, who managed to leave the Soviet Union for (West) Germany in 1980, has journeyed from a style that was jagged and modernist to something more simple. Again his music draws on spiritual roots. As he has put it:

> I have discovered that it is enough when a single note is beautifully played. This one note, or a silent beat, or a moment of silence, comforts me. I work with very few elements – with one voice, two voices. I build with primitive materials – with the triad, with one specific tonality. The three notes of a triad are like bells and that is why I call it tintinnabulation.

His style has been called 'holy minimalism' and has a great deal in common with Tavener's. They both represent the development of American minimalism in the 1970s and 1980s which had found classical composers adapting modernism to the challenge of popular culture and turning to driving rhythms and a mechanised atmosphere. Postmodernists wanted to be playful with the ideas which modernists had taken from high art and installed in their own temples. Instead, the kitsch, the commonplace, the ephemeral would be used as a kind of ironic commentary making the point that po-faced seriousness had passed away. It didn't stop any of the artists involved being precious to a degree that Stockhausen himself might have found pompous, but never mind. They were moving on.

They were like architects who gestured to the past, with affection and respect, but played with its legacy. Philip Johnson's AT&T skyscraper (now the Sony Building) in Manhattan is shaped like a grandfather clock of perfect design surmounted by a broken pediment from what might have been a Thomas Chippendale cabinet. As with architecture, so with music – it's a style that seems to carry the genes for its own destruction in its make-up, a piece of knowing transition. Yet it looks back while it looks forward, acknowledges debts and accepts lessons.

Michael Daugherty (born in 1954) is the perfect example of an American postmodern composer, one of whose best-known pieces is 'Dead Elvis', as Daugherty explains:

> For me icons serve as a way to have an emotional reason to compose a new work. I get ideas for my compositions by browsing through secondhand book stores, antique shops, and small towns that I find driving on the back roads of America. The icon can be an old postcard, magazine, photograph, knick-knack, matchbook, piece of furniture or roadmap. Like [Charles] Ives and [Gustav] Mahler, I use icons in my music to provide the listener and performer with a layer of reference. However, one does not need the reference of the icon to appreciate my music. It is merely one level among many in the musical, contrapuntal fabric of my compositions.

Daugherty incorporates the styles of great jazzmen like John Coltrane and Stan Getz in a piece called 'Philadelphia Stories'.

> I recreate the mood of walking down one of the most popular streets of Philadelphia where one finds numerous cafés, used book stores, ethnic restaurants, nightclubs and musicians from all walks of life . . . [it] begins with lush string melodies and glissing guitar chords evoking the soulful 1970s 'Philadelphia Sound' created by Kenny Gamble and Leon Huff . . . A pulsating woodblock suggests the snapping fingers of

1950s teenagers strutting down South Street . . . As night-time approaches, I introduce a cool, jazzy tune in muted brass, doubled in octaves by clarinets and flutes . . . This melody is punctuated in B flat major–minor by lower woodwinds, marimba, guitar, and pizzicato contrabass . . .

The spirit is similar to that of John Adams, probably the world's most performed living classical composer. He is a writer who has escaped from minimalism, and found an audience that wouldn't have followed him there. There is little severity in him. Born in 1948, he was a child of the 1950s and 1960s and has grown up on modernist techniques. His music, which has some of the ironic debris of the postmodernists in it, seems to be heading towards something new. Fundamentally different in style from Tavener, MacMillan, Turnage and Birtwistle, he nonetheless seems to be with them on a journey to a destination which he hasn't quite identified in his own mind. Along the way he has produced some memorable work, which will last. His opera *Nixon in China*, which would have struggled to get mainstream audiences in Britain when it was written in 1987 (though the production by Peter Sellars won the Grammy for Best Contemporary Composition in that year), is now firmly in the repertoire, a piece of riveting political theatre that has kept its edgy drama.

With the far-sighted minimalist Steve Reich (born in 1936) – myopia is not a precondition for the style – and Philip Glass (born 1937), Adams is in the vanguard. Reich's quest has been for simplicity, taking him back to medieval plainchant, where we began this journey. Modernists in the 1950s created structures that were meant to reorder or conceal the conventions of the past; Reich says he wants to reveal everything he does: 'The use of hidden structural devices never appealed to me. Even when all the cards are on the table and everyone hears what is gradually happening in a musical process, there are still enough mysteries to satisfy all. These mysteries are the impersonal unintended, psychoacoustic by-products of the intended process.'

Like Reich, Glass learned serialism as a student but he soon left modernists behind, saying in print that he thought Boulez and Stockhausen were 'crazy creeps'. You can't be much clearer. He saw minimalism as a way out of the ghetto. He had an encounter with the Indian master Ravi Shankar which influenced him greatly and he is another of the composers who have turned towards mysticism (in a mild form) for inspiration and a style.

Glass is a link between the modernists of the 1960s and our own time – a student who studied with those Paris musicians who wanted to dismantle their inheritance and reconstruct it in a modern way, then a minimalist searching for the bare sinews of music, a collaborator with inventive rock stars like David Bowie, an enthusiast for Indian music, and a writer of film scores. And in the last few years he has written symphonies, operas and concertos that embrace that whole story. He writes with a breadth that sweeps back, far beyond the arguments of our time: he seems to wrap them up and place them in a proper historical context so that they don't distort the way we look at a long, long story.

In the early 1960s he studied in Paris with the familiar figure of Nadia Boulanger, who had been a pillar of the Paris musical scene for as long as anyone could remember, the brilliant composer, conductor and teacher who was taught by Gabriel Fauré, knew Debussy and Stravinsky, and taught a sparkling *galère* of musicians from George Gershwin and Aaron Copland to Leonard Bernstein, Daniel Barenboim and the conductor John Eliot Gardiner. She was older than the Eiffel Tower, born in the 1880s when Brahms was still around, Verdi was writing opera and Richard Strauss hadn't started. She began to conduct before the First World War and was still teaching in the 1970s.

One of the first things her students were expected to do was to memorise the two books of J. S. Bach's *Well-Tempered Clavier*, the forty-eight preludes and fugues that explore music's nervous system and are the supreme example of the craft of composition, teaching pieces written for the harpsichord in the first half of the eighteenth century and still, in the second half of the twentieth century, speaking to modernists who wanted to reconstruct music in their own way, minimalists who were trying to reduce it to an essence, composers who were writing like late Romantics, neo-Classicists – maybe even post-postmodernists. All of them were connected to that past, involved in it because it revealed to them the reason for what they did.

The journey goes on. It was never true that the post-war modernists had an answer, nor that they would stop music dead in its tracks. How could they? But the spreading of a popular taste that was encouraged to avoid the challenging or the complicated, unless sold to them by a celebrity, meant that the experimental and the fresh was pushed into the shadows, even when it was original. A number of serious figures survived the experience and have prospered. Sir Harrison Birtwistle is – almost – a grand old man of the British musical scene, still writing with the dark but cheery passion that he says he developed when he used to wander through disused mine-workings as a boy in Accrington, Lancashire. Adams will be performed more and more; Glass will write for Hollywood again and take us on mystical journeys again; Pärt, MacMillan, Tavener will continue on their different spiritual odysseys. They believe that public taste may not be far behind them, and they may be right.

19

Survival

~

THE NIGHT THE Berlin Wall started to come down, on 9 November 1989, the cellist Mstislav Rostropovich heard the news in London. He booked two seats on the next plane, one for his cello and one for himself, and within a few hours a taxi was dropping him off at the Wall. He got a chair, found a place in what had been once been no-man's land under the searchlights, where in days gone by he might have been shot, and began to play a suite by J. S. Bach for the crowd.

A passageway was opening up across Europe's divide and a Russian exile, forced from his country following his dispute with the Soviet regime in the 1970s, was reaching into the continent's past for inspiration, because it was the natural response. Bach was a founding father of European music and a humanitarian, and no anthem would have sounded more appropriate for the beginning of the end of the two Germanys. Rostropovich, who had been a pupil of Dmitri Shostakovich when the composer was denounced in Stalin's Russia, and who had heard the knock on the door in the night, was marking a moment of hope with music that spoke of healing and survival and was a message from the heart, more eloquent than almost any words.

A few nights later, Daniel Barenboim played Beethoven's First Piano Concerto with the Berlin Philharmonic in its home near the Wall, and much of the audience came through from the east, to hear an orchestra from which they had been estranged since Wilhelm Furtwängler was music director during the Second World War before he abandoned Nazi Germany in Hitler's dying days. Barenboim was in tears, an Israeli citizen playing Beethoven for a German audience in Berlin, asserting the importance of their common inheritance. As a child, Barenboim remembers listening to orchestras in Israel and later, to his surprise, hearing precisely the same quality of sound and personality from the strings, like an echo, when he travelled to Europe for the first time. The violinists and cellists he had listened to as a boy were Jews who had fled from Germany, Austria and Poland and had carried with them the orchestral tradition in which they were reared. Back in Europe, he recognised it for what it was, in its home.

These are powerful images, revealing how music acts naturally as a conduit for the deepest feelings and the most profound reflections. It speaks its own language and offers solace, excitement and the chance to think. The writer and critic George Steiner posed a famous question about how, if it is true that music is uplifting and improving, Nazi guards in the death camps could listen to Beethoven quartets before going to bed and return the next day to the business of mass murder in the gas chambers. That was a fact, but it is not a conundrum. Music by itself improves nothing, guarantees nothing; it simply makes an offer.

The offer is a generous one. The composers who make up the European tradition, from (almost) the first named makers of music in Paris in the twelfth century through the long story to our own time, were drawn to their task because they understood the possibilities and felt an urge to explore them. Wagner and Brahms might have disagreed about whether music drama was the highest calling, and a semi-religious experience, but each was engrossed in his own act of creation with the same vigour; twentieth-century taste devalued Mozart for many years, but those musicians who were travelling a different road had in common with him the feeling of obligation to the tradition; when Pierre Boulez and the post-war modernists said they were pulverising Beethoven sonatas, they did it as an act of love, knowing that without that music they might have nothing to say for themselves. All of them knew, instinctively, that the tradition had to be refreshed, reinterpreted and kept alive.

The journey from the simple sounds of early polyphony to the cacophony of the end of the twentieth century and beyond, with music coming out of every machine and filling the streets, is a reminder of the visceral power of that instinct. Franz Schubert is said once to have written seven songs in one day; the output of Haydn or Wagner or Richard Strauss is extraordinarily rich and speaks of an irrepressible urge. It still stirs in contemporary composers, searching for their own language. They will never stop, and they will have successors. But will they be understood?

A culture that practises contempt is dangerous. There is a vast difference between the necessary arguments about the respective merits of a piece of music, which some may think rubbish and others cherish, and the tendency to label and stigmatise, which abandons argument in favour of implacable judgement. The music of an 'elite' can be sidelined and condemned to irrelevance. Alongside, there is a different danger which appears at first to work in another direction. The freedom of a society in which music is more available than ever before, increasingly summoned up by the click of a mouse, is also the opportunity for taste to be watered down to a point where discrimination between the good and the bad is no longer thought worth while. It is merely allowed to wash over us, unfiltered and almost unnoticed. Why listen to a symphony when you can catch the highlights? And as for opera, it's so *long*.

The two tendencies are wound into each other, like some con-catenation of weeds at the bottom of the garden. A celebrity-driven culture tends, paradoxically, to flatten the landscape. While pretending to spot talent and promote it, the drift is the other way. Success in the popular idiom is a matter of chance — a quirk of fashion, a pretty face, a singer who is oddly different — and doesn't reward talent with con-sistency. It is fickle and unsatisfying, even while it demands attention and money, almost because of its unpredictability. Spiralling upwards it demands more and more, and provides less and less. One consequence is that anything not conforming to the pattern — the music of serious composers, for example — is pushed further into the shadows, starved of investment and audiences and allowed to atrophy.

However, there is nothing like a little history to prove ourselves wrong. The crack of doom has not sounded; the end is not nigh. The tradition that tells the story of Europe in music is a mixture of individual craftsmanship and genius and a cultural understanding that still flows like an immense river, unstoppable and impossible to divert. It may well be true that a generation with a thousand things to do, games to play and texts to send, will not be attracted to a concert hall to sit quietly while a large number of people in white tie and tails perform an old piece of music, but it is just not true that the message is not being passed on. When BBC Radio 3 decided to broadcast a 'Beethoven Experience', then a 'Bach Christmas' and then a season of Tchaikovsky and other Russian masters, the requests for the temporarily available downloads were extraordinary in number, and from listeners who were not part of the network's regular audience. Even in the famously refined purlieus of Radio 3, well-known works were being discovered for the first time. And at the BBC Proms, night after night through every summer, relaxed audiences make the experience as open minded and rewarding as it has even been in its history, stretching back for well over a hundred years.

When the Royal Festival Hall reopened after its refit in summer 2007, London was excited. There was less division between the herbivores and the carnivores than there had been when the Festival of Britain opened its doors in 1951, much more of a sense of an arena in which entertainment and challenging art can live side by side.

That coexistence is the key. As our history shows us, it is misleading and wrong to try to separate completely the enjoyment of performance which is entertainment and that which aspires to something deeper. From the start, they have gone side by side. Italian audiences in the nineteenth century enjoyed the opera as they might a football match, but it did not stop them understanding the genius of a Rossini or a Verdi. The appreciation of an oral street tradition is not an alternative to the understanding of highly polished textured composition, but an experience that happens on a different part of the same spectrum. They need not cancel each other out.

Some will stay in thrall to music they believe to be serious, with only the occasional foray into more popular forms. Others will straddle the two quite happily, and will stretch out to the many traditions that are more closely interwoven than they sometimes appear. Many of us move happily among them, taking enjoyable detours as we go. Here is one.

In the 1950s in Scotland, a remarkable character called Hamish Henderson began to collect the sounds of traditional singing in the countryside. He wandered about with an early tape-recorder, trying to catch the oral culture. He made some remarkable discoveries, particularly among the families of travellers who would move from place to place with the season, berry-picking in the summer, potato-roguing in the spring, many joining the fish-gutters at other times. To his astonishment he found some singers who had been singing the great ballads – the 'muckle sangs' – all their lives, passed down through the generations over centuries and still intact. They had many verses, all learned by word of mouth, and the tunes were decorated by individual singers, sometimes with dazzling skill. As with folk collectors like Alan Lomax (with his expeditions through the Appalachians and in the Southern states), these recordings, held by the School of Scottish Studies at Edinburgh University, are a treasure trove.

Listening in the course of this journey to some of the songs that have been rescued from the fourteenth-century troubadours of the south of France, it has been extraordinary to realise how close the common roots are; how songs that are still sung by some old travellers in campsites in the Highlands, and are still passed on with care, carry the same echo – the same stories, tunes that spring from the same traditions, a method of singing that bridges the centuries.

These connections matter. As with jazz, and the torrent of popular song that it spawned for the musical and the crooners of the swing era, they are reminders of the nature of the inheritance. With the brilliant inventions of the classical composers, and their originality, we also inherit a tradition that speaks in other ways. It is not hard to explain that enjoying a Cole Porter song is a different experience from settling down to listen to the concentrated emotion of, say, Schubert's cycle *Die schöne Müllerin*. The difference is natural and obvious, because one is entertainment of the highest order and the other is an invitation to profound reflection. Each should be valued for what it is. That is not a relativist's cop-out, but a statement of the obvious: art comes in different forms, and that is how it should be enjoyed.

Musical history makes the case eloquently, because no one who explores the European tradition can avoid making judgements of the proper kind. Original music, a beautiful texture of sound, invites reflection and argument because it is a challenge. The mystery is enticing. How did Mozart, with the same number of notes available to him as everyone else, produce two short arias in *The Marriage of Figaro* that can be placed in the pantheon of the greatest written for the female voice? In Beethoven's later quartets, what is the quality that seems to turn them into endless journeys, different each time? In Bruckner's Seventh Symphony – or Shostakovich's Eleventh – what precisely is the secret of the grip it puts on you? We all enjoy entertainment, and we also value the kind of pleasure that carries with it an extra sense of adventure – the promise that the more you put into it, the more you will get back.

Few experiences can compare with a musical performance that transforms itself. Alfred Brendel playing Schubert will always be an event to savour, but sometimes it will be elevated on to a different plane for reasons that aren't easily explained. Hearing a singer of lieder enter a different world for a few minutes is an unforgettable sound; a string quartet that suddenly finds the sap and muscularity of the true ensemble can seem a thing possessed; an opera that turns in a moment from a limp piece of theatre with tunes into a true music drama is an unforgettable thrill. These are experiences that are bequeathed, in part, by our history. The skills are products of craftsmanship, and sometimes genius, but they are also the accumulation of a tradition that has been absorbed. It's as if a book is being taken down in a fine old library, opened at a favourite page and revisited because the reader knows that although each time the experience is different, it fits into a wider pattern that is being assembled piece by piece, day by day.

If the experience is available, it will do its work. If schools encourage music-making and the skills are passed on, the tradition will be sustained. It is also true of the recording industry, whose machinations have been the cause of considerable gloom. The big companies, watching the sales of classical CDs in steady decline (dipping under 2 per cent of total sales), have greatly diluted their commitment to recording new artists, and to re-recording masterworks. That process began in the 1980s and accelerated towards the end of the century. But small companies, led by Naxos and Hyperion, have been taking up the slack with more ingenuity than might have been expected. Their catalogues are now packed with the mainstream, the off-beat and the splendidly weird. In the age of the download and the MP3 player there is no reason why the availability of classical music should shrink. It may simply come from different sources.

The bigger danger is from the power of the celebrity culture. Instead of entertainment accompanying serious art, and overlapping as it should, the power of the market is so strong that many fear it will cause classical music to occupy a permanent place in the shadows, out of the sun, where it will die.

The threat is certainly there. If recording companies decide to invest in an inferior singer, whose efforts need to be patched together to make them sound acceptable, solely because he (or she) has some trait that will attract a wide public but that is unconnected with talent, then the essential belief in quality is diminished. It has always happened to a degree; the question is whether it is now a trend that cannot be reversed. Since the success of the Three Tenors concert in Rome before the football World Cup of 1990 the pace has quickened.

Plácido Domingo, José Carreras and Luciano Pavarotti were artists of distinction. In its length and breadth Domingo's career is a wonder, and in his prime (in the 1970s) the freshness and ringing tone of Pavarotti's singing, which had memorable dramatic bite, was sublime. But as Pavarotti limped towards his last years on the operatic stage he was a much sadder sight, and in his particular experience the darker side of the music business is revealed. His is a textbook example of the way the obsession with celebrity creates legends and destroys them, and in the process drains music of its integrity, without which it is weakened.

The rather sad caravan pulling up at the Royal Albert Hall for another circus performance as Pavarotti approached the age of seventy in 2004 was a depressing sight. The show did not have the sparkle of old. There was no athleticism and plenty of weariness. There were no plans for any more opera, the concerts being strung out to the end, involving trips to such places as Costa Rica and Panama, the places you go when time is running out. We were watching the last miserable shrinking of a great career, its artistry already spent.

This did not mean that Pavarotti could no longer sing, because from time to time he could, though to get his tuning right he had to pay a great deal of attention to the voice relayed back to him from the speakers in the flowers at the front of the stage, and there have long been signs of heavy wear and tear. The Neapolitan songs had some of the old spring in them and there were beautiful moments. But only a few. The performance was a desperate propping up of the legend, and the sight of him on stage made you wish that he'd decided long ago on an orderly and dignified retirement. His final appearance at the Met in New York in 2003 turned into a disaster. Having said at five o'clock on the night of the performance that his troubled throat was better, he cancelled just before curtain-up and stayed at his apartment. Joe Volpe of the Met told the audience that he had said to their old favourite: 'It's a helluva way to bring your beautiful career to an end.' He meant it. He was livid. For some years opera houses had been quietly excising him from their programmes, the trouble seeming to be more than the performance was worth. Throughout the 1990s his repertoire stayed limited to two or three roles, and even they proved a trial.

When he sang his last Cavaradossi in *Tosca* at Covent Garden the old Zeffirelli set had to be redesigned so that he didn't have to climb any steps in Act I. He couldn't. And Nemorino, the lusty peasant boy in Donizetti's *L'elisir d'amore*, his other standby in the last years, was a regular embarrassment. Opera audiences are trained to absorb some silly things – the art form demands it – but it was a trial, and a temptation to anyone with a good giggle, to watch a singer preparing cornfield seductions and lascivious partying when his stage movements are restricted to a few feet on either side from the spot from where he has decided to sing, all negotiated with the care of someone who is either infirm or alarmingly top-heavy.

Years ago the problem could be disguised. At Covent Garden he once wore what seemed to be a designer sack in *Aida* to hide his unheroic dimensions, and there was enough power and thrilling sap in the voice to let everyone pass over the spectacular immobility. Audiences would decide that although he couldn't move and acted badly there was enough of a dramatic surge in the voice to make it precious. They were right. At the height of his form, Pavarotti's ringing tone and the bite of his notes were marvels, and unmatched.

That is why the concerts are now so sad. They are reminders of how much better it once was. In the early 1970s the ageing Maria Callas and the broken but once magnificent tenor Giuseppe di Stefano embarked on a disastrous world tour which can still draw a shiver from those who saw the performances. She screeched and he hit every note except the right one. They were like a pair of washed-up singers in a bar, warbling to each other for old times' sake and it was horrible. Di Stefano (one of Pavarotti's heroes) had the world at his feet in the 1950s and the partnership with Callas had magic in it. But it was a fragile magic, a gift bestowed for only a few years, and without it the terrible ordinariness seemed unbearable to those who had heard them in their glory.

It happens so often. Rudolf Nureyev had to scuttle from the stage, to the sound of feet heading for the exit, in those last tours which took him to moth-eaten dressing rooms in seaside resorts; Sinatra, the nightclub necromancer, ended his career croaking his way through songs that he had to read from rickety music stands, wearing spectacles. Now Pavarotti, said by his recording company to have sold more classical records than any other artist (and why shouldn't we believe that claim?), was limping round the same track, to audiences who must hold in their minds a picture of what it once was like, without the amplification and the heavy breathing and the long pauses off-stage. They deserve better, and so does he.

The trouble with Pavarotti ('Fat Lucy' in the backstage patois of Covent Garden) is that he has tried quite hard to undermine the sympathy which he now needs. His tax case in Italy, in which he argued to general incredulity that his principal residence was in Monaco, was a miserable business. He was cleared of evasion, but he handed over $11 million to the Italian authorities (the second time he had to write a huge cheque). Even those who defend the vast fees to the great singers found it all rather revealing and uncomfortable. His annual fund-raising charity concert in his home town of Modena even turned out to have fallen victim to some creative accounting. There was no connection with the singer himself, but it was yet another embarrassment. The stories of extravagant demands from his promoters, never mind the cosseting that takes weeks of preparation for each performance, are the common stuff of theatrical gossip.

At some point inevitably it is time to bring the curtain down. Domingo, whose real age is a matter of frequent speculation, has managed his approach to the exit with considerable skill and delicacy. He sang his last *Otello* and began to move towards the conclusion of his career on stage with dignity and an artistic technique that was intact. You knew that he would see the end coming before we did. The contrast with his rival – for fierce rivalry it is, despite the hugging of the Three Tenors – was painful.

In the mid-1990s I watched Pavarotti performing with some younger opera singers at a charity concert for the Red Cross in the Albert Hall. The Princess of Wales was there, so it was a real weepy. But even then he struggled. Coming on and off the stage several times during the performance, and walking down three or four steps, was too much for him, so a tent was erected at the back of the stage in black cloth. When he swept through the curtains, as if to go to the dressing room, he flopped down immediately on chairs hidden there for the purpose. Though there were beautiful moments, he shouldn't have been doing it. Listen to a recording he made of *La Bohème* in the early 1970s, in a juicy and thrilling voice, possibly the most alluring of our time. These were sparkling days, when the sheer dramatic excitement of his voice was a revelation. But it was a long time ago.

The reason for caring about the last days of Pavarotti is that the effect can be contagious. Although there have always been stars with inflated egos and salaries, especially in opera, and audiences have always been fickle (remember Verdi on the opening night of *La Traviata*) the scale of the phenomenon is now formidable. Imagine the difference for a singer like Roberto Alagna, a few years ago a prized catch for EMI as one of the many singers given the putative title of the Fourth Tenor, now that he has been dropped by the recording company. Can he retain his status?

These pressures are immense and they have to be resisted. But just as it is wrong to be too gloomy about the future because of the changes in the way people are going to hear music and in their disc-buying habits, it is also wrong to condemn contemporary composers. Julian Lloyd-Webber, the cellist, made a passionate speech at the Davos World Economic Forum in Switzerland in 2007 railing against the failure of modern composers to write for the audience that was waiting to feel exalted:

> New music must be coming through, taking its listeners on fresh adventures, pushing at boundaries, exciting its audience. Yet for 40 years of madness, from 1945 to the early Eighties, classical music turned its back on its audience and shot itself in the foot with the result that, today, it remains seriously wounded.

After the war, everything had to be new. For example, instead of following through the plan to rebuild the beautiful, acoustically superb Queen's Hall in London, the decision was taken to move out of the city centre and create an entirely new concrete structure south of the river. British music is still paying for that mistake, as by common agreement England's capital city has no acoustically great concert hall for orchestral music.

Similar aberrations were happening all over the West as grey concrete mausoleums, which were hardly conducive to an enjoyable evening out, became synonymous with classical music. As the concert halls became more severe, so did the music itself. Suddenly it was only acceptable to write in one style.

He made an exemplary presentation of the case against the drift of composition in the last generation, and against the prevailing powers in the arts. But he overstated his case. The generation that includes Adès, Turnage and MacMillan are not writing in one style. Indeed, their ability to put behind them some of the grimmer exploits of the 1970s – in which Lloyd-Webber is right to identify a widespread habit of ignoring the audience as if it was an irritation – is surely a matter for admiration. John Adams's operas are listened to by huge audiences; Pärt and Tavener have created a mystical world of their own that has an enormous following. There is probably a more optimistic future ahead for composition than there has been since the 1950s.

The history of music-making is evidence that the ebb and flow of taste in the audience and invention among composers is the way of the world. It is simply not possible to follow a line of progress that does not deviate, because it takes detours and meanders, as it must. From that history emerges one overwhelming truth: that inspiration will come, in its own good time.

The urge to create music of originality and power will not be stifled. Commercial distortions might make life difficult for composers and arts administrators might make bad investments and build bad halls instead of good ones, but the passion is still there. While it remains, an audience will be assembled. It will not go away. It might shrink and expand from time to time, but it will argue, judge, assess. Stories will be passed on and experiences of a concert or a disc will be treasured.

These are experiences that are not temporary embellishments to day-to-day life, but part of it. They are embedded in our history and in our sense of the world we have come to know. As for generations of composers, musicians and audiences the trick is in remembering that what such moments and insights have brought before, they will bring again. The power of the music-makers survives.

Chronology

MUSICAL EVENTS	HISTORICAL EVENTS
	1115–42 King Henry IV of France makes Paris centre of religious learning
	1150 University of Paris founded
1151 Léonin begins to compose polyphonic music	
	1152 Eleanor of Aquitaine's marriage to King Louis VII of France is annulled; she marries Henry of Anjou (later King Henry II of England)
	1154 Henry II becomes king of England
	1163 Work on building the Cathedral of Notre Dame begins
	1215 King John signs Magna Carta at Runnymede
1260 First school of mastersingers opens in Mainz	
1280 'Anonymous IV' is working at Notre Dame	
1325 First organ pedals	
	1337 Start of the Hundred Years War between England and France

1369 John Dunstable born

1400 Gilles de Binchois born

1437 First records of counterpoint writing by John Dunstable

1450 Invention of the harpsichord; Josquin Desprez born

1465 First printed music

1495 Josquin becomes organist at Cambrai Cathedral

1499 Oxford University establishes a music degree

1501 First book of polyphonic music printed using movable type, Venice

1502 Josquin produces first book of masses

1347 Black Death ravages the population of Europe

1381 Peasants' Revolt in England

c.1387 Geoffrey Chaucer begins *The Canterbury Tales*

1415 King Henry V wins Battle of Agincourt

1419 Philip the Good becomes duke of Burgundy

1436 Consecration of the Duomo in Florence; completion of Filippo Brunelleschi's dome

1452 Leonardo da Vinci born near Florence

1453 Fall of Constantinople, end of Byzantine Empire

c.1455 Johannes Gutenberg invents the printing press

1475 Michelangelo born near Arezzo

1503 Leonardo begins *Mona Lisa*

1504 Michelangelo completes statue of David in Florence

1505 Thomas Tallis born

1517 Martin Luther nails his ninety-five theses to the door of a church in Wittenberg

1519 Magellan begins first round-the-world voyage

1532 Orlando Lassus born

1532 Machiavelli publishes *The Prince*

1534 King Henry VIII breaks with Rome and becomes head of the Church of England

1536 The dissolution of the monasteries of England begins

1543 Copernicus publishes his theory of a sun-centred universe

1545 Council of Trent begins

1551 Giovanni Pierluigi da Palestrina becomes music director at St Peter's, Rome

1557 Giovanni Gabrieli born

1558 Elizabeth I becomes queen of England and Ireland; Calais is lost to France

1564 William Shakespeare born

1565 Palestrina's 'Missa Papae Marcelli' performed

1565 Council of Trent ends

1572 William Byrd and Thomas Tallis become organists at the Chapel Royal

1575 Byrd and Tallis publish thirty-four motets in *Cantiones sacrae*

1585 Tallis dies

1587 Claudio Monteverdi publishes
first book of madrigals

1588 England repels the Spanish
Armada

1590 Publication of first part of
Edmund Spenser's *Faerie Queene*

1594 Jacopo Peri writes opera *Dafne*
(lost)

1599 The Globe theatre opens in
Southwark

1600 Three operas performed in
Florence at Medici wedding

1603 Death of Queen Elizabeth I;
King James VI of Scotland unites
the crowns and becomes King
James I of England and Ireland

1604 Monteverdi becomes music
director at St Mark's, Venice

1604 Jesuits banned in England

1614 Cardinal Richelieu dissolves
the States General, allowing King
Louis XIII absolute power

1626 St Peter's Basilica completed in
Rome

1642 English civil war begins

1648 The Peace of Westphalia ends
the Thirty Years War, and the
dominance of Spain and the Holy
Roman Empire

1649 King Charles I of England executed; Commonwealth established

1656 First English opera, *The Siege of
Rhodes*, performed privately in London

1660 British monarchy restored
under King Charles II; Samuel
Pepys begins to keep a diary

1661 Matthew Locke becomes court composer to King Charles II

1663 Jean-Baptiste Lully writes *Le Ballet des arts*

1666 Antonio Stradivari signs his name on a violin for the first time

1666 Great Fire of London; Christopher Wren produces first plan for St Paul's

1667 Milton publishes *Paradise Lost*

1670 John Blow becomes organist at Westminster Abbey

1678 Thomas Britton begins weekly concerts in an upstairs room in Clerkenwell, London

1680 Henry Purcell becomes organist at Westminster Abbey; first entertainment at Sadler's Wells, London; Stradivari makes his first cello

1685 Johann Sebastian Bach, George Frederick Handel, Domenico Scarlatti born

1687 Lully dies of gangrene after stabbing himself in the foot

1687 Isaac Newton publishes *Philosophiae naturalis principia mathematica*

1688 The Glorious Revolution; King James II flees and William of Orange becomes king of England, Scotland and Ireland

1689 Purcell writes *Dido and Aeneas*

1695 Purcell dies

1703 Tsar Peter the Great founds St Petersburg

1704 Bach publishes first cantata

1707 Handel visits Venice and meets Scarlatti

1707 Union of Parliaments of Scotland and England

1711 Handel's *Rinaldo* performed in London; clarinet appears in an orchestra for the first time

1714 Handel writes 'Utrecht Te Deum' at Queen Anne's request

1714 Death of Queen Anne; the Elector of Hanover becomes King George I of Great Britain and Ireland

1715 First Jacobite rising; King Louis XIV of France dies

1717 Handel's 'Water Music' performed for King George I on the Thames

1719 Handel becomes director of the Royal Academy of Music

1721 Bach writes six Brandenburg concertos

1722 Bach publishes first book of preludes and fugues, *The Well-Tempered Clavier*

1723 Bach takes up post at St Thomas's Church, Leipzig; writes *St John Passion*

1723–5 Handel writes *Ottone, Giulio Cesare* and *Rodelinda*

1725 First opera house opens in Prague

1726 Handel becomes a British subject

1728 First performance of John Gay's *The Beggar's Opera*

1728 Alexander Pope publishes *The Dunciad*

1729 Bach writes first version of *St Matthew Passion*

1732 Covent Garden Opera House opens in London

1733 Pergolesi's opera *La serva padrona* opens

1734 First performance of Jean-Philippe Rameau's opera-ballet *Les Indes galantes*

1737 Antonio Stradivari dies

1738 Bach completes Mass in B minor

1740 Joseph Haydn becomes choirboy in the court chapel, Vienna

1741 Handel writes *Messiah* (first performed in Dublin the following year)

1744 Bach publishes second book of *The Well-Tempered Clavier*

1748 Bach publishes 'The Art of the Fugue'

1749 Handel's 'Music for the Royal Fireworks' performed

1749 Henry Fielding publishes *Tom Jones*

1750 Bach dies

1751 'War of the Buffoons' breaks out in Paris

1755 Samuel Johnson publishes the first English dictionary

1756 Wolfgang Amadeus Mozart born

1759 Handel dies; Haydn's First Symphony performed

1760 King George III succeeds to the throne of Great Britain and Ireland

1761 Haydn becomes *Kapellmeister* to Prince Paul Esterházy

1762 Jean-Jacques Rousseau
publishes *The Social Contract*

1764 Mozart visits London, writes
First Symphony

1769 James Watt invents the steam
engine

1770 Ludwig van Beethoven born

1775 Mozart's opera *La finta
giardiniera* performed in Salzburg

1776 American Declaration of
Independence

1778 Thomas Linley drowns, aged
twenty-two; Teatro alla Scala
opens in Milan

1780 Joseph II becomes emperor of
Austria

1781 Haydn writes 'Russian' string
quartets

1782 Nicolò Paganini born

1783 Beethoven's first piano works
published; Mozart writes Mass in
C minor

1786 First performance of Mozart's
Le nozze di Figaro in Vienna

1787 First performance of Mozart's
Don Giovanni in Prague

1789 Fall of the Bastille in the
French Revolution

1790 First performance of Mozart's
Così fan tutte in Vienna

1791 Mozart dies

1791 Tom Paine publishes *The
Rights of Man*

1792 Giaocchino Rossini born

1793 Paganini gives his first violin
recital, aged eleven

1793 Reign of Terror in France

1795 Beethoven publishes three piano trios, Opus 1; Haydn completes the twelve 'London' symphonies

1798 William Wordsworth publishes *Lyrical Ballads*

1799 Beethoven's First Symphony performed; Haydn's *Creation*

1799 Consulate established in France; Napoleon takes power

1801 United Kingdom established by union of Great Britain and Ireland

1804 Beethoven writes Third Symphony, 'Eroica', striking Napoleon's name from the title page

1804 Napoleon crowns himself emperor

1805 First version of Beethoven's only opera, *Fidelio*, in Vienna

1806 Beethoven writes Fifth and Sixth symphonies ('Pastoral')

1810 Sir Walter Scott publishes *The Lady of the Lake*

1812 Napoleon marches to Moscow and retreats

1813 London Philharmonic Society founded; Giuseppe Verdi born; Richard Wagner born

1814 Final version of *Fidelio* performed in Vienna

1815 Battle of Waterloo, Congress of Vienna, end of Napoleonic era

1816 First performance of Rossini's opera *Il barbiere di Siviglia* in Rome

1821 Carl Maria von Weber's opera *Der Freischütz* performed in Berlin

1821 John Keats dies in Rome

1824 Beethoven's Ninth and last Symphony performed in Vienna

1824 George Gordon, Lord Byron dies in Greece

1827 Beethoven dies; Franz Schubert's song cycle *Die Winterreise* performed

1827 Percy Bysshe Shelley dies in Italy

1828 Schubert dies in Vienna, aged thirty-one

1831 Frédéric Chopin arrives in Paris

1832 Gaetano Donizetti's *L'elisir d'amore* performed in Milan

1833 Johannes Brahms born

1835 Donizetti's *Lucia di Lammermoor* performed in Naples; Vincenzo Bellini dies, aged thirty-three

1837 Queen Victoria comes to the throne of the United Kingdom

1838 Chopin meets George Sand

1839 First performance of Schubert's Ninth Symphony ('The Great') conducted by Felix Mendelssohn

1840 Robert Schumann marries Clara Wieck; Peter Ilyich Tchaikovsky born

1842 Wagner's first opera *Rienzi* performed in Dresden

1847 Verdi's *Macbeth* first performed in Florence; Mendelssohn, Donizetti die

1848 Uprisings in Paris spread across Europe; publication of *The Communist Manifesto*

1849 Wagner flees to Switzerland having joined uprising in Dresden

1850 Wagner writes *Lohengrin*

1851 Verdi's *Rigoletto* performed in Venice

1851 The Great Exhibition opens in London

1853 Verdi's *Il trovatore* and *La traviata* first performed; Wagner completes text of his Ring of the Nibelung

1857 Edward Elgar born; Hallé Orchestra founded in Manchester

1858 Giacomo Puccini born

1861 Italy unified under Victor Emmanuel; the American Civil War begins

1862 Music Society of St Petersburg founded

1863 *Les Troyens* by Hector Berlioz heard in Paris

1864 Richard Strauss born

1865 Wagner's *Tristan und Isolde* first performed in Munich

1865 Tolstoy publishes first part of *War and Peace*

1868 Tchaikovsky writes First Symphony

1869 First performance of *Das Rheingold*

1870–1 The Franco-Prussian war

1871 Opening of the Albert Hall in London

1871 Bismarck becomes chancellor of Germany

1871 Verdi's *Aida* performed in Cairo

1874 Arnold Schoenberg born; Bedřich Smetana's cycle of symphonic poems *Má Vlast* published

1874 First important exhibition of Impressionist paintings

1875 Tchaikovsky's Piano Concerto No. 1 first performed in Boston

1876 Brahms's First Symphony performed; first complete performance of Wagner's Ring cycle, Bayreuth

1878 George Grove begins his *Dictionary of Music and Musicians*

1882 Igor Stravinsky born; Tchaikovsky writes '1812' Overture; Berlin Philharmonic founded

1883 Royal College of Music founded in London; Wagner dies

1884 Bruckner's Seventh Symphony performed in Leipzig

1888 Gustav Mahler becomes director of the Budapest opera; Richard Strauss's tone poem *Don Juan* published

1889 Claude Debussy visits the Paris Exhibition

1889 The Paris Exhibition opens

1893 Tchaikovsky's Sixth Symphony first performed; Verdi's last opera *Falstaff* performed in Milan

1894 Debussy writes *L'Après-midi d'un faune*

1895 First Promenade concert at Queen's Hall, London, conducted by Henry Wood

1899 Elgar's 'Enigma' Variations first performed

1900 First performance of *Tosca* by Puccini, in Rome

1900 Sigmund Freud publishes *The Interpretation of Dreams*

1901 Verdi dies

1904 London Symphony Orchestra founded

1905 Michael Tippett born in London

1908 Elgar writes First Symphony; Schoenberg publishes *Book of Hanging Gardens*

1910 First performance of Stravinsky's *The Firebird*

1911 Richard Strauss's opera *Der Rosenkavalier* first performed

1913 Benjamin Britten born; first night of Stravinsky's *The Rite of Spring* in Paris

1914 First orchestral recording on disc, Berlin

1917 First performance of Sergei Prokofiev's 'Classical' First Symphony

1919 Elgar completes Cello Concerto

1901 Death of Queen Victoria

1903 First flight at Kittyhawk

1905 Albert Einstein proposes a theory of relativity

1907 Pablo Picasso completes *Les Demoiselles d'Avignon*

1914 First World War begins

1917 February Revolution in St Petersburg; October Revolution brings Bolsheviks to power

1918 First World War ends

1920 Prohibition introduced in the United States

1922 T. S. Eliot publishes *The Waste Land*; James Joyce finds a publisher for *Ulysses*; Joseph Stalin becomes general secretary of the Soviet Communist Party

1924 George Gershwin writes
'Rhapsody in Blue'

1935 Alban Berg completes his
Violin Concerto, his last piece; first
performance of Gershwin's *Porgy
and Bess*

1936 Dmitri Shostakovich
denounced after Joseph Stalin sees
his opera *Lady Macbeth of Mtsensk*

1937 First performance of Béla
Bartók's Music for Strings,
Percussion and Celeste

1939 Tippett begins *A Child of our
Time*

1941 Olivier Messiaen writes
Quartet 'For the End of Time' in
a prisoner-of-war camp in Silesia

1946 Britten's opera *Peter Grimes*
first performed

1923 The Charleston becomes a
dance craze

1924 V. I. Lenin dies

1927 The BBC is founded: first
feature-length 'talkie', *The Jazz
Singer*

1929 The Great Crash on Wall
Street

1932 Franklin D. Roosevelt elected
president of the United States

1933 Adolf Hitler becomes
chancellor of Germany

1937 Stalin's purges in the Soviet
Union reach their peak

1939 Second World War begins;
Gone with the Wind becomes the
most popular film to be made

1941 Siege of Leningrad begins

1945 Second World War ends in
Europe

1946 Winston Churchill speaks of
an 'Iron Curtain' dividing Europe

1948 Shostakovich and Prokofiev denounced by the Soviet Communist Party; Columbia Records produce the first long-playing record

1950 (for the next decade) Music courses at Darmstadt become rallying point for modernist composers

1953 Stalin dies

1956 Elvis Presley shocks America by gyrating on the *Ed Sullivan Show*

1957 First performance of Leonard Bernstein's *West Side Story*; the same year he becomes conductor of the New York Philharmonic Orchestra

1958 Decca begin first complete studio recording of the Ring cycle

1961 East Germany begins building Berlin Wall

1963 'Beatlemania' begins; President John F. Kennedy assassinated

1966 Mao Tse-tung launches the Cultural Revolution

1967 Peter Maxwell Davies and Harrison Birtwistle form the Pierrot Players (later Fires of London); Karlheinz Stockhausen appears on the cover of the Beatles' *Sergeant Pepper* album

1968 Student uprising in Paris; Martin King, Robert F. Kennedy assassinated; American protests against Vietnam war

1969 Man lands on the moon

1973 United States pulls out of Vietnam

1974 Richard Nixon becomes the first American president to resign, over the Watergate scandal

1975 Philip Glass completes 'Einstein on the Beach', important minimalist composition

1976 Benjamin Britten dies

1977 Elvis Presley dies

1979 John Paul II becomes the first Polish pope

1980 John Lennon murdered

1985 Mikhail Gorbachev starts programme of *glasnost* and *perestroika*, openness and reform, in the Soviet Union

1987 John Adams's *Nixon in China* first performed in Houston, Texas

1988 CDs outsell vinyl records for the first time

1989 Berlin Wall falls

1990 Leonard Bernstein dies

1990 Communist Party of the Soviet Union is dissolved

1995 Harrison Birtwistle's 'Panic' performed at the BBC Proms

2001 World Trade Center in New York destroyed

2004 Simon Rattle becomes conductor of the Berlin Philharmonic Orchestra

Sources and Further Reading

T HESE ARE THE principal sources used in the writing of this book, although naturally its drift and tone has been shaped by conversation: it is not intended as any kind of textbook. There are some obvious debts, of course. No one approaching music at any level will last long without consulting Grove – *The New Grove Dictionary of Music and Musicians*, edited by Stanley Sadie (London, 1980) – now, happily, available on-line through many public libraries, an invaluable resource and source of delight. I have also used extensively *The Oxford Companion to Music*, edited by Alison Latham (Oxford, 2002). Among other volumes that have always been to hand are the lovely collection of composers' letters edited by the composer Hans Gal, *The Musician's World: Great Composers in their Letters* (London, 1965), which is a cornucopia of the intriguing and the amusing, and the concise and exceedingly helpful *Dictionary of Composers*, edited by Charles Osborne (London, 1981).

I have tried to write for the general reader, with the music as the thread that holds the story together, and it was therefore inevitable that it would become something of a personal account of my reaction to music, rather than a history that tried to be comprehensive. I hope, nonetheless, that in so far as it tells a story through time it is accurate. For the main chapters of the book, these are the other sources that have been used, in some cases for a number of chapters, and I hope they provide some thoughts for further reading.

Chapter 2: Beginnings: Monks, Troubadours and Burgundians
Dunwell, Wilfred, *Music and the European Mind*, London, 1962
Headington, Christopher, *The Bodley Head History of Western Music*, London, 1974

Reese, Gustave, *Music in the Middle Ages*, London, 1941
Young, Percy M., *A History of British Music*, London, 1967

Chapter 3: The Renaissance: Florence, Trent and the First Opera
Fenlon, Iain (ed.), *The Renaissance*, London, 1989
Hale, John, *The Civilization of Europe in the Renaissance*, London, 1993
Mann, Nicholas (ed.), *Atlas of the Renaissance*, London, 1993

Chapter 4: A Seventeenth-Century Journey: Venice to Paris to Cremona
Arnold, Denis, *Monteverdi, Master Musician*, Oxford, 2000
Coryate, Thomas, *Crudities* (extracts), Bath, 1999
Hogwood, Christopher, *Music at Court*, London, 1977
Incherlse, Marc, *Vivaldi*, London, 1958
Pirrotta, Nino, and Povaledo, Elena, *Music and Theatre from Poliziano to Monteverdi*, trans. Karen Eales, Cambridge, 1982

Chapter 5: England: Elizabethans, Puritans and Purcell
Falkus, Christopher, *The Life and Times of Charles II*, London, 1972
Fraser, Antonia, *Charles II: His Life and Times*, London, 1993
Harley, John, *Music in Purcell's London*, London, 1968
Weston, William, *The Autobiography of an Elizabethan*, trans. Philip Caraman, London, 1955
Westrup, J. A., *Purcell*, London, 1947

Chapter 6: A Tale of Three Cities: London, Paris and Bath
Barzun, Jacques, *Pleasure of Music*, London, 1954
Butt, John, *The Age of Johnson*, Oxford, 1990
Cullen, Gordon, *Chiswick House*, London, 1986
Flower, Newman, *George Frederic Handel*, London, 1947
Young, Percy Marshall, *Handel*, London, 1947

Chapter 7: J. S. Bach: 'The Immortal God of Harmony'
David, Hans Theodor, and Mendel, Arthur (eds), *The Bach Reader*, London, 1967
Miller, Cynthia, *Bach and his World*, London, 1980

Chapter 8: Father and Son: Haydn and Mozart
Blom, Eric, *Mozart*, London, 1937

Blom, Eric (ed.), *Mozart's Letters*, Harmondsworth, 1956

Cairns, David, *Mozart and his Operas*, London, 2006

Einstein, Alfred, *Mozart*, Oxford, 1946

Gerardy, Riki, 'King of Instruments and Instrument of Kings', for *Haydn Baryton Trios*, EMI, London, 1977

Robbins Landon, H. C., *Haydn*, London, 1972

Robbins Landon, H. C. (ed.), *The Mozart Compendium*, London, 1990

Simpson, Robert (ed.), *The Symphony: Haydn to Dvořak*, London, 1966

Chapter 9: Beethoven the Revolutionary: From the Bastille to Vienna

Abrams, M. H., *The Mirror and the Lamp*, Oxford, 1971

Johnson, James H., *Listening in Paris*, London, 1995

Matthews, Denis, *Beethoven*, London, 1985

Praz, Mario, *The Romantic Agony*, trans. Angus Davidson, London, 1970

Chapter 10: Pain and Confidence: Romantics, the Virtuosi and the Masses

Best, Geoffrey, *Mid-Victorian Britain*, London, 1988

Einstein, Alfred, *Music in the Romantic Era*, London, 1947

Golby, J. M. (ed.), *Culture and Society in Britain 1850–1890*, Oxford, 1986

Mackay, Elizabeth Norman, *Franz Schubert*, Oxford, 2001

Opiensky, Henryk, *Chopin's Letters*, trans. E. L. Voynich, New York, 1988

Waissenberger, Robert (ed.), *Vienna in the Biedermeier Era*, London, 1986

Walker, Alan, *Franz Liszt: The Weimar Years*, London, 1989

Zamoysky, Adam, *Chopin*, London, 1981

Chapter 11: Viva Verdi! The Italian Love Affair with Opera

Budden, Julian, *The Operas of Verdi*, 3 vols, London, 1973–81

Budden, Julian, *Verdi*, London, 1993

Harewood, Earl of, *Kobbe's Complete Opera Book*, revised edn, London, 1983

Osborne, Charles, *The Complete Operas of Puccini*, London, 1981

Osborne, Richard, *Rossini*, London, 1986

Stassinopolous, Arianna, *Maria Callas*, London, 1981

Chapter 12: Wagner the Revolutionary: The Battle for Ideas in Music

Hartford, Robert, *Bayreuth: The Early Years*, London, 1980

Hodson, Phillip, *Who's Who in Wagner's Life and Work*, London, 1984

Millington, Barry (ed.), *The Wagner Compendium*, London, 1992

Sutcliffe, Tom, *Believing in Opera*, London, 1996

Wagner, Cosima, *Diaries*, vol. 1: 1869–1877, trans. Geoffrey Skelton, London, 1978

Wagner, Richard, *Actors and Singers*, trans. William Ashton Ellis, Lincoln and London, 1995

Chapter 13: Nations Everywhere: On the Neva, the Vltava and the Seine

Ekman, Karl, *Jean Sibelius*, Helsinki, 1955

Garden, Edward, *Tchaikovsky*, London, 1976

Large, Brian, *Smetana*, London, 1970

Marek, George, *The Eagles Die*, London, 1974

Zweig, Stefan, *The World of Yesterday*, London, 1944

Chapter 14: The Century of Wars: Vienna, Paris and the Trenches

Lockspeiser, Edward, *Debussy: His Life and Mind*, vol. 1: 1862–1902, Cambridge, 1978

Neighbour, Oliver, *Second Viennese School*, London, 1983

Nice, David, *Edward Elgar*, London, 1996

Osborne, Charles, *The Complete Operas of Richard Strauss*, London, 1992

Chapter 15: From War to War: Leningrad, Hollywood and the Diaspora

Ardov, Michael, *Memories of Shostakovich*, London, 2004

Bakst, James, *A History of Russian-Soviet Music*, New York, 1966

Devlin, James, *Shostakovich*, Sevenoaks, 1993

Hill, Peter, and Simeone, Nigel, *Messiaen*, London, 2005

Jackson, Stephen, *Dmitri Shostakovich*, London, 1997

Perrett, Geoffrey, *America in the Twenties: A History*, New York, 1982

Shannon, David A., *Between the Wars: America 1919–1941*, New York, 1979

Ulanov, Barry, *A History of Jazz in America*, London, 1958

Chapter 16: Out of the Rubble: Different Paths to Modernism

Carpenter, Humphrey, *Benjamin Britten*, London, 1992

Bowen, Meirion, *Michael Tippett*, London, 1982

Bridcut, John, *Britten's Children*, London, 1996

Stacey, Peter F., *Boulez and the Modern Concept*, Aldershot, 1987

Tannenbaum, Mya, *Conversations with Stockhausen*, Oxford, 1987

Chapter 17: A Golden Age: Two Visionaries

Burton, Humphrey, *Leonard Bernstein*, London, 1994
Lebrecht, Norman, *The Maestro Myth*, New York, 1991

Chapter 18: The Sixties and Afterwards: Popular Culture and Confusion

Fineberg, Joshua, *Classical Music: Why Bother?*, London, 2006
Fisher, Marc, *Something in the Air*, New York, 2007
Hewett, Ivan, *Music: Healing the Rift*, London, 2003
Levin, Bernard, *The Pendulum Years*, London, 1977
Schwarz, Elliot, and Godfrey, Dan, *Music since 1945*, New York, 1983
Tusa, John, *Engaged with the Arts*, London, 2007

These are a few other books, a musical potpourri, which will provide a mixture of fun and wisdom, occasionally at the same time:

Amis, John, and Rose, Michael (ed.), *Words about Music*, London, 1989
Cairns, David, *Berlioz*, 2 vols, London, 1988–99
Carey, John, *What Good Are the Arts?* London, 2005
Carhart, Thaddeus, *The Piano Shop on the Left Bank: The Hidden World of a Paris Atelier*, London, 2000
Conrad, Peter, *A Song of Love and Death*, London, 1987
Douglas, Nigel, *The Joy of Opera*, London, 2000
Drummond, John, *Tainted by Experience: A Life in the Arts*, London, 2000
Kenyon, Nicholas, *Simon Rattle: The Making of a Conductor*, London, 1987
Morrison, Richard, *Orchestra: LSO – A Century of Triumph and Turbulence*, London, 2003
Rosenthal, Harold, *My Mad World of Opera*, London, 1982
Rothenberg, David, *Why Birds Sing*, London, 2006
Wright, Donald (ed.), *Cardus on Music*, London, 1988

A Few Recommended Recordings

THIS IS A list of some fine or particularly interesting recordings of pieces mentioned in the text, although of course such a selection can only be a skim across the surface of the catalogues and can only hint at some other choices I would make. But it is a selection that would keep me happy for a very long time. Fortunately, despite the retreat from classical recording of some of the most powerful companies in the field, the output from small, sometimes specialist labels is immense and enticing, and the regular reissue of historic recordings is still a thriving business. On-line ordering has transformed listening for many people who are not lucky enough to have a specialist shop or a second-hand dealer near by – but I hope that it goes without saying that any retail outlet trying to keep an interesting stock, new or second hand, must be supported. Such places deserve everyone's gratitude and help. No doubt the following list – sparse though it is – will provoke some argument, but you will find it contains many worthwhile recordings. For those who want to browse there are several vital resources, prime among them *The Penguin Guide to Compact Discs & DVDs*, the website of *Gramophone* magazine (www.gramophone.co.uk) where its incomparable reviews are stored, and the website of *CD Review* on BBC Radio 3 (www.bbc.co.uk/radio3/cdreview) where the carefully judged recommendations in its weekly feature 'Building a Library' are available and always thought-provoking. Throughout c. = conductor.

Adams, John
Shaker Loops. Concerto for Violin and Orchestra – Gidon Kremer, violin, London Symphony Orchestra, St Luke's Orchestra, c. John Adams, Kent Nagano, Nonesuch 7559-79360-2

Adès, Thomas
Orchestral pieces – Asyla, Concerto conciso, These Premises are Alarmed, Chamber Symphony, . . . but all shall be well – Thomas Adès, piano, Birmingham Contemporary Music Group, City of Birmingham Symphony Orchestra, c. Simon Rattle, EMI 556818-2

Bach, Johann Sebastian
Cello Suites 1–6, Traditional El Cant del Ocells, 'The Song of the Birds' – Steven Isserlis, Hyperion CDA67541/2
Goldberg Variations, 15 3-Part Inventions – Glenn Gould, Sony Classical SMK52685
St Matthew Passion – Arnold Schoenberg Choir, Vienna Concentus Musicus, c. Nikolaus Harnoncourt, Teldec 8573-81036-2
Well-Tempered Clavier, Book I – Daniel Barenboim, Warner Classics 2564 61553-2
Well-Tempered Clavier, Book II – Daniel Barenboim, Warner Classics 2564 61940-2

Bartók, Béla
Divertimento, with Music for Strings, Percussion and Celesta – Chamber Orchestra of Europe, c. Nikolaus Harnoncourt, RCA 82876 59326-2
String Quartets 1–6 – Vermeer Quartet, Naxos 8 557543/4

Beethoven, Ludwig van
Complete Symphonies – Berlin Philharmonic Orchestra, Vienna Singverein, c. Herbert von Karajan, Deutsche Grammophon CD 453 701-2GCB5
Complete Symphonies – Berlin Philharmonic Orchestra, Bavarian Radio Symphony Orchestra and Chorus, c. Eugen Jochum, Deutsche Grammophon 474 018-2
Late String Quartets – Takács Quartet, Decca 470849-2
Concerto for Violin, Cello, Piano and Orchestra, with Brahms Concerto for Violin, Cello and Orchestra – David Oistrakh, Mstislav Rostropovich, Sviatoslav Richter, Berlin Philharmonic Orchestra, Cleveland Orchestra, c. George Szell, Herbert von Karajan, EMI 566902-2

Bellini, Vincenzo
Norma – Maria Callas, Joan Sutherland, Mirto Picchi, Giacomo Vaghi, Royal Opera House Chorus, Royal Opera House Orchestra, c. Vittorio Gui, EMI CD 562668-2

Berlioz, Hector
Symphonie fantastique, with Béatrice et Bénédict Overture – London Symphony
Orchestra, c. Colin Davis, LSO Live LS0007CD

Bernstein, Leonard
West Side Story – Kiri Te Kanawa, José Carreras, Tatiana Troyanos, etc,
Broadway Chorus, Broadway Orchestra, c. Leonard Bernstein, Deutsche
Grammophon 415 253-1GH2

Binchois, Gilles de
Motets – The Binchois Consort, c. Andrew Kirkman, Hyperion
CDA67474

Birtwistle, Harrison
Verses for Ensembles, with Refrains and Choruses – The Hague Percussion
Ensemble, Netherland Wind Ensemble, c. James Wood, Etcetera
KTC1130

Boulez, Pierre
Domaines – Michel Portal clarinet, Ensemble Musique Vivante, c. Diego
Masson, Harmonia Mundi HMA195930

Brahms, Johannes
The Four Symphonies – Concertgebouw Orchestra, c. Bernard Haitink,
Philips 442 068-2PB4

Britten, Benjamin
The Complete Purcell Realisations – Felicity Lott, Susan Gritton, Sarah
Walker, James Bowman, John Mark Ainsley, Ian Bostridge, Anthony
Rolfe Johnson, Richard Jackson, Simon Keenleyside, Graham Johnson
(piano), Hyperion CDD22058
Peter Grimes – Peter Pears, Claire Watson, James Pease, Chorus and
Orchestra of the Royal Opera House, c. Benjamin Britten, Decca 414
577-2
*4 Sea Interludes, The Young Person's Guide to the Orchestra, A Spring
Symphony* – Jo Vincent, Kathleen Ferrier, Peter Pears, Concertgebouw
Orchestra, Netherlands Radio Chorus, St Willibrord's Boys' Choir, c.
Eduard van Beinum, Decca 440 063-2DM

Bruckner, Anton
Symphony No. 7 – Berlin Philharmonic Orchestra, c. Otto Klemperer,
Music and Arts CD 4751, coupled with Richard Strauss, *Till Eulenspiegels lustige Streiche*
Symphony No. 8 – Berlin Philharmonic Orchestra, c. Gunter Wand, RCA
74321 82866-2 (live recording)

Byrd, William
The Great Service – Choir of Westminster Abbey, c. James O'Donnell,
Hyperion A67533
Complete Keyboard Works – Davitt Moroney, Hyperion CDA66551/7

Chopin, Frédéric
Nocturnes – Livia Rév, Hyperion CDD22013
Etudes, Mazurkas with Works by D. Scarlatti, Debussy, Haydn, Liszt, Poulenc, Rimsky-Korsakov, Schumann, Stravinsky – Vladimir Horowitz, Naxos 8
110606

Copland, Aaron
Clarinet Concerto – Richard Hosford, The Chamber Orchestra of Europe,
c. Thierry Fischer, ASV PLT8504

Debussy, Claude
Pelléas et Mélisande – Wolfgang Holzmair, Anne Sofie von Otter, Laurent
Naouri, Alain Vernhes, Radio France Chorus, Orchestre National de
France, c. Bernard Haitink, Naïve V4923
Prélude à l'après-midi d'un faune – Jonathan Snowden, flute, London
Philharmonic Orchestra, c. Serge Baudo, Classics for Pleasure CD-CFP 6022

Donizetti, Gaetano
Lucia di Lammermoor – Maria Callas, Luisa Villa, Giuseppe di Stefano,
Giuseppe Zampieri, Mario Carlin, Rolando Panerai, Nicola Zaccaria,
Berlin RIAS Orchestra. Chorus of La Scala Milan, c. Herbert von
Karajan, EMI CMS7 63631-2
Don Pasquale – Renato Bruson, Eva Mei, Thomas Allen, Frank Lopardo,
Bavarian Radio Chorus, Munich Radio Orchestra, c. Roberto Abbado,
RCA 09026 61924-2

Dunstable, John
Sacred Choral Works – Orlando Consort, Metronome METCD1009

Dufay, Guillaume
Sacred Works – Huelgas-Ensemble, c. Paul van Nevel, Harmonia Mundi
HMC90 1700

Elgar, Sir Edward
Second Symphony – London Symphony Orchestra, c. Sir Colin Davis, LSO
Live 3PD15
Cello Concerto, with Sea Pictures – Jacqueline Du Pré, Janet Baker, London
Symphony Orchestra, c. John Barbirolli, EMI Reissue CD 556219-2
Enigma Variations, with Falstaff – Royal Scottish National Orchestra, c.
Alexander Gibson, Chandos CHAN8431

Gabrieli, Giovanni
The 16 Canzonas and Sonatas from Sacrae Symphoniae – His Majestys
Sagbutts and Cornetts, Timothy Roberts, Hyperion CDA66908

Gershwin, George
Porgy and Bess – Willard White, Cynthia Haymon, Harolyn Blackwell,
Cynthia Clarey etc., Glyndebourne Festival Chorus, London Philharmonic
Orchestra, c. Sir Simon Rattle, EMI EX749568-1

Glass, Philip
Symphonies 2 and 3 – Bournemouth Symphony Orchestra, c. Marin
Allsop, Naxos 8 559202

Górecki, Henryk
3 Pieces in Old Style, Symphony No. 3, 'Symphony of Sorrowful Songs' –
Zofia Kilanowicz, Katowice Radio Symphony Orchestra, c. Antoni Wit,
Naxos 8 550822

Gurney, Ivor
Severn Meadows: Songs by Ivor Gurney, Paul Agnew, Julius Drake – Hyperion
CDA67243

Handel, George Frederick

Messiah – Arleen Auger, Anne Sofie von Otter, Michael Chance, Howard Crook, John Tomlinson, The English Concert Choir, The English Concert (recorded 1988), c. Trevor Pinnock, ARCHIV 423 630-2 (2-CD)

Rinaldo – Cecilia Bartoli, Gerald Finley, Luba Orgonasova, Bejun Mehta, Bernarda Fink, David Daniels, Academy of Ancient Music, c. Christopher Hogwood, Decca 467 087-2OHO3

Music for the Royal Fireworks, Water Music – Aradia Ensemble, c. Kevin Mallon, Naxos 8 557764

Haydn, Joseph

String Quartets Op. 42, Op. 103, 2 String Quartets, 'Lobkowitz', Op. 77 – Lindsay Quartet, ASV GLD4010

Symphony 103, 'Drumroll', 104, 'London' – London Classical Players, c. Roger Norrington, EMI C5 55002-2

Janáček, Leoš

Jenůfa – Janice Watson, Josephine Barstow etc., Welsh National Opera Chorus, Welsh National Opera Orchestra, c. Charles Mackerras, Chandos CHAN3106

Josquin Desprez

Josquin des Prés and his Contemporaries – sacred music by Josquin, Adrian Willaerts, and some pieces of disputed authorship, The Binchois Consort, c. Andrew Kirkman, Hyperion CDA67183

Missa de Beata Virgine, with Orlando Lassus, Passio secundum Matthaeum – Theatre of Voices, Paul Hillier, HMX2907376.77

Lassus, Orlando

Missa Bell' Amfitrit' altera, Festal Sacred Music of Bavaria – Westminster Cathedral Choir, His Majestys Sagbutts and Cornetts, c. James O'Donnell, Hyperion CDH55212

Linley (junior), Thomas

Ode on the Spirits of Shakespeare – Julia Gooding, Lorna Anderson, Richard Wistreich, The Parley of Instruments, The Parley of Instruments Choir, c. Paul Nicholson, Hyperion CDA66613

Liszt, Franz
A Faust Symphony, Von der Wiege bis zum Grabe – BBC Philharmonic Orchestra, c. Gianandrea Noseda, Chandos CHAN10375

Lully, Jean–Baptiste
Ballet Music for the Sun King – Aradia Baroque Ensemble, c. Kevin Mallon, Naxos 8 554003

MacMillan, James
The Confession of Isobel Gowdie, with The Exorcism of Rio Sumpúl, Tuireadh – BBC Scottish Symphony Orchestra, c. Osmo Vänskä, BIS BISCD1169

Mahler, Gustav
Symphony No. 2, 'Resurrection'. Symphony No. 4. Lieder including Das Lied von der Erde, 'Song of the Earth', Rückert-Lieder, No. 1 – soloists include Kathleen Ferrier, Vienna State Opera Chorus, Vienna Philharmonic Orchestra, c. Bruno Walter, Andante Historical 4973
Symphony No. 5 – New Philharmonia Orchestra, c. John Barbirolli, EMI 566910-2
Symphony No. 7 – New York Philharmonic Orchestra, c. Leonard Bernstein, Sony Classical CD SMK60564

Maxwell Davies, Peter
Sinfonia. Sinfonia Concertante – Scottish Chamber Orchestra, c. Peter Maxwell Davies, Regis RRC1148
The Martyrdom of St Magnus – Tamsin Dives, Christopher Gillett, Paul Thomson, Richard Morris, Kelvin Thomas, Scottish Chamber Opera Ensemble, c. Michael Rafferty, Unicorn-Kanchana DKPCD9100

Messiaen, Olivier
Quatuor pour la fin du temps – André Vacellier, Jean Pasquier, Etienne Pasquier, Olivier Messiaen, Accord 461 744-2
Eclairs sur l'au-delà – Paris Opéra-Bastille Orchestra, c. Myung-Whun Chung, Deutsche Grammophon 439 929-2GH

Monastic Chant
European Sacred Music, 12th and 13th Centuries – Theatre of Voices, c. Paul Hillier, Harmonia Mundi HMX 2907356.57

Monteverdi, Claudio

L'Orfeo – Paul Agnew, Pascal Bertin, Malcolm Bennett, Norbert Meyn, Carolyn Sampson, Christopher Maltman, Patrizia Ciofi, Ian Bostridge etc., Le Concert d'Astrée, European Voices, Les Sacqueboutiers, Virgin Classics 545642-2

Mozart, Wolfgang Amadeus

Four Concertos for Horn and Orchestra – Dennis Brain, Philharmonia Orchestra, c. Herbert von Karajan, EMI CDH7 61013-2
Complete Piano Concertos – Murray Perahia, English Chamber Orchestra, Sony SX12K46441
Adagio, Quintet for Clarinet and Strings, Quartets for Flute, Violin, Viola and Cello, Quintet for Keyboard, Oboe, Clarinet, Horn and Bassoon – Ensemble 360, SV GLD4022
Così fan tutte – Elisabeth Schwarzkopf, Hanny Steffek, Christa Ludwig, Alfredo Kraus, Giuseppe Taddei, Walter Berry, Philharmonia Orchestra, Philharmonia Chorus, c. Karl Böhm, EMI 567382-2
Le nozze di Figaro – Graziella Sciutti, Sena Jurinac, Monica Sinclair, Jeannette Sinclair, Risë Stevens, Hugues Cuénod, Daniel McCoshan, Franco Calabrese, Sesto Bruscantini, Ian Wallace, Gwyn Griffiths, Glyndebourne Festival Chorus, Glyndebourne Festival Orchestra, c. Vittorio Gui, EMI 573845-2

Orff, Carl

Carmina Burana – Lucia Popp, Gerhard Unger, John Noble, Raymond Wolansky, New Philharmonia Orchestra, New Philharmonia Chorus, Wandsworth School Boys' Choir, c. Frühbeck de Burgos, HMV Classics HMV5 72156-2

Palestrina, Giovanni Pierluigi da

Missa Papae Marcelli, Missa Brevis – Choir of Westminster Cathedral, c. David Hill, Hyperion A66266

Prokofiev, Sergei

Symphony No. 1, 'Classical', Cinderella – London Symphony Orchestra, c. André Previn, EMI CZS5 68604-2
Sonatas for Piano No. 4, No. 6, 10 Pieces from Romeo and Juliet – Nikolai Lugansky, Warner Classics 2564 61255-2

A FEW RECOMMENDED RECORDINGS

Puccini, Giacomo
La Bohème – Victoria de los Angeles, Lucine Amara, Jussi Björling, Robert Merrill etc, Columbus Boychoir, RCA Victor Chorus, RCA Victor Orchestra, c. Thomas Beecham, EMI 556236-2
Tosca – Leontyne Price, Giuseppe Taddei, Vienna Philharmonic, c. Herbert von Karajan, Decca 421 670-2DM2

Rameau, Jean-Philippe
Les Indes galante, opéra-ballet – Les Arts Florissants, c. William Christie, HMC901367.69

Ravel, Maurice
Concerto for Piano Left-Hand and Orchestra, Concerto for Piano and Orchestra, 8 Valses nobles et sentimentales – Krystian Zimmerman, Cleveland Orchestra, London Symphony Orchestra, c. Pierre Boulez, Deutsche Grammophon 449 213-2GH

Rimsky-Korsakov, Nikolai
Scheherazade, with Borodin's Second Symphony – Concertgebouw Orchestra, c. Kirill Kondrashin, Philipps 464 735-2 (Great Recordings Series)

Rossini, Gioacchino
Il barbiere di Siviglia – Leo Nucci, Cecilia Bartoli, William Matteuzzi, Enrico Fissore, Paata Burchaladze, Bologna Teatro Communale Chorus and Orchestra, c. Giuseppe Patane, Decca 425520-2

Schoenberg, Arnold
Verklärte Nacht, Op. 4 – The Hollywood String Quartet, Alvin Dinkin (viola), Kurt Reher (cello), c. Claudio Abbado, Testament SBT 1031 (CD)

Schubert, Franz
Sonata for Piano No. 14, D784. Sonata for Piano No. 15, 'Relique', D840. Sonata for Piano No. 18, D894. Sonata for Piano No. 20, D959. Sonata for Piano No. 21, D960 – Alfred Brendel, Philips 475 7191PX2
Symphony No. 9, 'The Great' – Munich Philharmonic Orchestra, c. Günter Wand, Profil Medien PH06014
Winterreise, D911 – Matthias Goerne, Alfred Brendel, Decca 467 092-2DH

Schumann, Robert
Quartet for Piano, Violin, Viola and Cello, Quintet for Piano and Strings –
Schubert Ensemble of London, ASV GLD4021

Shostakovich, Dmitri
String Quartets No. 10, No. 12 and No. 14 – St Petersburg Quartet,
Hyperion CDA67156
Symphony No. 7, 'Leningrad' – Rotterdam Philharmonic Orchestra, Kirov
Orchestra, c. Valery Gergiev, Philips CD 470 845-2PH

Sibelius, Jean
Symphonies Nos 3 and 7 – London Symphony Orchestra, c. Colin Davis,
LSO Live LSO0552

Smetana, Bedřich
Má Vlast – Czech Philharmonic Orchestra, c. Rafael Kubelik, Supraphon
(Koch International) 11 1208-2

Strauss, Richard
Der Rosenkavalier – Regine Crespin, Yvonne Minton, Helen Donath,
Manfred Jungwirth, Vienna State Opera Chorus, VPO (recorded 1968–9),
c. Sir Georg Solti, Decca 417 493-2 (3-CD)
Elektra – Birgit Nilsson, Marie Collier, Margareta Sjöstedt, Regina Resnik,
Gerhard Stolze, Tom Krause, Vienna State Opera Chorus, Vienna
Philharmonic Orchestra, c. Georg Solti, Decca 417 345-2DH2
Vier letzte Lieder – Felicity Lott, Royal Scottish National Orchestra, c.
Neeme Jarvi, Chandos CHAN7113

Stravinsky, Igor
Apollo, The Rite of Spring – City of Birmingham Symphony Orchestra, c.
Simon Rattle, EMI EL749636-1

Tallis, Thomas
Spem in alium – The Sixteen, c. Harry Christophers, Coro Corsacd16016

Tavener, John
Lament for Jerusalem – Angharad Gruffydd Jones, Peter Crawford, Choir of
London, London Orchestra, c. Jeremy Summerly, Naxos 8 557826

Tchaikovsky, Peter Ilyich

Eugene Onegin – Galina Vishnevskaya, Bolshoi Theatre Orchestra, Boris Khaikin, MELODIYA 74321 17090-2 (2-CD)
Symphony No. 6, 'Pathétique' – Oslo Philharmonic Orchestra, c. Mariss Jansons, Chandos CHAN8446

Tippett, Michael

A Child of our Time – Faye Robinson, Sarah Walker, Jon Garrison, John Cheek, City of Birmingham Symphony Orchestra, City of Birmingham Symphony Orchestra Chorus, c. Michael Tippett, Naxos 8 557570
Concerto for Double String Orchestra, with Fantasia Concertante on a Theme of Corelli, The Midsummer Marriage – Ritual Dances – BBC Symphony Orchestra, BBC Symphony Chorus, c. Andrew Davis, Teldec 8573 89098-2

Ventadorn, Bernart de (and other troubadours)

Songs of Love – Duo Trobairitz, Hyperion CDA67634

Verdi, Giuseppe

Falstaff – Ana Ibarra, Maria José Moreno, Marina Domashenko, Jane Henschel, Bülent Bezdüz, Peter Hoare, Alasdair Elliott, Michele Pertusi, Carlos Alvarez, Darren Jeffrey, London Symphony Chorus (amateur), London Symphony Orchestra, c. Sir Colin Davis, LSO Live LSO0055
Otello – Cheryl Studer, Denyce Graves, Plácido Domingo, Sergei Leiferkus, Hauts-de-Seine Maîtrise, Paris Opéra-Bastille Chorus, Paris Opéra-Bastille Orchestra, c. Myung-Whun Chung, Deutsche Grammophon 439 805-2GH2
Rigoletto – Maria Callas, Giuseppe di Stefano, Tito Gobbi etc, Milan La Scala Chorus, Milan La Scala Orchestra, c. Tullio Serafin, EMI 556327-2

Vivaldi, Antonio

5 Violin Concertos – Concerto in D, Concerto in B minor for 4 violins and cello, Concerto in C, Concerto in D 'L'inquietudine', Concerto in E minor 'Il Favorito' – Viktoria Mullova violin, Il Giardino Armonico, c. Giovanni Antonini, Onyx 4001

Wagner, Richard

Der Ring des Nibelungen – cast incl. Gustav Neidlinger, Eberhard Waechter, Walter Kreppel, Claire Watson, Kirsten Flagstad, Kurt Böhme, Hans Hotter, Régine Crespin, Birgit Nilsson, James King, Gottlob Frick, Joan Sutherland, Wolfgang Windgassen, c. Sir George Solti, Decca 455 556-2DHO2/559-2DHO4/564-2DHO4569-2DHO4

Tristan und Isolde – Birgit Nilsson, Christa Ludwig, Wolfgang Windgassen, Claude Heater, Erwin Wohlfahrt, Peter Schreier, Eberhard Waechter, Gerd Nienstedt, Martti Talvela, c. Karl Böhm, Bayreuth Festival Chorus, Bayreuth Festival Orchestra/Karl Böhm, Deutsche Grammophon CD 449 772-2GOR3

Weber, Carl Maria von Weber

Der Freischütz, with Oberon – Margaret Price, Helen Donath, Ingrid Bjoner, Júlia Hamari, Hanna Schwarz, Olivera Miljakovic, James King, Werner Hollweg, Andréa Snarski, Siegmund Nimsgern, Mario Machì, Karl Ridderbusch, Anton Diakov, Rome RAI Chorus, Rome RAI Orchestra, c. George Alexander Albrecht, Wolfgang Sawallisch, Ponto PONTO1045

Index